THICKER THAN OIL

THICKER THAN OIL

America's Uneasy Partnership
with Saudi Arabia

RACHEL BRONSON

A Council on Foreign Relations Book

OXFORD
UNIVERSITY PRESS
2006

OXFORD
UNIVERSITY PRESS

Oxford University Press, Inc., publishes works that further
Oxford University's objective of excellence
in research, scholarship, and education.

Oxford   New York
Auckland   Cape Town   Dar es Salaam   Hong Kong   Karachi
Kuala Lumpur   Madrid   Melbourne   Mexico City   Nairobi
New Delhi   Shanghai   Taipei   Toronto

With offices in
Argentina   Austria   Brazil   Chile   Czech Republic   France   Greece
Guatemala   Hungary   Italy   Japan   Poland   Portugal   Singapore
South Korea   Switzerland   Thailand   Turkey   Ukraine   Vietnam

Copyright © 2006 by Oxford University Press

Published by Oxford University Press, Inc.
198 Madison Avenue, New York, New York, 10016
www.oup.com/us

Oxford is a registered trademark of Oxford University Press

Library of Congress Cataloging-in-Publication Data
Bronson, Rachel.
Thicker than oil / Rachel Bronson.
p. cm. Includes bibliographical references
ISBN-13: 978-0-19-516743-6 (cloth)
ISBN-10: 0-19-516743-0 (cloth)
1. United States—Foreign relations—Saudi Arabia.
2. Saudia Arabia—Foreign relations—United States.
I. Title
E183.8.S25B76 2006
327.73053809′045—dc22
2005024834

Founded in 1921, the Council on Foreign Relations is an independent, national membership
organization and a nonpartisan center for scholars dedicated to producing and disseminating
ideas so that individual and corporate members, as well as policymakers, journalists, students,
and interested citizens in the United States and other countries, can better understand the
world and the foreign policy choices facing the United States and other governments. The
Council does this by convening meetings; conducting a wide-ranging Studies program;
publishing *Foreign Affairs*, the preeminent journal covering international affairs and U.S.
foreign policy; maintaining a diverse membership; sponsoring Independent Task Forces; and
providing up-to-date information about the world and U.S. foreign policy on the Council's
website, www.cfr.org.

THE COUNCIL TAKES NO INSTITUTIONAL POSITION ON POLICY ISSUES AND HAS NO AFFILIATION
WITH THE U.S. GOVERNMENT. ALL STATEMENTS OF FACT AND EXPRESSIONS OF OPINION
CONTAINED IN ITS PUBLICATIONS ARE THE SOLE RESPONSIBILITY OF THE AUTHOR OR AUTHORS.

2 4 6 8 9 7 5 3 1
Printed in the United States of America
on acid-free paper

For John.

Contents

Acknowledgments

This book would not have been possible without the help and support of many people. Les Gelb, the president of the Council on Foreign Relations when this project first took shape, ensured that I had the time and support necessary to pursue its research. I am grateful to Richard Haass, his successor, for continuing with the investment. The Carnegie Corporation of New York provided generous financial support, and Patricia Rosenfield, the chair of the Carnegie Scholars program, offered ongoing encouragement. Ellen Laipson directed my Council study group on U.S.-Saudi relations and helped bring together academics, policy analysts, and retired and active government officials who generously commented on draft chapters and contributed their own firsthand observations.

Colleagues at the Council selflessly contributed their own precious time, including weekends and vacations. I am particularly indebted to Isobel Coleman, Steven Cook, and Jim Lindsay for their thoughtful critiques. Irina Faskianos organized Council study sessions in Atlanta, Dallas, and Houston that provided useful contacts for developing the oil portion of this story. Rachel Abramson and Meredith Angelson provided tremendous research support. Both plowed through stacks of documents—often looking for (and somehow finding) what amounted to a needle in a haystack. In their efforts, they were ably aided by Kareem Idriss and Sarah Saghir. Leigh Gusts and her magnificent team at the Council's library did yeoman's work to make obscure reference materials magically appear and to fulfill my wide-ranging information requests.

I also must thank Fouad Ajami, Mike Ameen, Michelle Billig, Chris Blanchard, Ray Close, Helima Croft, Hermann Eilts, Greg Gause,

Patrick Heffernan, Larry Korb, David Kirsch, Richard Murphy, Mary Anne Weaver, and Frank Wisner for their encouragement and for making themselves available to a curious researcher. Two anonymous readers for the Council on Foreign Relations supplied extremely valuable comments. It is my hope that the book's endnotes offer a glimpse into the scores of others who made valuable contributions.

Wielding a ruthless pen, Tim Bartlett at Oxford slogged through successive drafts of this manuscript, demanding clarity while somehow remaining compassionate and encouraging. To my considerable relief, Peter Ginna seamlessly picked up this project and steered it through to completion after Tim left Oxford for Random House. Kate Hamill, Helen Mules, and Sue Warga made important suggestions from behind the scenes. My agent, Heather Schroder, joined this book halfway through its completion and has, since then, provided invaluable guidance.

One of the greatest pleasures in writing this book has been discovering America's presidential libraries. They are true national treasures, equal only to the people who staff them. David Knapp at the Energy Intelligence Group, Nicholas Scheetz of Special Collections at the Georgetown University Library, and Rima Hassan at the Saudi Embassy's photo archives also guided me to important documents and photos.

Many people in Saudi Arabia opened their homes and engaged in lengthy conversations about contemporary Saudi politics and the U.S.-Saudi relationship. They graciously accommodated an American scholar who overscheduled interviews rather than bask in the warm graces of their Arab hospitality. To them, often left nameless at their request, I extend my heartfelt gratitude.

I benefited from the insights provided by audiences and workshop participants at venues where portions of the book were presented, including the Rochester chapter of the American Council on Foreign Relations, the Center for Strategic and International Studies, the Columbia University Seminar Series, the Cosmopolitan Club of New York, the International Institute for the Study of Islam in the Modern World, Network 20/20, the Washington Institute for Near East Policy, and the Women's Foreign Policy Group.

There is no way that this one book can fully reflect the vast knowledge and experience of all who have contributed to it. I can only hope that it comes close. Any misreading of events or factual errors are, of course, solely my responsibility.

I reserve my greatest appreciation for my family, who has surrounded me with love and devotion. They suffered quietly as I left family gatherings to work on book chapters and as I interjected observations about the U.S.-Saudi relationship into otherwise easy dinner conversations. In particular, my wonderful husband opened his life to a country that he did not know and a history that he never expected to explore. In addition to keeping the home fires burning through this all-consuming task, he proved an invaluable debate and discussion partner. There is no way I can repay him for his unyielding support. It is to him that I dedicate this book.

"Put the stone back in its place in the stream of history," a wiser man told me. "Then that bit of rock will be joined by others to show its part in the flow of time and world events."

—Philip C. McConnell, one of Aramco's first "Hundred Men"

THICKER THAN OIL

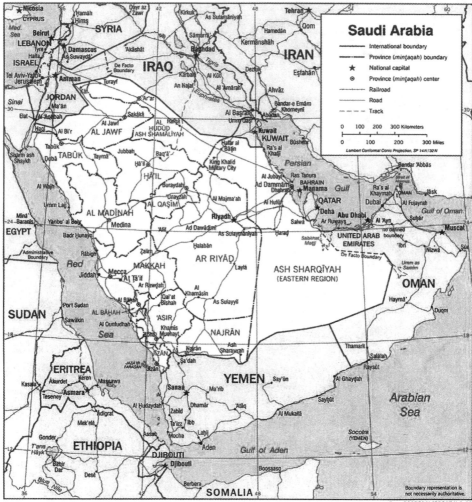

Prologue

The plane touched down on the hot and sandy Riyadh airstrip at 5 p.m., behind schedule. America's representative in Saudi Arabia, J. Rives Childs, stepped off the aircraft, followed by two young American foreign service officers, Donald C. Bergus and Hermann F. Eilts. It was March 1949, and Childs was in Riyadh to upgrade America's diplomatic presence in Saudi Arabia to an embassy, a step suggesting the evolving importance of that country.[1] Until that point, America had been represented by a legation, a small diplomatic mission operating out of Jeddah. The embassy Childs established would not move from Jeddah to Riyadh until 1984.

In 1949 Saudi Arabia was cautiously engaging the modern world. Jeddah, one of its most cosmopolitan and dynamic cities, was an old walled city of about thirty thousand people. It didn't have a single paved street, and camels wandered through the middle of town. There were no public utilities of any kind—no electric lights, running water, or sewage system. Fifty-gallon tanks from Wadi Fatimah, twenty miles away, were hauled in each morning to provide the legation with water. The tanks usually ran dry by about two in the afternoon.[2]

Royal escorts met Childs' flight and guided his small team to the king's guest house, a simple mud hut with straw-filled mattresses. Until the early 1940s fewer than a hundred American and Europeans had set foot in Riyadh. According to convention, each visitor received a gift of traditional Arab clothing. One did not meet the king in Western attire. Childs had his own Arab costume, but the two young officers gratefully accepted the gifts.

A tailor arrived to shorten the oversized garments, but since the plane had arrived late and it was now nearly prayer time, he left with a promise

1

to return shortly. The meeting with the king approached, but the tailor did not, leaving poor Bergus and Eilts with no choice but to don the untailored extra-long thobes—the traditional shirt dress still worn today by many Saudi males. Bergus and Eilts hiked up their thobes and went off to meet the king, who was waiting for them at the Murubba palace, his main residence. The bedraggled Americans cut quite an image for the amused, if somewhat surprised, members of the royal entourage, including men such as Youssef Yassin, Fouad Hamza, and H. St. John Philby (the king's confidant and the father of the notorious British double agent Kim Philby), sent to accompany the visitors.

The trio approached the nearly blind sixty-nine-year-old king, who was sitting in a high-backed chair in the royal palace's main receiving room, illuminated by kerosene lamps. Childs presented his credentials to the king, who made a brief comment about the importance of close ties between their nations. Childs then bowed, shook hands with the king, and backed out of the room. Don Bergus, who, unlike Childs, had been properly instructed on what to do, bowed, shook hands, and then turned to exit properly. Finding himself face-to-face with a receding Childs, he did what any good underling would do: he whirled back around to mimic his boss. Eilts did the same. The seasoned diplomat, flanked by two minions with "evening gowns in hand," slowly backed down the corridor.

Halfway out of the room, the ambassador bumped into one of the hall's many pillars and lost his balance. Bergus, whose garment was much too long, stumbled onto Childs, toppling him to the floor. Eilts, himself destined to become U.S. ambassador to Saudi Arabia in 1966, tripped next, landing atop both his colleagues. "*Shoo heatha, shoo heatha*"—what's going on, what's going on? cried the Saudi king, hearing the commotion, but unable to see clearly the heap of Americans on the floor—or, perhaps, able to see it all too clearly. The Saudi foreign minister and future king, Prince Faisal, along with a number of other well-positioned Saudis, surged forward, disentangled the Americans, and hastily ushered them out. As Hermann Eilts remembers it, "Five minutes after the American embassy was established in Saudi Arabia, we were flat on our collective butts."[3] Childs didn't speak to his young staffers for weeks.

"An Accident Waiting to Happen"

Few relationships are as vital, under as much pressure, and as poorly understood as that between the United States and the Kingdom of Saudi

Arabia. The 865,000-square-mile kingdom, equivalent in area to more than one-fifth of the United States, sits astride one-quarter of the world's proven oil reserves and neighbors two of America's foreign policy hot spots, Iraq and Iran, and one of its closest friends, Israel. Every devout Muslim turns toward its holy city, Mecca, five times a day to pray.

Traditionally the United States' relationship with Saudi Arabia has been characterized as a basic bargain of "oil for security." For its part, since the mid-1970s, Saudi Arabia has ensured the free flow of oil at reasonable prices. The kingdom's ability to put oil on the market quickly during times of crisis is the most obvious benefit the United States gains from good relations. Immediately after September 11, for example, Saudi Arabia increased oil shipments to the United States in order to keep prices stable. It also augmented oil production just before Operation Iraqi Freedom commenced, a time when political strife in Venezuela and Nigeria threatened to elevate oil prices dramatically. In return for this, the United States extends to Saudi Arabia's leadership a security umbrella, including a commitment to its territorial integrity. Since 1950 the United States has explicitly vowed to help defend the kingdom against external threats—including, over the years, the Soviet Union, Yemen, Egypt, Iran, and Iraq. Since the fall of the shah of Iran in 1979, this commitment has evolved into implicit support for the Saudi regime against internal challenges, including today's al-Qaeda.[4]

Although the notion of oil for defense is a compelling shorthand for describing the relationship between the United States and Saudi Arabia, it ignores overlapping strategic interests that drove together successive Saudi kings and American administrations. A critical, if often overlooked, aspect of the U.S.-Saudi relationship has been the shared interest in combating the Soviet Union. After all, who better for the United States to partner with in its fight against "godless Communism" than a religiously motivated state such as Saudi Arabia? Successive Saudi leaders were similarly concerned about the ideological threat posed by the atheistic Soviet Union and its proxies in the region. Their concern was driven by the fact that the ruling family's domestic legitimacy was based on a long-standing bargain with religious clerics. Saudi Arabia and the United States' mutual fear of the Soviet Union's expanding global influence, predicated on strategic and religious realities, provided a protective political layer that enveloped oil and defense interests. It also left behind a legacy that today enflames the Middle East.

For most of Saudi Arabia's recent history, the two states shared important geostrategic interests that drove together leaders from both states, despite real differences. During the 1960s America helped Saudi Arabia defend its borders against Soviet-supported Egypt, which repeatedly bombed Saudi territory during a proxy war in Yemen. America and Saudi Arabia worked together to beat back growing Iranian influence during the Iran-Iraq War between 1980 and 1988. Most importantly, during the Cold War Saudi Arabia was one of the few Middle East countries the United States could regularly rely upon for military access, financial assistance, and political support. Furthermore, Saudi Arabia never seriously played the United States off the Soviet Union, as many of its neighbors such as Egypt and Iraq tried to do.[5] For over three decades, Saudi Arabia actively supported anti-Communist insurgencies and governments, influencing politics from Central Asia to Central America. But Saudi Arabia's political support was conjoined with religious proselytizing. Mosques, schools, and the education of local clerics who enrolled in Saudi Arabia's austere religious universities followed in the wake of Saudi assistance.

Contrary to the myth repeated regularly by diplomats on both sides, relations between the two states have not always been smooth. The United States and Saudi Arabia have weathered deep differences with respect to the Arab-Israeli conflict. Saudi leaders and citizens, like other Arabs, usually focus on America's "unflinching" support for Israel. Less than two months after the 2001 terrorist attacks, Saudi Arabia's foreign minister, Saud al-Faisal, declared that the Bush administration's approach toward the Arab-Israeli conflict "makes a sane man go mad."[6] When Americans think of Saudi Arabia, they tend only to envision a country that raises vast sums of money for the most extreme anti-Israel groups such as Hamas. Almost every major U.S. weapons sale to Saudi Arabia in recent history has caused protesters to gather outside the White House, often carrying placards linking Saudi Arabia to anti-Israel funding. However, even within this controversial arena, each capital has pursued over the years a much more nuanced set of policies than is usually acknowledged. The United States has at times pushed hard for a peaceful settlement, either withholding financial assistance from Israel, bringing leaders together at Camp David, or, most recently, calling for a Palestinian state. Saudi Arabia used its financial leverage to cool Egypt's once fiery rhetoric (especially after 1967), moderate Syria's intransigent foreign policy, and twice put forward plans that suggested a recognition of Israel, although not as unambiguously as some would have liked. Saudi Arabia's late King Fahd, who for all intents and purposes ruled the kingdom from the Ford presidency until 2005, quietly told successive presidents that his government would support a two-state solution if agreed upon by both parties. In 1981 he publicly put forward the Fahd Plan, which included the controversial (at least inside Saudi Arabia) assertion that "all states in the region should be able to live in peace in the region." Still, it is equally clear that Saudi leaders will not sacrifice the House of Saud in order to achieve Israeli-Palestinian peace.

While the events of September 11 unleashed a wave of criticism of, and profound questioning about, the U.S.-Saudi relationship, relations between the two had been deteriorating for almost a decade prior. As one prominent Saudi businessman poignantly described it to me in an e-mail shortly after the attacks, the public furor "was an accident waiting to happen." Since the end of the Cold War, government leaders on both sides allowed the relationship to coast on autopilot, even as changing global realities weakened the relationship's basic pillars. The acrimony between Saudi Arabia and the United States that burst forth at the beginning of the twenty-first century is directly attributable to the September 11 terror attacks. But the roots of the U.S.-Saudi disassociation stem back to November 1989, when the Berlin Wall came down.

When it comes to the U.S.-Saudi relationship, Middle East policy makers have a striking case of historical amnesia, in part because so little serious work exists on the official bilateral relationship between the two states. Books and movies that spotlight a particular president's close relationship with Saudi Arabia miss the point that almost *every* administration since that of Franklin Delano Roosevelt has had close ties to the kingdom. Roosevelt set the warm tone for the official relationship in 1945 when he met with Saudi Arabia's King Abdel Aziz on the Great Bitter Lake just south of the Suez Canal. Even Eisenhower and Kennedy ended up with strong relations with Saudi Arabia, despite initial efforts to distance their administrations. Both Democratic and Republican administrations, before and after the 1973 oil boom, built close ties to the kingdom. Saudi Arabia's kings Abdel Aziz, Saud, Faisal, Khaled, and Fahd all sought the same with the United States. The reason for this has much to do with Saudi Arabia's oil holdings and vulnerable security situation, but also with a set of mutually shared global interests defined during the Cold War, interests that have since crumbled.

Recent books seem more intent on feeding public outrage than on seriously probing the relationship.[7] Only a handful focus seriously on oil or succession.[8] Still fewer try to figure out what the world looks like through the lens used by Saudi decision makers.[9] Politics and history seem all but absent from the debate over the U.S.-Saudi relationship.[10] Why have we been partners for sixty years? How have politics, the oil business, and religion commingled? When did the relationship go sour? Should we, can we, salvage what worked? Could we, must we, jettison the whole relationship?

The attacks of September 11, 2001, caused an unprecedented public outcry on both sides, with many arguing that the benefits of close ties did not warrant the overwhelming costs. A July 2002 briefing to the illustrious Defense Policy Board, an advisory committee of American strategic luminaries devoted to assisting the secretary of defense, defined Saudi Arabia as "the kernel of evil, the prime mover, the most dangerous opponent" in the Middle East and advised U.S. forces to target Saudi Arabia's oil fields and seize its assets.[11] While campaigning for the presidency, Senator John F. Kerry made it clear that while "the truth is that we have deep, and for the moment inescapable ties" with Saudi Arabia, he nonetheless had "specific concerns," most notably that the kingdom's "officially sanctioned bigotry breeds terrorism."[12] In August 2002 Hassan Yassin, a longtime Saudi government official, penned an op-ed piece in the *Los Angeles Times* acknowledging that "the United States of America and the Kingdom of Saudi Arabia are drifting apart."[13] As late as June 2005 Secretary of State Condoleezza Rice stated emphatically that "for 60 years, my country, the United States, pursued stability at the expense of democracy in this region here in the Middle East—and we achieved neither."[14] The reference to sixty years, coming as it did around the time of the sixtieth anniversary of the first meeting between Roosevelt and Abdel Aziz, was a direct message to the Saudi leadership that Washington wanted change, and was reportedly interpreted as such in Riyadh. In Saudi Arabia, members of the royal family are actively debating the utility of close relations with the United States.

As it pursues its war on terror America faces the central and difficult question of what policy to build vis-à-vis Saudi Arabia, especially as the Cold War justification has fallen away. New issues, including counterterrorism, political reform, and stability in Iraq, populate today's political agenda and are rarely interpreted the same way by both capitals. Saudi Arabia's religious credentials, something Washington once deemed a strategic asset, are today a much more obvious, controversial, and potentially dangerous issue. At the same time, the kingdom poses one of the toughest challenges to the George W. Bush administration's political reform agenda, one of the administration's highest priorities. The kingdom lags behind on almost every indicator of political openness, and reform there would have an immediate positive effect throughout the region. Yet because the kingdom figures so prominently on issues such as oil, Iraq, and counterterrorism, there are limits to how hard the United States can push. Reformers inside the kingdom also worry that a frenetic push toward reform will backfire and result in increased religious radicalism, as occurred in Iran and Algeria, or outright chaos, as in Iraq.[15]

For its part, Saudi Arabia is no longer the impoverished, insular country that American oil companies and diplomatic representatives first engaged nearly seventy-five years ago. It has emerged as a major regional player and a significant global one, able to influence the price of oil—one of the world's most important commodities. Demand from oil-hungry states such as China and India, not just the requirements of traditional markets such as Europe and the United States, now influences Saudi decisions. Religious institutions that were constructed four decades ago today serve as powerful political transmission belts for Saudi Arabia's influence across the globe.

With the end of the Cold War, economic, political, and geographical circumstances have changed so dramatically that neither the U.S. nor Saudi leadership should expect the continuation of the same kind of relationship that existed for more than half a century. Still, there is good reason for each to work to ensure that the relationship does not collapse entirely, nor become so strained that cooperation on existing problems becomes impossible.

Today's all-important strategic question is whether Saudi Arabia will use its foreign aid and the global pulpit provided by Islam's two holiest mosques to turn the tide in the ideological battle of our age: the spread of Islamic radicalism. Since May 2003, when simultaneous bombings occurred in Riyadh, the Saudi government has aggressively cracked down on homegrown radical religious cells, the existence of which had been previously denied. The government has clamped down on charitable giving and has instituted legislation in order to monitor the outflow of money more effectively. It also initiated a series of domestic reforms aimed at broadening its domestic legitimacy. Such actions are extremely important. As Frances "Fran" Fragos Townsend, assistant to the president and homeland security advisor, stated at a 2005 conference on counter-terrorism in Riyadh, "The world cannot defeat terrorism without Saudi Arabia defeating terrorism on its own grounds."[16] But is the Saudi government willing and able to act as determinedly on the international stage, where Islamic radicalism flourishes? Can it control a new generation of religious firebrands who garner considerable popular support? Neither the United States nor Saudi Arabia, alone or in partnership, has yet developed a convincing strategy for reducing Islamic radicalism's global influence.

There are many reasons why the United States could walk away from decades of close relations, chief among them a fact that the Saudi leadership was hard-pressed to acknowledge: fifteen of the nineteen September 11 hijackers were Saudi citizens. Many of the schools and mosques once supported by Saudi charitable assistance still spew out virulent anti-Americanism. A 2005 report by the Center for Religious Freedom highlighted intolerant and at times violent material from a number of U.S. mosques, much of which was printed with Saudi support. The materials, collected between November 2003 and December 2004, provide disturbing evidence of "the content of Wahhabi indoctrination within the United States."[17] Although the report's authors give only passing mention to the fact that most of the "titles were published in the 1980s and 1990s" (until 1989 many in the United States government were actively encouraging the proliferation of religious fighters in order to confront the Soviets in Afghanistan) and "that some of the titles were published by groups and entities that in the last two years have been shut down or have broken ties with the Saudi government," a secondhand market for virulent materials published with onetime Saudi support still exists, even in the United States. These are problems that will not go away anytime soon. As one senior Saudi asked me somewhat provocatively, what does the United States have in common with "a country where women can't drive, the Quran is the constitution, and beheadings are commonplace?"—a question echoed by countless American and Saudi citizens.

In spite of very real differences between the two countries, turning our backs on Saudi Arabia risks abandoning reformers inside the kingdom, both within the royal family and in the broader population, and producing the very reality we seek to avoid—a clash of civilizations between the West, represented by the United States, and the Muslim world, led by Saudi Arabia. It also denies the role that both the United States and Saudi Arabia together played in creating many of today's most pressing political problems, problems that could be best solved if the United States and Saudi Arabia worked together.

One important finding of the National Commission on Terrorist Attacks Upon the United States (the 9/11 commission), the highly effective group appointed to probe the causes of the September 2001 terrorist attacks, is that both Riyadh and Washington "must determine if they can build a relationship that political leaders on both sides are prepared to publicly defend—a relationship about more than oil."[18] This will be impossible without (1) a common knowledge base about the relationship's history, (2) a better appreciation for the many ways in which each state has contributed to the foreign policy goals of the other, (3) an unvarnished understanding of the long-term effects of these policies, and (4) more than just a caricature of the very complicated role that oil has played.

Both Saudis and Americans have been markedly uninterested in acknowledging how their own policies have contributed to today's dangerous world. Each finds it easier to shine the spotlight of responsibility on the misdeeds of the other. This has vexed the search for an effective political response. In fact, the fight against al-Qaeda and Islamic radicalism flows directly from policy choices America and its Middle East partners took to win the Cold War and concurrent local political conflicts. Extremism's appeal is not simply the result of a primordial clash of civilizations, nor a political response to globalization, nor even the consequence of authoritarian regimes stifling outlets for peaceful political dissent—the current operating assumption of the Bush administration. Rather, Islamic radicals have been created and cultivated by political leaders for political ends. As the respected Middle East scholar Fred Halliday states, the power of today's Islamist movements is "not a product of the *end* of the Cold War, but a pervasive, influential legacy of *the Cold War itself*."[19]

The recent focus on Saudi religious zeal has allowed Americans to ignore the role that American policy has played in the problems confronting the post-September 11 world. Afghanistan is the best-known case, with the United States and Saudi Arabia each pouring no less than $3 billion into a fight that empowered religious extremists. During the 1980s, American leaders believed that bringing down the Soviet Union was worth the costs of empowering religious radicals in Afghanistan and elsewhere. In the words of Zbigniew K. Brzezinski, an early proponent of arming Afghanistan's mujahideen: "What was more important in the world view of history? The Taliban or the fall of the Soviet Empire? A few stirred-up Muslims or the liberation of Central Europe and the end of the Cold War?"[20] But Afghanistan is hardly the only case where the politicization of religion was useful in combating the Soviet threat. Throughout the 1970s and 1980s, a series of Afghanistans dotted the regional landscape, albeit on a smaller scale. In Somalia, Sudan, Pakistan, and beyond, Saudi Arabia contributed money either in lieu of or to complement American efforts. Today such places are often the most vexing for counterterrorism experts. In many ways September 11 was the price we paid for winning the Cold War and the strategies we chose. And so are our complicated ties with Saudi Arabia.

Halfway across the globe in Saudi Arabia, the late King Fahd's decision to empower religious extremists inside Saudi Arabia after 1979 also endangered international stability. His policies had as much to do with international threats, viewed similarly by many opposing the Soviet Union, as it did with the long-standing alliance between Saudi Arabia's political and religious establishments. It is true that the political and religious establishments in Saudi Arabia have been allied for over two centuries. Throughout history, however, the relationship between the two has been much more conflicted than many of today's commentators would have us believe. In fact, the political agenda has tended to dominate the religious one.

This began to change in 1979 with the unfolding of three dramatic events. First, in February 1979 the Iranian revolution brought to power Ayatollah Ruhollah Khomeini, a Shi'a cleric who threatened to spread his version of Islam (as opposed to the Sunni interpretation prevalent in many Arab states) to the Persian Gulf and Central Asia. The Iranian situation took a notably violent turn in November of that year when U.S. hostages were seized. During that same month, a group of Saudi religious extremists seized the Grand Mosque of Mecca, the holiest shrine in Islam. For the first time since the late 1920s, the religious credentials of Saudi Arabia's ruling family were openly contested. Then, weeks later, the Soviet Union invaded Afghanistan, a predominantly Muslim state, in a move that brought the Soviets one step closer to the Persian Gulf. Religion emerged as an obvious and effective counter to the three disparate challenges.[21]

Accordingly, all aspects of Saudi Arabian life after 1979 became infused with the spirit of jihad, no longer defined purely as "exertion" or "endeavor" or "struggle" but rather as "holy war."[22] Flyers recruiting religious fighters appeared everywhere. Fiery religious clerics stirred up their followers across the country to volunteer for the fight against the infidels and to pursue a more ascetic life at home. The king regularly appeared with them in public. Women's hairdressing salons were shuttered, women's clubs were closed down, and female announcers were dismissed from their jobs on television. New regulations prohibited girls from continuing their education abroad.[23] As one Saudi journalist described it to me during a 2005 trip to Riyadh, "We are now dealing with the effects of 1979."

The king began pouring money into the region's religious institutions, created years earlier, to contest Iranian influence, beat back the Soviet Union, and bolster his domestic legitimacy. By some accounts Saudi Arabia spent more than $75 billion underwriting schools, mosques, and charities worldwide.[24] One direct benefit was that this politicization of religion helped check Soviet influence, an advantage not lost on the American leadership. The curse, of course, is that it also poisoned the minds of those who "benefited" from such largesse. Whereas during past conflicts the Saudi leadership had either wiped out religious opposition or negotiated with and subordinated it, in 1979 the king embraced and bolstered the most austere interpretation of Islam.

Like Saudi Arabia's government, many Middle East and South Asian regimes (usually American allies) funded religious opposition in the mid- to late twentieth century for their own political purposes, thus contributing to the intolerant strand of Islamic interpretation the world is today witnessing. In Pakistan between 1971 and 1988 the number of registered religious schools increased from nine hundred to eight thousand, which doesn't include the twenty-five thousand unregistered ones.[25] The trend was greatly accelerated under Pakistan's president Zia ul-Haq, in office from 1978 to 1988. In Egypt during the 1970s President Anwar el-Sadat channeled state money to political-religious groups in order to build his own indigenous pillar of support and to counter the more threatening Nasserist opposition to his rule. Even Israel allowed money to flow to Islamic groups in order to counter the then more threatening national opposition of the Palestinian Liberation Organization and Yasser Arafat. But it was Saudi Arabia, with its vast fortune and very real foreign threats, that altered the global course of political Islam. In doing so, it received the tacit approval of the United States.

There is a silver lining to seeing today's challenges as the result of past political decisions. If the problem were Islam or some other basic identity, the situation would be hopeless. A true clash of civilizations would be in the offing, auguring a dark and dangerous future. If, however, the problem is political, then there exists a glimmer of hope. Policies are malleable and can be changed. But it will take time and courage to undo the damage that has been done. It will also require the United States and Saudi Arabia to realign their foreign policies to more effectively address current challenges.

This book will put the high-stakes U.S.-Saudi relationship under the microscope to expose its cracks and fissures. It will look closely at not only American foreign policy but also the woefully underexamined topic of Saudi foreign policy.[26] The book attempts to retrace decisions made by leaders on both sides, and to highlight the different incentives pushing together both leaderships at the uppermost political levels. It is a story of presidents, kings, senior cabinet officials, royal confidants, and chief intelligence officers. Publics on both sides, which have become more influential in the policy process as a result of satellite television and twenty-four-hour news cycles, were for most of this story kept at bay.

But before beginning, we ought to consider the larger political context in which the relationship is now operating. Many of the alliances that have helped steer American foreign policy over the past fifty years are deteriorating. Anti-Americanism has become the flavor of the decade in the political circles of America's closest friends. Talk to anyone focused on the transatlantic relationship, the crucial partnership between the United States and its European partners, and you will undoubtedly confront stories of anger, frustration, and failing confidence, notwithstanding Secretary Rice's recent efforts to woo European leaders. A 2005 report from the Pew Global Attitudes Project found that "most Europeans surveyed want a more independent approach from the U.S. on security and diplomatic affairs" and that "opinion of the U.S. continues to be mostly unfavorable among the publics of America's traditional allies, except Great Britain and Canada."[27] Secretary of Defense Donald H. Rumsfeld's description of France and Germany as "old Europe" exacerbated already frayed relations. During his 2002 election campaign, German chancellor Gerhard Schroeder campaigned on an anti-American platform. The chancellor got so far ahead of himself and his own diplomatic corps that he went on record that Germany would not follow America into Iraq, even with a United Nations Security Council resolution. Germany was president of the United Nations Security Council in the days immediately preceding the war.

The situation is hardly better in South Korea, long considered a reliable U.S. partner. In December 2002 hundreds of thousands of South Koreans took to the streets to protest a variety of issues, ranging from acquittal of two American servicemen accused of running over two fourteen-year-old girls with their armored vehicle to American policy toward North Korea. While Korean experts made clear that such protests were not unprecedented, the timing, coinciding with German and Saudi protests, suggests that something very troubling is brewing within many of America's traditional relationships.

It is fair to say that George W. Bush's administration has exacerbated international tensions, but it did not create them. Anti-Americanism has been on the rise since the end of the Cold War.[28] This increase stems in part from controversial American policies but also from the collapse of the Soviet Union. Today America is damned if it does and damned if it doesn't. It is criticized for failing to intervene in Chechnya but condemned for invading Iraq. It is criticized for not doing enough to spread democracy and human rights but then rebuked for taking small measures in Egypt or Kuwait to do just that. In interviews and speeches I gave in the late 1990s in the small Arab states that abut the Persian Gulf, I was grilled by dismayed audiences asking when the United States would see fit to rid the region of one of the world's worst monsters, Iraq's Saddam Hussein. When the Bush administration finally ousted Saddam in 2003, it received little public support from all those who knew better than we how destructive and destabilizing his regime actually was. It seems that everyone wants American intervention until it happens in their own backyard.

Many of the readily understood justifications for America's Cold War relationships no longer apply. Today American decision makers must determine which relationships to sustain, and how to sustain them. The story and future of the U.S.-Saudi relationship is thus a story about how America should understand and realign its relationships in the post–Cold War, post–September 11 world.

1

Oil, God, and Real Estate

O h Philby," sighed the king almost beseechingly. "If anyone would offer me a million pounds, I would give him all the concessions he wanted."[1] In the autumn of 1930 King Abdel Aziz bin Abdel Rahman al-Faisal al-Saud, known in the West as Ibn Saud, could barely sustain his vast territorial holdings—which ranged east to west from the Red Sea to the Persian Gulf and north to south from Iraq to Yemen—through traditional sources of revenue including British financial assistance and taxes on the hajj, the traditional Muslim pilgrimage to Mecca.[2] Hajj revenues were down significantly because of the Great Depression. Between 1929 and 1931 the number of pilgrims dropped from a hundred thousand to only forty thousand as travelers from India and Indonesia stopped taking the expensive trip. At the same time, expenditures were increasing. Revenues were needed to pay government salaries, cover army expenses, and keep tribal elders loyal. Early nation-building efforts such as installing radio-telegraph stations across the country and improving Jeddah's water supply strained the kingdom's coffers. During these difficult times Abdullah Suleiman, Abdel Aziz's close aide and the fledgling kingdom's finance minister, dragged the king's fortune around in nothing more than a tin trunk, usually doling out more than he took in.

H. St. John Philby, the king's trusted British confidant, tried to energize his despondent friend. He quoted back to the king a Quranic passage, "God changeth not that which is in people unless they change that which is in themselves." It was a comforting thought, but what the king really needed was a miracle.

As it turned out, the king's price was less than a million pounds— £50,000 ($250,000), to be exact—and a miracle was indeed in the offing. In return for two interest-free loans payable in gold, Standard Oil of California (Socal, later Chevron) would win Saudi Arabia's oil concession in 1933, strike oil in 1938, and transform the desperately poor, newly fashioned kingdom into one of the most important countries in the world.

Black Gold

The story of America's relationship with Saudi Arabia begins with oil, first established as a strategically vital commodity in the days prior to World War I. Winston Churchill, then the most senior civilian representing the British Royal Navy, oversaw a series of programs to convert Britain's fleet from coal to oil. The switch made the British fleet a faster, more agile counter to the increasingly adversarial German navy. But without its own indigenous oil supply, Britain's conversion irrevocably tied it to the Persian Gulf, its cheapest source of oil.[3]

World War I would highlight the strategic importance of oil. In 1916 it spurred Germany's invasion of Romania, a minor global oil power but at the time Europe's largest producer outside of Russia. It also fueled the newly introduced military tank, which increased the flexibility of British forces against the rail-bound German army. The petroleum-dependent tank, used dramatically in the summer of 1918 at the battle of Amiens, ended the "primacy of the defense," which had paralyzed European forces inside muddy trenches for most of the war.[4] By the war's end, British army vehicles included 56,000 trucks, 23,000 motorcars, and 34,000 motorcycles and motor bicycles, all powered by gasoline. As oil historian Daniel Yergin rightly describes it: "The victory of the Allies over Germany was in some ways the victory of the truck over the locomotive." Oil was central to this success.

Because 80 percent of the Allies' oil during the war came from Standard Oil of New Jersey (later Exxon) in the United States, U.S. officials worried that their country would run out of the precious commodity. One United States senator grew so concerned that he called for the U.S. Navy to revert from oil to coal. The director of the U.S. Geological Survey described the American oil situation as "precarious." Shortly after the war, American oil executives and government officials turned their attention to newly promising oil fields around the Persian Gulf.

But in the Gulf, American oil companies confronted a virtual British monopoly on access to foreign oil fields, backed by Britain's fierce determination to retain its exclusionary position in places such as Iran, Iraq, and the smaller Gulf States. "The British position is impregnable," boasted British oil man E. Mackay Edgar in the 1919 summer edition of *Sperling's Journal*, an economic journal of that time. "All the known oil fields, all the likely or probable oil fields outside of the United States itself, are in British hands or under British management or control, or financed by British capital."[5]

There appeared to be only two ways for American companies to break the British stranglehold: either gain access to Britain's exclusive Iraq Petroleum Company (IPC), which held most of the concessions in the Middle East states of the former Ottoman Empire, or proceed independently, outside the IPC framework. Big oil companies such as Standard Oil of New Jersey and Socony-Vacuum Oil Company (later Mobil) pursued the first course. Backed by the U.S. Department of State, which found it intolerable that U.S. companies were denied economic access anywhere by its former World War I allies, the oil companies embarked on arduous negotiations with the owners of IPC. The State Department advocated an "open door policy" that would allow American companies access to an area circumscribed on a map by a red line encompassing most of the old Ottoman Empire, including Turkey, Iraq, Saudi Arabia, and most of the lands along the Persian Gulf's western shores.[6] In 1929, with U.S. government help, Standard Oil of New Jersey and Socony-Vacuum joined IPC and were granted a combined 23.75 percent share. Remaining shares were distributed evenly between British Petroleum, Royal Dutch/Shell, and Compagnie Française Pétrole, a state-owned firm established in 1924 to represent French interests in IPC.

Now signatories to the Red Line Agreement, as it was then called, American oil companies had finally penetrated the Middle East. In joining IPC, however, the companies had to sign on to a stringent preexisting arrangement: members agreed they would not embark on independent exploration or cut any deals inside the red line without the express approval and cooperation of the other members of IPC.

This "self-denying clause" had the unintended consequence of keeping the British, and most major American companies, out of Saudi Arabia during the crucial years of the 1930s. With an increasing oil supply coming onto the market and no corresponding upsurge in world demand anticipated, IPC shied away from new deals or concessions that would increase the global oil supply and thus reduce prices. In the early 1930s the American company Gulf Oil won a concession to explore for oil in Bahrain, a tiny island off the Arabian Peninsula, but relinquished it when it joined IPC. IPC restrictions demanded that no independent drilling could take place by IPC members, and no member wanted to begin jointly drilling in Bahrain.

Standard Oil of California followed the second course available to international oil companies in the Middle East. It chose to operate outside of IPC restrictions, which increased its autonomy but kept it from the more lucrative IPC-controlled areas such as Iraq. Socal bought Gulf Oil's Bahrain concession for $50,000. This purchase significantly altered the future course of U.S.-Saudi relations.

In 1932 Standard Oil of California struck oil in Bahrain. Saudi Arabia, situated less than twenty miles away and displaying a similar geological profile, suddenly appeared as a potential oil producer. Until that time, no major oil company had taken much interest in the kingdom. With the Bahrain discovery, that began to change.

King Abdel Aziz, now courted by Socal and IPC for rights to explore and drill for oil, did not expect the companies to find much of anything under his sandy lands.[7] A few years earlier he had awarded a concession to a New Zealander by the name of Frank Holmes, with little result. Unable to convince any major oil company to invest in his Saudi project, Holmes faced bankruptcy. He departed the kingdom owing Abdel Aziz £6,000. Still, the cash-strapped monarch was not about to turn away IPC or Socal, both of which were now seeking an oil concession.[8]

Socal was aided in its concession negotiations by St. John Philby. Once a member of Britain's Foreign Office, Philby was deeply distrustful of his own government's imperial designs on Saudi Arabia. After playing IPC and Socal off each other in order to ensure the king a good price, Philby passed to the king proprietary information that he had gathered from IPC negotiators. It seemed that IPC's primary goal in obtaining the concession was not to make money for Saudi Arabia, or itself for that matter, but rather to keep Socal out of the Middle East oil hunt. Because of the global oil glut, IPC did not intend to explore for oil if it won the Saudi concession. This hardly endeared IPC to the impoverished king. Philby also withheld from IPC Socal's final offer to the king, thus denying IPC negotiators the opportunity to outbid their adversary.

In 1933 the king—who was partial to the Americans anyway, given their success in Bahrain and their apparent disinterest in Middle East colonial intervention—awarded Socal the concession. In return, the company agreed to provide the king with a £30,000 interest-free loan in gold and a second loan of £20,000 within eighteen months. Saudi Arabia agreed to pay back the loan in future oil revenue if it ever materialized. The king also secured an annual payment of £5,000. "Put your trust in God and sign!" King Abdel Aziz exhorted Abdullah Suleiman, the second most powerful man in the fledgling government.[9]

The Saudi concession, roughly the size of Texas, New Mexico, and Arizona combined, was the only important oil concession in the Middle East that was exclusively American-owned and operated. Shortly thereafter a handful of Socal employees landed on Saudi Arabia's eastern shore. They included men such as the burly and "much loved" Max Steineke, a savvy geologist who could identify oil fields from Saudi Arabia's challenging landscape, and Floyd W. Ohliger, Socal's superintendent of Arabian operation. Both were "good eggs," according to Thomas C. Barger, who arrived shortly after the others and eventually rose to head the oil company's impressive government relations department and then the entire Arabian-based company. Barger himself came to Saudi Arabia in December 1937 on a rickety barge from Bahrain, disembarked at a half-finished pier at Khobar, then just a small fishing village, and drove six miles along an oiled road to Dhahran, the hot and rugged company town. Barger, who had cut his teeth as a professional geologist around the rough-and-tumble copper mines of Butte, Montana, was assigned to assist Steineke in his geological pursuit. "I'm awfully glad to have you here with us," Steineke enthused when Barger arrived. "I don't know what I am going to do with you, but I am certainly glad to have you on board." Barger's Arabic eventually became so fluent that he was occasionally mistaken for a Bedouin, an Arab nomad. After witnessing Barger's language proficiency, the king blurted out, "*Mashallah!*"—a phrase expressing wonderment and amazement.[10]

Almost immediately, Socal's newly formed and wholly owned subsidiary, the California Arabian Standard Oil Company (Casoc), faced a quandary. If the company's investment in Saudi Arabia's fields paid off and the company struck oil, it would not have markets available to sell its product to. Fiercely competitive, IPC denied Casoc access to its markets. Partly as a result of this, Casoc merged in 1936 with Texas Oil—a company that had markets in Asia but only a limited supply of American oil to service it. Together in 1944 the two companies renamed their subsidiary the Arab American Company (Aramco), which would become a principal actor in U.S.-Saudi relations.

Between 1933 and 1938 Casoc struggled. The landscape proved difficult to decipher, and no one was quite sure how deep the oil was located, or even if there was any. The Americans began drilling at an area called Dammam, a few miles north of Dhahran. The first holes produced little of note; on occasion the wells showed traces of oil, but not enough to give them commercial value. The seventh hole proved a different story. On March 4, 1938, after a series of disappointing drills, Saudi Arabia's Dammam-7 well "blew," producing more than 1,500 barrels per day. At the time, an average U.S. well produced about 100 barrels per day, although Saudi Arabia's neighbor, Bahrain, was producing a total of 13,000 barrels per day.[11] Still, Saudi Arabia now had one commercially viable well and its future as an oil producer appeared bright.

The Dammam-7 blow corresponded with a visit to Dhahran by Princess Alice, the granddaughter of Britain's Queen Victoria, and her husband, the Earl of Athlone, the brother of Queen Mary. Both had crossed the entire width of Arabia from Jeddah in a sort of goodwill tour. For the Americans, isolated from much of civilization in eastern Saudi Arabia, the arrival of royalty overshadowed the excitement of the oil discovery. Although those involved did not realize it at the time, the visit of Princess Alice, corresponding as it did with the discovery of oil in Saudi Arabia, foreshadowed the handover of British influence in the Gulf to the Americans. The cordial letters that later passed between the princess and Dhahran's American women, discussing among other things an angel food cake recipe, preceded a higher-stakes and much terser set of letters exchanged six years later between Roosevelt and Churchill arguing over whether the United States was seeking to "deprive" Britain of its oil assets or whether Britain was trying to "horn in" on Casoc's Saudi oil concession.[12]

The 1938 oil discovery and subsequent finds shocked and delighted King Abdel Aziz. His first royalty check topped $1.5 million. Months later, on May 1, 1939, the king, along with a retinue of more than two thousand people in five hundred automobiles, journeyed out to the eastern oil fields and turned the spigot that began the flow of oil into the first tankers. On the return trip, the king, along with some of his brothers and older sons, boisterously sang Bedouin raiding songs from their youth.[13] Impressed with American ingenuity and seeming to genuinely like the American oil workers, the king augmented Casoc's concession by nearly 80,000 square miles, increasing Casoc's area to about 440,000 square miles, a little over 50 percent of Saudi territory.[14] "Do you know what they will find when they reach Mars?" the king asked Tom Barger after he had heard a radio report predicting that men would someday travel to the distant planet. He then proceeded to answer his own question: "They will find Americans out there in the desert hunting for oil."[15]

In 1939 Casoc produced approximately 11,000 barrels per day. Ten years later that number hovered around 477,000 barrels, accounting for slightly more than 5 percent of total world production and about 35 percent of all Middle East production.[16]

Oil would play an even larger role in World War II than it had in World War I, as new technologies demanded ever more "black gold."

Cordell Hull, Franklin D. Roosevelt's secretary of state for most of his presidency, acknowledged that "the Near East, in which our government had evinced only a slight interest for a century and a half, became through the demand of WWII a vital area in the conduct of our foreign relations. . . . Iran (once known to us as Persia), Iraq, Saudi Arabia, Lebanon and Syria began to appear more and more in American print, not as lands of the ancients but as cogs in the machine of war."[17] In Saudi Arabia, the United States had important interests to protect, "principally the vast oil concession."[18]

World War II had a direct impact on oil development in eastern Arabia. Oil's importance was obvious. But the machinery needed to get it out of the ground was required elsewhere. Spare parts, trucks, and other equipment were requisitioned for the war effort. One boat filled with crucial parts sank en route to the Eastern Province, where Saudi Arabia's oil resources were located. Then in November 1940 Italian planes bombed the oil fields in Bahrain and eastern Saudi Arabia. Although the bombs somehow missed both sites' oil fields, and Benito Mussolini later publicly apologized for the attack, it was enough to scare Casoc's employees and spur many to return home. The camp of 371 American employees, 38 wives, and 16 children decreased in size in the weeks after the bombing to only 226 employees, 19 wives, and 5 children. Eight months later the camp emptied of its remaining women and children as German troops threatened to converge on Dhahran from El-Alamein, Egypt, in the west and the Caucasus in the north.[19] Promising Saudi fields such as the ones at Abu Hadriya and al-Abqaiq were left for future probing if and when the political situation stabilized.

In 1948, after the war's end, Aramco's drillers (Casoc was renamed Aramco in 1944) returned to a site that had long fascinated Max Steineke and other Aramco geologists. The company struck oil at Ghawar, southwest of Dhahran and east of Riyadh. The Ghawar field was soon classified as the world's largest oil deposit. Saudi Arabia was now on the map as a very serious oil player. In need of even more markets and capital given the vastly expanding Saudi output, Aramco was joined by Standard Oil of New Jersey and Socony-Vacuum, which slipped out of their IPC contracts on a technicality in November 1948. One of the king's only conditions was that whatever the face of the bigger company, it had to be 100 percent American, rather than include European (particularly British) companies. He did not trust European designs on his country.

Between 1944 and 1950 Aramco's gross production of crude oil increased from 21,000 to 548,000 barrels of oil per day.[20] Cheap Persian Gulf oil became a central component of America's postwar strategy, as the reconstruction of Europe depended on it. In 1948 the United States imported only about 6 percent of its oil, with only about 8 percent of that coming from Saudi Arabia.[21] In contrast, Western Europe was almost entirely dependent on Persian Gulf oil. U.S. planners busily determined how best to ensure its flow.

The U.S. government by and large took a backseat to Aramco's relations with Riyadh. The State Department let Aramco take the lead in interacting with the Saudi government, particularly around oil and local development issues. In the early days of the relationship Aramco handled oil, while the embassy (after it was established) handled politics, including the fallout from America's 1947 decision to support the partition of Palestine and difficulties in managing Saudi-British tensions given Washington's warm relations with both. The arrangement was partly a result of Aramco's legacy in the kingdom, but it also fit nicely with the determined efforts of successive U.S. administrations to stay out of local politics rather than re-create Britain and France's colonial experience.

This division of labor between the U.S. government and U.S. oil companies was evident in how America's diplomatic and economic interests were physically located inside the kingdom. Aramco dominated eastern Saudi Arabia and the majority of oil issues that emerged from there. The U.S. embassy operated out of Jeddah, on Saudi Arabia's west coast, and handled most of the nettlesome foreign policy issues from there. Aramco kept the State Department and CIA apprised of its initiatives, but it largely operated independent of official U.S. channels. Over time, however, especially as ownership of Aramco passed to Saudi Arabia over the course of the 1970s and the American economy became increasingly dependent on Saudi oil, the U.S. government took a more dominant role in U.S.-Saudi relations.

America's Three Pillars

Oil, of course, is a significant factor in the U.S.-Saudi relationship, as it is in all other Saudi dealings. It can hardly be otherwise for a country that sits astride one-quarter of the world's proven oil resources and relies on oil exports for 90 to 95 percent of its total export earnings.[22] But while oil explains a good portion of America's interest in the kingdom, it does not explain the strength of the relationship. After all, America's relationships with other major oil-producing states such as Russia, Iran, Iraq, Libya, and Venezuela have been exceedingly troubled. Politically and militarily, the United States and Soviet Union were at odds for the entire Cold War period. For thirty of the thirty-six years between 1967 and 2003, the United States had no official political relations with Iraq, a country whose oil holdings are estimated at 115 billion barrels of proven reserves, second only to Saudi Arabia. Iran, with 10 percent of the world's oil, has lived under U.S. sanctions for twenty-five years. Libya experienced nineteen years of American-led sanctions. In 2002 the Bush administration quietly encouraged an unsuccessful extralegal effort to remove Venezuela's president, Hugo Chávez. In the fall of 2004, the United States actively encouraged international sanctions against Sudan's oil exports in response to egregious human rights abuses taking place in that country. Successive administrations have shown a clear willingness to bear the costs of poor relations with oil-rich states.

It is true that Saudi Arabia's ability to bear the cost of maintaining spare oil capacity and its willingness to put oil onto the market in times of crisis give it a unique standing among producers. It is the world's "swing producer" and has a disproportionate influence over global oil prices. Saudi Arabia holds around 85 percent of OPEC's spare capacity, which, given problems in Iraq, Venezuela, Nigeria, and elsewhere, has come to mean about 85 percent of the world's spare capacity.[23] If any single problem hits a big producer elsewhere (Iraq descends further into chaos, Nigeria's political situation devolves, Venezuelan oil workers strike, hurricanes damage U.S. oil facilities), the only place that has been able to quickly make up those volumes is Saudi Arabia. Still, American policies of sanctioning and cutting off relations with other oil producers have reinforced Saudi Arabia's position. Good U.S.-Saudi relations have given Washington decision makers the latitude to curtail the production of others. This then begs the question of why relations were so good in the first place.

When it comes to the Middle East, America's relationship with Saudi Arabia is more similar to its relationships with Egypt (after 1973), Jordan, and even Israel (politically friendly but oil-poor) than to its ties with Iran, Iraq, or Libya (traditionally hostile but oil-rich). Thus when Thomas Friedman states in the pages of the *New York Times* that the United States has treated Arab oil-producing states "like big, dumb gas stations, and all the U.S. cared about was that they kept their pumps open and their prices low," he misses a good portion of the politics and political context of the past half century.[24] Oil by itself does not explain why, in the late 1950s, the United States sought to transform the Saudi king into a globally recognized Muslim leader. The Saudi leadership's claim to Mecca and Medina and the importance this had for America's anti-Communist agenda is a more powerful explanation. Oil hardly explains why relations between the two countries became exceptionally close during in the 1980s, even as Saudi debts began to mount and oil prices fell dramatically. Mutual interest in countering Soviet expansion provides a better accounting. Most importantly, oil alone does not anticipate the kingdom's spending billions of dollars on anti-Communist activity around the globe, decisions that were not preordained by its resource holdings but were greatly valued in Washington. As *Newsweek* reported in 1978:

> It is the Saudis using their oil money as an ideological weapon, who have scored the most significant foreign policy successes in recent years. By funneling $2.5 billion into the Egyptian economy each year, Saudi Arabia has been able to rid a key Arab country of Soviet influence. By pumping large doses of cash into Morocco, Riyadh's rulers helped check a Marxist movement in the Maghreb and enabled the Moroccans to help Zaire, another Saudi client state, turn back an invasion launched by the Communist rebels.[25]

That Saudi Arabia had money to spend is directly attributable to oil. How it chose to spend it is not. "God help us if we couldn't count these people among our closest allies," said one senior American diplomat in Riyadh during this time.[26] Riyadh's willingness to invest its revenue in American-supported causes earned it considerable favor at the highest levels in Washington.

To understand why and how the United States and Saudi Arabia became such close partners over the course of the last half century, two factors other than oil must also be considered: strategic location and religious identity. Saudi Arabia's claim to speak for Muslims worldwide and the legitimacy the Saudi leadership derived from its own religious establishment ensured that anti-Communism figured prominently in the Saudi decision calculus, something U.S. leaders greatly appreciated. Saudi Arabia's strategic location and religious identity, especially the latter, conditioned how American policy makers came to define their oil interests and the policies that emerged from them.

A singular focus on oil misses the way in which a broader convergence of interests helped to cement the relationship between the United States and the Saudis during the Cold War. It also overlooks the genesis of a number of problems that decision makers are grappling with today. Until the Berlin Wall came down in 1989, Saudi Arabia's extensive proselytizing of a fundamentalist interpretation of Islam—commonly referred to as Wahhabi Islam outside of Saudi Arabia—was not a source of considerable concern because it had an anti-Communist justification. For Saudi Arabia, America provided security, markets, and a shared antipathy toward Communist expansion—something that threatened Saudi borders directly, indirectly through proxies such as Egypt and Yemen, and through subversion of the population. Mutually supporting interests gave leaders on both sides opportunities to weave their way through complicated international situations and benefit from the support of the other. The U.S.-Saudi relationship became a testing ground for how Washington would apply varying Cold War policies in the Middle East.[27]

Location, Location, Location

During World War II, the Persian Gulf provided an important staging ground for resupplying the desperate Russians, then allies of the United States. The Arabian Peninsula was also located along the logistical route for supplying troops fighting Japan. America's War Department was an early and strong advocate of building Saudi Arabia's Dhahran airfield, first proposed in 1944 in order to shorten the air route to the Pacific theater. Dhahran provided a much-needed stop between Libya and Karachi. A year earlier, in 1943, the State Department anticipated the War Department's interests and advocated extending lend-lease assistance—a World War II program that authorized the president to transfer food, military services, and industrial parts to countries considered vital to American national security—to Saudi Arabia. As Dean G. Acheson argued:

> Saudi Arabia lies between the vital Red Sea and Persian Gulf shipping routes and across the direct air route to India and the Far East. The Government of Saudi Arabia has been highly sympathetic to the cause of the United Nations [Allied forces] and has accorded United States Army aircraft the right to fly over certain uninhabited zones of Saudi Arabia. Furthermore, the Army may at any time wish to obtain extensive air facilities in Saudi Arabia. However, the Department is of the opinion that it will be difficult to obtain additional privileges from the Government of Saudi Arabia unless we are prepared to furnish certain direct assistance to that country.[28]

The State Department was aided by American oil officials in the kingdom who pressed Harold L. Ickes, the secretary of the interior, to find a way to counter British foreign aid to the kingdom, lest the British steal away the American concession. James F. Byrnes, President Roosevelt's director of the Office of War Mobilization from May 1943 until April 1945, testified that FDR had "determined that in view of the strategic location of Saudi Arabia, the important oil resources of that country and the prestige of King Ibn Saud throughout the Arab world, the defense of Saudi Arabia was vital to the defense of the United States."[29] Saudi Arabia became one of only three Arab countries to be designated eligible for lend-lease assistance.

After the war, the commercial value of the Dhahran airfield, near the Dammam oil fields, increased as Egypt's Payne Field was turned over to Egyptian control and Trans World Airways began using Dhahran as a hub between Europe and growing markets in South and East Asia. In 1946 the *New York Times* reported that the potential strategic value of the base was "enormous because of its geographical position and indefinite possibilities for expansion as well as its ability to handle any size aircraft."[30] A military survey team that was sent to Saudi Arabia in the autumn of 1949 reported that training a small Saudi military force as part of the Dhahran leasing agreement would "be a useful force for our purposes in the event of war with Russia."[31] In 1951 the National Security Council articulated its views on what made the area so important. In order of priority, the report listed the geographic position of the area (with respect to the Mediterranean, Western Europe, Africa, and European and Asiatic Russia), oil resources, military bases, and communications and facilities.[32]

During the Cold War the importance of Dhahran again increased, given that it was within a thousand miles—striking distance—of the Soviet Union. According to Parker "Pete" T. Hart, America's venerable ambassador to Saudi Arabia during the early 1960s, "Dhahran was of potential value as a strategic backup—a hinterland in the evolving security structure that in 1955 became the Baghdad Pact."[33] During the 1980s Dhahran served as a transit hub for American-procured weapons headed for Afghanistan.

Saudi Arabia would become even more important after 1979, when the Iranian revolution removed from American orbit one of the twin pillars it relied on for regional security. Under President Richard M. Nixon, Saudi Arabia was to act as a junior partner to Iran in preserving stability over the Persian Gulf and the region. Once Iran could no longer be counted on, the Reagan administration came to rely on Saudi Arabia to serve as a bulwark against Iranian expansion and Russian meddling.

Finally, permission for the American military to fly over Saudi territory and pre-position material in the Persian Gulf region has been a valued asset. During the Cold War the denial of air space to the Soviet Union was very important to U.S. planners. Even today military planners view access to Saudi airspace as "essential" to all operations in the region.[34] The U.S. military has no viable cost-efficient alternative to flying over Saudi Arabia. There are not enough tanker aircraft or bases to easily avoid flying over the kingdom. America's heavy reliance on the small Persian Gulf states would also be rendered irrelevant without tacit Saudi support.

Finding Religion

In addition to oil and geography, America has since the dawn of the Cold War valued Saudi Arabia's religiosity. In a neat division of labor, Saudis attacked godlessness while Americans fought Communism. Because Soviet-inspired Communism was based on a hostility toward religious belief, the more religious a country, the more likely it would be to rail against Communism and look toward the United States. As early as 1954 historian Bernard Lewis predicted that "pious Muslims— and most Muslims are pious—will not long tolerate an atheist creed."[35] Saudi Arabia, a deeply religious state, was the perfect prophylactic against the spread of Communism and a natural American partner.

"Who is testing you in China? Who is testing you in Japan? Who is testing you in Germany?" Abdel Aziz rhetorically asked one of President Truman's emissaries in 1948.[36] The answer, of course, was the Soviets. The king was clear that he "would never abandon his people or his religion" to it. His religion, and his role as ruler of Islam's two holiest mosques, dictated an anti-Communist stance.

Initially during the early 1930s, Prince Faisal, the king's second-oldest living son, explored the possibility of establishing ties with the Soviet Union. Moscow was in fact the first capital to officially recognize his father's newly founded state. But King Abdel Aziz wanted little to do with the Soviets and banished the Soviet ambassador from Jeddah in 1938. Official relations between Russia and Saudi Arabia were not reestablished until 1990. Faisal eventually became one of the most intensely anti-Communist warriors American leaders would find. He concocted a wild conspiracy theory that intimately connected Communism and Zionism. "Communism . . . is a Zionist creation designed to fulfill the aims of Zionism," he told *Newsweek* in 1970. "They are only pretending to work against each other."[37] Although a succession of American presidents, secretaries of state, and senior oil executives would raise their eyebrows when confronted with Faisal's convoluted theory, his earnest hatred of America's mortal foe largely caused them to hold their tongue.

The benefits of Saudi Arabia's religiosity to the United States were real. During the Cold War religiosity was synonymous with anti-Communism. In the 1950s the words "under God" were added to the Pledge of Allegiance to differentiate the United States from the Soviet Union. During the 1960s senators such as Tennessee's Albert A. Gore Sr. (former Vice President Gore's father) asked witnesses appearing before Congress whether they believed in God, on the grounds that if they answered affirmatively they could not be Communist.[38] Religion was integral to the debate, and a religiously inspired state was a natural global partner.

When President Dwight D. Eisenhower's secretary of state, John Foster Dulles, toured the Middle East, he brought letters of introduction from Eisenhower to the leaders in the region. Of these letters, the one written to the Saudi king, Abdel Aziz, was the only one to mention a shared interest in fighting "godless communism."[39] American presidents also hoped that religious Saudi Arabia could serve as a counter to the more revolutionary secular nationalism that swept through the region in the 1950s, 1960s, and 1970s. In 1954, Gamal Abdel Nasser assumed the reins of power in Egypt and mobilized citizens across the Arab world to throw off the shackles of colonialism and old-fashioned monarchical rule and embrace an Arab republican national identity. Nasser hurled invectives against the French, British, Saudis, and Jordanians, and eventually the Americans. He also received considerable Soviet aid. During the late 1950s President Eisenhower encouraged Saudi Arabia's King Saud (reigned 1953–64) to become a political and religious counter to the charismatic Nasser, and the White House began referring to King Saud somewhat optimistically as "an Islamic pope." Such shared interests established a strong foundation that supported close relations at the highest political levels for decades. It was done at the expense of democratization, human rights, and the promotion of religious freedom, goals that drove American policies elsewhere.

The View from Riyadh

Washington's interests in Saudi Arabia boiled down to oil, God, and real estate. But why did Saudi Arabia choose America? Why did King Abdel Aziz award American companies Saudi Arabia's major oil concessions only a year after he formally declared the patchwork of political alliances and military victories the Kingdom of Saudi Arabia? Why did he turn to the American military in 1946 to build his country's first major airfield? Why did he seek American companies and foundations to build Saudi Arabia's education and economic institutions, rather than those of other interested and experienced countries? The answer says much about why successive Saudi Arabian leaders have similarly turned to the United States, year after year, crisis after crisis. It also lies deeply in the kingdom's history.

The roots of modern Saudi Arabia stretch back to 1744 and the desert town of Diriyah, just outside of Riyadh. It was there, deep in the Nejd, the central province of Arabia, that Muhammad ibn Saud, a local

potentate and patriarch of the House of Saud (and a direct forefather
of today's rulers), and Muhammad ibn Abd al-Wahhab, an ascetic religious cleric committed to a literal interpretation of the Quran, swore an
oath of allegiance. The area that in 1932 came to be called Saudi Arabia
was then under nominal Ottoman control. While the Ottomans were
active on the desert's periphery, they mostly ignored the peninsula's harsh
interior. Warring Bedouin tribes populated its vast desert tracts. It was
hardly worth Ottoman effort to assert greater political control.

The alliance between Muhammad ibn Saud and Muhammad ibn
Abd al-Wahhab proved potent. For seventy years they and their
descendants recorded victories and converts as far north as Karbala,
Iraq, and Damascus, Syria. They pushed deep into Yemen and into the
Hejaz, Arabia's western province and home to the holy cities of Mecca
and Medina. It was the behavior of the zealous soldiers in the Hejaz
that caused their downfall. The followers of Abd al-Wahhab terrorized
the residents of Mecca and Medina for not practicing the ascetic version of Islam of the warriors. They attacked and turned away Muslims
making the hajj who practiced Islam in a different manner. This enraged Muslims throughout the area and unnerved the Ottomans, who
benefited from taxes generated during the hajj. The Ottomans, already
in decline, encouraged Muhammad Ali, their Egyptian proxy, to do
battle on their behalf against the troublemakers from Diriyah. In 1818,
after a decade's worth of fighting, Muhammad Ali defeated the Nejdi
warriors and pushed them back to their home base of Diriyah. This
marked the end of the first Saudi state.

No sooner had they been defeated than the descendants of
Muhammad ibn Saud began organizing to reassert their rule. They
retained their alliance with the descendants of Muhammad ibn Abd al-
Wahhab (commonly referred to collectively as "Al al-Sheikh"), though
now placing limits on their missionary zeal. The area they eventually
conquered, which constituted the second Saudi state, was smaller than
the original; this time its rulers stayed clear of Mecca and Medina, the
area that had antagonized the Ottomans and other Muslims the first
time around. Still, seventy years later, in 1884, the Saud/Al al-Sheikh
alliance was once again defeated, this time by a local tribal leader,
Muhammad ibn Rashid, who was nominally backed by the Ottoman
Empire. Ibn Rashid's victory was facilitated by incessant internal bick-
ering among the al-Saud family, which irrevocably weakened the second Saudi state. Ibn Rashid stripped away possessions and claims
but did allow Abdullah al-Faisal al-Saud, then the head of the al-Saud
clan, to continue on as governor of Riyadh. His brother Abdel Rahman
al-Faisal al-Saud succeeded him. When Abdel Rahman revolted against

Rashid domination in 1891, his forces were decimated and he fled to Kuwait. He took with him his young son Abdel Aziz, the future king of Saudi Arabia.

The young Abdel Aziz absorbed the lesson, painfully learned by his father and uncle, of how devastating unresolved internal political tensions could be. When he eventually became king, he insisted on his sons' fealty and drummed into them a loyalty to each other and an obsessive commitment to keeping interfamilial disagreements private that is readily apparent even today.

Abdel Aziz spent his formative years exiled in Kuwait, learning international politics at the knee of its ruler, Emir Mubarak. Kuwait at the time was a relatively cosmopolitan area, located on a trade route that attracted Christians, Jews, Indians, Arabs, British, and others. Unlike his ancestors, Abdel Aziz was introduced to both foreigners and non-Wahhabi Muslims. He studiously observed Emir Mubarak, a savvy politician, artfully balance Ottoman and British territorial claims, a lesson that the young Saudi internalized and later practiced.[40]

While living in Kuwait, Abdel Aziz never gave up his claim to his ancestral home. In 1902 Abdel Aziz's men, sixty-three in total, approached Riyadh. A few, led by Abdel Aziz, penetrated the city's walls. Abdel Aziz's cousin Abdullah bin Jiluwi threw a dagger at the local governor but missed. Abdel Aziz sprung out, grabbed the governor, and kicked him in the groin. As the Rashid governor stumbled away, Abdullah ran him down and murdered him. In time, King Abdel Aziz appointed Abdullah bin Jiluwi the governor of Saudi Arabia's oil-rich Eastern Province. His descendants maintained the post until riots broke out there in 1979. Thus began the formative years of today's Saudi Arabia, the third Saudi state.

After the attack, Abdel Aziz began a protracted effort to expand his realm in all directions. He drew his strength from the towns that dotted the Nejd. To promote his rule, he also set about subduing the Bedouins, whose incessant raiding throughout central Arabia had prevented the development of any sustained commerce or socioeconomic development in the region. To encourage them to settle permanently, he sent money, seeds, and other agricultural support to a series of villages to attract wandering Bedouins and encourage them to forgo raiding and their itinerant lifestyle. The first hijrah (Bedouin settlement) was established in early 1912, and there would eventually be 120 or more. Abdel Aziz encouraged their development in order to harness the destructive power of the Bedouin tribes and bend them to his rule. He employed a long-term strategy of proselytization in order to curb the violent practices of the Bedouins.[41]

To these settlements Abdel Aziz also sent religious teachers to inculcate the rough residents with an extremely ascetic interpretation of the Quran and an intense desire to return to a life replicating exactly that of the Prophet Muhammad. As new converts often are, the Ikhwan, as members of the new Bedouin fighting force were called, were religiously resolute and fanatical.[42] Some even went so far as to challenge Abdel Aziz for his contact with outside powers and his seemingly lenient religious interpretations (although Abdel Aziz had been schooled in religion by a direct descendant of Muhammad ibn Abd al-Wahhab). Hafiz Wahba, Abdel Aziz's representative to the British, recalls that the king "dealt with this by raising an 'army' of scholars well versed in religious debate to go out to the different hijrahs to repair the mischief wrought by the earlier teachers, whom he promptly dismissed. He [however] was not able to eradicate fanaticism entirely."[43] Still, as one scholar of the movement acknowledges, "the unalterable fact is that [the Ikhwan] did what they did not out of inherent cruelty and maliciousness, but as the logical result of their religious training at the hands of people who should have and probably did know better."[44]

From these settled Bedouin villages, which included subsets of existing tribes, Abdel Aziz raised a powerful religious fighting force that supplemented his core fighters.[45] In a heavily tribal environment such as Arabia, what was notable about the Ikhwan was their loyalty to each other rather than to their tribe more generally, and this was something that Abdel Aziz actively cultivated.[46] Zealously religious, they sought to spread their interpretation of Islam—Wahhabi Islam. They were a violent and determined group.

Whereas raiding was a fact of life on the peninsula, certain long-standing norms applied. Raiders looted but rarely pillaged. Unless there was an existing blood rivalry, killings were rare, especially of women and children. The Ikhwan, however, disregarded such norms. They ransacked villages and murdered those whom they deemed insufficiently pious. They were after purity, not plunder.[47]

With the help of the Ikhwan (who at the time made up a small but growing portion of Abdel Aziz's fighters), loyal townsmen, the core of his army, and local tribes, the future king brought Hasa, the eastern portion of Saudi Arabia (now called the Eastern Province), under his command.[48] With eight thousand men, Abdel Aziz overran a small Turkish garrison there in 1913. The Ikhwan fighters involved were only too happy to conquer Hasa, as they viewed the largely Shi'a population there as apostates. They scorned Abdel Aziz's victory pledge to the population that he would allow them some freedom to practice their religion as they always had.

The British grew increasingly enamored of Abdel Aziz's growing strength and military prowess, although they maintained closer ties with Sharif Hussein, the ruler of Mecca, Medina, and the rest of the Hejaz.[49] In 1916 London offered Abdel Aziz a monthly subsidy of £5,000 and a shipment of machine guns and rifles. This augmented the three hundred rifles and 10,000 rupees that the British had provided Abdel Aziz a year earlier to help him overcome a tribal revolt.[50] Abdel Aziz was now formally receiving protection from the British, something he had been courting for over a decade. In return for protection, the British expected Abdel Aziz to resist Ottoman entreaties and harass, if not defeat, the Ottoman-supported Ibn Rashid.[51] The British remained neutral in the Arabian contest between the Hashemite leader in the west and Abdel Aziz in the Nejd, both of whom were friendly with the British crown.

After Hasa, Abdel Aziz returned his attention to the Turkish-backed Rashid clan to defeat them once and for all at the town of Hail in 1921. (In what was his usual fashion, the king married a Rashidi girl to minimize the chances that the family's descendants would come back to fight another day. Their son, Abdullah, is today the king of Saudi Arabia.) But at Hail, fissures that already existed between Abdel Aziz and the Ikhwan became even more apparent. The Ikhwan viewed fighting the Rashid clan as a distraction. They wanted to focus efforts on the Shi'a of Hasa, and they wanted the Hejaz, the home of Mecca and Medina. Religion, not Abdel Aziz's second-order political agenda against the Rashid clan, motivated the Ikhwan. As Mutluq al-Sur, the right-hand man of one of the Ikhwan's most notorious leaders, recalled, it was at this point that he began questioning the religious conviction of Abdel Aziz. "It was in 1920 at the siege of Hail by the Imam [Abdel Aziz] that I first found out that we were political tools."[52]

More trouble arose with the Ikhwan when Abdel Aziz conquered the Hejaz in 1924. With the victory, Abdel Aziz sent packing the Hejaz's historical rulers, the British-backed Hashemites, direct descendants of the Prophet Muhammad. The Hashemites lost considerable international support when their leader, Sharif Hussein of Mecca (who eventually fled the kingdom and whose great-great-grandson Abdullah is today the king of Jordan), declared himself caliph (leader of the worldwide Muslim community). His move antagonized Egypt's King Fouad, who sought the title for himself; the Saudi Ikwahn, who interpreted the move as a direct challenge to Abdel Aziz; Muslims in India, who were themselves divided over whom to support; and others who opposed Sharif Hussein for any number of reasons.[53] Rampant corruption and increasing heavy-handedness also alienated the local population, causing some to defect to Abdel Aziz. Perhaps sensing Arabia's shifting balance of power, London had been distancing itself from the Hashemites since the end of World War I—especially after Sharif Hussein began constantly complaining about Britain's evident betrayal.

Ikhwan leaders objected to the constraints Abdel Aziz placed on their behavior during the sacking of the Hejaz in 1924. During the fighting the Ikhwan disregarded Abdel Aziz's cautionary warnings and rampaged through Mecca and Medina, smashing shrines that they considered sacrilegious and once again terrorizing Muslim pilgrims whose traditions differed from their own. Many of the king's closest allies, including Abdullah bin Jiluwi and members of his family, pressed the king to crack down on the marauding religious fighters. But the king replied that "the Ikhwan were his children and that it was his duty to bear with them and advise, not punish them. Their intentions were good, he insisted, and sooner or later they would mend their ways."[54]

The king tried to placate the Ikhwan by turning their attention elsewhere. But the Ikhwan grew frustrated, especially after Abdel Aziz failed to include any of their leaders in the new Hejaz government and did not appoint any of them governor in newly occupied towns. Worse still, the king made his own son Faisal viceroy of the area.[55] Abdel Aziz's blatant nepotism offended the Ikhwan, especially when it involved such a religiously coveted position. Matters came to a head when the Ikhwan appeared determined to confront the British in Iraq, a move that Abdel Aziz deemed reckless. He rallied loyal Nejdi leaders who were exasperated by Ikhwan extremism, various frontier tribesmen, a few Bedouin tribal members who chose to fight against their kinsmen, and the ulema (serious religious scholars who acted as the guardians of legal and scholarly traditions); the last of these issued a fatwa (religious edict) recognizing the king's right to set foreign policy. In the spring of 1929, at the fateful battle of Sibila, the king took the offensive to counter growing Ikhwan power. After an hour of brutal hand-to-hand combat, with Abdel Aziz leading the charge, his brother Mohammed to his left and his eldest son (the future King Saud) on his right, the battle was decided in Abdel Aziz's favor.[56] The Ikhwan's influence was all but destroyed with this loss. The Ikhwan leaders surrendered within months, an outcome that was hastened by British military support. The government proceeded to destroy many hijrah, although for decades afterward those not destroyed received government grants and subsidies. Perhaps not surprisingly, one of the leaders of a 1979 revolt in Mecca that would shake the Saudi regime to its core was born in one of these remaining settlements.[57] Abdel Aziz followed the battle of Sibila with a set of regulations forbidding anyone but the ulema from issuing religious rulings. For the short term, he was able to dampen religious extremism. But once created, the force could not be stamped out completely. Over the course of the following decades Saudi Arabian leaders engaged in trying to steer, subdue, and at times encourage the religious radicalism stoked in these early days.

The 1929 battle provides an early and powerful example of the tension between Saudi Arabia's political and religious establishment despite nearly two centuries of mutual dependence. Such tension courses through Saudi Arabia's political veins up to the present.[58] The religious extremism that the settlements produced puts pressure not only on the royal family but also on the more establishment-leaning clerics within the ulema. A point that most casual observers of Saudi Arabia often overlook is that the ulema has frequently played an important role in mediating between the fanatics and the government; it is not synonymous with either. The government has often been supported by important tribes and townsmen who believe that the al-Saud's courtship of religiously radical groups is not only dangerous but counterproductive, as their intolerance inflames outside powers against the kingdom.[59]

Enter America

On September 23, 1932, Abdel Aziz formally declared his massive territorial acquisition to be the Kingdom of Saudi Arabia. The United States recognized it in 1933, the same year Socal won the Saudi oil concession.

As the king welcomed American oil workers to his lands, relations with Britain, now the dominant force in the region, grew testy. The British provided Abdel Aziz with an important stream of income, and they resented his courtship of the Americans.[60] But what Abdel Aziz found attractive about the newly arriving Americans was that they were not colonialists, like the British, and therefore were uninterested in restructuring Saudi domestic politics. They were first and foremost businessmen who represented their companies, not government policy. Happily, they also lived very far away. America's lack of interest in Saudi Arabia's domestic institutions became even more important in the 1950s, when anticolonial movements swept the region. Part of America's attractiveness throughout the Middle East was that it was not bent on occupation. It was not Great Britain. Ironically, this legacy is now used against the United States by critics pointing out that American allies are often brutally authoritarian, a characteristic that is an outgrowth of previous U.S. policies of noninterference.

The United States, already active in Saudi Arabia's oil fields, pro-vided a natural counter to British hegemony in the region. British influence surrounded the kingdom. The British had treaty obligations with every Persian Gulf state, maintained a colony at Aden with pro-tectorates around it (which eventually became South Yemen and then eventually merged with North Yemen), placed its allies on thrones in Iraq and Jordan, and held the Palestinian Mandate. A fear of encirclement, which guides Saudi Arabian foreign policy even today, pushed the new king away from the British and toward the Americans.

Later, just as the Americans helped to offset the British, Saudi leaders relied on Washington to offset Soviet power. The United States never had to convince Saudi Arabia that the Soviets were a threat, as they needed to do with Saudi Arabia's neighbors. True, Saudi leaders often viewed other threats as more compelling, such as the threat posed by Egypt, Yemen, and Israel (the first two eventually receiving consid-erable Soviet support). But the Saudi leadership took seriously Soviet machinations and held an anti-Communist outlook that was much more similar to the Americans' than it was to the points of view of many of their counterparts in the developing world.

In addition to America's anticolonial and later anti-Communist ideology, the United States also offered security and eventually access to markets. King Abdel Aziz worried about the British. His successors worried about Egypt, Iraq, Yemen, and Iran. From the beginning, America offered a military alternative. In the very first set of military agreements, the Dhahran airfield agreement, the United States offered Saudi Arabia a mission to begin training a military force. By 1950 President Truman had publicly committed the United States to the pre-servation of the independence and territorial integrity of Saudi Arabia. America remained the primary source of Saudi Arabian weapons until the 1980s.

If overlapping threat perceptions and the need for security pushed Saudi Arabia toward the United States, differences over Israel pulled them apart. These differences were never significant enough to lead Saudi Arabia into the Soviet camp, but Israel would remain a pressing issue for all Saudi Arabian leaders. As early as the 1930s, King Abdel Aziz vocally opposed increased Jewish immigration to Palestine. The king, like other Arab leaders, was against the partition of Palestine when it occurred. America's support for Israel gave a stick to Saudi Arabia's enemies to wield against the kingdom. Over the course of the last half century, Saudi Arabia's neighbors have relentlessly pointed out that the kingdom has the same international benefactor as the Arab archnemesis, Israel. America's support for Israel has also stoked anti-

Americanism among Saudi citizens, a phenomenon that the Soviets tried for years to exploit. As early as the 1940s the king warned that anti-Americanism would be the natural outcome of America's recognition. America's competing interests provided an ongoing difficulty for Saudi Arabia, from the 1940s until today. They have yet to find a way to reconcile them effectively. In 2001 Crown Prince (now King) Abdullah threatened to abrogate the long-standing relationship between the two countries unless Washington devised a way to reduce the violence between Palestinians and Israelis.

Setting the Stage for the Next Fifty Years

From 1902 until 1933 Arabia emerged from a disparate group of tribes backed by various world powers to a unified state under the command of King Abdel Aziz. From 1933 until 1948 the king struggled to keep hold of his kingdom as financial hardship threatened to bankrupt his rule. Unlike their British counterparts, American oil companies appeared willing to risk desert hardships to search and dig for oil and possibly make the king some money. Their energy, business acumen, and notable lack of interest in reconfiguring Saudi domestic politics drew the king toward them.

The U.S.-Saudi political relationship was born at the end of World War II and grew up during the Cold War. The Cold War environment informed everything about the relationship, from why oil was important to whom it was to be kept from, whom it was to be directed toward, and how its profits were to be employed. But Saudi Arabia became a particularly valuable U.S. Cold War partner not only because of its oil but also for its strategic location and religiously inspired antipathy toward Communism. Unlike Iraq, Syria, and Egypt, it never seriously flirted with the Soviet Union or credibly played the United States off the Soviet Union. Saudi Arabia's anti-Communist activity was particularly helpful during the 1970s when the United States was licking its wounds from the fighting in Vietnam. Confronted by an inward-focused America, Saudi Arabia, France, and others built a coalition to challenge Soviet adventurism, independent of American efforts. This was both welcomed and encouraged by the White House when it rejoined the fight after President Reagan took office in 1981.

But this was for the future. In 1945 the king was delighted to receive an invitation to meet the great American leader Franklin Delano Roosevelt. It was an opportunity that he would not pass up. The meeting would set the tone for the next fifty years of U.S.-Saudi relations.

2

Dropping Anchors in the Middle East

On February 14, 1945, President Franklin D. Roosevelt and King Abdel Aziz bin Abdel Rahman al-Faisal al-Saud met for the first and only time aboard the USS *Quincy*, a state-of-the-art military cruiser that was anchored in the Great Bitter Lake, north of the Suez Canal. The president was on his way home from Yalta, where he, Joseph Stalin, and Winston Churchill had started sketching the outlines of post-conflict Europe. King Abdel Aziz slipped out of his country under the cover of air raid sirens, worried that his absence would incite revolt. He returned home to wild rumors that he had abdicated or been kidnapped.[1]

The president's decision to sail south from Malta, where the *Quincy* was anchored, rather than immediately head home was not a decision he or anyone on board would have taken lightly. In the waning days of World War II the president made a fine target for the German navy and air force. At the same time, the president and his team were exhausted and not all in the best of health—Roosevelt's military aide of nearly twelve years, Major General Edwin "Pa" Watson, would die aboard the *Quincy* two weeks after meeting the king. For his own health reasons and to his lasting regret, the president's close advisor Harry L. Hopkins departed the ship midcourse and checked into the Mayo Clinic upon his return to the United States. It was the last time he would see his friend the president. Roosevelt himself disembarked from the *Quincy*, addressed a joint session of Congress sitting down, the first and only time, and died six weeks later.

There were a number of hardheaded security reasons Roosevelt wanted to meet the Saudi monarch, and also why King Abdel Aziz wished to meet Roosevelt. The president no doubt wanted to meet the ruler of the country whose oil was helpful to the war effort and whose territory was anticipated to become an important staging ground for the war in the Pacific. Although officially neutral until March 1945, the king leaned toward the Allies. In April 1941 he had turned down requests from Iraqi saboteurs to support a Nazi-inspired coup in that country. He also ignored a request from Adolf Hitler for Saudi Arabia to rise in protest against British influence. Starting in 1942, the king provided Allied air forces with access to air routes across the massive Arabian Peninsula. This was particularly vital, as fighting in North Africa forced the Allies to resupply troops in the Pacific from the more southern airfields in Sudan, which put Saudi territory directly along the preferred air route. Saudi Arabia also provided safe passage for significant wartime resupplies that flowed up the Persian Gulf waterway from the United States and Europe to the embattled Soviet Union. Accordingly, almost exactly two years prior to the meeting, Roosevelt declared Saudi Arabia eligible for lend-lease assistance.

But in addition to all the sensible reasons the two should meet, each leader was also filled with a profound curiosity about the other. As one of his secretaries of state remembered: "The president himself was drawn to the powerful personality of King Ibn Saud, and looked forward eagerly to making his personal acquaintance."[2] A less charitable Harry Hopkins acknowledged that "the president was going to thoroughly enjoy the colorful panoply of sovereigns of this part of the world" and that the trip was nothing more than "a lot of horseplay."[3] The king, for his part, wanted to meet the U.S. president whom he regarded as "the greatest man of the century."[4] As remembered by Hassan Yassin, who was taken as a young boy by his father, Youssef Yassin, the king's foreign minister, to meet the president aboard the *Quincy*, it was an opportunity for the desert king to "deal with the world's problems . . . with a giant, sitting eye to eye."[5]

During his 1943 trip to Tehran two years earlier, the president had twice flown over Saudi Arabia. The vast kingdom fascinated him, and he began envisioning agricultural and technical programs America could offer the kingdom for its own development. He wrote to the king of the possibilities and his "lasting regret" at not meeting. He hoped to meet in the future if his travels took him to the Near East, as "there are many things I want to talk with you about."[6] The king concluded that the message was a "good letter from a good person" and sent his sons Faisal and Khaled, both future kings, to the United States for a visit.[7]

Towering somewhere between six foot two and six foot four, approximately 260 pounds, and with "piercing luminous eyes," the "picturesque" Saudi king was indeed a formidable and charismatic leader. His heavy limp and outsized cane were a reminder to all that he had survived somewhere on the order of nine serious battlefield wounds. He lived a devoutly religious life, which was especially notable given that toward the end of it he was one of the wealthier men in the region. He was regularly attired in flowing black robes with the red and white checked head scarf characteristic of the Nejd, Saudi Arabia's central region, and, like other members of the royal family, he used gold head ropes to hold it in place.[8] As the captain of the USS *Murphy*, the ship sent to bring the king to the president's vessel, later recalled, "The immediate impression that you got was great majesty and dignity. You knew that you were in the presence of a powerful man."[9] Another American later described him as "a patriarch of the biblical mold."

After receiving the invitation to meet the president, Abdel Aziz embarked on his trip to Jeddah, using the excuse that he was making a pilgrimage to nearby Mecca. The king traveled six hundred miles in less than two weeks to meet the president on what was a dangerous journey. A set of Western journalists who had taken the reverse trip from Jeddah to Riyadh two years prior had had their own vehicle stall in the desert, witnessed their escort van capsize (killing two), had their car flooded with water in a swollen streambed, been marooned for several days, and eventually been forced to dispatch a runner to Riyadh in order to stave off dehydration.[10] On his yearly trips to Mecca, the king traveled slowly and carefully, often accompanied by a five-hundred-person retinue. Still, it was not unusual to find him sitting by the side of the road waiting for breakdowns and malfunctions to be reversed. His unexpected stops provided Bedouins the opportunity to approach and discuss with him their local problems.

Once in Jeddah, the king met up with the captain of the USS *Murphy*, the first American destroyer to dock in the Saudi seaport. The king's organizers began making preparations for the two hundred people and eighty-six sheep the king planned to take with him to meet the president. After plenty of agitated haggling between American and Saudi planners, it was agreed that only twenty Saudis would accompany the king, though forty-three ultimately made it aboard. The Saudis also managed to bring along eight sheep for feasting upon, surely straining U.S. naval regulations.

The king had only twice before left his country, once as a boy when he sought refuge in Kuwait and once when the British invited him to Basra in an attempt to co-opt him. But for the president of the United States of America, he was willing to make the journey. Domestic revolt was a serious enough risk that when he left Saudi Arabia a direct circuit was established from the *Murphy* to his son Prince Faisal, his representative in Mecca. Each half hour a radio operator would call Mecca and ask, "OK?" Mecca would reply, "OK," and sign off.[11]

Probably the greatest testimony to the almost larger-than-life stature of Saudi Arabia's king was his ability to keep his dinner down as the *Murphy* pitched back and forth on its journey along the Red Sea. One by one the king's men were excused and were later found "draped over the side of the ship emitting unpleasant sounds."[12] As his entourage strained to manage their seasickness, the king sat impassive.

That Valentine's Day, the ship carrying King Abdel Aziz pulled up beside Roosevelt's. The king's vessel was festooned with rare and valuable carpets, sheep bleating on the fantail, and at the bow a large tentlike structure referred to as "the big top" by American seamen manning the boat. Regular prayer sessions and the wafting smell of coffee had transformed the ship into a floating desert caravan.

President Roosevelt intended to discuss energy matters. A mere two weeks before, the president had summoned the cruiser's captain and asked him to arrange a meeting with the king "in regard to oil."[13] America's dwindling oil supply preoccupied the president and the secretaries of war, state, and the interior. During the war, U.S. consumption was increasing at a faster rate than new oil sources were being discovered. "Since 1938," the indomitable interior secretary, Harold Ickes, told a radio audience,

> We in the United States have been using up our oil reserves faster than we have been discovering new ones. . . . [W]e don't have enough oil right now—*tonight*—so that we can supply the military and essential industry with all that they require, and still have enough left for normal civilian consumption.[14]

During World War II, American forces in Europe used one hundred times more gasoline than they had throughout World War I.[15]

Foreign oil sources, particularly Middle East ones, were needed to supplement American output and relieve the demands on the nation's crude oil reserves. In 1943, President Roosevelt created the Petroleum Reserve Corporation (PRC) "to acquire petroleum, petroleum products and petroleum reserves outside of the continental United States." Under its auspices, Roosevelt asked Ickes to negotiate with the American oil company operating in the kingdom, Casoc (soon to be renamed Aramco), and purchase a majority of shares in the company. Ickes, a peppery and scrappy bureaucratic fighter, had no reservations about taking on the powerful oil industry. For Ickes, oil was too important to be left to the oil companies. He regarded World War II as being as much an oil war as anything else, and intended to ensure the commodity's supply. He repeatedly told the president, "Next to winning the war, the most important matter before us as a nation [is] the world oil situation."[16] The Middle East presented "an important key to postwar economic problems and to basic international political arrangements."[17]

America needed oil, and Ickes wanted to better position the nation vis-à-vis the British government, which had stakes in British oil companies operating in the Gulf and seemed to be pressing aggressively on America's relationship with the king of Saudi Arabia. Had he been successful, the deal would have marked the first time that the U.S. government owned a participating share in a foreign oil property. The oil companies, not surprisingly, were not forthcoming. They declined early government offers to buy a controlling portion of Casoc's stock.

The king also shared an interest in matters of oil. It was his primary revenue source, made all the more important given that revenue generated by the hajj, the annual Muslim pilgrimage, had dried up during the war. Running a huge kingdom and keeping important tribal leaders satisfied required more money than the king was bringing in. Aramco officials estimated that the king needed approximately $10 million per year to run his country effectively. It was unclear whether he would be able to hold on to the kingdom in the absence of increased American foreign aid.

Up until 1942, Great Britain had made up the shortfall between what the king needed and what was available. But because the United States underwrote Great Britain's treasury, the king's aid was indirectly provided by the United States. In 1942, the oil companies came knocking on Washington's doors. Britain was benefiting from Washington's aid, and the oil companies worried that unless the United States took a more direct role in supporting the king, they would be shut out of postwar oil discussions. On February 18, 1943, for reasons of oil, strategic location, and the king's influence in the region, President Roosevelt made Saudi Arabia eligible for U.S. assistance through the valuable lend-lease assistance program. Between 1940 and 1947, the United States provided Saudi Arabia with $99 million in aid, only 25 percent of which was meant to be paid back.[18]

At their meeting on the *Quincy* the president also hoped to secure the king's help in averting conflict between Jews and Arabs in Palestine. In 1938 the king had been the first Arab head of state to write directly to the president expressing concern over the devolving situation. His letter generated considerable attention in the State Department and was passed up to the president with a note that

> in view of the special position of the Arab States in respect of the Palestine question, and in view of the position of King ibn Saud as the outstanding Arab ruler and as the person most qualified to speak

on behalf of the Arab people, it would seem that something more than a perfunctory acknowledgement should be made of his present communications.[19]

Prior to meeting, the president wrote on occasion to the king soliciting his advice about how to reduce skirmishes between Jews and Arabs over land purchases and immigration. Each time the king replied that the only way to avert conflict was to stop the ongoing Jewish immigration to Palestine. According to King Abdel Aziz, if the Jews were "reinstall[ed in Palestine] . . . the Heavens will split, the earth will be rent asunder, and the mountains will tremble at what the Jews claim in Palestine, both materially and spiritually."[20] Face-to-face on the ship, the king reiterated what he had long stated privately—that conflict was all but inevitable unless the president considered resettling the Jews in Europe, the continent that had caused their problems in the first place.

Roosevelt tried to bring up other subjects, such as the economic development of Saudi Arabia, but the king responded that "he could not engage with any enthusiasm in the development of his country's agriculture and public works if this prosperity would be inherited by the Jews."[21] This, despite the fact that in 1942 Saudi Arabia had requested that the United States dispatch "a mission of technical experts to assist in the agricultural development of Arabia."[22]

The Saudi king also had a number of other issues he wanted to raise. He wanted to ensure his country's independence and obtain assurances that the Americans would never become occupiers like their British counterparts.[23] Although he welcomed American backing, the Saudi leader was so nervous about colonial designs on his country that when the U.S. consulate in Dhahran was established in 1944, the consul general was not allowed to sink a flagpole into Saudi sand but rather had to grapple it to the side of a building. In addition to America's intentions, the king wanted to discuss inter-Arab politics, including French influence in Lebanon and Syria and the dangerous situation emerging between Jews and Arabs in Palestine.[24]

After their meeting, Roosevelt declared that he had learned more about the Arab-Israeli conflict in one meeting with the Saudi Arabian monarch than he had in repeated briefing papers from his own State Department. He left the meeting promising Abdel Aziz two things. First, the U.S. government would make no change in its basic policy in Palestine without full and prior consultation with both Jews and Arabs. This was consistent with pledges made previously. Second, Roosevelt promised that he would never do anything that might prove hostile to the Arabs.[25] One week before his death, Roosevelt reconfirmed his pledge in writing.[26]

Shortly after meeting the Saudi Arabian king, the president told Secretary of State Edward R. Stettinius Jr. that "he must have a conference with congressional leaders and re-examine our entire policy on Palestine." The secretary remembered that Roosevelt was convinced "that if nature took its course there would be bloodshed between the Arabs and Jews. Some formula, not yet discovered, would have to be evolved to prevent warfare."[27] But in a letter to her good friend Joseph P. Lash, Eleanor Roosevelt also reported that despite his statements to the king and Stettinius, her husband said to her that "his one complete failure was with Ibn Saud on Palestine."[28] The president had not been able to move the king toward a more compromising position. Three years later, when the United States recognized the State of Israel, King Abdel Aziz viewed it as a direct betrayal of Roosevelt's pledge.

The meeting between Roosevelt and Abdel Aziz had lasting symbolic and practical importance. It marked the beginning of political relations between the two countries, overshadowing Washington's recognition of Saudi Arabia in 1933. The meeting also established a high-level personal relationship between the leaders of the two countries. There was a notable chemistry between Roosevelt and Abdel Aziz, and the two seemed genuinely to enjoy each other's company. Upon his departure, the hobbling king received from Roosevelt one of the president's extra wheelchairs. The king regularly acknowledged it as one of his most cherished possessions. Accompanying aides played only a marginal role, a role still adopted by much of the U.S. and Saudi foreign policy establishments in the bilateral relationship. Differences over Palestine were discussed, although not resolved.

As soon as it ended, the meeting spawned a nostalgic larger-than-life mythology, something that future leaders have been unable to approach. Leaders on both sides still reference this meeting when discussing a history of close working relations at the highest political level. A 2005 joint statement by President George W. Bush and Saudi Arabia's Crown Prince Abdullah begins by referring to the meeting and stating that "in six hours President Bush's predecessor and the Crown Prince's father established a strong personal bond that set the tone for decades of close relations between our two nations."[29] To this day, the U.S. embassy in Riyadh showcases a glass-enclosed replica of the USS *Quincy* on special occasions.

On April 12, 1945, Roosevelt died in Warm Springs, Georgia, one month before Germany's surrender and four months before Japan's. It was left to President Harry S. Truman to end the war and construct the peace. With the end of the war, and the need for oil and air routes greatly reduced, Saudi Arabia became a lesser priority for Washington.

Ending the War and Constructing the Peace

Truman readily acknowledged that he was not the most experienced man for the job of president of the United States. A two-term senator from Missouri, he had been a compromise vice presidential candidate during a contentious 1944 Democratic national convention. His eighty-three days as vice president provided scant training for the enormous responsibility that descended upon his shoulders. When the president died, an April exploratory trip Truman had planned to familiarize himself with the Middle East was canceled, something he "regretted immeasurably."[30] Upon taking office, Truman did not share Roosevelt's hard-earned experience engaging Middle East leaders.

Upon World War II's conclusion Truman confronted three thorny postwar realities that ultimately shaped his views on Saudi Arabia. First, he faced an expansionist Soviet Union that came to dominate all other foreign policy concerns. After World War II the Soviet Union began aggressively asserting control over Eastern Europe and seemed poised to abrogate its 1943 Tehran Declaration commitments to respect the sovereignty of Saudi Arabia's neighbor across the Persian Gulf, Iran. Only with significant U.S. support did Iranian troops successfully reclaim its northern territory from Soviet forces stationed there. Shortly thereafter Stalin challenged Turkish sovereignty over the strategic Black Sea Straits and initiated a war of nerves on Turkey's eastern border. It actively stoked domestic opposition groups in Greece. Moscow's action at the edges of the Middle East appeared designed "to deny to Western Powers the strategic facilities available in the Near East, such as bases, Suez Canal and oil."[31] Unlike some Democrats who comfortably conceded to Moscow a sphere of influence, Truman and his team determined to contain the rising Soviet tide.[32]

Truman's options for dealing with Soviet moves in Europe and the Middle East were circumscribed by a second political reality: weak congressional support for an internationalist agenda. The United States at the time was undergoing a massive demobilization to "bring the boys home." A strong isolationist wing within the Republican Party, led by Senator Robert A. Taft, drew significant support and called for keeping resources at home. At the same time, a large number of Democrats, including James Roosevelt, the late president's son, wanted to turn international problems over to the newly formed United Nations. Truman was thus stuck between those in Congress whom Eisenhower later called the "stupid isolationists" and those Truman considered "crackpot liberals." The domestic divide increased his admiration for President James K. Polk, who regularly told Congress "to go to hell on foreign policy matters."[33] In November 1945, shortly after assuming the presidency, Truman assured a delegation of U.S. Middle East officials, including the director of Near Eastern and African affairs, Loy W. Henderson, and the minister to Saudi Arabia, William A. Eddy, that "in spite of campaigns waged in the press by various isolationist publicists," his administration would pursue an activist foreign policy in the Middle East.[34] For the moment, this calmed America's Middle East diplomats, who feared that Washington's interests would once again recede behind its borders, as had happened after World War I, and that the United States would thus turn the region over to Soviet domination.

In 1947 a third set of challenges emerged that had a direct bearing on Middle East politics and U.S.-Saudi relations. That February Britain made two startling announcements that added to Truman's Middle East problems. First, on February 14, exactly two years after the meeting between Roosevelt and Abdel Aziz, London announced its plans to end its Palestine Mandate, withdraw its troops by the summer of 1948, and turn all deliberations over to the United Nations. Then, one week later, on February 21 Britain revealed that it would no longer help defend Greece and Turkey from Soviet aggression. London had neither the will nor the ability to manage the growing anticolonial sentiments sweeping the region. It would dramatically scale back its commitments to southeastern Europe and the Middle East. Over the course of its two terms, the Truman administration wrestled with how to manage Britain's withdrawal from empire.

These three realities—an expansionist Soviet Union, a constrained United States, and declining British power—defined Truman's foreign policy challenges in the Middle East. The State Department identified two available options. The United States could distance itself from Great Britain and let the empire collapse under its own weight. This risked the Soviet Union filling the vacuum, since America did not have the military or financial wherewithal to replace the British. Alternatively, Washington could use the goodwill it had amassed over the years in the Middle East to help stanch Britain's decline. This threatened to tether America to Britain's sinking ship. Paul H. Nitze of the State Department's newly created Policy Planning Staff warned that choosing the latter option ran the danger of "becoming involved in the general decline in the Middle East without being able to effectively halt it."[35] Nonetheless, Truman threw his lot in with the British. He simply did not believe that America had the resources to make any other decision.

In financial, political, and security matters, the United States began assuming increased influence in Middle East politics in order to help manage Britain's withdrawal. Saudi Arabia welcomed Britain's retreat, although it chafed at the close American-British coordination.

Although Saudi Arabia did not occupy a significant portion of Truman's attention, he did view the kingdom as an important player in a complicated and confusing neighborhood. After a meeting with Crown Prince Saud, the king's oldest living son, at the White House in January 1947, he confided in his diary that the "Arabians [are] jealous of Syrians, Iraqis, Egyptians and Turks. They seem to like us but are suspicious of the British. They hate the Bolsheviks."[36] He was unclear how to square Saudi political concerns with the competing American interest of working with the British, Turks, and other Arabs. An even greater challenge was how to reconcile Arab and Jewish claims to Palestine. Still, the strategic advantages of Saudi Arabia's geographic position, petroleum resources, and the "general antipathy of the Saudi Arabs for Communism" provided strong incentives for deepening existing ties.[37] In doing so, the Truman administration set the stage for the next half century of U.S.-Saudi relations.

Truman and Saudi Arabia

During the Truman years, the United States and Saudi Arabia initiated a series of military agreements that laid the groundwork for U.S. training of Saudi forces (which continues until today) and access to a military airstrip on Saudi Arabia's eastern shores. During the late 1940s and 1950s the airfield formed part of an emerging ring of American strategic air commands built to contain the Soviet Union. It also provided a defensive shield around Saudi Arabia's nearby oil fields, which assumed an important role in Europe's postwar reconstruction.

In 1946 77 percent of Europe's oil supply came from the Western Hemisphere. Strategic planners at that time anticipated that within a few years 80 percent of that supply would come from the Middle East.[38] Saudi oil, along with other Gulf sources, was to become the lifeblood of Europe's economic and political recovery.

The Truman administration also ramped up financial assistance to the Middle East. Battling a thrifty Congress, the administration offered massive financial assistance to Greece and Turkey in order to defend the Middle East from Soviet penetration. The State Department also advocated varying forms of indirect aid. In Saudi Arabia this took the form of the controversial "50/50 agreement," so called because it evenly divided Aramco's profits between the company and Saudi Arabia and controversial because it shifted oil revenues from the U.S. Treasury to the government in Riyadh.

In return for financial and military support, the king offered broad political backing for America's activities in the region, outside the Arab-Israeli conflict. In 1951 the State Department concluded that "while US policy has been the target of adverse criticism and bitterness in some countries of the Near East, Saudi Arabia has remained firm in its friendship for the United States. It has served as our spokesman and interpreter to less friendly Arab states, and has, through the prestige and conservative nature of its King, exerted a stabilizing influence on the Near East generally."[39] The administration also deemed King Abdel Aziz's steadfast anti-Communism genuine and helpful, especially during the Korean War, when Soviet-American tensions were running high. "If you could find a Communist in Saudi Arabia, I will hand you his head," King Abdel Aziz assured Brigadier General Edwin M. Day, the commanding general of the Dhahran airfield, when they met in 1951.[40]

For these strategic, economic, and ideological reasons, the president of the United States repeatedly assured the king in writing that the United States was "interested in the preservation of the independence and territorial integrity of Saudi Arabia [and that] no threat to your Kingdom could occur which would not be a matter of immediate concern to the United States."[41] This was interpreted by both Saudis and Americans as an implicit security guarantee.

While the Truman administration would lay the foundation for the future of U.S.-Saudi relations, the global situation that the president inherited presented significant challenges to the relationship. In addition to the close Anglo-American coordination on Middle East policy, something the Saudis viewed as troublesome, America's support for the partition of Palestine in 1947 and its recognition of Israel in 1948 prompted enormous protests from senior Saudis. Prince Faisal, the titular head of the Foreign Ministry, viewed the action as a personal betrayal, and King Abdel Aziz dispatched a series of angry letters. The king never threatened to withdraw the oil concession, as many diplomats feared he would. The king understood the American concession as key to his country's economic survival. Still, American support for Israel created problems for the king and limited the outward support he would offer the United States. It gave ammunition to the king's detractors at home and abroad. They pointed out repeatedly that the king's principal ally was also Israel's. So began a balancing act that both Saudi and American leaders would undertake for decades after.

"A Miserable Place"

In August 1945 Saudi Arabia and the United States reached their first major military accord, the Dhahran Air Field Agreement. It permitted the United States to build an air base near the small Aramco company town, once described by an American diplomat as "a miserable place; nothing but sand and sandstorms."[42]

The request for an air base came not from Saudi Arabia but from the United States War (later Defense) Department, which desperately sought shorter and cheaper air routes between North Africa and the fighting in the Pacific. A base at Dhahran promised to shorten the route between Cairo, Karachi, and the Pacific by nearly two hundred miles. The U.S. War Department also hoped that local Saudi oil would help refuel its Pacific-bound air fleets. James S. Moose Jr., America's representative in the region, and William Eddy, the minister to Saudi Arabia and a well-regarded linguist who had interpreted the conversation between King Abdel Aziz and President Roosevelt on the *Quincy*, began a prolonged set of negotiations with the king for a base at Dhahran to assist the American war effort.

The king was uneasy about the precedent of a base on his soil. He feared it would become the first drip in an unstoppable flow of imperial intervention. He was also worried that a base would unnecessarily provoke the British. Prince Faisal reflected his father's concern in explaining that "the Americans are our friends and we like them; but Britain is the power with which to deal."[43] Nonetheless, in May 1945, because of the harsh toll that World War II was taking on Britain's financial and military position, London reluctantly informed the king that it had no objections to an American airfield. Taking the king's concerns into account, the August agreement called for an "airfield" rather than an "air base" and ensured that full ownership would revert to Saudi Arabia after the war. Americans were granted operating rights for three years after the war ended.

The timing of Saudi and British acquiescence to a military outpost at Dhahran could not have been worse. When Allied forces declared victory in Europe in May 1945, Dhahran immediately lost its wartime relevance. American commanders no longer needed to deploy Asian-bound troops eastward, via Saudi Arabia. After the European victory, troop movement shifted westward, from the United States.

On June 25 the acting secretary of state, Joseph C. Grew, informed Eddy that the War Department was pulling its support for the Saudi airfield. It could no longer justify paying for a base of "diminishing military necessity."[44] Also, given that victory against Japan appeared imminent, the War Department did not think that Dhahran would be completed in time to be useful. Their concerns proved justified. Dhahran was not completed until 1946, almost a year after the war's end.

Colonel Eddy, who was so decorated from his World War I pursuits that when General George S. Patton Jr. first laid eyes on him he reportedly grunted, "I don't know who he is, but the son of a bitch has sure been shot at enough," was frustrated with the War Department's about-face.[45] He had logged countless hours negotiating the basing arrangement. He prodded Grew to inform the president that the air-field was still in America's national interest, even if the War Department no longer supported it. In his subsequent memo to the president, Grew insisted that the United States did not want to give the king "the impression that our policies with regard to Saudi Arabia are of wavering character."[46]

Three days after the War Department's about-face and two days after Grew sent his memo to Truman, the president approved the Dhahran agreement. The vulnerability of Saudi Arabia's oil fields and the opportunity for America to use Dhahran as a civilian air travel hub in the postwar period persuaded President Truman of its utility. And then, much to State's surprise, the king rejected the offer.

Just like the U.S. War Department, the king hesitated when the military justification for the base disappeared. According to Eddy, he preferred "to have foreign cooperation in developing his country achieved through civilian agencies," rather than the U.S. military.[47] As long as there was a wartime necessity, the king could stave off protests from the ulema, his neighbors, fanatical elements within his own society, and the British by invoking national security concerns. As Prince Faisal told Grew when he met him in Washington in July 1945, "Rumors were circulated, not only throughout Saudi Arabia but also throughout the whole Arab world, to the effect that the American soldiers in Saudi Arabia were the forerunners of the American military imperialism in the Near East."[48] Without a military justification, the airfield seemed little more than a traditional colonial base.

Despite the war's end, the State Department kept pushing for a base in order to demonstrate America's support for the kingdom of Saudi Arabia. It had no other nonmilitary carrots to offer the cash-strapped king, who was asking for development aid in areas such as water and electricity infrastructure. Congress had already made it quite apparent that "outright grants specifically to Saudi Arabia are out of the question."[49] In August 1945 the two sides agreed to complete the construction of Dhahran only after Congress reluctantly agreed to generous budgetary aid for Saudi Arabia's economic development, a sum amounting to more than twice the total allocated by Great Britain. The War Department was saddled with the cost of constructing the Dhahran site. The State Department got a base that the War Department did not want but had to pay for, and Saudi Arabia got from Congress its nonmilitary assistance as an add-on to the considerable American military investment it had not sought. The State Department did not have to use its own resources in order to increase aid to Saudi Arabia, resources it did not have in any event. The base resulted from convoluted bureaucratic logic that did not serve any party particularly well in the long run, not even the State Department.

The War Department made the best of it. Within a year, the *New York Times* called the Dhahran field "the most important air base in the sprawling area of the Middle East."[50] Three years after the Joint Chiefs of Staff had questioned the utility of Dhahran, Secretary of Defense James V. Forrestal wrote that "our world-wide strategic position would be greatly improved if, in the event of war, the means could be developed to defend successfully, and to conduct sustained air operations from Dhahran Air Base."[51] Come 1949, Dhahran was the only airfield in the region that could handle the U.S. Air Force's massive B-29 bombers.

What changed between 1945 and 1949 was concern over Soviet behavior. By the late 1940s American planners were more anxious about Soviet intentions, and Saudi Arabia seemed a natural place to build defenses. As the American consul general in Dhahran recalled, by 1949

> the containment policy of President Truman was in force . . . the mood in the United States Government was tense and the military were doing an awful lot of planning pursuant to the Soviet takeover of Eastern Europe, the Soviet threat to Iran, the threat to Turkey, etc. . . . The result was an upgrading of Dhahran airfield, an identification of that field in our strategic planning.[52]

Because of Saudi ambivalence toward the airfield, Dhahran would cause considerable heartburn for future U.S. negotiators. The king welcomed the security it provided, but he detested its political symbolism. Given this, the United States would probably have been better off abandoning the air base in 1945, when the War Department originally lost interest. Instead, a series of painful negotiations continued until 1962, when the United States finally gave up all claims. Dhahran served only to create and exacerbate tensions in the U.S.-Saudi relationship. It never provided the political anchor that bases did elsewhere around the globe.

"Muddling the Situation as Completely as It Could Possibly Be Muddled"

On February 21, 1947, the British ambassador to Washington, Lord Inverchapel, notified the State Department that within six weeks Great Britain would suspend foreign aid to Greece and Turkey. By London's estimation, Greece immediately required up to $280 million in foreign exchange lest the government collapse and attract Soviet involvement. Turkey too required significant assistance, although not of the same order of magnitude. Washington had to decide quickly whether it wanted to replace Great Britain's financial contributions to Greece and Turkey and make its first foray into Middle East great-power politics.

Secretary of State George C. Marshall was out of town when Inverchapel's message was delivered, leaving Marshall's undersecretary, Dean Acheson, to begin drafting America's response. According to Robert J. Donovan, a brash and colorful newspaper reporter, Acheson was "a man of intellect wit, snobbery, arrogance, high style and charm . . . [He] was imbued with esteem for the British Empire and the stable world order of the nineteenth century."[53] He, like Truman, feared that British weakness provided the Soviet Union an opportunity to move on three continents: Europe, Africa, and Asia.

Taking over the British position in Europe to deter Soviet expansion would require massive American financial assistance at a time when Congress was cutting the budget by several billion dollars. If anyone could sell the idea of increasing foreign assistance to Congress, it was Marshall, the man Truman considered "the greatest living American." The old general was so popular that the Republican-controlled Senate unanimously approved Marshall's nomination as secretary of state only hours after Truman submitted it.

Yet according to Acheson, Marshall "most unusually and unhappily flubbed his opening statement" to the congressional leaders.[54] He hardly convinced any of them that only massive American aid could save "the entire independent structure of the eastern Mediterranean and the Middle East."[55] Acheson, a Marshall devotee, took a second shot, arguing that

> like apples in a barrel infected by one rotten one, the corruption of Greece would infect Iran and all to the east. It would also carry infection to Africa through Asia Minor and Egypt, and to Europe through Italy and France. . . . [T]he Soviet Union was playing one of the greatest gambles in history at minimal cost . . . we and we alone were in a position to break up the play. These were the stakes that British withdrawal from the Eastern Mediterranean offered to an eager and ruthless opponent.[56]

Afterward, awed lawmakers led by Republican Senator Arthur H. Vandenberg quietly committed to support what ultimately became known as the Truman Doctrine. The United States began its path to replace the British in the Middle East.

The British decision on Greece and Turkey would have been difficult for any administration to handle, but it coincided with the United Kingdom's decision also to extricate itself from the problems of Palestine. Only one week prior to the announcement about Greece and Turkey, the British Embassy had informed the State Department that London was turning the Palestinian Mandate over to the United Nations.[57] Now Washington would have to manage the fallout directly.

For nearly a decade King Abdel Aziz had been warning that problems between Jews and Arabs in Palestine would engulf the region. In the winter of 1946–47 the king had sent two of his sons, first Prince Faisal and then Prince Saud, to the United States. Prince Faisal and President Truman earnestly discussed the problem of Palestine, but the two talked past each other. Faisal focused on the injustice of increased immigration and the negative regional consequences that a Jewish state would have. The president addressed his comments to the deplorable conditions of displaced Jews in Europe and the need to fashion a refuge for them in Palestine. The backdrop to their conversation was the ongoing violence in Palestine, which threatened to escalate. Dean Acheson remembered that "neither really grasped the depth of the other's concern; indeed, each rather believed the other's was exaggerated. The conversation ended in platitudes, which were seized upon as agreement."[58]

Crown Prince Saud's visit was even less consequential, as he did not broach the subject of Palestine with the president, as expected, or much else of interest. He did, however, sit incredibly still, which mesmerized Dean Acheson, who later tried to mimic the prince's immobility when "the boredom of presiding over public meetings would overcome me."[59]

The United Nations, then a young and fragile organization, was in no way prepared to deal with the emotional and complicated crisis of Palestine. Loy Henderson, Truman's director of Near Eastern and African affairs and a strong UN backer, was "appalled" that Britain was turning such a problem over to it. He did not expect that an organization of some fifty-odd nations could solve a problem of this kind. "It seemed to us," Henderson recalled, "that the British should at least work out what they considered to be the best solution and then present their plan to the United Nations on approval."[60] Without such a plan, responsibility for constructing a political solution fell by default onto the desk of the American president.

But the British saw no way to reconcile increased Jewish immigration and regional stability. Truman, like Roosevelt before him, viewed the problem as one of Britain's own making. Both believed that there was a British commitment to create a Jewish state.[61] As far as Truman was concerned, the constant stream of British commissions and overlapping commitments on Palestine only served to "muddl[e] the situation just as much as it can be muddled."[62]

On November 29, 1947, the United Nations passed a resolution supporting the partition of Palestine. Prince Faisal, who had expected the United States to either delay such a decision or endorse a UN trusteeship over the entire area, sat shocked. He not only was Saudi Arabia's representative at the UN but was dual-hatted as the UN spokesman for Arab representatives. He had been assured by Ambassador Henry A. Byroade, America's Middle East hand at the UN, and others that the United States would not support partition. He had shared those assurances with other Arab leaders, and his credibility was now in question. Eventually the stunned Faisal took the podium. According to D. Dean Rusk, the State Department's director for special political affairs, Faisal "stood there erect and tall, a man whose honor had been insulted and his pride wounded, and he spoke with passion and clarity about this great injury that had been done to the Arab people."[63] For Prince Faisal, who had represented his father at the 1919 Versailles Peace Conference in Paris, when he was only fourteen years old, and who had already witnessed firsthand thirty years of great-power machinations, America's support for partition was a staggering personal and political blow. He had assured his Arab counterparts that Americans would not make such a decision, and his miscalculation was now on full display.

King Abdel Aziz was also angry, but he remained pragmatic. A few days after partition passed, he summoned the U.S. representative in Jeddah, J. Rives Childs, and made clear that there were still many areas in which the two countries could work. The king told Childs that the U.S.

> government had taken [a] decision with respect to Palestine which was most distasteful for the Arab world [but] . . . that was past and the Arabs would take such measures as they deemed necessary for the defense of their interests. . . . Although [the U.S. and Saudi Arabia] differ enormously on the question of Palestine we still have our own mutual interests and friendship to safeguard. . . . I occupy a position of preeminence in the Arab world. In the case of Palestine I have to make common cause with other Arab states. Although the other Arab states may bring pressure to bear on me I do not anticipate that a situation will arise whereby I shall be drawn into conflict with friendly western powers on this question.[64]

But the king failed to anticipate how difficult it would be to stay removed from the impending conflict.

Between November 1947 and May 1948, when the United States recognized the State of Israel, President Truman mulled over a variety of options to solve the Palestine problem. These included recognizing a sovereign Jewish state and delaying such a decision through a temporary UN trusteeship, an option still circulating even after the United Nation's endorsement of partition.

There existed no easy solution. Trusteeship posed significant challenges. The UN was too weak and divided to manage the problem. In February 1948 Secretary of Defense Forrestal reported that "any serious attempt to implement the General Assembly's recommendation on [a trusteeship for] Palestine would set in train events that must finally result in at least a partial mobilization of U.S. forces, including recourse to Selective Services."[65] There was little public support for a U.S. military mobilization.

Yet almost the entire U.S. foreign policy establishment, including pivotal players such as George Marshall, Dean Acheson, and Loy Henderson, was against the alternative: recognizing a Jewish state. Henderson well summarized the State Department's concern that a Jewish state

> would cause much bloodshed and suffering, would alienate the people of that world who have been placing much trust in the United States, might result in the loss to the free world of the use of the great resources of the Middle East, and that the continued existence of such a State could cause suffering, expense, bickering and damage to the United States internally and internationally for many years to come. The Soviet Union would also try to take advantage of the situation by penetrating into the Middle East.[66]

Forrestal, who clearly saw the dangers of both options, feared that if, or more likely when, war broke out, America would have to come to the aid of the Jews with forces that Washington simply did not have. He was also deeply concerned about the possibility of losing access to the region's oil, particularly Saudi Arabia's, "one of the three great puddles left in the world."[67] The president later told the defense secretary that, notwithstanding Saudi resources, he wanted to handle the problem in the light not of oil but of justice.[68]

On May 14, 1948, the British mandate expired and Israel declared independence. The United States recognized it minutes later. The U.S. ambassador to the United Nations, Warren R. Austin, was informed of the decision fifteen minutes before he was to cast the vote. Upon hearing the news, Austin left the building, muttering, "To hell with it." The rest of the U.S. delegation found out about the decision from a UN delegate who read it off an Associated Press report. Pandemonium broke out on the floor of the United Nations. Dean Rusk recalls a despondent Faisal stating that "with the creation of Israel, the Arabs were being forced to pay for the crimes of Adolf Hitler. He held the United States responsible."[69]

From Jeddah, Minister Childs reported that the Saudis were "profoundly shocked," and he warned of "ominous possibilities."[70] Childs believed that in the future the government of Saudi Arabia would have little confidence in "our policy assurances," and Washington should expect a "break" in U.S.-Saudi relations and orders to evacuate the Dhahran air base. Neither threat materialized. What did happen was war. Upon recognition of Israel, Egypt, Syria, Transjordan, Lebanon, and Iraq invaded the newly declared state. Saudi Arabia also participated but sent only a small battalion, two companies, to Palestine and put them under Egyptian command.[71] In that way, it seems that the king was trying to keep his earlier commitment to Childs to join the Arab cause without threatening relations with Western powers. Abdel Aziz remained true to assurances that he viewed U.S. policy as distinct from U.S. corporate interests.[72] The 1948 war was the first of several times that Saudi Arabia refrained from sending significant forces to fight for Palestine. Relations were not suspended, Aramco's concession remained intact, and America continued to operate from Dhahran.

Still, the king was bitterly opposed to recognition. He spoke about it constantly with visiting Americans, although never as acerbically as Faisal. Until his death the Saudi monarch believed that Truman had betrayed Roosevelt's promise to consult with him and other Arabs on the problem of Palestine and avoid taking actions detrimental to their cause. However, he tried to redirect attention to other areas where U.S. and Saudi interests overlapped. Although distressed, the king made it clear that he was not going to act against official relations, the oil concession, or the Dhahran airfield.[73] When Abdel Aziz was pushed, the security and development of his own kingdom were what mattered most. "It outweighed Saudi unhappiness, which was always there, about our policy toward Palestine and Israel."[74]

The Israeli-Palestinian conflict became, and remains to this day, one of the most significant challenges between the United States and Saudi Arabia. As the king rightly acknowledged in 1947, the two sides differed enormously on the question of Palestine. From 1948 on, the king and his successors had to manage the fact that both Israel and Saudi Arabia shared the same international backer. The king's detractors, both inside and especially outside the kingdom, made it the relentless focus of their propaganda against the royal family. In 1948 the legation in Jeddah reported back to Washington that Abdel Aziz was "under heavy attack in the Arab world for what is regarded already as his excessive leniency toward US interest, in view of what is regarded as our hostility to Arab world by our Palestine policy."[75] Whenever possible, the king tried to show his neighbors that there was some daylight between his country and the United States, if only to quiet the critics. To the United States, he made apparent his preference that Palestine should not come between them. The conflict, however, exacerbated his many other regional challenges.

The 50/50 Agreement

Partly in response to its decisions around Palestine, Washington sought ways to try to ease the pressure on its regional partners from angry critics. Toward Saudi Arabia in particular, the State Department looked for ways to increase economic support for the king. Oil profits, while growing significantly, were not enough to cover the increasing costs of running the kingdom and keeping full the pockets of influential tribal leaders. The American public, however, was not predisposed to help the king out of his troubling financial situation. During Truman's time the U.S. Congress was reluctant to provide foreign aid to any country, particularly Saudi Arabia, which seemed to have enough money if only it spent it more wisely. Congress was not persuaded by King Abdel Aziz's argument that he needed to spend liberally in order to ensure quiescence at home and build influence abroad.

Particularly galling to the Saudi government was that the U.S. Treasury received higher taxes from Aramco's income than Riyadh received in total oil revenue. In 1949 Aramco paid $43 million in U.S. income tax but only $39.1 million in fees and royalties to the Saudi government. Fred A. Davies, head of Aramco, reported that the Saudis "weren't a darn bit happy about that."[76] In 1950, following a precedent set by Venezuela earlier that year to receive more equitable profits, the king demanded an equal share of Aramco's revenues, a 50/50 split between company and host country. The Saudis sought to augment their own profits by taxing Aramco's and leveraging the American tax code, which stipulated that a company operating in a foreign country could deduct the amount of taxes it paid to a host government. This meant that Riyadh's increased profits came not at the expense of Aramco's bottom line (economically reliant on Aramco, the king did not want to bankrupt the company) but rather from a redirected tax flow from the United States to Saudi coffers.

The State Department backed Saudi Arabia's position. State saw the demand as an inevitable outgrowth of the Venezuela precedent and therefore sought to manage rather than resist the fallout. State was also looking for ways to increase foreign assistance to Saudi Arabia, something made difficult by a cost-conscious Congress. But perhaps most important to State's position was the fact that in June 1950 the Korean War broke out. According to oil historian Daniel Yergin, "The American government was now even more worried about communist influence and Soviet expansion in the Middle East and about regional stability and secure access to oil. . . . [T]he State Department wanted to see more revenues going to Saudi Arabia and other oil producing countries in the region, in order to maintain pro-Western governments in power and to keep discontent within manageable bounds."[77] Thus the Department ardently and successfully backed the "50/50 agreement," as it came to be called. In 1950 Aramco paid the U.S. Treasury $50 million in U.S. taxes, while Saudi Arabia received $60 million in fees and royalties. In 1951, once the 50/50 agreement fully kicked in, Aramco paid the U.S. government $6 million while Riyadh received nearly $110 million.[78]

More than twenty years later, at congressional hearings on the subject, angry lawmakers accused Truman administration officials of using the 50/50 agreement to increase foreign aid to Saudi Arabia without congressional consent. Although the State Department's motivations were vulnerable to such charges, the Saudi financing arrangements were consistent with existing U.S. tax law. The public outrage around the 50/50 agreement did, however, reflect a deep and abiding American cynicism about both oil companies and Saudi Arabia, one that continues until today. The 50/50 agreement also set off a scramble among neighboring oil producers to secure a similar deal. Oil producers were beginning to flex their growing political muscle in the emerging petroleum-dependent postwar economic order.

The Security Dimension

By 1948 it was time to renegotiate the Dhahran airfield agreement. Three years had passed since the end of World War II, and America's stipulated right to occupy the facility was expiring. As the Cold War heated up, Saudi Arabia and its Dhahran military base played an increasingly prominent role in American strategic calculations. The State Department worried that "the area is highly attractive to the USSR because of oil, its strategic location at the air, land and sea crossroads of Eurasia and its vulnerability to attack from without and within."[79]

The U.S. ambassador to Saudi Arabia, Raymond A. Hare, spent most of his time negotiating Dhahran's year-to-year lease. He viewed the negotiations as the main reason he had been assigned to the kingdom in the first place. As Hare recalled, "The Russians were acting in a very alarming manner. Dhahran airfield was particularly important as a staging point in the event there was trouble with the Russians."[80] As American threat perception shifted from World War II to the Cold War, the justification for Dhahran changed from a link in a chain of military bases connecting the United States and the Far East to a potential poststrike base from which to defend against Soviet attacks. There was little certainty and much debate around Soviet intentions in the Middle East. Ambassador Hare remembered that in those days "you could practically hear the Russian boots clumping down over those desert sands."[81]

As anticipated by the original Dhahran agreement, the United States and Saudi Arabia began renegotiating the terms of agreement in 1948. The Americans offered a twelve-year lease, which the king declined. Although he liked the security provided by the American military stationed on his territory, a long-term lease too closely resembled a colonial base.

Still, the king's security situation seemed precarious, and he feared encirclement. In 1948 the king was greatly concerned about being squeezed by Yemen in the south and the Hashemites in Iraq and Transjordan to his north. The Hashemites provoked particular angst since the king had sent the Hashemite family fleeing when his soldiers conquered the Hejaz in 1924. Until his death in 1953 Abdel Aziz feared that one day they would try to reclaim their ancestral lands, a Saudi fear that extended until as late as 1990. To make matters worse, the British had ties with all of Saudi Arabia's neighbors. In 1948 these ties caused the king to throw out the British military training mission in Saudi Arabia. To replace them, he first turned to the Egyptians, which did not work out, and then to the Americans.

The Saudi and American negotiators fashioned a solution that ensured American presence without creating an imperial base. They agreed that actual ownership of the base would pass from the United States to Saudi Arabia. To ensure Saudi control, the king approved only year-to-year agreements, rather than longer-term ones. In return for access to the airfield, the United States approved the dispatch of a military survey team to assess the kingdom's defense requirements. Washington also agreed to pay rent for Dhahran. As Ambassador Parker Hart remembered, it "became apparent that the Saudis wanted a US training mission as the *quid* for the Dhahran *quo*."[82] Although Dhahran looked, acted, and smelled like a base, for Saudi political purposes it was never officially considered one by either Riyadh or Washington.[83]

As a result of the 1948 agreement Truman sent a military survey team led by Colonel Richard J. O'Keefe, a man King Abdel Aziz grew quite fond of, to the kingdom in May 1949. The resulting O'Keefe Report was, according to Saudi diplomatic historian David Long, "the first comprehensive U.S. plan for building a modern Saudi armed forces."[84] It recommended the creation of a 43,000-member Saudi Arabian fighting force, consisting of 28,000 combat troops and 15,000 air force troops. The $107 million price tag was substantially more than the Saudis could afford at the time. This massive sum caused future American negotiators profound headaches, as it became the baseline for subsequent Saudi military financial assistance requests.[85]

In 1951 the United States and Saudi Arabia finally moved beyond the inefficient year-to-year agreements and concluded a five-year understanding. The Mutual Defense Assistance Agreement (MDAA), as it came to be called, also brought to the kingdom a hundred army, navy, and air force personnel for joint training with Saudi forces. The MDAA's recommendations ultimately led to the establishment of the United States Military and Training Mission (USMTM) on June 27, 1953, a program devoted to advising and assisting the Saudi armed forces on military planning, organization, and training methods. It remains today the cornerstone of U.S. military relations with Saudi Arabia.[86]

Simultaneous to the Dhahran negotiations, a more ominous set of contingency plans evolved for handling Saudi Arabia's oil in the event of a Soviet attack. Quietly, at the highest levels, the U.S. military and National Security Council (NSC) began devising plans to plug and destroy Saudi oil fields.[87] A 1949 NSC document urged active efforts to "deny" Soviet control over Saudi Arabia's oil deposits. President Truman later approved NSC 26/4, which stated that in the event of an attack on Saudi Arabia's oil, "wells should be permanently plugged with material which would make it impossible to reopen them."[88] In late 1949 and early 1950 the CIA secretly shipped explosives into the kingdom in preparation for the doomsday scenario. Ultimately no less than ten tons arrived. Marines stationed off the Saudi coast were expected to come ashore in small boats and lay down explosives.[89] These plans were contentious within the Truman and, later, Eisenhower administrations. After all, Washington was contemplating plans to destroy the resources of a partner it was claiming to defend. Both administrations explored possibilities to limit the damage, including temporarily, rather than permanently, rendering the fields inoperative—leaving open the opportunity to restart the wells when the United States prevailed.[90] A 1951 document advocates "moderate plugging," or plugging that could be later reversed.[91] The United States also briefly considered using radiological weapons to limit Soviet access; however, those plans were scrapped when they proved impractical. Such weapons would likely kill their handlers.

American planners also believed that even if the radiological elements could be controlled after deployment, a dubious proposition, the Soviets would simply compel Saudis into the toxic environment and restart production.[92] All such information was kept from the Saudis, although not from key Aramco officials, some of whom stored explosives under their beds for years.[93]

Concern that Washington might seize Saudi oil fields has recurred throughout the relationship's history. It surfaced in the mid-1970s when Secretary of State Henry A. Kissinger and Secretary of Defense James R. Schlesinger made reference to military options if escalating oil prices were not controlled. The subject again emerged after the 2001 attacks, when some in Washington pointed to the vulnerability of Saudi Arabia's oil-rich Eastern Province. The existence of contingency plans in no way suggests that such plans were ever near realization. However, these NSC documents, uncovered by the dogged *Kansas City Star* reporter Steve Everly, between 2002 and 2004, do show that since 1949 the United States government has been deeply concerned about the security of Saudi Arabia's fields.

Conclusion

By January 1953, when Truman left office, many of the building blocks for future U.S.-Saudi relations were in place. Eight years prior, on the Great Bitter Lake, Roosevelt and Abdel Aziz had set the tone for the relationship, one of warmth and mutual respect. Roosevelt also approved the lend-lease program for Saudi Arabia, something that provided financial assistance to the economically struggling king. Under Truman, the bilateral relationship was institutionally deepened with military training programs and access to the Dhahran airfield. The king appreciated Washington's commitment to Saudi Arabia's territorial integrity, although he regularly tested it to see how far that commitment extended.

Still, profound challenges persisted. Congress made it difficult to get nonmilitary aid to the kingdom. Hermann Eilts, then a young U.S. Foreign Service officer, remembers a series of futile efforts to attract official U.S. civilian support for an agriculture program inside the kingdom.[94] Aramco did its part in providing considerable developmental assistance programs, particularly in the Eastern Province. But this alone could not substitute for U.S. government aid.

Real disagreement also continued to percolate around Palestine, U.S. cooperation with the British, and the status of the Dhahran air field.

Washington also demonstrated deep concern about the security of Saudi Arabia's oil fields and developed doomsday contingency plans that involved radiological weapons and destruction of the Saudi fields.

Despite these differences, the relationship continued evolving. It was, however, about to enter into a dizzying series of events that would include two wars, two oil embargos, and a U.S. focus on Saudi political, social, and economic reform. Such events tested each government's commitment to the relationship.

3

An Islamic Pope

Secretary of State John Foster Dulles would recall a great sense of frustration during his 1953 trip to Saudi Arabia. His aides had somehow forgotten to schedule time for a dip in the Persian Gulf. An avid swimmer, Dulles collected swimming hole memories as others accumulated stamps. His aides had been so preoccupied with finding him a comfortable bed—a difficult task in the rough oil town of Dhahran, which he visited after a stop in Riyadh—that they had overlooked this readily accessible luxury. The newly appointed secretary of state was deeply disappointed to be so tantalizingly close to Saudi Arabia's exotic desert shores, yet unable to experience the Persian Gulf's refreshing waters. His disappointment would be minor compared to his later efforts to turn Saudi Arabia and King Abdel Aziz's son Saud into a pro-American globally recognized Muslim leader.

The Eisenhower, Kennedy, and Johnson administrations would all experience considerable frustration trying to build a sustainable Middle East policy as anticolonialism and anti-Zionism swept across the region. During this period America cast about for allies in a region that seemed to be steadily drifting toward the Soviet camp. Although no administration initially sought Saudi Arabia's support, each ended up cultivating it. Saudi Arabia, for its part, explored different international alternatives. It preferred to work closely with Egypt, the Arab powerhouse, but turned to the United States when that proved unworkable. By the end of President Johnson's tenure the shifting alliances of the 1950s and 1960s had given way to a steadier U.S.-Saudi bilateral relationship, one that revolved around oil and anti-Communism.

In the election of 1952 Americans had put their faith in President Dwight D. Eisenhower, hoping that the retired general would lead the

West to victory against the Soviet Union, much as he had led Allied forces against Axis powers during World War II. Signaling his commitment to international affairs, Eisenhower's first appointment was Dulles as secretary of state. Dulles had been active in foreign policy since the 1919 Versailles Peace Conference, which he had attended as a thirty-one-year-old junior diplomat. He had been a front-runner in the race to become Thomas E. Dewey's secretary of state had Dewey defeated Truman as expected in the 1948 presidential election. The grandson of an established statesman and the son of a Presbyterian minister, Dulles was didactic and intense. He plodded through the endless minutiae of foreign policy, building lawyerly briefs that left Eisenhower glassy-eyed. The British, rarely known for their flair, would bemoan their dealings with "dull, duller, Dulles." Still, for Eisenhower, no man was more seasoned in or knowledgeable about foreign policy. Eisenhower's military prowess and Dulles' foreign policy experience presented a formidable combination.

Political and military expertise was sorely needed during the turbulent 1950s and 1960s. In the developing world the U.S.-Soviet rivalry became enmeshed in anticolonial struggles and emerging nationalist movements. The erosion of European colonial control was evident from Africa to Asia to the Middle East. Between 1945 and 1965 United Nations membership jumped from 51 to 117 nation-states. Both Eisenhower and Dulles worried that British and French imperial policies in the Middle East and elsewhere would drive newly independent countries into the arms of the Soviets, and they set out to build an alternative. Saudi Arabia would become a key player in this effort.

To manage the challenge, Eisenhower and Dulles adopted an overtly anticolonial posture. In Asia the United States resisted backing French claims in Indochina in 1954. In 1956 the United States also stood against its European partners during the Suez crisis when Britain, France, and Israel attacked Egypt. Eisenhower believed that the "moral position" of the United States' anticolonialism was one of its greatest assets in opposing the Soviet Union and managing global politics more generally.[1]

But it was with the crisis in Buraimi, a small desert oasis on Arabia's eastern boundary, where Washington would favor Saudi Arabia in a territorial dispute between Riyadh and London, that Eisenhower would first confront the challenges of European imperialism in the developing world. At Buraimi, Washington would make clear that it would not back its traditional European allies so long as their policies remained inspired by colonialism. This marked a significant change from Truman's administration, which had tried to ease Britain and France gently out of its colonial entanglements.

In economic policy Eisenhower also charted a new course. He gave private companies, including oil companies, greater latitude in representing American interests abroad. President Roosevelt's secretary of the interior, Harold Ickes, had relished his legendary battles against big oil.[2] Truman also had been skeptical about oil company motives. In contrast, the Eisenhower administration allowed corporate interests to represent American interests abroad. Nathan J. Citino, a professor at Colorado State University and the author of an impressive book on U.S.-Saudi relations during the Eisenhower years, argues that U.S. officials under Eisenhower "promoted private initiative as an enlightened way of doing business, as a means to differentiate the American presence abroad from that of the Europeans and the Soviets, and as a way to advance economic growth and pacify Arab nationalism."[3] Aramco, already playing a dominant role in Saudi Arabia's Eastern Province, came to influence some key decisions during the Eisenhower period, especially during the Buraimi conflict, which was brewing when the president took office early in 1953.

Plugging the Holes

Dulles aimed to "plug the many holes in the free world's line of defense against Communism."[4] Nowhere was the task more urgent than in the Middle East. Libya's Wheelus Air Force Base and Saudi Arabia's Dhahran airfield represented the only two reliable military staging grounds available to the United States should the Soviet Union push south to secure its historic ambitions.

Less than four months after assuming office, Dulles embarked on a three-week comprehensive tour of the Middle East; he was the first U.S. secretary of state ever to do so. His trip illuminated two overarching problems that would vex the Eisenhower administration for its entire tenure. First was the power of anticolonial sentiments sweeping the Middle East. The colonial legacies of America's European allies were fast becoming geopolitical liabilities. In the Middle East, America risked becoming collateral damage in the struggle between colonizer and colonized. Dulles cautioned that unless Washington distanced itself in the Middle East from its Cold War partners, Moscow would eventually represent the only viable anticolonial alternative. He moved the administration away from the Truman-era inclination of closely coordinating with the British, which had immediate ramifications for Saudi Arabia around the Buraimi conflict and set the stage for the 1956 Suez crisis.

In addition to anticolonialism, Secretary Dulles got his first whiff of how local problems could complicate global objectives. Six weeks after Dulles returned, the National Security Council acknowledged that the key security threats to the region would come not from direct Soviet military attack but rather from "acute political and economic instability; military weakness; widespread unrest; Arab-Israel tensions; the UK controversies with Egypt, Iran and Saudi Arabia," and the French North African problem.[5] Throughout Eisenhower's two terms in office, the president and his secretary of state struggled to reconcile regional realities with global Cold War necessities. At different points they looked to Saudi Arabia to contribute both ideologically and financially to various schemes they developed.

Buraimi: "An Interesting Little War Between Us and the Limies"

As part of his regional tour, Dulles stopped in Jeddah to meet the "old and crotchety" King Abdel Aziz. In Dulles' letter of introduction to the king, Eisenhower stressed the shared American and Saudi interests in fighting Communism, writing that "your support in the common cause against godless communism has been a source of inspiration to me and the American people."[6] It was the only letter to a Middle East leader to mention the shared interest of combating Communism.

But anti-Communism was not the conversation's centerpiece. Instead Dulles received an earful about a percolating territorial conflict between Saudi Arabia and Great Britain in Buraimi. Buraimi was a "cluster of rather miserable little villages in the sands," according to the venerable U.S. ambassador Parker Hart.[7] Situated about 110 miles inland from Abu Dhabi (a small sheikhdom that would join six others between 1971 and 1972 to form the United Arab Emirates) and equidistant between Abu Dhabi and the Gulf of Oman, Buraimi was key to asserting political authority over eastern Arabia and accessing potential (although in the end nonexistent) oil reserves in Yemen.[8] Britain claimed the area belonged to Oman and Abu Dhabi, territories bound to Britain by treaty. British prime minister Winston Churchill, the man who had driven the Royal Navy's conversion from coal to oil, well understood the area's strategic value for Britain's national security. He adopted an unyielding stance on Buraimi both to secure British access to oil and to stanch the more general deterioration of Britain's worldwide colonial holdings. King Abdel Aziz, for his part, was still testing the outer boundaries of his national conquest and argued that the remote area was, and had always been, loyal to Riyadh.

When Dulles returned to Washington, he cautioned Eisenhower that the seemingly minor scrape could spiral uncontrollably. Without active U.S. engagement, the secretary warned that the escalating conflict could cause the king to "throw away" his alliance with the United States, "cancel the oil concession and the air base, and throw in his lot with some other nation which he might feel would be a more faithful ally."[9] Dulles feared that Riyadh would come to define American interests in the area as indistinguishable from British ones, and punish Washington for London's colonial practices. Throughout its two terms, the Eisenhower administration sought to avoid such guilt by association.

Although Eisenhower and Dulles were predisposed to support Saudi Arabia for anticolonial reasons, the Buraimi conflict also illuminated Aramco's important hold on both U.S. and Saudi decision-making processes. Aramco helped Abdel Aziz build his case, believing no doubt that a larger kingdom meant a larger Aramco concession. By interviewing local residents, Aramco researchers discovered that local Buraimi tribesmen had on occasion paid taxes to Riyadh, bolstering Saudi political claims to the area. The company fed this information back to both Washington and Riyadh, influencing views on the conflict in both capitals. What Aramco investigators failed to discover, or perhaps conveniently omitted, was that those same leaders who paid taxes to Riyadh had also paid taxes to Abu Dhabi and at times Oman, undermining their seemingly persuasive tax argument.[10]

At the time the U.S. government maintained few independent intelligence-collecting assets and was largely reliant on Aramco for its information. The company, in fact, had the best American intelligence on, and insights into, Saudi Arabia. As Phebe A. Marr, then a young Aramco employee recalls, the company "was very powerful" in the Eastern Province.[11] It was organized to relate to the emerging Saudi government at all levels. Its Department of Government Relations, which mirrored the U.S. State Department, had representatives living in the few important Saudi cities. Its active Arabian Affairs Division replicated the State Department's Bureau of Intelligence and Research.

Created in 1946, Aramco's Arabian Affairs Division collected a wide array of information, including biographies of leading Saudi personalities, chronicles of important historical events such as eyewitness accounts from Abdel Aziz's 1929 battle against the Ikhwan, and press clippings about the kingdom. It supported a translation bureau responsible for daily summaries of Saudi radio and press, and a full-time librarian. Its original director, George S. Rentz, who had attended Princeton Theological Seminary and later wrote his doctoral thesis at the University of California at Berkeley on the life and times of

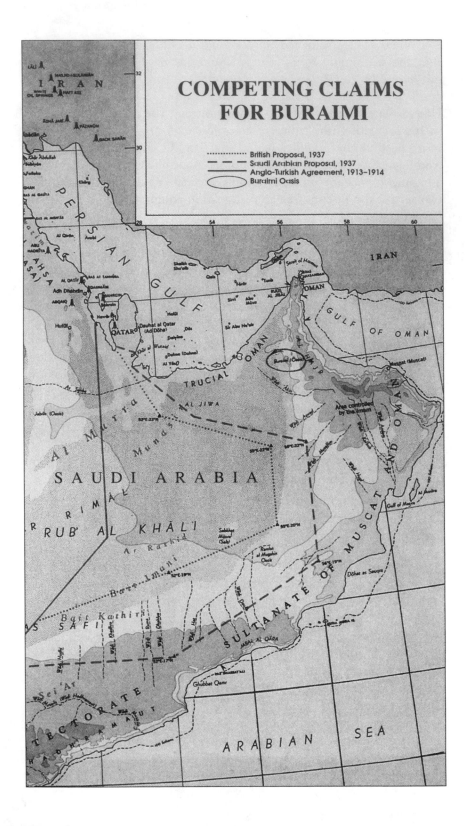

COMPETING CLAIMS
FOR BURAIMI

················ British Proposal, 1937
--------- Saudi Arabian Proposal, 1937
————— Anglo-Turkish Agreement, 1913–1914
⬭ Buraimi Oasis

Muhammad ibn Abd al-Wahhab, hired anthropologists to report on Saudi society's social fabric, document local political practices, and even better understand the role of women. His researchers spent long hours over coffee in the homes of local residents while their colleagues worked doggedly in the oil fields. In one incident Rentz sent Marr, who was conducting research on Saudi government administration in the health field, to Riyadh to determine whether a single woman could operate professionally in Saudi Arabia. "The Saudis were fine," remembers Marr. "They all treated me like gentlemen."[12]

The Saudis often found it easier to work with Aramco than the U.S. government. In 1953, for example, Arab Aramco employees began pressuring the company to build better schools for their children. Instead of approaching the U.S. consulate to develop pilot schools and curricula, Aramco sought out the Ford Foundation, a major granting agency in New York that was committed to helping developing countries. Little came of the effort, largely because Saudi Arabia's Crown Prince Saud refused any non-Muslim involvement in local education. However, Riyadh hired the Ford Foundation to assist in restructuring Saudi Arabia's unwieldy political bureaucracy in areas such as planning, accounting, and public administration.[13] The U.S. government did not figure prominently in these efforts.

Attempts to separate Aramco from the government would not be entirely successful, however: over the course of the 1950s and 1960s Aramco headquarters would become a lightning rod for anti-American protestors. The most dramatic incident occurred in 1953 when thousands of non-American workers protested poor wages and living conditions.[14] At Buraimi, Aramco officials hoped to prove their reliability and usefulness to the government of Saudi Arabia. As one Aramco historian discovered, "there is no lack of evidence that Aramco allied itself with Saudi officials to make mischief for Britain during the crisis."[15] The Buraimi scrape was viewed by Aramco as "an interesting little war between us and the Limies."[16]

The Eisenhower administration, although officially neutral, supported Saudi Arabia's claims to the area. Based on both Aramco's research and a visceral reaction to British colonial concerns, Secretary of State Dulles argued that there was "some degree of justice in the grievance felt by the Saudi Arabians." The director of the CIA, Allen W. Dulles (John Foster Dulles' younger brother), believed "that the Saudi Government had acted with considerable moderation on the Buraimi problem." Treasury secretary George M. Humphrey saw little benefit to intervening in a conflict that was nothing more than "a matter of British prestige." For Eisenhower, Buraimi was just "one more instance of this perennial problem" of the British trying to shore up their colonial position at the expense of sound regional policy. Eisenhower urged Dulles to "press the British pretty hard."[17]

Buraimi would mark the end of any real British influence inside the kingdom for the next several decades. Britain's influence in Jordan, Iraq, Yemen, and now Buraimi stoked the king's fears of encirclement. Great Britain's star had fallen three years earlier when Saudi Arabia let lapse its British military training program.

In October 1955 Britain unilaterally evicted Saudi Arabia from Buraimi, drawing displeasure, but no military response, from either the United States or Saudi Arabia. The Saudis broke relations with Great Britain a year later during the Suez crisis. Crown Prince Faisal made some threatening remarks about turning to the Soviet Union in response but never acted upon them.[18] The Buraimi conflict simmered until 1971, when Britain withdrew all its forces east of Suez. On July 29, 1974, the United Arab Emirates and Saudi Arabia signed a border agreement in which the UAE obtained the Buraimi oasis but in return ceded to Saudi Arabia a coveted land corridor to the Gulf. The agreement put the Buraimi matter to rest for more than thirty years.[19] In the winter of 2004–05, however, tensions flared once again when the president of the United Arab Emirates raised the border issue while on a trip to Saudi Arabia. According to the *Arab News*, Saudi Arabia's defense minister, Sultan bin Abdel Aziz, "tried to cool things down" when he visited the Emirates one month later.[20]

In addition to destroying any remaining trust between Saudi Arabia and Great Britain, the military confrontation at Buraimi reinforced the United States' (and Aramco's) emergence as Saudi Arabia's undisputed international partner.

The King Is Dead

Wary of Great Britain, King Abdel Aziz did not live to see its military response at Buraimi. On November 9, 1953, he passed away quietly at the age of about seventy-three, at the home of his son Prince Faisal.[21] His arthritis had become severe in the waning years of his life, and his physical and mental capabilities failed rapidly. Shortly before he died, the king called to his bedside his two oldest sons, Saud and Faisal, and ordered them to swear to work in harmony and keep any discord away from the public eye. "Don't fight among yourselves," their younger brother Talal recalled the king saying. "Beware of differences."[22] Political infighting had destroyed a previous Saudi effort to assert hegemony across the Arabian Peninsula. It later weakened Abdel Aziz's nemesis, Rashid clan, which allowed him to reclaim his ancestral lands. The ailing king was determined that his realm and legacy not succumb similarly. The two sons, very different yet loyal to their father and committed to continuing their family's reign, took an oath to avoid this problem.

American concern that Saudi Arabia would spiral into chaos upon the king's death was quickly alleviated when Faisal took an oath of allegiance to his brother Saud, who immediately recognized Faisal as crown prince. This was followed by the male members of the royal family taking oaths of fealty to both the new king and the new crown prince.[23]

The fifty-one-year-old King Saud would prove a far cry from his near-mythical father. Whereas King Abdel Aziz was revered and feared, King Saud was wasteful and politically inept. Upon assuming office, he began using state money to build huge palaces and distributed enormous sums with little regard to existing assets. Ministries that he created soon folded due to budgetary shortfalls.[24] Personal and state funds bled together indiscriminately. King Saud's proclivity to give his sons plum government slots such as the post of minister of defense also antagonized his brothers. He also took up drinking. In foreign policy, he vacillated between working closely with the United States and flirting with Arab nationalist movements. In the end his policies resulted in alienating both without building up an alternative to either. King Saud would quickly run the kingdom into the ground.

One of the few checks on Saud was his younger brother Prince Faisal, who had an alternative vision for Saudi Arabia. Faisal's religious lineage set him apart from his other half brothers. His mother was the daughter of King Abdel Aziz's childhood Quran instructor and a descendant of Muhammad ibn Abd al-Wahhab. The relatively cosmopolitan Faisal had represented his father abroad starting at the age of fourteen, traveling throughout Europe, the United States, and elsewhere. Recognizing his son's political aptitude, King Abdel Aziz once lamented, "I only wish I had three Faisals."[25]

Along with his stark features and deeply sunken eyes, a stomach condition that limited his food intake gave Faisal a haunted appearance. Hardworking, taciturn, and rather tightfisted, Faisal tried to limit the damage caused by Saud's loose spending and indecisive foreign policy. Although he never directly challenged Saud's decisions (King Abdel Aziz had too deeply embedded in his sons an intense reverence for age and position, which is still on display today), Faisal and his supporters did thwart the efforts of King Saud's subordinates, thus indirectly yet meaningfully challenging the king's rule.[26]

Although the brothers were often at odds, it is unlikely that at their father's deathbed either Saud or Faisal would have predicted that within five years Saudi Arabia's external debt would double, domestic unrest would increase, both Egypt and the United States would become estranged from the kingdom, and members of the royal family would defect to Egypt. Nevertheless, the pair soon spiraled into a fierce decade-long power struggle.

"The End of Western Civilization"

Like Saudi Arabia and the United States, Egypt underwent a leadership change in the early 1950s, one that had far-reaching consequences. In 1952 a group of military leaders forced out Egypt's King Farouk. Within two years Gamal Abdel Nasser was fully in charge, riding to power on a crest of anticolonialism and Arab nationalism. His charisma, populism, and rhetorical commitment to Arab nationalism electrified Egyptians and other Arabs throughout the region. Nasser directed his oratorical ammunition at Arab monarchs and other Western-leaning regimes, accusing them of perpetuating colonialism by their close ties with imperialist powers. Over the airwaves of Egypt's far-reaching Voice of the Arabs, Nasser and his supporters urged the downfall of "reactionary" governments in the region, including those in Iraq, Jordan, and Saudi Arabia. Because Voice of the Arabs broadcasted far beyond Egypt's borders, Nasser was able to further extend his influence.

Saudi Arabia and Egypt were soon fully engaged in what has been called the "Arab Cold War," a bruising battle that pitted Saudi Arabia, Iraq, and others against Egypt, the most influential and powerful Arab state, and its supporters.[27] Both the Egyptian and Saudi leaderships sought to leverage their ideological strengths and their great-power partners to gain a regional advantage. Egypt promoted Arab nationalist, often anti-Western, movements. Saudi Arabia for its part began organizing opposition to Nasser in the Muslim world along religious lines. Saudi Arabia gave safe harbor to fleeing members of Egypt's Muslim Brotherhood, a grassroots Islamist organization, in an effort to keep pressure on Nasser. Over time King Saud and then later King Faisal each would try to co-opt Nasser and then, when that failed, work actively to oppose him.

On October 29, 1956, the Middle East again descended into crisis when Israel, with France and England's full support, attacked Egypt. Responding to an ongoing Arab blockade and escalating Egyptian violence, Israel surged toward the Suez Canal. The attack was designed to draw British and French intervention.

The Suez crisis brought to a head the difficulties Washington faced in trying to support both its traditional European allies and the developing world's anticolonial movement. Although initially attracted by the young Egyptian nationalist, Eisenhower was no fan of Nasser by 1955. In that year, to the great shock of Washington and Riyadh, Nasser accepted from Czechoslovakia $200 million worth (nearly $1 billion in today's currency) of advanced Soviet military equipment in exchange for Egyptian cotton. It was a major blow to the Eisenhower administration. It marked the first major Soviet arms deal to a non-Communist state, and Eisenhower viewed it as the first evidence of serious Communist penetration in the Middle East.[28] Soviet-backed Egypt now seemed poised to become a major arms supplier to the region. Few doubted that Nasser would soon target Saudi Arabia, Syria, and North African states.

Still, Nasser galvanized the developing world, and both Eisenhower and King Saud believed that the joint attack at Suez would alienate newly independent states. Dulles warned that "we [can] not walk this tightrope much longer."[29] He urged his colleagues to decide "whether we think the future lies with a policy of reasserting by force colonial control over the less developed nations, or whether we will oppose such a course of action by every appropriate means."[30] The administration chose the latter course. "How [can] we possibly support Britain and France if in doing so we lose the whole Arab world?" the president asked his staff.[31]

King Saud also wavered on how to approach the situation. Nasser was a menace. He was turning the entire Arab world against the House of Saud. And yet it was difficult if not suicidal for Riyadh to remain quiet while two colonial powers and Israel attacked the most powerful Arab state. King Saud decided to back Egypt, no doubt hoping that after the war the kingdom would face either a defeated or a less anti-Saudi Nasser.

On November 7, in support of Egypt, Saudi Arabia embargoed all oil destined for the United Kingdom and France. The whole of Western Europe depended upon British and French supplies, as no other country had the facilities to receive or store large amounts of petroleum.[32] It was the first of three times over a period of twenty years that Saudi Arabia used oil as a political weapon. It would do so again in 1967 and 1973.

European leaders petitioned Washington for support, urging Washington either to compel the Saudis to relax the embargo or to use its own oil to make up the supply disruption. When Washington resisted both options, Britain's chancellor of the exchequer, M. Harold

Macmillan, approached U.S. Treasury secretary George Humphrey to request financial assistance but was told that first Britain must accept the cease-fire at the Suez Canal. Like his European counterparts, Eisenhower wanted to "deflate the ambitious pretensions of Nasser," but he believed that the Europeans were challenging him on the wrong issue.[33] The way he saw it, the Canal Company "lay completely within Egyptian sovereign territory and under Egyptian sovereignty" and the attack would only fuel anti-Western sentiment.[34] In a virtual death knell for the European position in the Middle East, the president refused to offset the embargoed oil by increasing American supplies to Western Europe. Some inside the administration, such as Vice President Nixon, argued that while the European position was egregious, France and Britain were still vital allies, deserving of support. But Eisenhower, backed by Dulles, thought otherwise. "Those who began this operation should be left to work out their own oil problems—to boil in their own oil, so to speak."[35]

Macmillan captured European despondency when he told the American ambassador to Britain that at Suez "we are probably witnessing the end of western civilization; that in another 50 years yellow and black men would take over civilization and that, on the whole, we had all had a very good time of it for about 500 years."[36] There was little for England, France, and Israel to do but withdraw.

Eisenhower rebuffed his allies at Suez in order to limit Soviet influence in the Middle East. Some have characterized Eisenhower's decision as one of the crowning glories of his administration. Many Saudis still do, especially because Washington stood so firmly in opposition to Israel and European colonial powers.[37] For the next few months American popularity in the Arab world was at an unprecedented high. But one of the greatest failings of the Eisenhower administration was that it was unable to capitalize on this overwhelming public relations victory and translate it into any larger political benefit. After the crisis Soviet-Egyptian relations remained strong and, as the British feared would happen, an emboldened Nasser continued to spread his influence, uniting with Syria in 1958, inspiring a bloody coup in Iraq that same year, and engaging in a proxy war with Saudi Arabia in Yemen a few years later.

Britain and France emerged from the crisis battered. Yet Eisenhower and Dulles expected them to resume their prior role as dominant powers in the Middle East, as the White House had neither the interest nor the capacity to invest in the region as those two countries had once done. The Soviet Union sat poised to exploit the vacuum. It was exactly the situation that Truman and Acheson had hoped to avoid half a decade earlier. As the earlier administration had calculated, allying with Britain had its drawbacks, but it was the only non-Communist power willing to bear the financial and strategic burden in the Middle East. Now it was Washington's responsibility to devise an alternative framework.

The Best Counter to Nasser

Far from solving the administration's Nasser problem, Suez exacerbated it. Washington's strong-arming of Britain and France showed that it was possible for the developing world, Arabs in particular, to split the Western alliance.

To check Soviet power in the region and counter Egypt's growing influence, on January 5, 1957, the White House rolled out what became known as the Eisenhower Doctrine, offering to "secure and protect the territorial integrity and political independence of such nations, requesting such aid, against overt armed aggression from any nation controlled by International Communism."[38] The president proposed setting aside $200 million a year for countries domestically threatened by Communist insurgents.

The Eisenhower Doctrine received little support at home or abroad. In the Middle East, the phrase "any nation controlled by International Communism" was correctly interpreted as a veiled reference to Egypt. At a time when Nasser's prestige was at an all-time high, the administration was asking local leaders to take a daring domestic stance in return for American financial assistance.

Domestically, the Eisenhower Doctrine ran into trouble and languished for several months in Congress, which was in no mood to channel $200 million to Arab states that had just embargoed Western Europe. The response from Congress to the Eisenhower Doctrine was immediate. On the floor of the Senate Hubert Humphrey exhorted:

> I am not against economic assistance. But I want to know how much King Saud is going to get. I want to know how much these oil-rich countries are going to get. I think the American taxpayer has a right to know how much these countries that have fabulous resources of oil are going to get out of the American treasury.[39]

Without real financial legs, and receiving only halfhearted domestic and international support, the Eisenhower Doctrine was a flop, and in fact was a great propaganda victory for Moscow and Cairo.

In addition to its failed financial inducements, the administration began looking to King Saud to develop an ideological alternative to pan-Arabism. John Foster Dulles viewed King Saud as "the best counter to Nasser."[40] For Dulles, Saud was "the only figure in the area with sufficient presence and potential assets to serve as a counterpoise to Nasser."[41] The president believed that "we should work toward building up King Saud as a major figure in the Middle Eastern area."[42] In a briefing book prepared before King Saud's 1957 visit, the president was told that "as King of the country which nurtured the Islamic religion, [Saud] commands the respect of more than 200 million Muslims throughout the world."[43] Washington began exploring whether King Saud might be able to develop a widespread religious following based on his control over Mecca and Medina. Some within the administration began referring to King Saud hopefully as the "Islamic pope."

Had Dulles known more about Saudi Arabia and his newly chosen protagonist, he would have immediately understood the folly of expecting too much. One long-serving American diplomat recounts that the administration was "desperate," noting that "to believe that Saud ever could have been an alternative leader to Nasser, in terms of pan-Arabism, was just unbelievable."[44]

Saud, at the time, was embattled domestically and internationally, and Saudi Arabia's precarious financial situation exacerbated his problems. Just before King Abdel Aziz died in 1953, most of Aramco's non-American workers went on strike, protesting wages and conditions.[45] While this action never directly challenged the ruling family, it unnerved them. In time Aramco conceded to some of the workers' demands, but not before many were rounded up, severely beaten, and imprisoned by Saudi police. Soviet papers hopefully acknowledged Saudi Arabia's "emerging working class," which was said to be playing a "more and more active role in political life."[46] The uprising was put down, but political unrest continued to simmer just below the surface. In October there was another workers' strike, this one spreading to employees at the Dhahran airfield. Aramco officials worked in coordination with Saudi officials to break up the protests.[47] Not immune to Arab politics, pro-Nasser Saudi Arab nationalist groups began quietly emerging inside the kingdom. Members of the royal family grew increasingly convinced that Saud could not handle the mounting challenges.

Faced with domestic problems and frustrated by Nasser's growing appeal abroad, King Saud vacillated over whether to accept the role presented to him by the Eisenhower administration or pursue a more pan-Arab policy. He was torn between religious extremists at home who favored continuing relations with the United States and its fight against international atheism, and Arab nationalists who urged closer relations with Egypt.[48] In the end, Saud decided to cast his lot with Washington, hoping to lead the region against Communism and Arab nationalism.

In Washington, the king was met with huge banners draped across the route of his motorcade, proclaiming, "Welcome King Saud!" Cheering spectators, touched by the paternal affection Saud displayed for his young handicapped son, who accompanied him on the trip, hailed the arriving desert monarch. The president met the king with great expectations. Saud did not inspire Eisenhower, as many had hoped, but the king did appear earnest in his distaste for Communism and affinity for America, which carried a lot of weight in Washington in the late 1950s. Still, from the meetings it became apparent that Saud had neither the gravitas nor the charisma to contest Nasser. The Eisenhower Doctrine and the administration's Middle East policy had no anchor.

"I Accept"

A year later King Saud was implicated in a botched attempt on Nasser's life. In March 1958 Syrian intelligence chief Abdel Ahmed al-Sarraj publicly displayed copies of checks totaling £1.9 million issued to him by Saud.[49] Such recklessness was about as much as the royal family could take. Even before the assassination attempt, many inside the kingdom were losing patience with King Saud. The king's health was deteriorating. The kingdom's finances were in disarray. The king spent wantonly on royal residences and luxury items. He was known to drive through the desert throwing money out of his car to watch locals chase after it. He provoked his brothers by placing his sons in key government posts. Such appointments eroded the House of Saud's base of support, both domestically and internationally.

Saudi Arabia's public attack on Nasser compounded its growing domestic problems. Nasser was capturing the imagination of citizens throughout the region, and King Saud did not appear to have the political strength to take him on directly. Prince Talal, King Saud's half brother, confronted Saud about Sarraj's charges. The king denied responsibility, but his arguments were unconvincing. Talal reasoned that if he did not have confidence in his own brother's story, no one else could be expected to believe it. Quietly the sons of Abdel Aziz, along with important members of the ulema, began lining up behind Prince Faisal. Saud retained strong backing from the Bedouins and some important tribal sheikhs who benefited from his compulsive generosity, the same munificence that was bankrupting the country. But the religious authorities, some other tribal elders, and most of the king's brothers had had enough.

On March 24, 1958, in Riyadh, twelve senior princes, led by Prince Fahd (later to become king himself), approached the king just before an early Ramadan breakfast. The king, sitting between his brother Faisal and a beloved and revered uncle, listened to their ultimatum. Speaking for the group, Prince Muhammad stated that they were calling for change. "What do you want me to do?" asked the king. Muhammad replied, "We decided to demand your abdication, but your brother Faisal opposed the idea and asked that you remain on the Throne. We have accepted on one condition, that you hand over all your power to Faisal." The king, with little choice, responded, "I accept."[50] One week later a royal decree was published codifying a transfer in power. Although Saud remained king, Faisal was named prime minister and would be in charge of the Council of Ministers, the political body established just before King Abdel Aziz died in 1953.

Once it was clear that the House of Saud would not fall as a result of the 1958 internal power struggle and that Prince Faisal would assume significant responsibility uncontested, the Eisenhower administration breathed a collective sigh of relief. Contrary to press reports that branded Faisal pro-Nasser and a supporter of Arab nationalism, CIA chief Allan Dulles reported that Faisal "should not be put down as anti-American. He was definitely anti-Communist." The secretary of state believed that Faisal had "mellowed" with age. Vice President Nixon thought Faisal was "smart as hell."[51] It was generally agreed that if anyone could save Saudi Arabia, it was Prince Faisal.

Almost immediately, Faisal directed Saudi Arabia onto a fiscal austerity program that put the country back in the black.[52] He also both reduced Saudi Arabia's foreign aid program and began making overtures toward Egypt in an effort to reduce the hostility Nasser directed at Saudi Arabia. While there was some concern in Washington about Faisal's overtures toward Nasser, most understood that Faisal's actions were intended to quiet serious domestic dissent at home rather than mark any real pro-Egypt (and thus pro-Soviet) leanings.[53]

Unwilling to operate as a figurehead, however, Saud reasserted control in 1960. He refused to sign Faisal's budget, one of the few powers still accorded him. The budget proposed drastic reductions in domestic spending, including many of the subsidies allotted to members of the royal family and tribal leaders who were at the heart of King Saud's political support. Faisal resigned from his responsibilities of running the day-to-day operations of the kingdom: "As I am unable to continue I shall cease to use the powers vested in me from tonight and I wish you every success."[54]

The governing elite in Saudi Arabia was at that point divided into three rival camps. King Saud relied on a group of princes and tribal sheikhs. Crown Prince Faisal enjoyed the support of other princes, many of the ulema, and the influential merchants of the Hejaz. This group advocated greater centralization in order to push through a coherent economic and social development program orchestrated from above. The third group, led by Prince Talal, Abdel Aziz's twenty-third son, was supported by the nascent intelligentsia (the graduates of foreign universities), the younger generation of Abdel Aziz's sons, and some officials.[55] Prince Talal advocated turning Saudi Arabia into a constitutional monarchy, believing that such a governing system would increase the regime's legitimacy and allow it to modernize more quickly.[56] Prince Talal hoped that King Saud would give him the power to push through political and economic liberalization. Although both Faisal and Saud had rejected his earlier calls for a constitution, Talal helped convince the other brothers to accept Saud's return. Too respectful of age, too worried about open conflict, and some certainly hoping for better governmental positions in any new government and a return to the lavish spending of the pre-Faisal days, the brothers offered King Saud a second chance. Talal became the minister of finance and vice president of the Supreme Planning Board.

Even though members of Saud's cabinet championed more liberal politics, the shift back from Faisal to Saud did not impress Washington. Like the Eisenhower administration before it, the incoming Kennedy administration regarded Faisal as the better man. But they would not get a chance to work with him directly for another two years, and in the interim the Kennedy administration had to deal with vicissitudes of Saudi domestic politics and weak political leadership.

Eisenhower turned over to Kennedy a Middle East mess. France and Britain were no longer the dominant powers they had been when Eisenhower took office. At the same time, Washington had not replaced them with a compelling economic, political, or military alternative. By backing Egypt at Suez, Eisenhower had emboldened Nasser, who went on to target America's allies in the region. When the White House threw its weight behind Saudi Arabia in the hope of turning Saud into a powerful religious leader who could inspire the region's Muslim population to identify politically along religious lines, the king had proved lacking. The Soviets seemed to be gaining new ground in the strategic Middle East. It was left to Kennedy to devise a new approach—one that would prove painful for Saudi Arabia.

4

Shifting Sands

The Kennedy administration entered office with a strong emphasis on supporting modernizing states, a focus that would push the U.S.-Saudi relationship to one of its lowest points between 1960 and 1962. Kennedy's global outlook emphasized building ties to countries such as India, Indonesia, and Egypt. It left little room for conservative monarchies such as the kingdom of Saudi Arabia. A deep personal rift also soon developed between King Saud and President Kennedy after the king sent Kennedy a blistering letter on Palestine. Ideologically and personally, the U.S.-Saudi relationship was in trouble. What could not have been anticipated was that by the end of Kennedy's short tenure, the United States would be strongly backing Saudi Arabia in a proxy war against Egypt in Yemen, after initially trying to remain neutral.

Upon assuming office, Kennedy sent a round of letters to Middle East leaders. The letters were intended to "make clear the desire of this administration to deal with Middle East matters on as fair and friendly a basis as possible."[1] However, local leaders were unprepared to turn over a new leaf in their relations with Washington around the Arab-Israeli conflict simply as a result of the inauguration of a new president, and angry responses from leaders such as King Hussein of Jordan stunned Kennedy; Nasser and Libya's King Idriss did not even bother to respond. But it was the reply by King Saud, one of America's supposed partners in the region, that caused the young president's face to turn "white with rage."[2] A ten-page meandering diatribe about the "liberation of the Arab homeland" from "so-called Israel," the letter denigrated Kennedy's grasp on Middle East politics and charged Washington with siding "against the Arabs from first to last and on every occasion."[3] Kennedy summoned his new secretary of state, Dean Rusk, and demanded to know why the State Department had recommended sending the letters in the first place. Rusk tried to explain away a number of the responses, but he was unable to do so with King Saud's letter. He conceded that King Saud's letter was indefensible and "undiplomatic to the point of being insulting," and he concluded that "no one can condone the harshness such as that expressed by King Saud's reply."[4] The new secretary of state dispatched the U.S. ambassador to Saudi Arabia to speak with the king. A few months later the king tried to repair relations by blaming the letter's tone on the advisor who drafted it.[5]

Relations further deteriorated when King Saud betrayed a carefully crafted understanding involving the Dhahran air base. In December 1960 Prince Faisal quietly but ardently urged the U.S. ambassador, Douglas R. Heath, not to seek the renewal of America's Dhahran lease when it came up in 1962. In a revolutionary age, with monarchies such as Iraq collapsing and Nasser and his allies targeting foreign bases, Dhahran was too politically costly for the kingdom to maintain. Faisal proposed that the two capitals find a way to gracefully terminate the lease. Three days before an agreed-upon joint statement was to be delivered in March 1962, it became clear that Saud, with his brother Prince Talal's backing, was not going to renew the lease and planned to release a statement that "his majesty's government does not intend to renew the agreement."[6] As the Americans indignantly packed up and shipped out from what had become one of the largest airfields in the world, the king tried to prevent them from repatriating the base's equipment. Though the situation was quickly resolved and the Americans were ultimately able to get their equipment out, it hardly endeared Saud to Kennedy.

Within a year King Saud went even further and violated one of the most sacred tenets of the U.S.-Saudi relationship by beginning to seek an accord with the Soviets. Against Prince Faisal's recommendations, King Saud sent an emissary to Moscow to explore arms sales and improved relations.[7] An increasingly erratic Saud now seemed to be working at cross-purposes with American interests without effectively constructing alternative bases of support.

But the sour personal rapport between the king and the president does not on its own explain why U.S.-Saudi relations deteriorated so dramatically between 1960 and 1962. A strategic shift was taking place as Kennedy's team replaced Eisenhower's. Uncomfortable with America's support for conservative status-quo-oriented powers, the new administration sought to engage rather than oppose the developing world's nationalists and reformers. Scholars such as John K.

Galbraith and Walt W. Rostow joined the administration, providing a theoretical justification for supporting third-world nationalist movements. They argued that nationalism and Communism were not interchangeable and that nationalism could serve as a positive force for development. Such nationalism was something to cultivate rather than oppose, as they believed Eisenhower had done. In a special address to Congress the new president made clear that "no amount of arms and armies can help stabilize those governments which are unable or unwilling to achieve social and economic reform and development." The administration intended to work with reformers in Asia, Latin America, Africa, and the Middle East—"the land of rising people."[8]

More specifically, those responsible for the Middle East, including the hard-charging Robert W. Komer at the National Security Council (NSC) and the able Phillips Talbot at the State Department, strongly believed that conservative monarchies that only slowly embraced change, such as Saudi Arabia, invited domestic unrest and Soviet penetration. As John S. Badeau, Kennedy's ambassador to Egypt, observed, snail's-pace political change might have been acceptable if the status quo was stable. However, "the status quo in the Middle East is not a state of peace; it is perilously close to a *status belli*—a state of war."[9]

This new approach produced a pro-Egypt tilt. In 1962 Kennedy pushed through a massive increase to Egypt in Public Law 480 funding, which allowed surplus American food products to be sold at cut-rate prices. Egypt had received $254 million in total aid from the Truman and Eisenhower administrations. During Kennedy's two and a half years aid to Egypt exceeded $500 million.[10] In 1962 Washington allocated to Saudi Arabia a mere $1.8 million (down from $25 million), a point not lost on Riyadh.[11] In supporting Egypt, Kennedy was turning America's anti-Communism policy on its head.

The Saudis were apprehensive about the United States' shifting priorities and its drift toward Egypt. Prince Faisal was not pleased with "the professors" who were guiding America's new foreign policy.[12] Not only was Nasser's foreign policy increasingly militant and revolutionary and his invective against the Saudi regime more shrill, his appeal to young Saudis was seen as a growing threat to stability.[13] During a meeting with Kennedy in February 1962 King Saud warned that Washington's Egypt policy served only to "aid states which have pronounced leftist tendencies and sympathize more with the Soviet Union than with the U.S." The king exhorted the president that history "had revealed Nasser as a Communist who presents a real danger to the Arab World." Prince Faisal believed that Nasser was either a Communist, a rabid madman, or schizophrenic.[14]

At home in the United States, Kennedy's pro-Nasser tilt cut against powerful domestic pressure groups that urged a very different policy direction. Many in Congress questioned the wisdom of supporting one of Israel's most implacable foes. Others viewed Nasser as a Soviet proxy. Defense officials and leading oil executives argued that Kennedy's shift toward Nasser threatened pro-American oil producers, particularly Saudi Arabia. By 1962 American oil executives were arguing that continued aid to Egypt was in effect throwing Saudi Arabia and Aramco "to the dogs."[15] With a single-minded focus, Kennedy held off these powerful domestic pressures, including pro-Israel and oil lobbyists.

"The Saudi Monarchy Declines with Every Passing Day"

Saud's 1960–62 government was probably the nearest that the nationalists and constitutionalists ever got to gaining power in Saudi Arabia.[16] Under Saud, Prince Talal became minister of finance and economy. Thirty-five-year-old Abdullah Tariki, one of the young reformers associated with Talal, became the director-general of petroleum and mineral affairs in the Ministry of Finance and National Economy. Tariki would use his platform to call for greater Saudi control over its oil resources and increased Saudi autonomy from Aramco. Aramco officials tracked his movements carefully.

The son of a Nejdi tribesman and a Bedouin mother, Tariki was schooled in Egypt and later received a master's degree from the University of Texas. His role as director-general gave him almost complete control over relations between the Saudi government and Aramco. He was an ardent Saudi nationalist who combined bluntness with great personal charm. "He [could] say the most drastic things with the most pleasant smile," observed Wanda Jablonski, a reporter for *Petroleum Week* with unrivaled access to Saudi Arabia's oil community.[17] His detractors claimed that at times he seemed to look more toward Nasser than King Saud for inspiration.[18]

By the time Tariki was appointed minister in 1960, Aramco viewed him as potential trouble, a firebrand and a thorn.[19] In 1954 he had advocated a deal with the Greek shipping magnate Aristotle Onassis that would have allowed Onassis' company instead of Aramco to transport Saudi oil. In 1958, after years of litigation, depositions, and forays into Hanbali law (the school of Islamic law followed in Saudi Arabia), Aramco won its case at the International Court of Justice. During this

time Tariki had also vocally endorsed renegotiating the Aramco concession, arguing that it was signed when Saudi Arabia was a fledgling
country and therefore too unsophisticated to protect its own interests.

Like Aramco officials, Prince Faisal (Tariki's onetime mentor)
closely monitored Tariki's activity. When Faisal became prime minister in 1958 he instructed Tariki "to be reasonable and fair, and to protect not only Saudi Arabia's interests but also Aramco's."[20] Like his father
before him, Faisal understood that Saudi Arabia benefited from cordial
relations with the United States. Faisal recognized that Saudi Arabia could
not independently produce its own oil, globally distribute it, defend its
own interests, and continue to modernize without outside assistance,
and no other global power could easily substitute for the United States.
To Faisal, Tariki seemed cavalier, willing to antagonize Washington and
Aramco unnecessarily. When Saud appointed Tariki to be minister of
petroleum, Faisal argued that Tariki had too much discretion over oil
policy and risked rupturing Saudi Arabia's relations with Aramco and
the United States.

Tariki is best remembered for the ideas that led to the creation
of the Organization of Petroleum Exporting Countries (OPEC) in
September 1960. A year earlier, at the Arab Petroleum Congress in Cairo,
Tariki had floated the idea of oil producers forming a bloc to defend
against oil company price slashing. His proposal was a response to a
global oil surplus that caused the oil companies to drastically reduce
prices. Without prior consultation with the oil-producing countries,
the companies twice reduced the posted price of oil between February
1959 and August 1960, averaging a reduction of 27 cents per barrel.[21]
Standard Oil of New Jersey, the most powerful member of the Aramco
consortium, cut the price it paid for Arabian oil by 10 cents per barrel
on August 8, 1960, and then cut it again without consulting the Saudi
government, which had little control over oil pricing. Such action infuri-
ated government officials such as Tariki who were ultimately responsible to the king on matters pertaining to oil. At the Cairo meeting, oil
ministers from Iraq, Kuwait, Iran, Saudi Arabia, and Venezuela concluded
a secret agreement to draft recommendations to their governments to
defend against the oil companies' pricing onslaught.

In September the five countries created OPEC with the goal "to
defend the price of oil—more precisely, to restore it to its precut level."
Still, OPEC was unable to organize until the 1973 oil embargo.

Almost immediately after Saud wrested control back from Prince
Faisal in 1960, Saudi Arabia's political and financial situation again began
to spiral out of control, and low-level domestic dissent continued to
percolate. Faisal and his supporters relentlessly concentrated attacks on

Talal as a way of checking the powers of King Saud. They were joined by members of Saudi Arabia's religious establishment who feared Talal's liberal leanings. As Alexei Vassilev, a noted Saudi Arabia historian, observed, "Conservative princes in the royal family and high-ranking officials formed a bloc with religious circles [against Talal], which feared that reforms might diminish the *ulema*'s role in the country."[22]

By 1962, Prince Talal and others who had originally backed Saud in the 1960 power struggle were also growing disillusioned by the lack of real political reform.[23] In August 1962 Talal and a small group of brothers left for Lebanon, where they publicly called for a constitutional monarchy. They eventually took up residence in Egypt after they were barred from returning home to Saudi Arabia. Tariki visited with them there. A few months later, shortly after a coup in Yemen that brought Egyptian troops onto the Arabian Peninsula and terrified Saudi officials, several Saudi air force pilots and their crews defected to Cairo. The combination of both military and political elites leaving Saudi Arabia for Egypt put on display the kingdom's mounting troubles. The CIA reported that inside Saudi Arabia there was a "general feeling [among] businessmen that King Saud may be overthrown at any time, probably by a military coup . . . Saudi businessmen as well as members of the royal family are liquidating their assets and transferring money and capital to Beirut. Import orders are being cancelled."[24] In a memo to national security advisor McGeorge Bundy, Robert Komer wrote, "The staying power of the Saudi monarchy declines with every passing day."[25]

In October 1962, while Saud was away for medical treatment, Faisal instigated a government shake-up and replaced several of King Saud's sons, putting in place those he believed more competent and less beholden to the king. He replaced Tariki with Sheikh Ahmed Zaki Yamani as minister of oil. Yamani, another member of Saudi Arabia's new guard, was as impressive as Tariki but more cautious. Yamani would orchestrate the 1973 oil embargo eleven years later.

The October 1962 reshuffle brought to prominence many still in power today. Faisal promoted Prince Fahd, who became king in 1982, from minister of education to minister of the interior (Faisal made him second deputy prime minister in 1965—a presumptive heir to the throne). Prince Sultan, the current Saudi minister of defense and aviation, assumed his post during the reshuffle. Within three months Prince Abdullah, today's king, became the commander of the Saudi National Guard, a position he still holds today. Many others in prominent positions today got their real start in the early 1960s under Faisal.

Upon his return Saud threatened to mobilize the royal guard unless Faisal withdrew his appointments. Faisal responded by threatening to mobilize the National Guard against the king. The ulema, along with senior brothers, stepped in to resolve the situation in Faisal's favor.[26]

Washington welcomed the 1962 changes. As far as the United States was concerned, Saudi Arabia's deterioration under Saud invited domestic instability and Soviet penetration. The Kennedy administration had all but washed its hands of Saudi Arabia. The future, they believed, lay with Egypt and the Arab nationalists, not the conservative monarchies of Saudi Arabia and elsewhere.

In 1964 Prince Talal returned to Saudi Arabia. Having antagonized Faisal by supporting Saud, he never again played a major political role. His son Prince Alwaleed bin Talal bin Abdul Aziz al-Saud, however, became a world-renowned businessman who presciently invested in Citibank and the Internet early on; in 2005 he was ranked by *Forbes* magazine as the fifth richest man in the world. Prince Alwaleed made national headlines in New York shortly after the September 11 terrorist attacks when New York mayor Rudolph Giuliani rejected Alwaleed's $10 million gift to the city after the prince tied the attacks to America's Middle East policy.

"We Won't Save Our Oil Just by Giving Faisal a Blank Check"

A seemingly insignificant event in a far-off corner of the world quickly overshadowed Saudi Arabia's domestic turmoil and undermined President Kennedy's Middle East policy of leaning toward Egypt while distancing the United States from Saudi Arabia. The overthrow of Yemen's leader, Muhammad al-Badr, by Egyptian-backed republican soldiers in September 1962 eventually led the United States to confront Nasser and forsake a serious reform agenda in Saudi Arabia. As Robert Komer, Kennedy's Middle East point man at the National Security Council, remembered, "Kennedy had some very deep personal convictions on a lot of issues. Like Yemen. My God! If there was ever a backward corner of the Arabian Peninsula, Yemen is it! But he was very actively engaged in the war between the Yemeni Royalists and the Republicans." Kennedy, it was said, could give an excellent briefing on Yemen to anybody.[27]

On September 18, 1962, Yemen's autocratic leader, Imam Ahmed, died, and his son Muhammad al-Badr assumed power. Nine days later

Badr was deposed in a swift coup led by his erstwhile friend and protégé Brigadier General Abdullah al-Sallal. Proclaiming Yemen a republic, Sallal ended ten centuries of the imamate, making Yemen the first nonmonarchy on the Arabian Peninsula. Badr escaped to the Saudi border and rallied local tribes to his royalist cause. The Yemeni battle between royalists and republicans evolved into a proxy war between Saudi Arabia and Egypt in defense of their preferred regime type. This brought with it increased U.S.-Soviet attention.

In Jeddah and Washington it was immediately apparent that Nasser was behind the operation. The U.S. embassy estimated that Egypt contributed around £E 35,000 for use by the rebels for propaganda and subversion.[28] Egyptian troops arrived in Yemen shortly after the coup, and Nasser reportedly planned to intervene militarily in support of the coup the day after it occurred.[29] Within weeks of the coup, two senior Egyptian officials, Field Marshal Abdul Hakim Amer and Colonel Anwar el-Sadat, arrived in Yemen.

Prince Faisal arrived in Washington nine days after the coup. He had planned the trip months earlier to convince the president that "all Saudis [were] not like the King [his brother Saud]."[30] He used the opportunity to discuss Yemen. In preparation for the meeting, Komer briefed the president that "the Yemen revolt has brought to a boil all Saudi fears of Nasserism (the House of Saud well knows that it might be next)."[31] The Saudis grew even more nervous when the United States later recognized the new Yemeni government. During his meeting with Kennedy, Faisal told the president that "Nasser had one sole aim, namely, to crush the authority of the Saudi Arabian Government."[32]

Rather than offer Faisal arms packages or military support, as Eisenhower and Dulles might have done, Kennedy pushed Faisal on domestic reform.[33] Yemen, after all, was one of the most backward countries in the world. Kennedy and his advisors worried that Saudi efforts to reverse the coup would only drain Saudi attention and resources away from its own domestic reform. The State Department predicted that "major Saudi military participation seems likely to lead to violent repercussion at home, very possibly even the demise of the Royal Family."[34] Komer wrote to Kennedy that "we think the Saudis themselves must press forward with modernization and development. Deliberate, controlled internal reform is the best antidote to Nasserism. We're pleased with the signs of progress to date, but wonder if it's fast enough."[35] There was little self-reflection that perhaps Tariki and Prince Talal had represented more fundamental change. The Joint Chiefs of Staff, recalling the recent defection of the seven Saudi pilots to Egypt, similarly concluded that "military measures in support of the present Saudi Arabian

Government may be largely ineffective unless that Government is capable of sustaining the loyalty of the armed forces and finding an effective base of support within Saudi Arabia."[36]

The White House believed that "instead of idling around in Yemen Faisal need[ed] to shore himself up domestically as the chief means of protecting himself against Nasser [and the Communist] virus." Komer argued that "in the long run we won't save our oil just by giving Faisal a blank check on us. Nor will we necessarily lose it if we let Faisal get bloodied a bit." Washington offered nothing like the covert support that Britain intended to provide the royalists, its proxy in Yemen.[37] Because of this, Faisal reinitiated contacts with Britain, which had been severed as a result of the Buraimi and Suez crises. This roused little attention in Washington.

Urged on by Kennedy, Faisal issued a ten-point program for domestic reform upon returning home from his meeting at the White House. It laid down what was termed the "Basic Law for the Government" and promised forthcoming legislation around decentralizing power to the local level and a Supreme Judicial Council operating with immunity. At the same time it proposed a Judicial Council of twenty appointed scholars and members of the ulema. Some close to Prince Faisal have suggested that this latter creation was an attempt to keep the members of the ulema debating among themselves, rather than issuing policy dictates, ultimately weakening their position in society.[38]

The ten-point plan promised to attract capital for economic development and to "make available innocent means of recreation for all citizens."[39] Most dramatically, the program also called for the abolition of slavery, then still prevalent and a constant source of embarrassment for Saudi Arabia on the world stage. The program brought Faisal domestic support from local reformers, and it also impressed the Kennedy administration. But Faisal offered the program with a "wink and a nod."[40] Reforms in the end were slow in coming—aside from the abolition of slavery, the first set of real reforms did not appear until the early 1970s, nearly a decade later.

On November 3, 1962, Saudi Arabia reported that "combat aircraft supplied by the government of the UAR [Egypt]" bombed five areas inside Saudi Arabia in response to Riyadh's support of royalist forces. Saudi Arabia's defense minister immediately sent word to the head of the U.S. Military Training Mission that he planned to request "US assistance to establish an active air defense system, for the maintenance of internal security." In February Egyptian planes dropped 119 bundles of small arms and ammunition along a 100-mile corridor up the Saudis' western coast (which was where the Saudis ran supply lines to the Yemeni front but which was otherwise of little military value) in an attempt to aid Nasser's supporters inside the kingdom.[41] The Saudis pleaded for help, but Kennedy continued to insist that Faisal focus on internal security and let the Americans negotiate an Egyptian withdrawal. The president believed that domestic reform, not military hardware, would save the kingdom. Kennedy authorized a major mission led by the established American diplomat Ellsworth Bunker to arrange a UN-supported cease-fire.

Faisal came to believe, with good reason, that the Kennedy administration was generating cease-fire proposals that were more amenable to Nasser, showing again the administration's pro-Egypt tilt. Both the American ambassador to Saudi Arabia and Vice President Johnson were skeptical of this approach. As the leader of the Senate during the Eisenhower years, Johnson had watched Nasser thwart the Eisenhower administration, and he later questioned Kennedy's wooing of the Egyptian. Johnson, however, was in the minority when it came to Egypt. Still, the White House had one red line—the territorial integrity of Saudi Arabia. Egypt could not abide by even this. In one of the last messages associated with Kennedy's progressive reform agenda vis-à-vis Saudi Arabia, Secretary of State Rusk cabled John Badeau, the U.S. ambassador to Egypt, authorizing him to make clear to Nasser that Egypt's "bombings of Saudi Arabia and airdrops of weapons . . . are forcing US close to point where we will have no alternative but to make good our obligation to Saudis." The secretary advised Badeau that "we wish avoid rancorous dispute with UAR [United Arab Republic/Egypt] if possible but unless UAR stops overt attacks on Saudi Arabia USG will be forced review its policy toward UAR."[42]

When it became apparent that Nasser would not change course, President Kennedy approved Operation Hard Surface, the deployment to Saudi Arabia of eight F-100D tactical fighter aircraft and one transport-type command support aircraft.[43] It was intended to "demonstrate to the Saudi and Egyptian governments and peoples continued US interest in and support for Saudi Arabia and to provide a deterrent to Egyptian operations in Saudi airspace."[44]

Shortly before the planes were due to deploy, however, Congressman Emanuel Celler (D-N.Y.) sent an inquiry to the Defense Department asking whether Jewish personnel were being excluded from the mission. Celler had gotten wind of an original U.S. Air Force directive, later retracted, ordering that "personnel of Jewish faith or Jewish extraction will not be selected."[45] Celler leaked to the press the department's response, which stated that Jewish servicemen were not prevented from serving in Saudi Arabia. On June 10, as the pilots prepared to depart, the *New York Times* reported that Jewish personnel would possibly serve in Saudi Arabia.[46]

Such news traveled quickly to Saudi Arabia, and officials there urged President Kennedy to denounce it—which he would not do. The Joint Chiefs of Staff "directed that the movement of all U.S. forces going to Saudi Arabia be halted" until the controversy was resolved. After two weeks of wrangling and a "crisis of confidence" in the relationship, a face-saving statement was agreed to. The administration issued a statement noting that while Saudi Arabia retained its anti-Jewish visa policy, the issue had "not arisen in cases of U.S. servicemen serving in Saudi Arabia and the United States upheld a nondiscrimination policy in this matter." American planes landed in Saudi Arabia two weeks later. [47]

Kennedy had long warned the king that his country's anti-Jewish policies would prove self-defeating. During a 1961 meeting at the White House, the president put King Saud on notice that Saudi Arabia's decision to prevent Jewish American citizens from transiting the Dhahran airport and the refusal of visas to Jewish congressmen was "grist for the propaganda mill." It "hurts the Saudi cause," Kennedy told the king, and was "more extreme than that pursued by other Arab states." The king promised that he "would give the matter consideration upon his return."[48] Nothing changed.

For all intents and purposes, Operation Hard Surface marked the end of Kennedy's reform agenda. He had hoped to withhold military assistance to compel Saudi reform efforts. Once the planes were dispatched, the White House lost its leverage. Faisal's reform plans slowed thereafter. The Egyptians cheated on their disengagement, replacing departing soldiers and equipment with fresh ones.

Seven months after the coup in Yemen, Kennedy's approach to the Middle East was in tatters. Trying to work more closely with Egypt provided no appreciable political benefit but carried a considerable cost. The UN mission repeatedly confirmed that Nasser was acting in bad faith. In accordance with UN dictates, Riyadh did initially reduce its financial support to the royalists, only to reinitiate it when confronted with Egyptian provocations.

Like Eisenhower before him, Kennedy eventually grew disenchanted with Nasser. The most obvious alternative to Egypt was Saudi Arabia, with its anti-Egypt, anti-Communist stance. But Saudi Arabia was itself going through a series of domestic crises and was unable to provide Washington with a strong and viable Middle East alternative. It was unable to rise to Washington's hopes of it playing a major role in regional politics.

Unlike the Eisenhower administration and most others, Kennedy's team strongly pushed domestic reform in Saudi Arabia. No American president until possibly President George W. Bush would again be as committed in practice to Saudi reform as Kennedy. Kennedy withheld military support to focus Faisal's attention on the domestic environment. There were limits, however, to how hard Washington could press. Nasser's relentless assaults forced Kennedy to dispatch planes and military support to Saudi Arabia. With the deployment, Kennedy lost leverage over Saudi Arabia's reform agenda.

It was not that oil and anti-Communism did not matter to Kennedy, but rather that he believed that without reform, the West's access to Saudi oil was vulnerable and Communists would ultimately subvert the kingdom. At their White House meeting Kennedy pushed the crown prince to adopt a ten-point reform program and abolish slavery, something Faisal seemed to want to do anyway. Kennedy's insistence changed Faisal's political incentives and gave him good political reasons to make hard choices. However, there were limits to what the United States could do from the outside, both because of the intrinsic limits to American power and because the United States needed Saudi Arabia in so many other realms.

With Vietnam a mounting concern, the nagging problem of Yemen was absorbing too much American time and resources. Perhaps had he lived longer, Kennedy would have found a way to continue to press for Saudi domestic reforms, although it seems unlikely. The balance had already shifted away from defending Egypt and pushing reform.[49] In any event, Kennedy's successor, Lyndon B. Johnson, was much less interested in reform. In Johnson's estimation, Faisal had acted in good faith in Yemen, while Nasser regularly violated international agreements.[50] Johnson abandoned America's courting of Egypt and positioned American support squarely behind Saudi Arabia.

Shifting Gears

As vice president, Johnson had privately questioned Kennedy's pro-Egypt leanings. He did not find Nasser as initially compelling as his two predecessors. A seasoned political fighter and a man whom *Time* magazine once called "a tornado from the Southwest, a Texas-size hunk of perpetual motion," Johnson was a horse trader, expecting to receive concessions in return for favorable political decisions. Yet despite massive amounts of aid and some risky political maneuvering on his behalf, Nasser seemed intent on making life difficult for America and its allies. Johnson had too many pressing international and domestic problems to spend his time soliciting unlikely Egyptian support. In fact, the whole of the Middle East assumed a relatively low priority for the Johnson administration, offering as it did only the possibility of getting "kicked in the shanks by both the Arabs and the Jews."[51]

Over the course of the following year the Johnson administration shifted gears in three key areas. First, it significantly reduced aid to Egypt. Johnson had never been an enthusiastic supporter of Kennedy's Egypt aid program, but when in November 1964 Egypt's security forces allowed students in Cairo to burn to the ground the newly christened John F. Kennedy Memorial Library and ransack the U.S. embassy compound in response to a U.S. airlift operation in Congo, the president was furious. The U.S. ambassador to Egypt, Lucius D. Battle, called Nasser's complicity a "dastardly deed."[52] A month after that, a plane owned by one of Johnson's Texas oil friends was downed near the Red Sea by an Egyptian fighter jet. Although in retrospect there is reason to believe it was an accident, the timing was inauspicious. Ambassador Battle delayed previously scheduled discussions around economic assistance to Egypt.[53] A few days later Nasser made yet another anti-American speech, saying the United States should "drink the water of the sea." In February 1965 Johnson opposed his Kennedy-era advisors and suspended food aid to Egypt. Aid was reactivated four months later, but the president eventually let the money run out. In November 1965 Komer, Bundy, and Rusk proposed new aid to Egypt. Even though it was substantially less than Kennedy had offered in 1962, Johnson halved it.

The second area in which the administration began to shift policy was in Arab reform. Johnson distanced himself from Kennedy's drive for political and economic reform (a drive that had been losing steam anyway since Operation Hard Surface). Secretary Rusk, now vested with more power, ordered the U.S. ambassador to Saudi Arabia, Hermann Eilts, "to stop making these [reform] representations to [the king] . . . the Saudis know what their best interests are. They'll handle them accordingly."[54]

The third major change in U.S.-Saudi relations came in terms of arms sales. During the Kennedy administration Saudi Arabia's military expenditures steadily increased. Between 1962 and 1964 arms sales to both Saudi Arabia and Iran doubled, and they continued increasing over the course of the Johnson years and beyond.[55]

Concurrent with Johnson's changing Middle East emphasis came a dramatic changeover in his administration's staff. The reform-minded crowd exited, and a more realpolitik-oriented group entered the scene. John Badeau, Kennedy's ambassador to Egypt and a driving force between the Egyptian-American rapprochement, left the Foreign Service in May 1964 and was replaced by Lucius Battle. Parker Hart accepted the ambassadorship to Turkey in May 1965, and Saudi Arabia did not have an ambassador for another eight months, until Eilts assumed the post in January 1966. In 1965 Phillips Talbot, assistant secretary of state for Near Eastern and South Asian affairs, assumed the role of ambassador to Greece. With his departure, "the Near East bureau at State had lost its prestige and power."[56] Between 1966 and 1967, the State Department's Policy Planning Staff did not have anyone assigned to the Middle East.[57] The activist Robert Komer bowed out as the president's Middle East advisor after his boss, McGeorge Bundy, left for the Ford Foundation in spring 1966. The NSC had three different Middle East directors between April 1966 and June 1967. The Middle East team was not really replenished until April 1967, when Battle was transferred from Cairo to Washington to fill Talbot's vacated position of assistant secretary of state. Johnson's Middle East team was finalized only weeks before the 1967 Arab-Israeli war, four years after Johnson took over. The changes were the clearest example that the days of wooing Nasser and distancing Washington from conservative Arab regimes were over.

"Never Do Anything Like This to Us Again"

In Saudi Arabia, the political struggle between Saud and Faisal continued. By late 1963 senior princes and members of the ulema were growing increasingly worried about the lack of an effective king. King Saud regularly left the kingdom for medical treatments. While he was gone, Faisal would take over and try to resolve the kingdom's numerous challenges, including spiraling financial problems and the crisis in Yemen. But when Saud returned, inevitably a new round of problems began. Faisal constantly was performing triage. "Every time I treat a wound, another one opens," he once remarked.[58]

In December King Saud sensed his family's loyalty turning against him. He retired to the Nasiriyah palace outside of Riyadh along with fifteen hundred bodyguards. Concerned about his intentions, Princes Abdullah and Sultan (then and now the commander of the National Guard and minister of defense, respectively) put the National Guard and armed forces on alert to signal their displeasure and make clear that Saud did not have control of Saudi Arabia's military forces. Then Saud did the unthinkable. Defying the oath taken beside his father's deathbed, he sent a message to Faisal warning that "when my enemy has his hands around my neck, then I strike at him with all my strength."[59] Prince Muhammad, Abdel Aziz's third-oldest son and long associated with Prince Faisal, stormed into the Nasiriyah palace.

He tore the letter up and threw it in Saud's face, demanding, "Did you send this letter to our brother?" Saud accepted responsibility, and Muhammad raged, "Never, never do anything like this to us again." Much later an old friend of Prince Muhammad's asked him why he had sided with Faisal rather than Saud, and the prince bristled. "I did not favor Faisal," replied the prince. "If Faisal had sent Sa'ud such a challenge I would have thrown it back in his face also. Challenges are not the way we settle our differences inside the Al Sa'ud."[60] Prince Muhammad would make headlines in the United States twenty-five years later when the movie *Death of a Princess* dramatized his behind-the-scenes role in the execution of his adulterous granddaughter.

The immediate crisis was resolved but peaked again in March 1964 when Saud sent Faisal a letter demanding full restoration of his kingly powers. For the next six months Riyadh braced for civil war. In October 1964 the senior brothers, who were (and today still are) in constant communication with each other, agreed that Saud must go. Within days of the momentous decision no less than sixty-five members of the ulema, representing all parts of Saudi Arabia, and one hundred princes gathered in Riyadh. Senior princes such as Muhammad, Fahd and his full brothers, and Abdullah along with the late king's trusted brother Abdullah bin Abdel Rahman withdrew their loyalty from Saud and gave it to Prince Faisal. In an interview with *Al-Haya*, a Lebanese publication, one Saudi prince explained that "we preferred to sacrifice Saud rather than the country."[61] The ulema, led by Saudi Arabia's grand mufti, Muhammad ibn Ibrahim Al al-Sheikh, legitimized the brothers' decision with a fatwa.

In early November 1964 Faisal took an oath on the Quran to serve his nation as monarch. With a departure ceremony fit for a king, and Faisal bestowing all the appropriate symbolic respect on his brother, Saud left his kingdom for retirement elsewhere.

The ex-king did not go quietly. In one of the more bizarre episodes of the U.S.-Saudi history, Saud assembled an armada of cargo aircraft and bombers and tried to ship them secretly into the kingdom to retake power. The CIA broke up the plot. Then the ex-king appeared in Egypt, following in his younger brother Talal's footsteps, and harangued King Faisal on Cairo's Voice of the Arabs. He criticized Faisal for "boldly and wantonly selling himself to imperialism and conspiring with the enemy against the Muslim Arab nation." "Know[,] Faisal," he fumed, "that Arabs and Muslims have washed their hands of you."[62] Saud later traveled to Yemen to lend moral support to the Egyptian-backed republicans against the Saudi-backed royalists. Still, Saud never again presented a serious challenge to the throne. He died in Greece in 1969.

Islamic Solidarity

To counter Nasser's pan-Arab appeal, one of Faisal's first efforts after becoming king was to draw on his religious credentials and promote the notion of Islamic, rather than Arab, solidarity. Faisal had been developing the idea of using religion to organize politics since the early 1950s. King Saud had welcomed to the kingdom Nasser's religious opponents a decade prior. But it was Faisal who sought to make Islam a constituent part of Saudi foreign policy. Beginning in December 1965, a year after he became king, Faisal visited nine Muslim states in nine months to promote the idea of an Islamic bloc. Iran joined in December 1965, as did Jordan, Tunisia, Sudan, Turkey, Pakistan, and Morocco subsequently. They all attended a conference in Jeddah shortly thereafter. The group was never intended as a military pact or an alliance to put troops on the ground. Rather, Faisal was trying to build a religious counterpoint to Nasser's pan-Arabism.

In February 1966 Nasser launched his biggest Yemen offensive to date. With Soviet material support and renewed commitment to Yemen, Nasser was in a position to sustain pressure on Saudi Arabia indefinitely, and perhaps even to extend his position in south Arabia.[63] Faisal responded by redoubling his efforts to pursue Islamic solidarity, traveling to Pakistan, Turkey, Morocco, Guinea, Mali, and Tunisia between April and September 1966. Washington viewed Faisal's attempts with ambivalence, as they did not expect much to come from the visits. However, if Faisal could use religion to keep certain countries out of Nasser's orbit (and by extension the Soviets'), it was a useful exercise.

Islamic solidarity was exactly what Dulles and Eisenhower had hoped Saud would create six years prior. If constructed then, the effort would undoubtedly have received higher-level attention in Washington. But by the mid-1960s Washington had become more realistic about what a Saudi leader could actually accomplish in the region vis-à-vis Nasser. In a 1966 background paper the State Department concluded that "because of his potential weaknesses, the narrowness of his political base and his small and still backward population, Faisal cannot be considered a viable counterweight to Nasser in the Middle East."[64] He would prove more successful, however, than his half brother Saud and Washington's predictions.

While Faisal was busy organizing Saudi Arabia's foreign policy around religion, he was making some interesting decisions at home. Deeply religious, Faisal nonetheless had some concern about the influence of the more radical strand of Saudi thought.

At home, Faisal deliberately eroded the ulema's power and independence. He left vacant and practically abolished the key positions of
judicial power held by the ulema, such as the Grand Mufti and Chief
Qadi. . . . Moreover, Faisal entrusted his newly established Ministry
of Justice in 1970 to an 'alim of Hijazi origin (usually more moderate
than the Najdi ones) and gradually established secular administrative
(non-Sharia) tribunals of different kinds. Frequently he ignored the
ulema's opposition to aspects of his accelerated modernization,
sometimes even in matters that they considered to be major issues.
Last but not least, he curbed the authority and activities of the
Committees for Encouraging Virtue and Preventing Vice.[65]

Faisal's religious foreign policy road map was laid out early in his
kingship. But he fully understood that ideas alone could not fend off
Nasser and the Soviet tide. Saudi Arabia also needed arms. For those
he turned to the United States.

The McNamara-Jenkins Agreement

Until the mid-1960s, arms sales to Saudi Arabia were limited mostly to
supplying the U.S.-led training mission that worked with Saudi forces.
Imports, including bombers, tanks, and ammunition, were usually
purchased in small amounts and often haphazardly at that. This type
of slow and controlled buying changed dramatically under President
Johnson.

Relentless Egyptian air strikes compelled the Saudis to take more
seriously their defense acquisition and training. With Prince Sultan newly
in charge of the defense ministry, the Saudis began looking to purchase
a more capable air defense system and military transports, which they
did in the spring of 1965, spending $15 million for four C-130 trans-
port planes. In late 1963 Ambassador Hart noted the change that the
"activist, dynamic approach" of Prince Sultan brought to defense.[66]

The largest arms purchase of the period occurred in December 1965,
when the Saudi government negotiated the purchase of more than $300
million worth of British military equipment, most notably Lightning
supersonic fighter jets, and another $125 million of American equip-
ment, largely in the form of Hawk missiles. In a subsequent deal the
United States also agreed to sell the Saudis $100 million in trucks,
troop transports, and spare parts. The deal more than quadrupled the
total U.S. sales to the regular Saudi armed forces in the previous fifteen
years.[67]

The deal was partially a response to the fact that four months prior
Nasser had openly invited Soviet support in his Yemen adventure,

turning the hitherto regional problem into one between the superpowers. It was also a response to Britain's long-standing balance of payments problem.

On the surface, the package deal was a strange one, given that the United States had long protected its privileged arms export position in Saudi Arabia, and the deal with Britain constituted the largest defense contract in Saudi Arabia's history. One scholar recently argued that the arms sale was a result of Jewish lobby pressure: "Unwilling to risk another bitter fight on Capitol Hill, the State Department advised the Saudis to 'split the package' between Britain and the United States."[68] The *New York Times* attributed the Saudi choice of a joint arms deal to Britain's formal announcement of its withdrawal from Aden, something that threatened to create a vacuum on Saudi Arabia's southern border.[69] The real reason is more nuanced and is better explained by Cold War alliance politics.

In November 1963 the U.S. Air Force recommended that Saudi Arabia acquire either Northrop F-5s or Lockheed F-104s. A fierce battle between the two companies ensued, with Kermit Roosevelt representing Northrop and the twenty-six-year-old Adnan Khashoggi (who went on to become a internationally renowned arms dealer and a leading protagonist in the Iran-contra controversy) representing Lockheed.[70] The State Department lobbied against the sale because it felt that the F-104s were potentially lethal for less experienced pilots (which the Saudis were), thus earning the plane the nickname "widow maker." Robert Komer at the NSC argued to the president that the planes requested were simply "too complex" for the Saudis.[71] State also lobbied against the sale. The Defense Department broke ranks and argued for it.

The British, however, were also willing to provide fighter aircraft, weakening Komer's and the State Department's case. The Lightnings were in fact easier to fly but were ill-equipped for the long flight paths required over the desert kingdom.[72] Behind the scenes the British approached Washington inquiring whether the United States "would agree to offer a joint defense package [to Saudi Arabia] as a means of offsetting British balance of payments problems."[73] At the time the British wanted to buy F-111s, a top-of-the-line U.S. fighter jet, but did not have the necessary cash available. In what came to be called the Jenkins-McNamara Agreement, U.S. secretary of defense Robert S. McNamara and British air minister Roy H. Jenkins concocted a plan in which the Saudis would spend $100 million on Raytheon's Hawk ground-to-air missiles and approximately $300 million on British Lightnings and maintenance service.[74] Britain would use the profits to buy F-111s.

Upon hearing about the back-room deal, Prince Sultan, the new Saudi defense minister, was livid. He rightly felt that Saudi Arabia was paying a high price for a less desirable system so that the British could have "an addition of 90 million to [their] exports."[75] As one arms industry watcher put it, "The Saudis in the end had been persuaded to buy British planes they did not want, to allow Britain to pay for American planes they could not afford."[76]

Because the weapons package was not delivered until after the 1967 war, data on Saudi military expenditures do not register a real increase until the 1967–68 period, when the weapons were paid for in full. Not surprisingly, most interpret this rise as a response to the June war, the need to replenish stocks, and a new fear of Israeli power. But actual Saudi purchases were notably low between 1967 and 1970, a fact that was masked by the earlier purchases finally being delivered.[77] The real jump in Saudi spending, and in what Washington was willing to sell, came during the middle of Johnson's tenure, before the June 1967 war. Several years later the Nixon administration would continue the pattern of selling significant arms packages to the Saudis. But it was under President Johnson, even before the 1967 war, that the arms pipeline to Saudi Arabia was pried wide open.

"Gobbled Up by the Communists"

In June 1966 King Faisal came to Washington worried about Nasser and hoping to establish a personal connection with the president and get from him some renewed assurances of American support for Saudi independence, security, and territorial integrity. In an earlier letter to Johnson, Faisal had made it clear that "Egyptian forces in Yemen create a mortal danger for us. . . . With all my power I will fight against the UAR in the Yemen, if the situation requires, whether we win or lose."[78] Arguing that Nasser supported a wellspring of communism and instability in the region, the king pressed Johnson to further limit America's remaining commitments to Egypt.

The one-on-one meeting between president and king started off slow and stilted. Johnson, having been advised by Walt Rostow that "under those robes, you will find a sharp mind and deep devotion to education and social progress," decided to open the meeting with a bit of friendly banter, referring to his days as a schoolteacher and stressing the importance of educational reform.[79] King Faisal agreed and laid out the key educational challenges facing Saudi Arabia, noting that the greatest problem facing the kingdom was

> the shortage of teachers who, of necessity, have had to be imported from neighboring Arab countries. Problem number two [is] the need

to revamp the educational curriculum for elementary schools because the original education plans were drawn up with the assistance of non-Saudi experts [particularly from Egypt]. . . . [W]e have discovered that some of the subjects suggested according to those old plans included matters which would fashion the tender young minds of our youth in a way prejudicial to the interests of our countries.[80]

Saudi statesmen blame foreign influences in their educational system to this day. The problem is at least four decades old.

A long period of silence followed. At one point Johnson stood up and walked over to the water cooler. Faisal, trying to energize the conversation, asked, "How is Vietnam going?" Crushing his cup in his hand, Johnson hissed, "If I could get a clear indication from Westmoreland I could give you a better answer."[81] Another period of silence ensued.

Despite the meeting's awkward beginning, the two were able to find common ground around their mutual distrust of Nasser and Communism. Faisal made his resolve for fighting Communism absolutely clear. A few months prior, in preparing for the meeting, Faisal had sent Johnson a letter stating, "I would like to exchange views with you concerning our joint efforts to halt the Communist advance . . . just as we fight it on the basis of our religion, and you fight against it as a doctrine."[82] During the meeting, Johnson promised Faisal that "as long as I am in office I will not permit your country to be gobbled up by the Communists."[83]

During the follow-up meeting with other officials, the president characterized their talk as "delightful" and said that "he did not know when he had so enjoyed such a visit."[84] After the meeting, the king told the press that his talks with the president were "the happiest, most delightful in my life."[85] Although likely an exaggeration, reports back from the embassy in Saudi Arabia suggest that the trip was viewed there as a "complete success."[86] The ambassador further reported that the visit boosted the king's spirits and enhanced his prestige at home.

One flap did occur as the king was planning to leave Washington for a week of meetings in New York with UN and business officials, New York governor Nelson Rockefeller, and New York City mayor John Lindsay. On the eve of his trip to New York, the king made a set of strongly anti-Israel comments at a National Press Conference briefing. The governor and mayor promptly canceled their meetings with the king. Advised by the State Department, Johnson approved extending the king's Washington visit and holding further follow-up meetings to "take the sting out" of the New York snub. The king, however, decided to head to New York anyway, perhaps sensing that the rebuff in New York could help him at home (the king had in fact met with the president shortly after a major arms deal had been concluded with the Israelis, and he was taking some heat domestically). This resulted in the absurd situation of the king's car passing Governor Nelson Rockefeller's car on the way to David Rockefeller's estate, where the king had been invited for a visit. The governor was no doubt leaving his brother's residence to avoid meeting the king.

The American public was furious over Faisal's remarks. It seemed to have little effect on relations between the two leaders.

War and Embargo

By November 1966 the State Department had begun calling attention to escalating regional tensions. Over the course of 1966 and early 1967, violence increased between Syria, Israel, and Egypt. Harold H. Saunders, then a junior staffer on the National Security Council, warned of a growing crisis on the Israel-Syria border.

Saudi Arabia, exhausted by Nasser's ceaseless quest to bring down the monarchy, joined Jordan and Syria in egging on the Egyptian leader. Broadcasting over Saudi state-controlled radio, announcers chastised Nasser for doing little for the Palestinian people, failing to honor Egypt's defense agreements with Syria when Syria was attacked by Israel, and weakening Arab strength by sowing dissension in Yemen.

On May 21, 1967, Egypt mobilized its armed forces and the next day blockaded Israeli shipping through the Straits of Tiran, an act of war as far as Washington was concerned. Aramco reported that "the King was openly criticized by heretofore silent segments of the population for Saudi Arabia's role (or more properly, lack of a role) in the struggle against Israel."[87] Aside from its anti-Nasser rhetoric, Saudi Arabia remained relatively quiet until May 24, when Riyadh ordered a full mobilization and put the Saudi armed forces on alert. Eventually a brigade of three thousand Saudi soldiers made their way to southern Jordan, where they settled far from the front.[88] Hermann Eilts, now U.S. ambassador to Saudi Arabia, cabled back to Washington that if war broke out, the United States and Saudi Arabia would lose regardless of whether Egypt or Israel won the war. If Israel won, the United States and by implication Saudi Arabia would be castigated for its victory. If Egypt won, a victorious Nasser would assume an even more powerful position in the Middle East and developing world.[89]

King Faisal, who had been in London for a state dinner on May 8, did not rush home, but rather stretched out his stay to include an unscheduled stopover in Paris to discuss the crisis with General

1. *King Abdel Aziz meets U.S. president Franklin D. Roosevelt aboard the USS* Quincy *on February 14, 1945. The two established a strong personal bond that set the tone for the next sixty years of bilateral relations. To the left of King Abdel Aziz, the dynamic Col. William A. Eddy kneels to interpret.* Courtesy of the Franklin D. Roosevelt Library, Hyde Park, New York.

2. *The slaughter of one of the eight sheep that the Saudi delegation brought aboard the* USS Murphy, *the military destroyer carrying King Abdel Aziz to meet President Roosevelt. The king's organizers had hoped to bring along eighty-six sheep while the Americans had been surprised that any sheep were expected to come aboard.* Courtesy of the Franklin D. Roosevelt Library, Hyde Park, New York.

3. Permanent representative to the United Nations Prince (later King) Faisal bin Abdel Aziz arrives at LaGuardia Field on September 9, 1947, with his brothers and young son, two months before the UN voted for the partition of Palestine. As the leader of the "free princes," Prince Talal would go into brief exile in Egypt in 1962. Faisal's son is the current foreign minister. Left to right: Talal bin Abdel Aziz, Saud al-Faisal, Prince Faisal, Abdel Rahman bin Abdel Aziz, and Abdel Mohsin bin Abdel Aziz al-Saud. Photo by Bettmann/CORBIS.

4. President Truman awards Prince (later King) Saud a medal for Saudi Arabia's declaring "war against the Axis in March 1945" and "keeping the land, sea, and air routes open for use." Courtesy of the Harry S. Truman Library, Independence, Missouri.

THE WHITE HOUSE
WASHINGTON

October 31, 1950

Your Majesty:

Upon sending to you my new Ambassador to reside near your Court, I wish to take occasion to renew to Your Majesty expressions of my sincere and lasting friendship toward yourself, the Royal Family and your people.

Your steadfast loyalty and good will, alike in times of stress as in days of happiness and well-being, have ever been sources of pride and pleasure to me and to the American people. Our countries have been comrades in arms together and we have common cause in opposing the godless forces of Communism which are endeavoring to destroy freedom throughout the world. I count it a high tribute to the United States to have the support of so illustrious a warrior as yourself in this struggle.

The efforts you are making to develop your country and improve the standards of living for your people are admirable and praiseworthy. I am proud that American enterprise has been able to assist you in such worthy projects.

I wish to renew to Your Majesty the assurances which have been made to you several times in the past, that the United States is interested in the preservation of the independence and territorial integrity of Saudi Arabia. No threat to your Kingdom could occur which would not be a matter of immediate concern to the United States.

The health of Your Majesty is a subject of no less importance and I pray that you will be long preserved for the welfare of your country and the happiness of your people.

Faithfully yours,

(Sgd) HARRY S. TRUMAN

His Majesty
King Abdul Aziz ibn Abderrahman
al Feisal al Saud,
Riyadh,
Saudi Arabia.

5. *This letter from President Truman to King Abdel Aziz in October 1950 assures Abdel Aziz that "no threat to your Kingdom could occur which would not be a matter of immediate concern to the United States." It became the backbone to the security component of the U.S.-Saudi relationship.* Courtesy of the Harry S. Truman Library, Independence, Missouri.

Your Majesty:

It was a great privilege for me to meet and discuss matters of mutual interest with your son and Foreign Minister, His Royal Highness Prince Faisal. I am now sending Secretary Dulles and Mr. Stassen to meet you and to gain a further understanding of the problems which confront both of us.

I have long shared the widespread admiration of your Majesty's outstanding political and military qualities which have so eminently fitted you to be the leader of your people. Your constant friendship and loyalty and your support in the common cause against godless communism have been a source of inspiration to me and the American people. I have also observed with great interest the progress being made in the economic development of Saudi Arabia and take pride in the fact that American citizens are collaborating with your Government in this important enterprise.

I pray that God may have your Majesty in His safekeeping and that you may long be preserved for the welfare and happiness of your people.

                    Your sincere friend,

His Majesty

    King Abdul Aziz al Saud,

        Kingdom of Saudi Arabia.

6. *In his letter introducing Secretary of State John Foster Dulles to King Abdel Aziz, President Eisenhower acknowledged Saudi Arabia's "common cause in opposing godless communism." It was the only letter of the thirteen that Dulles carried during his comprehensive tour of the Middle East to explicitly mention this shared interest.* Courtesy of the Dwight D. Eisenhower Library, Abilene, Kansas.

7. *Secretary of State John Foster Dulles and Harold E. Stassen, director of the Mutual Security Agency, are met by Prince Faisal in Riyadh, May 18, 1953. Ambassador Raymond A. Hare is behind Dulles and Stassen.* Courtesy of Princeton University Library, Princeton, New Jersey.

8. *The White House welcomed King Saud to Washington with a large banner across his motorcade's route during a visit in January 1957. Eisenhower and Dulles had hoped that King Saud would use Saudi Arabia's religious credentials to counter the influence of Egypt's President Gamal Abdel Nasser.* National Park Service photo, courtesy of the Dwight D. Eisenhower Library, Abilene, Kansas.

9. President Eisenhower and Vice President Nixon attend a dinner at the Mayflower Hotel hosted by King Saud, February 1, 1957. National Park Service photo, courtesy of the Dwight D. Eisenhower Library, Abilene, Kansas.

10. Thomas C. Barger, Aramco's chairman of the board, and Sheikh Abdullah Tariki, minister of petroleum and mineral affairs, tour an Aramco oil facility in the Eastern Province, Saudi Arabia. Fluent in Arabic, Barger met regularly with Saudi kings, princes, and other high-level officials. Tariki's ideas laid the foundation for the formation of OPEC. Courtesy of Michael R. Crocker.

11. *On October 5, 1962, days after a coup in Yemen, Kennedy and Faisal met at the White House to discuss regional events. At the meeting President Kennedy pushed the king to implement internal reforms, the first U.S. president to ever do so.* Courtesy of the Information Office, Embassy of Saudi Arabia, Washington, D.C.

12. *President Johnson never liked speaking through interpreters because they prevented him from establishing a personal connection with his counterparts. Here he is with King Faisal and America's renowned interpreter Isa Sabbagh, June 21, 1966.* Courtesy of the Lyndon B. Johnson Library, Austin, Texas.

13. On February 16, 1974, with the oil embargo eased but still formally in place, King Faisal met with Frank Jungers, director of Aramco. The tension between the two is palpable. Photo by Alain Nogues/CORBIS.

14. As the Watergate scandal reached its climax, Nixon traveled to the Middle East to discuss American foreign policy, a much safer topic for him than domestic politics. Nixon and Kissinger met King Faisal in Jeddah on June 15, 1974. Brent Scowcroft, deputy assistant to the president for national security affairs, stands off to Nixon's left. Courtesy of the Nixon Presidential Materials Staff, National Archives II, College Park, Maryland.

Charles de Gaulle.[90] There was much grumbling inside Saudi Arabia that the king did not return home sooner from Europe. An opinion piece in the British *Observer* suggested that "King Faisal's visit to Britain was not very wisely timed." But Faisal's prolonged absence from the region allowed him to keep his country somewhat removed from the impending disaster. It allowed him to avoid directly responding to the public outcry against Israel and the United States. On June 2, for example, local Saudi saboteurs attacked a machine shop in the U.S. embassy compound in Jeddah, along with a USMTM house and a compound belonging to an American-owned printing firm. Faisal, just returning home, was able to distance himself a bit from the outpouring of anti-American, and by extension anti-regime, sentiment. Still, Americans in the kingdom grew increasingly worried about the restive Saudi population. Riyadh assured Aramco officials that it would assume full responsibility for the safety of expatriate employees and dependents.

On June 5, 1967, Israel attacked Egypt's and Jordan's air forces, wiping them out in a matter of hours. Within days Israel seized the West Bank, Golan Heights, and Gaza Strip. On June 6, the day after Israel's attack, Nasser falsely accused the United States and Great Britain of providing Israel with air cover. The rumor spread through the region like wildfire, and Egypt, Algeria, Sudan, Syria, Yemen, and Iraq quickly broke relations with the United States.[91] Iraq, Kuwait, and Algeria suspended oil deliveries to the United States and United Kingdom.

Unlike other Arab media outlets, the official Saudi press did not carry Nasser's charges, although King Faisal did issue a statement that Saudi Arabia would cut off the flow of oil to any country that aided Israel. By not mentioning the United States by name specifically or immediately cutting off supplies, the king may have hoped Washington could quickly establish its lack of involvement. By June 7, however, Saudi Arabia joined the embargo when the oil minister, Sheikh Ahmad Zaki Yamani, informed Aramco executives that "you are requested hereby not to ship oil to the United States of America or the United Kingdom."[92] Aramco officials complied, believing that if they did not, their company faced nationalization. In case there was any doubt about the risks, on May 25, in only a half-jesting manner, Yamani asked his deputy minister, Hisham Nazer, in the presence of Aramco representatives from Riyadh, how Aramco should be punished for U.S. government assistance to Israel. Nazer suggested nationalization, to which the minister responded, "Not yet."[93] Saudi Arabia thus supported the second international oil embargo in eleven years—the first having occurred in 1956, during the Suez crisis.

The security situation for Americans and oil infrastructure grew precarious. Protests had been occurring on and off throughout the 1950s and 1960s, but they swelled around the 1967 war. On the morning of June 7 small groups began forming at Aramco's offices in Dhahran, Dammam, al-Khobar, and Ras Tanura. The American consulate was stoned. The emir of the Eastern Province arrived and assured Aramco officials that "everything was under control." But, according to one observer, things were "definitely not under control." There were not enough forces left in the Eastern Province to mobilize a convincing show of force, as the area had been stripped of soldiers to fight in Yemen, to fight the Israelis in Jordan, and to protect the oil pipeline in the north of the country.

The emir of the Eastern Province, Emir bin Jiluwi (a direct descendant of the late King Abdel Aziz's cousin, who had helped him take Riyadh at the turn of the century), was reluctant to contact Riyadh, notwithstanding Aramco's pressure on him to do so. Marauding mobs began targeting the vehicles, offices, homes, and personal effects of USMTM officers. There were some reports that Saudi military personnel were joining with their compatriots.

The emir did not call Riyadh until late on the morning of the seventh, and even then he withheld information regarding the full extent of the damage. According to an Aramco report, "officials were playing down the seriousness of the demonstrations, presumably because the officials were concerned that the demonstrations had gotten out of hand, and they were unable to handle them." By midafternoon the chaos was undeniable, and the emir finally called Riyadh to report the extent of the damage. Two thousand Saudi National Guard members were deployed to the Eastern Province, scheduled to arrive at midnight.[94] Aramco began evacuating four hundred of its most vulnerable employees, including the sick and children, the next day.

On June 8 President Johnson sent a telegram to Faisal stressing that he was "disturbed" about the mob action. He assured the king "that it is not my desire to take any action which would focus attention on your problem."[95] Still, if the king did not find a way to protect the Americans on his soil, the president would support an evacuation, a decision the king did not want and that Ambassador Eilts did not believe was necessary. Almost immediately the CIA reported that "the Saudis are apparently dealing harshly with those participating in mob action against the American consulate and other American installations in Dhahran. Two were killed and others injured when security police fired into the crowd during one disturbance, and most of those involved in the rioting have apparently been arrested. It is popularly believed that they are being severely punished, and this has helped stabilize the tense situation."[96]

In a review after the riot, Aramco concluded:

> The Government, manifestly, misjudged the temper of the population. It also learned that it could not depend upon many of the people whose trust it was trying to buy, e.g., members of the educated class who had benefited most from recent progressive steps and reforms. In the final analysis, the Government was thrown back to its earliest and most constant basis of support—the Bedouins of the National Guard.[97]

Despite the fact that Saudi Arabia was now engaged in its second embargo against Britain in eleven years, and the first one against the United States, the king did not sever official relations. Johnson made clear that he "recognized the imperatives" of King Faisal's position.

Johnson, however, could not abide any decisions that affected America's abilities in Vietnam, and U.S. troops in Vietnam were vulnerable to the oil embargo. As in 1956, the United States maintained a large unused spare capacity and economically could ride out the oil embargo. What it could do militarily was another story. In 1967 the Defense Department bought 450,000 barrels of petroleum products per day, or 45 percent of its needs, abroad.[98] American troops in Vietnam alone consumed 200,000 to 300,000 barrels of Persian Gulf oil per day. Sixty percent of U.S. overall petroleum requirements for Vietnam and East Asia, and 80 percent of its aviation fuel, came from the Gulf. Recognizing this, Faisal quietly allowed J-9 jet fuel shipments to reach the U.S. Air Force in Vietnam, the embargo notwithstanding.[99]

Two warships in the Red Sea were also vulnerable. Ambassador Eilts pleaded with the king that "we've got to bunker [fuel] these ships, otherwise they are dead in the water." Faisal told Eilts and Yamani that they should send out barges to assist the ships, but quietly and out of the public eye. "In that way," remembered Ambassador Eilts "he was assisting us. He recognized that, but he was not doing it in a visible fashion, which might have stirred public opinion."[100]

To minimize the embargo's global effect, the United States increased its oil production and rerouted oil shipments. By early August the British and Germans had expressed their gratitude for the speed of the American response and reported that the immediate effects of the oil crisis were "manageable."[101]

Officially the embargo was not lifted until September 1 at the Arab League summit in Khartoum, Sudan, when Arab states decided to "resume the pumping of oil."[102] But the real turning point came on June

11, six days after the war began. On that day Sheikh Yamani and his Kuwaiti counterpart announced that in return for written guarantees that oil would not go directly to Britain or the United States, oil would again flow. Yamani knew full well that as long as oil flowed somewhere, others could supply individually embargoed countries. The destination of the oil was less important than the amount available. Had American policy makers fully grasped this reality, they would have been much better prepared to manage the next, more detrimental oil embargo six years later.

Throughout the summer, Saudi officials released a number of trial balloons to end the oil embargo, which was still officially in place. In late June Yamani broadcasted that Saudi Arabia was losing $350,000 per day to the embargo, "and if such losses continued, they would be no less serious than Arab territorial and human losses in the war with Israel." The comments were the first of their kind to come from an Arab country.[103] Each new Saudi proposal was countered with vicious Egyptian and Iraqi responses and then quickly buried. American officials closely monitored Saudi efforts to roll back the embargo.

Although Saudi efforts were somewhat helpful on the oil front, the political and military situation was significantly more conflicted. U.S.-Saudi military and social contacts were suspended for months, although diplomatic ones continued. The Saudis were furious that Israel was being allowed to keep territory taken by force. From Truman through Johnson, successive American presidents had assured Saudi Arabia that Washington was committed to the territorial integrity of all Middle East states, something Saudi leaders took very seriously. After the June war, such pledges appeared hollow. Secretary of Defense McNamara realized this, noting to his staff, "We're in a heck of a jam on territorial integrity."[104]

The Saudis pressed Washington hard to condemn not only Egypt but also Israel for starting the war, something Washington refused to do. The CIA reported that Saudi Arabia was vulnerable to Arab charges that they had not provided any fighting force for the June war. "The Saudis themselves are aware that their image is tarnished in the eyes of other Arab states as a result of their inaction. The US Ambassador in Jeddah reports that King Faisal now feels that he must push hard for the US to take positions which will protect Arab interests in order to demonstrate that his policy of friendship with the US 'pays off.' "[105]

The Saudis, along with the Arab world, were also dismayed that the United States did not insist in UN Resolution 242 that Israel withdraw from "those territories occupied" but rather only from "territories occupied," which allowed Israel to define which territories were to be ceded back.

The anger went both ways. Faisal hoped Johnson would appreciate that at the Khartoum summit Arab leaders had not issued their usual statements about the elimination of Israel, but rather called only for Israel to withdraw from lands "which have been occupied since the aggression of June 5." But as far as Johnson was concerned Khartoum provided only a list of what the Arab states would not do, such as "no peace with Israel, no recognition of Israel, no negotiations with it, and insistence on the rights of the Palestinian people in their own country." The president wanted to know what the Arabs would do.

Johnson was reluctant to press for an Israeli withdrawal. He was acutely aware that the 1956 decision to compel Israel's retreat had not resulted in peace. Rather than urging Israel to withdraw, Johnson's staff instead decided to pursue a comprehensive peace for the region.

After the war, Johnson turned his attention back to Vietnam and did little else in the Middle East. Undersecretary of State George W. Ball did tour the region, hoping to garner Saudi financial and political support for a peace between Arabs and Israelis and for Nasser to clear the sunken ships from the Suez Canal. Ball made no headway. Other than the failed mission, little else happened between the Americans and Saudis for the rest of Johnson's tenure. The American foreign policy staff was engaged elsewhere.

The Effects of the Six-Day War

Saudi Arabia emerged from the June war in a substantially stronger regional position. Nasser had been discredited, his military humiliated, and his country economically broken. He was no longer the omnipotent Arab leader inspiring followers from across the region. Once the subsidizer of pan-Arabism, Nasser's Egypt now had to scrounge for cash.

At the September Arab League summit in Khartoum, Arab states lifted the oil embargo and Egypt announced that it would pull twenty thousand troops out of Yemen. In return, the oil-producing countries agreed to subsidize Jordan and Egypt to the tune of $329 million per year, with Saudi Arabia providing nearly half the total amount. Egypt, the once dominant force in the Arab world and the country that had posed a direct threat to the Saudis' territorial integrity, was now on the Saudi payroll.

After the war, the regional balance of power began migrating across the Red Sea from Egypt to Saudi Arabia. At the same time, Arabs began turning toward political Islam to replace discredited ideas of Arab Nationalism. This was the result of the crushing defeat that religiously inspired Israel dealt its Arab neighbors, many of whom were led by secular national leaders. But the rise of Islamic politics also directly correlates to the rise of Saudi Arabia, a country that regularly sought to use religion as a base of its power. Fouad Ajami best captured the dynamic at play when he stated, "Few struggles for power are ever waged without pretensions to ideological or normative stakes. The protagonists drag ideas into the game because they take the ideas seriously and because they wish to invest their quest with moral worth and to provide a cover for what otherwise would seem to be narrow and selfish goals."[106] Thus Saudi Arabia "dragged" Wahhabi Islam into Middle East politics.

In addition to the shifting regional balance of power, the war had an important if rarely acknowledged effect on American domestic politics as it related to Saudi Arabia. Until 1967, what was good for Saudi Arabia was, ironically, often good for Israel. Although the animosity between Israel and Saudi Arabia ran deep, both were first and foremost threatened by Nasser's Egypt. When Kennedy attempted to woo Nasser, both pro-Saudi and pro-Israel groups lined up against him. When Johnson eased such support, pro-Saudi and pro-Israel groups breathed a sigh of relief. But 1967 spelled the end for Nasser, and with their goal of his demise realized, pro-Israel and pro-Saudi domestic groups were no longer aligned on one of their most prominent foreign policy goals.

The embargo and war also had significant consequences in Great Britain, highlighting the costs of direct involvement in the Middle East. On November 30, 1967, after nearly 130 years of close association, the British withdrew from Aden. Within three years, the newly named People's Republic of South Yemen was under the control of revolutionary Marxist leaders. The new Yemeni leadership proclaimed its dedication to the overthrow of all the traditional regimes in the Arabian Peninsula and its interest in reuniting with North Yemen. This presented Saudi Arabia once again with the threat of a large, populous, irredentist, revolutionary neighbor to the south.[107] On January 16, 1968, British prime minister J. Harold Wilson went even further and announced that within three years Britain intended to withdraw from its commitments east of Suez. This threatened to create a power vacuum on Saudi Arabia's eastern border, where the British had asserted control for decades.

A Steadier Course

During the 1950s and 1960s the United States and the Soviet Union sought to influence their regional partners, respectively Saudi Arabia and Egypt. Over the course of these two decades, the United States exper-imented with various ways to contain the Soviet Union. Each had dif-ferent implications for Saudi Arabia, whose leadership was expected to adjust to shifting American policy immediately. At times Washington sought to embrace the kingdom, often by encouraging religious pro-selytizing. At other points, when Washington tried to woo Egypt, it kept Saudi Arabia at arm's length. By the end of the 1960s, President Johnson put an end to America's wavering allegiances. Under Johnson, Saudi Arabia came to be seen as a reliable partner in the struggles against Nasser and Communism, due in part to Prince Faisal's assumption of the monarchy in 1964, American's increasing focus on Vietnam, and a steadier U.S. anti-Communist approach. This did not prevent the two states from ending up on opposite sides in the June 1967 war, the third Arab-Israeli war in less than two decades. But Johnson's decisions laid the foundations for President Nixon's twin pillars policy, which domin-ated much of the 1970s.

After the 1967 war, President Johnson turned his attention back to Asia, bequeathing to his successor a changed and changing Middle East. Israel was now in a much stronger position, controlling the strategically important West Bank, Golan Heights, and Sinai Peninsula. With Nasser vanquished and prized Arab territory conquered, the Arab world was in crisis. Making matters worse, Saudi leaders could no longer trust America's commitment to the territorial integrity of the Middle East, a promise made during the Truman administration and reconfirmed by each president thereafter.

The 1967 war challenged America's relationship with all Arab countries, Saudi Arabia being no exception. But oil interests and anti-Communism were able to override the stresses of regional politics and cause the two countries to operate much more closely over the course of the following decades.

5

Double, Double, Oil and Trouble

An urgent early morning message passed over Henry Kissinger's desk, one that required presidential attention. It was October 10, 1973, day five of the fifth Arab-Israeli war in two and a half decades. The Israelis, surprised by Egypt and Syria's joint attack, did not appear to be faring well. As Kissinger was heading off to meet President Richard Nixon, the secretary of defense called, wanting to discuss a number of urgent issues, including Saudi Arabian troop movements. "They have requested rights to move other brigades from Saudi proper through Jordan and Jordan can't really resist it," James Schlesinger reported in his deep and deliberate voice. "We are going to get into a position in which all of our interests in Saudi Arabia are at risk and it might be desirable to examine the fundamentals of our position."

"Well," asked Kissinger, "what are the fundamentals of our position, as you see it?"

The defense secretary's response focused Kissinger's attention. "The fundamentals are that we may be faced with the choice that lies cruelly between support of Israel [and] loss of Saudi Arabia and if [our] interests in the Middle East are at risk, the choice between occupation or watching them go down the drain."

"Occupation of whom?" Kissinger, somewhat alarmed, wanted to know.

"That would remain to be seen—it can be partial," Schlesinger replied.

"But which country are we occupying?" Kissinger pressed.

"That's one of the things we'd like to talk about."

"Who's we?"

"Me," responded Schlesinger.

Kissinger promised to get back to him after he met with the president.[1]

A week and a half later Saudi Arabia would orchestrate a five-month embargo on all Arab oil shipping to the United States, one that lasted well past the cease-fire between the belligerents. Thirty years later the British national archives would release documents showing that the head of Britain's Joint Intelligence Committee, Percy Cradock, considered the scenario of American forces seizing Saudi Arabia's and other Gulf states' oil facilities so plausible that he penned a report that made it all the way up to British prime minister Edward Heath's desk. The seizure might "be executed without any prior consultation of allies," warned Cradock's December 1973 report. London's concern was due in no small part to the fact that, in November, Schlesinger warned the British ambassador to Washington, Lord Cromer, that Washington would not tolerate threats from "under-developed, under-populated" countries and that "it was no longer obvious to him that the United States could not use force." Upon reading the report Heath penciled in a single word: "ominous."

U.S.-Saudi relations had hit a new low. Yet within six years not only would Saudi-American relations rebound, but the foreign policies of both would align from Angola to Afghanistan as never before.

The Middle East After 1967

When Richard Nixon assumed the presidency on January 20, 1969, the Middle East was again in crisis. The quick collapse of Arab forces in the Six-Day War had left Arab nationalism in tatters—a discredited ideology unable to defend, let alone augment, Arab territory. Although Egypt's president Gamal Abdel Nasser limped along politically for another three years, he was unable to regain his aura of invincibility, especially as he had become dependant on Saudi aid. Saudi Arabia, for its part, was beginning to flex its economic and political muscles.

Middle East leaders faced serious political challenges that had their origins in the 1967 war. Within two years of the 1967 war Egypt and Israel locked horns in a bloody war of attrition, hostilities that cost both sides thousands of lives. For the first time, modern American-made fighter jets appeared as part of Israel's fighting force—until then such equipment had come primarily from France. Soviet officers piloted MiG fighters flying from Egypt.

In Libya, Colonel Muammar al-Qadhafi overthrew King Idriss, re-energizing antimonarchical tendencies in the Arab world. An ambitious eccentric, Qadhafi worked actively to replace Nasser as the pan-Arab leader, and like Nasser he reserved particular venom for Saudi Arabia's leaders, whom he considered the "renegades of Islam." A self-appointed messiah, he promised a different kind of Islamic foreign policy, one independent of Saudi influence. Saudi Arabia's King Faisal was determined to prevent the emergence of another anti-Saudi firebrand, having finally chastened Nasser only a couple of years earlier. Within a few years Saudi Arabia and Libya were engaged in a decades-long power struggle that played itself out viciously, if stealthily, across Africa. As late as 2003, American, Egyptian, and Saudi officials uncovered a Libyan attempt to assassinate Crown Prince Abdullah.[2]

The 1967 war also gave rise to a new Palestine Liberation Organization (PLO) leadership and structure. At its founding in 1964, the PLO was the creation of and subservient to the Arab League—Egypt in particular. The Arab League countries used the PLO both to express their ongoing support for Palestinian rights and to restrain Palestinian activity when it threatened parochial national interests. After the war, Palestinian groups such as Yasser Arafat's Fatah adopted a more forceful approach to resisting Israeli occupation, one that was more independent of larger Arab control. By 1969 Fatah had captured most of the important offices within the PLO.[3]

Along with Fatah's rise to prominence, Saudi Arabia became a vital backer of the PLO. The loss of Jerusalem during the war enraged King Faisal, who was determined to win back for Muslims Islam's third holiest site. Until 1967 Saudi Arabia's financial support for Palestinian groups had been tepid, largely because the PLO had been so closely associated with Egypt, Saudi Arabia's nemesis. Fatah provided a means for King Faisal to support the Palestinians while counterbalancing Marxist groups such as the Popular Front for the Liberation of Palestine. Faisal also began incorporating the Palestinian struggle into Saudi Arabia's larger foreign policy goals. According to James Piscatori, a close observer of Islamic politics, "Faisal proved remarkably successful at transferring the Arab-Israeli conflict from the exclusively Arab plane to the broader Islamic one."[4]

The rise of Palestinian nationalism and the deterioration of pan-Arab nationalism challenged states with large Palestinian populations. In 1970 Jordan's King Hussein barely survived "Black September," a civil war fought between the Jordanian armed forces and the Palestinian Liberation Organization in Jordan. Although never completely trustful of their Hashemite neighbors, the Saudi leadership did not want to see the fall of a neighboring monarchy, as that would likely encourage opposition to the kingdom's own monarchy. An emboldened PLO began undertaking raids on Israel from Jordanian territory, and Israel responded by targeting Jordan. This is one reason why Jordan's King Hussein decided to crush the PLO operating in Jordan.[5] Defense Minister Hafiz al-Asad seized power in Syria after the reigning Syrian leader, Salah Jadid, unsuccessfully attempted to back the PLO during the Jordanian civil war.

Although the external environment appeared treacherous for the kingdom, domestic life provided no respite. At home, King Faisal staved off several coup attempts.[6] In June 1969 a group of Saudi air force officers began meeting quietly in what looked like early efforts at challenging the government. Faisal took prompt action, spurring mass arrests, executions, and torture in jails. Throughout the summer and early fall hundreds of civil servants were arrested; the Saudi air force was temporarily grounded and its officers purged. The *New York Times* reported that "the revolutionary movement is . . . the largest ever uncovered in Saudi Arabia."[7]

During the same year Crown Prince Khaled, Faisal's half brother, announced that he no longer wanted to continue as crown prince or to be next in line for the throne after King Faisal. Khaled dreamed of returning to a simpler life among the tribes of the kingdom's heartland. But it was precisely his Bedouin spirit and his wide-ranging domestic support that made him his family's choice to succeed King Faisal. There were powerful members of the royal family who also saw Khaled as a way to keep power from Prince Fahd—the number two behind Khaled—and Fahd's reputedly Western-oriented full brothers. In the end, the family averted this potential internal crisis by convincing Khaled to stay on.

An overworked and increasingly harried King Faisal juggled competing threats. Washington hardly seemed to notice.

"More than Enough on Our Plate"

In Washington, Nixon was much more preoccupied by Vietnam and U.S.-Soviet relations than by Middle East regional crises. Nixon thought "Middle East diplomacy was a loser," remembered Henry Kissinger, and therefore "sought to deflect its risks from himself."[8] This was evident in how Nixon distributed responsibilities among his foreign policy team.

Even before taking office, Nixon had made clear that he intended to direct foreign policy from the White House and that he wanted Henry Kissinger, the protégé of his Republican rival Nelson Rockefeller, in the hot seat as national security advisor—except when it came to the Middle East. For that troubled region, Nixon gave prime responsibility to Secretary of State William P. Rogers and Assistant Secretary of State for Near Eastern and South Asian Affairs Joseph J. Sisco. Nixon was concerned that Kissinger's Jewish background would interfere with improving relations with Arab states, one of his key objectives in the region. He also believed that he and Kissinger had "more than enough on our plate with Vietnam, SALT, the Soviets, Japan and Europe" and that the Middle East required the focused attention of a full-time operator.[9]

To the extent that he considered the Middle East, Nixon hoped to improve relations with the Arabs to counter Soviet gains in the Middle East. Although he valued Israel's role in combating Communism, as well as the model of freedom it provided, Nixon intended to chart a more "even handed" (i.e., less pro-Israel) strategy than his predecessors. But such even-handedness was to take a backseat to U.S.-Soviet relations if the two conflicted. As he made clear in a memo, " 'even handedness' is the right policy—but above all our interest is—what gives the Soviet[s] the most trouble—don't let Arab-Israeli conflict obscure that interest."[10]

The Nixon administration also began looking toward Saudi Arabia with greater interest. The Vietnam War was sapping American resources, and the White House began a global search for local proxies through which America could operate. In the Middle East, Washington began relying increasingly on Saudi Arabia and Iran to provide regional stability and stem the Soviet tide. It was a role Iran embraced with alacrity and Saudi Arabia with caution. Saudi Arabia rarely took public stands outside its borders, preferring to operate quietly from the shadows. The policy became known as the "twin pillars," with Saudi Arabia serving as one pillar and Iran as the other. When in 1979 the Iranian revolution collapsed America's dominant pillar, Saudi Arabia assumed an even more important role in Washington's calculations.

As Kissinger emerged as a powerful figure within the government during Nixon's first term, he chafed under the system that gave Rogers responsibility for Middle East policy. He violently disagreed with what he viewed as the State Department's predisposition to distance the United States from Israel in order to prompt concessions from the Arabs. Kissinger believed this would only encourage Arabs to blackmail the United States. Rogers, on the other hand, believed the only way to ensure peace was to inject more equity into the Arab-Israeli balance of power. A peace initiative launched by Rogers that eventually bore his name was "deflected," "defeated" and "spiked" by Kissinger and the White House.[11]

In late 1971 Nixon began shifting responsibility for the Middle East to Kissinger. This shift culminated in September 1973, less than one month before the 1973 Yom Kippur War, when Rogers resigned and Kissinger assumed the role of both national security advisor and secretary of state.

"Never-Never Land"

Though it went largely unnoticed by either Kissinger or Rogers, the global energy market experienced profound changes during the late 1960s and early 1970s, ones that would redefine America's and Saudi Arabia's standing and set the stage for the 1973 Arab oil embargo. In a February 1970 report the White House predicted continued energy self-sufficiency over the course of the next decade and steady or decreasing prices.[12] The forecast proved spectacularly wrong.

The White House believed that it could, in theory, restrict oil coming from the Eastern Hemisphere to 5 percent of total imports.[13] In practice, by 1972, the United States imported no less than 15 percent of its oil from the East. A host of other trend lines also pointed in the wrong direction. Between 1967 and 1973 the nation's total natural gas reserves had dropped from a fifteen-year supply to one of less than ten years.[14] Gas shortfalls could only be covered by increased oil imports, putting further pressure on petroleum demand. Between 1955 and 1972 the number of wells drilled in the United States plummeted from 31,567 to 11,306 a year, in part a result of increasing environmental legislation.[15] By the summer of 1973 U.S. imports were 6.2 million barrels per day (mbd), compared to 4.5 mbd in 1972 and 3.2 mbd in 1970.[16]

Until the early 1970s, a complicated system of import quotas and domestic production controls regulated the American energy market. Eisenhower-era quotas rationed global imports into the United States. The Texas Railroad Commission, one of the country's oldest regulatory agencies, regulated oil production in Texas, the country's dominant production area, determining American overall output.[17] In 1972 the Texas Railroad Commission acknowledged for the first time that local supplies were not keeping pace with domestic consumption. It removed all restrictions on domestic production. American oil companies began producing at full capacity, no longer maintaining spare reserves to put on the market in times of crisis.[18] The United States was no longer the supplier of last resort. This simple fact is central to why the 1973 embargo was so much more painful for consuming countries than the Arab embargos of 1956 and 1967.

In response to growing global demand, the market price for crude doubled between 1970 and 1973.[19] Aramco increased production from

1.3 mbd to 2 billion barrels daily between 1970 and 1972.[20] Between January and June 1973 it increased production another 40 percent.[21] The kingdom now vied with the Soviet Union for the number two slot among world producers, behind the United States.

Changing dynamics in the oil sector also gave OPEC real leverage for the first time. Starting in 1960, when he co-founded the organization, Abdullah Tariki worked assiduously for better local representation in, or control over, multinational oil companies. His successor, Sheikh Ahmed Zaki Yamani, a personable and handsome man with a Vandyke beard whom Faisal once referred to as "a wily fox," pursued similar goals, albeit more quietly, cautiously, and ultimately successfully. In 1972 he engineered an OPEC plan to transition ownership of the multinational oil companies to local hands, something Tariki could not do back in the early 1960s, when oil companies had greater leverage over their sovereign hosts. Yamani's plan, which he referred to euphemistically as "participation" rather than gradual nationalization, called for an initial transfer of 25 percent ownership into local hands and a gradual transition to 51 percent by 1983.[22] He wanted to proceed cautiously in order not to unnecessarily antagonize the United States, a tempo Faisal supported. Saudi Arabia's actions stood in contrast to those of Libya and Algeria, which immediately took 51 percent ownership of local companies.[23] The Arab oil embargo of 1973–74 further hastened the nationalization process for other countries, with most OPEC members fully nationalizing their industries between 1973 and 1975. Saudi Arabia did not fully nationalize Aramco until almost a decade later, around the time first anticipated by Yamani.

As demand for international supplies of oil increased, oil-producing countries considered how to translate their growing economic leverage into comparable political power. In 1972 Arab states made no less than fifteen different threats to use oil as a weapon against their "enemies, and almost all of them singled out the United States as the prime enemy," observed the State Department's oil expert and future ambassador to Saudi Arabia, James E. Akins, in a prescient April 1973 article in the foreign policy journal *Foreign Affairs*.[24] Saudi Arabia was not one of them. King Faisal steadfastly refused Arab entreaties to use oil against the West. "Oil isn't a weapon," argued King Faisal throughout 1972. "It is an economic force with which we can buy weapons which can be used in battle."[25] Faisal's position began to change in the spring of 1973 as Israeli-Palestinian violence escalated and the region seemed to be drifting toward war. Faisal did not believe that the monarchy would survive if Saudi Arabia remained outside the fight.

What is most remarkable about this period is that few in the Nixon administration appreciated the magnitude of the shifts under way.

"It really is true that in the early 1970s there were not many people who understood how the oil market worked," remembered William B. Quandt, a staff member for the Middle East on the National Security Council under Presidents Nixon and Carter.[26] In Kissinger's words, the Nixon administration operated in a "never-never land" of cheap and available energy. All danger signs, including Yamani's statement in the early fall of 1973 that there would be intense OPEC pressure for a significant price increase at the upcoming meeting in Tehran, scheduled for October 8, were "much clearer in retrospect."[27] Akins was one of the few who did sense impending danger, arguing that "the oil crisis is a reality that compels urgent action."[28] But even he did not anticipate the speed and fury with which production cuts and the embargo were to be visited upon the United States.

A Rivalry in Africa Takes Shape

Changes in the oil market combined with a realignment in inter-Arab politics to create a perfect energy storm. Like the shifts in the energy sector, the Arab realignment was recognized only in hindsight.

Nasser's death in 1970 and his replacement by the politically weaker Anwar el-Sadat provided a set of new opportunities for Saudi Arabia. Faisal was well acquainted with Sadat. The two had first worked together fifteen years prior at the Islamic Conference in 1955. They had dined together on occasion at Sadat's home near the pyramids.[29] Faisal hoped to use his easy relations with Sadat and the fact that Saudi Arabia subsidized Egypt to lure Cairo away from both the Soviet Union and Libya.

Weeks after Sadat assumed power in October 1970, Faisal sent his trusted brother-in-law Kamal Adham to Egypt to explore closer relations between Egypt and Saudi Arabia. Adham, a capable negotiator with high-level contacts throughout the Muslim world, was one-quarter Albanian and three-quarters Turkish and had been raised in the Ottoman court with his half sister Effat, King Faisal's favorite, and eventually only, wife. Well versed in great-power politics from his time in Turkey, he became Saudi Arabia's director of intelligence and mentored his two young nephews, Faisal's sons Saud and Turki, the future minister of foreign affairs and director of Saudi intelligence, respectively.[30]

The king dispatched Adham to Cairo to urge Sadat to reduce Egypt's dependence on the Soviet Union. In the 1970s Soviet customs officers worked in Cairo's airport, allowing Soviet planes to take off and land at will. Thousands of Soviet advisors served throughout the country. At his first meeting with Sadat, Adham explained that such a large

Soviet presence was a strategic liability. It only alarmed the Americans and hindered Faisal's ability to push for the United States to use its influence with Israel and urge a withdrawal from territory conquered in the 1967 war.[31] Little came of these initial efforts, as Egypt signed a treaty of friendship with the Soviet Union in 1971.

Over the course of the next several years Adham shuttled regularly between Jeddah and Cairo, trying to lure Egypt from Soviet clutches. To provide Egypt the freedom to purchase arms from outside the Soviet bloc and increase its bargaining power over the Soviets, Saudi Arabia almost doubled its subsidies to Egypt, to $200 million a year, or slightly more than $1 billion in 2005 dollars. Faisal ordered Saudi officers to purchase French Mirage aircraft on Egypt's behalf. Faisal even promised to put Saudi-owned British Lightning fighter jets at Egypt's disposal (the ones resulting from the McNamara-Jenkins Agreement, detailed in chapter 4), a promise he never fulfilled.[32] Saudi Arabia, along with other Gulf states, extended new low-interest loans to Egypt to allow it to purchase weapons and jump-start its economy. Saudi and Gulf businessmen began actively investing in Egypt's emerging private sector, helping the Egyptian economy to shed its socialist influences.

Sadat's daring, supported by Saudi resources, culminated in a dramatic geopolitical shift. In July 1972 Sadat ordered home the approximately twenty thousand Soviet advisors operating inside his borders.[33] Both Prince Sultan, Saudi Arabia's minister of defense, and Kamal Adham were in Cairo when Sadat gave the order. Based on a message passed by Washington that hinted that the solution to Egypt's problems was already in Egypt, Mohamed H. Heikal, the powerful editor of the Egyptian daily *Al-Ahram*, speculated that the Saudi presence in Egypt was a sign of U.S. and Saudi tacit support for Sadat's bold gesture.[34]

Kissinger remembered being surprised that Sadat did not try "to obtain any reciprocal gestures" from the United States for such a bold move.[35] Upon hearing the news, an elated but nervous King Faisal mused, "I hope [Egypt] got something for it."[36] They did not, although it allowed Henry Kissinger to establish a short-lived back channel to communicate with Egypt's Hafiz Ismail, Sadat's national security advisor.[37] Faisal's son, who became Saudi Arabia's ambassador to the United States in 2005, remembered that the king felt personally betrayed when America offered little in response.[38] In retrospect, however, it is clear that Sadat had in mind a well-conceived plan. In the longer term, he hoped to establish closer U.S.-Egyptian relations. In the short term, he was setting the stage for a surprise attack against Israel. Close Egyptian-Saudi relations would be instrumental to both.

"Playing for Real Marbles"

At the end of August 1973 Sadat and Syrian president Hafiz al-Asad met in Damascus. Motivated by a deep desire to regain the territory and political standing each had lost in the 1967 war with Israel, the two leaders agreed that the next Arab-Israeli war would begin on October 6. After Damascus, Sadat traveled to Riyadh. Faisal promised that if Egypt required it, Saudi Arabia would use oil as a weapon against Israel's supporters. But "give us time," urged Faisal; "we don't want to use our oil weapon in a battle which only goes on for two or three days and then stops. We want to see a battle which goes on for long enough time for world public opinion to be mobilized."[39]

Faisal's pledge marked a departure from more recent Saudi foreign policy practices. Since 1967 Saudi Arabian leaders had steadfastly committed to keeping oil separate from politics. In providing Cairo with a generous monthly allowance, Faisal had hoped to convince the Arab states that the free flow of oil was in their own self-interest and that an embargo would only bring about self-inflicted wounds. In spring 1973 Saudi Arabia's position began to change.

The reasons for the change are complex. Faisal and others had hoped that Nixon's second term would bring greater American engagement with the Arab-Israeli dispute. Nixon, after all, had given a speech shortly before the presidential elections saying that the Middle East would have "a very high priority" in his second term. In the early 1970s Palestinian radicals, angry at the lack of momentum toward a restoration of their homeland, set off a number of bombs that ineffectually targeted Saudi Arabia's oil infrastructure, resulting in the deportation of many Palestinians from the kingdom. The U.S. inspired Rogers Plan for an Arab-Israeli settlement—the one "spiked" by the White House—was dead and there was little momentum toward an Arab-Israeli settlement. From Riyadh's perspective, the situation of increasing Palestinian radicalism and a disengaged White House was growing untenable. Even those working the Middle East portfolio most closely have subsequently acknowledged that "throughout 1972, the United States appeared to have virtually no Middle East Policy other than supporting the status quo."[40]

In April Yamani met with U.S. officials and warned of a possible Saudi change in oil policy if the United States did not put more pressure on Israel to withdraw from its 1967 conquest.[41] In June Saudi foreign minister Omar Saqqaf issued two statements while in Latin America that echoed Yamani's warnings. That same month in a meeting in Geneva between Sheikh Yamani and high-level officials of

Aramco's American owners, the king made a surprise appearance and warned that if America did not change its foreign policy, "you will lose everything."[42] In July the king summoned journalists from the *Washington Post* and the *Christian Science Monitor* to make clear that Saudi Arabia was seriously considering blocking future oil production increases because of all-out American support for Israel.[43] "We are not asking for the destruction of Israel," said a Saudi minister. "We want a reasonable policy to bring a settlement."[44]

In mid-August 1973 Nicholas G. Thacher, the U.S. ambassador to Saudi Arabia, met with Prince Fahd, then minister of the interior. Fahd told Thacher that Saudi Arabia's Council of Ministers had met and agreed not to use oil as a weapon. Relieved, Thacher relayed this message to Washington. Shortly thereafter Yamani summoned Aramco's chief liaison in Riyadh, Michael A. Ameen, to a meeting. Yamani showed him his copy of Thacher's secret memo, which had been written for high-level U.S. eyes only. Ameen, a congenial Lebanese American and retired U.S. Marine, was shocked to see the document in Saudi possession and listened carefully to what Yamani had to say. According to Yamani, Washington needed to know that Fahd's message was not the final word. Yamani told Ameen that the king would have to institute an embargo if there was fighting between Arabs and Israelis.[45] The monarchy was not strong enough to weather the severity of domestic opposition that was likely to follow if Saudi Arabia did not participate. The monarchy's survival took precedence.

In September, in an interview with *Newsweek*, the king again warned that oil was at stake. American oil officials in the kingdom urged Washington to take the king's threats seriously. "Faisal is no bluffer," urged one. "We're playing for real marbles now."[46] Saudi officials minced no words about their intended course of action should Israel and the Arabs engage in another serious showdown. "If there is a battle, we are in it . . . people had better understand that now."[47]

Still, until the actual embargo was imposed, Faisal's threats were dismissed. It was widely recognized that Saudi Arabia was under increasing pressure from radical Arab states to do something, but that had been true since 1967. Also, the local situation was not as threatening as the Faisal/Nasser rivalry of the 1960s. Many inside the administration pointed out that previous embargos had been ineffective, and the Arabs needed to sell their oil to someone. American diplomatic officials remained noncommittal. The State Department interpreted Saudi Arabia as "making an entreaty rather than a threat."[48] Secretary of Defense Schlesinger recalls that Faisal's warnings were considered little more than "hot air."[49]

In their last meeting before the war, Faisal promised Sadat that if Egypt attacked and continued fighting for long enough to galvanize international attention, Saudi Arabia would undertake an embargo. Those circumstances came together between October 18 and 20, two weeks after Egypt and Syria coordinated a surprise attack on Israel on the Jewish holy day of Yom Kippur and during the Muslim fast of Ramadan. Sadat gave Faisal the time he requested.

War and Embargo

On October 6, 1973, Syrian and Egyptian forces attacked Israel. During the war Israeli and Arab forces engaged in the largest tank battle since World War II. The war cost the two sides over 500 aircraft and 2,700 tanks—an average of one tank every ten to fifteen minutes and a plane every hour of the nearly three-week-long war.[50] The United States and the Soviet Union delivered enormous supplies of weapons to their respective sides. Nixon and Brezhnev used the "hot line," a communications link meant to reduce the risk of nuclear war.

Syrian and Egyptian forces were quickly supplemented with Arab support. During the war Iraq deployed 18,000 men, several hundred tanks, and a number of MiG fighter planes to the Golan Heights. Violating Paris' ban on the transfer of French-made weapons, Libya sent Mirage fighters to Egypt. Algeria dispatched three aircraft squadrons and an armored brigade with 150 tanks. Approximately 1,000–2,000 Tunisian soldiers were positioned in the Nile Delta. Sudan stationed 3,500 troops in southern Egypt. Morocco sent three brigades to the front lines, including 2,500 men to Syria. Jordan ordered to Syria two of its best units.

Saudi Arabia made its own contribution to the Arab cause. Four days after war broke out, Saudi Arabia sent a brigade of 3,000 troops to Syria; this was the deployment that so worried Schlesinger in his phone call to Kissinger. But the brigade did not reach Damascus until after the fighting ended. Prince Fahd summoned the CIA station chief and made clear that Saudi troops were under strict instructions not to become involved in the fighting.[51]

Early in the war, as losses mounted, the Soviet Union began actively resupplying Egypt and Syria. As the Arab front stood poised to again break through Israeli defenses, the United States began its own massive airlift to Israel. By October 13, when the airlift became fully operational, Washington was delivering one thousand tons of equipment a day, with flights landing almost every hour.[52] Kissinger had two goals, for which he received Nixon's backing. First, Arab states should fully understand that working with the United States brought benefits far in excess of what the Soviets could provide. This required the United States to ensure an Israeli victory. The message rang loud and clear in the kingdom. In a story relayed to Robert W. Jordan, U.S. ambassador to the kingdom between 2001 and 2003, the minister of the interior, Prince Fahd, summoned his security officers to a meeting during the massive American airlift. There he showed them clips of American matériel flowing to Israel. "This is why we need to maintain close relations with the U.S.," he explained. "They are the only ones capable of saving us in this manner should we ever be at risk."[53] Prince Fahd, a future king, anticipated a time seventeen years in the future when America would undertake an even more massive airlift to defend the kingdom against Saddam Hussein's Iraq in 1990.

Kissinger's second goal was that Israel's victory should not be so overwhelming that it would leave that country impervious to American entreaties to negotiate. For Kissinger, there should be neither victor nor vanquished.[54] Kissinger told Schlesinger that the best result "would be if Israel came out a little ahead but got bloodied in the process, and if the U.S. stayed clean."[55]

What Kissinger did not fully anticipate was that Saudi Arabia would use oil to alter the equation. On October 8, two days into the war, OPEC representatives met with their oil company counterparts in a previously scheduled meeting to negotiate pricing. Oil company representatives offered a 10 percent price increase, while OPEC representatives called for a 100 percent increase. The gap in proposals was insurmountable, and negotiations broke down. A little over a week later, at a meeting in Kuwait, delegates from the Gulf states (five Arabs and an Iranian) unilaterally decided on a whopping 70 percent increase in the posted price of oil, from $3.01 to $5.12 per barrel.[56]

The next day Arab oil ministers met to consider punishing the United States and others backing Israel. Iraqi president Ahmad Hassan al-Bakr called for the nationalization of all American assets in the Middle East, a liquidation of Arab funds from American banks, and an embargo on all countries friendly to Israel. Yamani was under strict orders from Faisal to avoid spiraling into economic warfare with the United States, and the Saudis did not support nationalization.[57] Instead, Arab oil ministers agreed to a 5 percent cut in production for every month that the United States and others continued backing Israel. The next day Saudi Arabia upped the ante, announcing that it planned to cut production by another 5 percent per month. Two days later Nixon agreed to provide the Israelis with $2.2 billion to pay for the resupply of weaponry that Washington was rushing to the region. Two days after that, the king announced a full embargo on all oil exports to the United States and other Israel supporters.[58]

Frank Jungers, Aramco's president, recorded the detailed embargo arrangements that Yamani insisted upon.

> At the head of the list were The Netherlands, and the United States, and so on. Then there were degrees of boycott. It got more and more complicated as the countries who were boycotted or who were about to be boycotted made their way to Saudi Arabia and pled their case and the degree of the boycott changed. We were given day-by-day instructions of what the boycott order was and who could buy what. . . . So we set up a system that determined where the oil actually ended up, every barrel . . . we knew exactly where every barrel went, and monitored it. This was under threat of complete Nationalization. There was no doubt about this. And we [obeyed] in order not to give them [the chance of nationalization]. We had no choice.[59]

In reality, the production cuts were much more significant than the embargo, although it was the embargo that caused mass panic. An embargo without production cuts is costly but manageable. At a price, embargoed countries can always shift from one supplier to another, as long as others accommodate by also shifting supplies. Sheikh Yamani was well aware that it was difficult to track oil once it was loaded onto a tanker. When confronted with this reality, Yamani merely shrugged and said, "What else can we do?"[60] Production cuts, on the other hand, were much more transformative. Less oil on the market squeezed all consumers. In addition, the way Saudi Arabia and others calculated their reductions made the situation even more severe than it originally appeared. Saudi Arabia calculated the 10 percent reduction from the total production originally destined for the embargoed countries, reduced its export by the embargoed amount, and then subtracted the original 10 percent cut. The result was a real reduction of between 17 and 25 percent.

King Faisal ordered the embargo to include the U.S. Sixth Fleet in the Mediterranean. Shortly thereafter Riyadh instructed Aramco to stop all supplies to the U.S. military.[61] U.S. military planners panicked, as there was not enough oil available to fuel American ships and provide for ongoing global activity. In a November 30 memo the Pentagon advised the White House that "DoD petroleum shortage is very serious . . . [Without finding a way to meet our demand] we will soon be forced to begin standing down operational forces."[62] Undersecretary of Defense William P. Clements called in senior Aramco executives. "Find a way to get fuel to Vietnam," he insisted. "Our kids are dying out there fighting Communists."[63] There was also the problem of fueling American ships in the Mediterranean, operating very close to Soviet ones. Back in Saudi Arabia, Frank Jungers, the president of Aramco, explained the situation to Faisal. Caught between his hatred for Zionists and Communists, Faisal, picking at his bisht (a loose black robe), as was his habit, told Jungers, "God help you if you get caught, or if it becomes a public issue." Aramco had veiled permission to allow Saudi oil to flow toward American warships and bases.[64]

Only Yamani, his then deputy oil minister, Prince Saud al-Faisal, and Aramco vice president Mike Ameen were privy to the conversation between Faisal and Jungers.[65] As Jungers remembered, "We did figure out some ways to do this, and it was done. Everyone was happy and not a word was ever said and it was, of course, a secret thing for years afterward."[66]

Quietly Aramco lined up ships from nations not targeted by the embargo. They came into port at Ras Tanura and then departed for Singapore.[67] From there they were sent to key American naval ports across the globe. As Aramco historian Anthony Cave Brown concludes, "Though shrouded in secrecy, this partial lifting of the embargo did show that Faisal did not intend to make difficulties for the U.S. Navy as it attempted to hamper Russian military operations in the Eastern Mediterranean," or for American operations in the Pacific.[68]

As he had in 1967, the king made an exception to continue containing the Soviet Union.[69] The Saudi leadership considered its geostrategic competition with the Soviets and its relationship with the United States more important than the Arab-Israeli one, and viewed the United States as its long-term central partner in that larger struggle. Nixon had also sublimated the Arab-Israeli crisis to the global struggle against Communism. Under conditions of duress, Riyadh would not subjugate its global interests to more local ones. Riyadh did of course try to serve both its regional and global interests. But when the two clashed, as they did in 1973, its global self-interest prevailed.

The fighting ended with a final cease-fire on October 25, with the Egyptian Third Army surrounded, Israel still in control of the Sinai Peninsula and the Golan Heights, and the Israelis bloodied by Egypt's and Syria's initial advances. The cease-fire was not enough to lift the embargo. King Faisal made clear that he would neither lift the embargo nor increase production unless America seriously committed to ending the Arab-Israeli conflict.

And so began, in early November 1973, Kissinger's now-famous "shuttle diplomacy," taking him to the Arab world for the first time. In a dazzling diplomatic tour de force Kissinger negotiated disengagement agreements between Israel and Egypt and between Israel and Syria.

He traveled regularly between Cairo, Jerusalem, and Jeddah, eventually making at least eleven trips to the kingdom. His itinerary also included Damascus and Amman. He rarely, if ever, made a trip to the Middle East without at least touching base with Saudi officials. He was the first American secretary of state to make any effort to engage the kingdom in a sustained manner.

Although Kissinger got along well with Egypt's President Sadat and Syria's President Asad, it took time for him and the Saudis to warm up to each other, which they eventually did. In his first set of meetings with King Faisal he twice sent the Saudi leader into moments of despondency. First, at a dinner in Jeddah, he tried to change the subject in the midst of one of King Faisal's by now routine diatribes about the connection between Communism and Zionism. As Kissinger recalled, "This faux pas threw Faisal into minutes of deep melancholy, causing conversation around the table to stop all together." To add insult to injury, Kissinger then referred to Sadat as the leader of the Arabs, which not surprisingly rankled his host, who at the time was funding Sadat to the tune of $200 million a year.[70]

Relations improved somewhat over the following weeks and months. One regular participant remembers that "after a while the long Saudi dinners became very comfortable."[71] Still, the situation was far from calm. Oil prices were at an all-time high, up 70 percent overnight. The production cuts meant that even at such high prices, petroleum was not available to energy-thirsty consumers. Lines snaked around corners at American gas stations. Throughout the fall and winter European leaders introduced different austerity measures. In Britain, Prime Minister Heath announced a three-day workweek for most British industries, a move that drastically reduced the salaries of thirteen million workers. In Italy and West Germany governments banned Sunday driving. Inflation rates doubled in many Western European nations. The Western world was nearing a breaking point.

In a November 19 speech, Kissinger issued a dire warning: "It is clear that if pressures continue unreasonably and indefinitely, that then the U.S. will have to consider what countermeasures it may have to take."[73] He ordered a number of studies undertaken to devise retaliation against Arab members of OPEC. This was the natural evolution of the phone conversation he and Schlesinger had had on the fifth day of the war.[74] Yamani responded to some of the more public threats with his own speech in Europe warning that if the United States followed through on its "countermeasures," Arabs would blow up their own fields. To underscore the seriousness of the matter, Thomas Barger, Aramco's retired president, penned an op-ed article stressing the dangers of a "military adventure far from home," and the likely Arab response, including rendering wells inoperable and hindering rehabilitation.[75]

In December 1973, at an OPEC meeting in Tehran, the shah, who had not participated in the embargo, pushed hard for what some oil executives referred to as "the Christmas Eve massacre," an oil price rise from $5.12 to $11.66 a barrel effective immediately. Although a partner of the United States, the shah had long wanted more money for his modernization and defense programs. The increase constituted another doubling of prices, the second in two months. It was a "colossal blow" that "cost the [struggling oil-dependent] developing countries more than the entire foreign aid programs extended to them by the industrial democracies, re-creating the desperate conditions that foreign assistance was supposed to cure."[76] Between 1972 and 1973 the U.S. bill for foreign oil jumped from $3.9 billion to $24 billion.[77]

King Faisal realized that the Iranian-led price increase on top of a production cut could ruin Western Europe and severely weaken America's ability to deter the Soviet Union. Soviet leaders were reveling in the "crisis of capitalism" that the oil embargo was causing. Yamani and other Saudis pressed Washington to bring the shah into more intense discussions to ease prices.[78] Three days after the price increase, Arab OPEC members, led by Saudi Arabia, agreed to increase oil production, substantially easing the embargo.

Western chaos and Soviet aggrandizement did not serve Riyadh's interest. Riyadh could live with friction in its relationship with the United States within the Arab-Israeli context. It could not, however, countenance problems spilling over into the larger geostrategic arena, and worked actively to prevent that from happening. This was different from the tack taken by Arab countries such as Syria, Iraq, and Egypt before 1972, whose leaders cultivated Soviet support.

The embargo was not officially ended until mid-March 1974, when Kissinger could show progress toward an Israeli-Egyptian disengagement and promise to work toward a Syrian one as well. On March 18 Arab oil ministers unconditionally lifted the embargo, and Saudi Arabia announced an oil production increase of one million barrels per day.

The Effects of the 1973 War

The embargo represented the worst crisis in U.S.-Saudi history, with the exception, perhaps, of the 2001 terrorist attacks. Only a few years prior, the balance of power in the petroleum sector had shifted in the kingdom's favor, when American producers began pumping at full capacity. Without the means to ease the embargo, the American and global economies stumbled through a painful recession.

At the popular level, Americans were angered by Saudi Arabia's wartime decisions. Saudi Arabia, for its part, confronted American contingency plans that involved an outright assault on the kingdom.

And yet the relationship seemed to recover with unprecedented speed. The leaderships of both countries acknowledged that it was far too dangerous and costly to willfully oppose the other. Almost as if nothing had happened, high-level officials on both sides began closely working together toward goals such as Saudi infrastructure development, military modernization, and American economic recovery. Common interests around anti-Communism provided a balm that soothed the deep wounds. But it could not root out an infection that had settled deeply in the recesses of the relationship. As we will see, anger and resentment at the popular level continued to fester for years to come.

The balance of power in the region, which had begun to shift from Egypt to Saudi Arabia after 1967, was solidified after 1973. With revenue now reaching well beyond what had been imaginable only a few years prior, Saudi Arabia began flexing its political and economic muscles. Religion became its chosen instrument. As Gilles Kepel, a French expert on political Islam acknowledges, after 1973 "the transnational Saudi system insinuated itself into the relationship between state and society in the majority of Muslim countries."[79] Such proselytizing brought benefits to the shared American and Saudi anti-Communist agenda.

6

"A New and Glorious Chapter"

In the years following the quadrupling of oil prices, Saudi Arabia Monetary Agency (SAMA) officials scrambled to invest the avalanche of cash descending on the kingdom. David C. Mulford, an Illinois native who at the time headed SAMA's investment advisory group through a contract that was eventually taken over by Merrill Lynch, was responsible for finding investments for tens (sometimes hundreds) of millions of dollars a day. At one point Mulford noted his anxiety around a potentially lengthy morning meeting with the Malaysian finance minister, realizing that when it was over he would be $300 million behind in his day.[1] OPEC countries were piling up reserves at the rate of $115,000 a second.[2]

The primary goal of the Nixon administration and later the Ford administration, which began August 9, 1974, was to break OPEC and recoup the American dollars flowing toward oil-producing capitals, soon dubbed "petrodollars." The story of their effort to do so, and of their engagement with Saudi Arabia on this front, marks one of the turning points in U.S.-Saudi history. Through hard political work, abetted by market forces, U.S. and Saudi leaders set the stage for the next three decades of the U.S.-Saudi special relationship.

In the spring of 1974, U.S. treasury secretary William E. Simon teamed up with Henry Kissinger to lure American dollars back home. Simon and Kissinger were a powerful ideological duo. Simon, a hard-charging free marketeer, embodied the conservative wing of the Republican Party, while Kissinger represented the more mainstream realpolitik crowd. As a team, they squashed dissent from within the Republican ranks over close working relations with Saudi Arabia.

Simon's motivations were clear. As treasury secretary, he was responsible for closing America's growing balance-of-payments deficit. Kissinger, for his part, understood that the massive hemorrhaging of funds toward the Middle East had troubling geopolitical consequences. In 1974 Arab oil producers preferred investing their money in short-term investment vehicles and considered floating their money between countries whose foreign policies were most sympathetic to Arab causes. While difficult to coordinate, the mere threat of such activity unnerved U.S. planners. Kissinger decided that in order to prevent Saudi Arabia from blackmailing the United States, as such tactics would allow, and from ever again embargoing the United States, he would make Saudi Arabia a stakeholder in America's economic success. He wanted to "create incentives for the producing nations to become responsible participants in the international economy."[3] Kissinger believed that the only thing that could truly neutralize the oil weapon was heavy Saudi investment in the U.S. economy, since an embargo that raised oil prices would only exacerbate American balance-of-payments problems, which would in turn hurt Saudi investments in the U.S. economy.

Simon and Kissinger's interest in tethering Saudi Arabia's financial future to that of the United States was matched by a similarly motivated Saudi Arabia. King Faisal and Prince (later King) Fahd, along with members of Saudi Arabia's nascent business class, seized the opportunity to rebuild economic and military relations with the United States through a series of joint ventures. In Prince Fahd's words, he set out to begin "a new and glorious chapter in relations between Saudi Arabia and the United States," notwithstanding the recent oil embargo and American threats to strike at the kingdom.[4] While many within Saudi Arabia's business and political elite supported the pro-U.S. tilt, Fahd would become one of the most active proponents of close U.S.-Saudi relations. He was more committed to building an intimate working relationship than any of his predecessors or his successor.

There were many things Saudi Arabia wanted from relations with the United States. Security was an important component. Dizzying oil wealth would necessarily bring predators that Saudi Arabia's population of approximately five million could not single-handedly defend against. "We are a very appealing piece of cake," said Saudi minister of information Muhammad Abdel Yamani. "There are lots of people who would dearly love to get a slice of us." Another high-level Saudi official commented at the time, "In our dealing with the industrialized world, we must cultivate friends who will look after our interests and protect us."[5]

Saudi leaders also hoped that the United States would assist in their economic modernization plans. Saudi Arabia was still very much a developing nation in the early 1970s. Oil wealth provided a route out. After the 1973 price increases, Saudi Arabia's ports were suddenly so clogged that perishable imports regularly rotted aboard cargo ships before receiving entry clearance. Prominent global investors traveling to Saudi Arabia, as in the case of the co-chairman of Goldman Sachs, John C. Whitehead, and Lyndon Johnson's secretary of the treasury, Henry H. Fowler, ended up sleeping on cots in dimly lit hotel hallways, as scarce rooms were often double-booked.[6]

By the mid-1970s Saudi Arabia had drawn up an ambitious $480 billion five-year internal development program. The previous five-year plan had rested on a mere $45 billion in revenue.[7] With money to spend, Saudi Arabia sought out the United States. "In the underdeveloped world we see the threat of radicalism," one Saudi official explained, "and we can put our money where the Communists' mouths are."[8]

In June 1974, only three months after OPEC lifted the oil embargo, Prince Fahd and other high Saudi officials arrived in Washington to codify a multipronged agreement in the fields of economics, technology, industry, and defense. The agreement called for the establishment of a Joint Commission on Economic Cooperation and a Joint Security Cooperation Commission that brought together officials from the U.S. and Saudi governments to devise strategies for Saudi economic development and defense modernization.

By virtue of this decision, practically every major industrial project within the kingdom from 1973 to 1993 fit within the U.S.-Saudi joint-venture formula, which attracted the largest and most reputable multinational corporations—precisely what the Saudis wanted, needed, and were willing to pay for. One American businessman benefiting from Saudi largesse exuberantly told *Newsweek*, "They're going to fuel our industry and keep our economy afloat. I say make the place the goddam 51st state."[9] Even in retrospect, the joint commissions were a rather stunning accomplishment in light of the pain the embargo caused and the U.S. public's palpable hostility toward embargoing countries.

While actual figures are exceedingly hard to determine, it appears that in 1974 alone Saudi Arabia invested almost $5 billion of its $26 billion in oil revenue in the United States.[10] By 1976 Saudi Arabia had invested $60 billion in the United States.[11] By 1979 Saudi Arabia had the largest single holding of dollars and U.S. government securities.[12] One Citibank analyst involved in a study for SAMA remembers that "the U.S. capital market was the only one at that time that afforded sufficient depth for them to invest significantly without overshadowing other investors and moving prices." But such agreements were needed because "Saudi investment did not happen as fast as it should have."[13]

Like its economic sibling, the Joint Security Cooperation Commission aimed to recoup dollars via the defense industry and to cement U.S.-Saudi ties. In a meeting with Prince Fahd, Secretary of Defense Schlesinger turned to the CIA's station chief in Saudi Arabia and directed him to "work with our brother to knit together the fabric of this security relationship . . . be creative."[14]

The weapons pipeline was fully opened. One American military officer in Saudi Arabia commented, "I do not know of anything that is nonnuclear that we would not give the Saudis."[15] A U.S. government official more attuned to popular sensitivities characterized the arrangement in less bombastic terms, suggesting that "nothing spectacular" should be expected to come from the arrangement.[16] The numbers suggest that the military officer was both more honest and accurate. The value of foreign military sales agreements jumped from $305 million in 1972 to more than $5 billion in 1975.[17]

Defense contracts began pouring into American companies. The contracts provided a much-needed economic stimulus to the cash-strapped American arms industry. It allowed defense companies to increase production, provide new jobs, and reduce the per-unit cost charged to the American military. Through the Joint Security Cooperation Commission, Saudi contracts became integral to the welfare of the United States arms industry. Defense industry officials became vocal advocates for strong U.S.-Saudi relations.

Contracts ran the gamut from a $1.5 billion deal to provide naval training and equipment to buying defense equipment for Egypt (to continue to woo the country away from the Soviet Union) and hiring U.S. Vietnam veterans to train Saudi Arabia's National Guard, an internal security force under Prince (later King) Abdullah.[18] In February 1975 the U.S. Defense Department subcontracted to Vinnell Corporation a $77 million program to train Saudi National Guard forces. It was the first such contract ever given to a private American company to train a foreign army.[19] Vinnell made news again in 1995 and May 2003 when al-Qaeda terrorists bombed its Saudi-based facilities.

The table below provides a year-by-year comparison of the amounts flowing into the kingdom for Saudi oil versus the amounts flowing into the United States through commodity markets, military sales and services, oil company profits and dividends, and Saudi investment funds. Although some of the funds included in the table were

Saudi-owned, more money was returning to the United States than any other country. The joint programs helped ensure this outcome.

United States–Saudi Arabia
Balance of Payments (in $ millions)[20]

Year	U.S. Payments for Saudi Oil	Flow of Saudi Funds to the United States
1974	1,671	8,486
1975	2,625	7,124
1976	5,213	10,589
1977	6,358	11,016
1978	5,307	10,060

From these numbers, one banker concluded that the "US oil deficit with Saudi Arabia is more than covered by the reflow of funds from Saudi Arabia to the US."[21]

On the military and economic front, American officials intentionally integrated Saudi Arabia into America's orbit. The Saudis, led by Prince Fahd, joined with enthusiasm. Some, such as Prince Abdullah, cautioned that Fahd was moving too quickly, losing touch with society's conservative base and risking a backlash. But Fahd disregarded such concerns. The kingdom, after all, had to do something with all that money.

The gushing revenue stream enabled significant corruption among Saudi Arabia's leadership and those well positioned to benefit from the exorbitant spending within society. Corruption ran rampant—in particular throughout Saudi Arabia's armed services. Lavish arms deals resulted in huge cash transfers that benefited a select few at the top of the power chain. Years later Saudi Arabia's ambassador to the United States Prince Bandar, a son of Saudi Arabia's Defense Minister, would dismiss the severity of the problem: "If you tell me that [in] building this whole country, and spending $350 billion out of $400 billion, that we misused or got corrupted with $50 billion, I'll tell you, 'Yes.' But I'll take that any time. . . . We did not invent corruption."[22]

"A Helpful Saudi Footprint"

One of the most important, if overlooked, aspects of Saudi Arabia's newfound wealth was how the leadership chose to invest it internationally. The record shows that Saudi Arabia supported anti-Communist efforts not simply as a favor to the United States, as is often implied, but because it viewed such efforts as integral to its own national security. With revenue reaching tens of billions of dollars ($24 billion in 1974, $100 billion by the end of the decade), there was more than enough cash available to finance foreign operations. Saudi Arabia put its money into three main baskets: Islamic organizations (such as the World Muslim League, a worldwide Islamic charity based in Saudi Arabia, and local mosques and Islamic schools), pro-Palestinian groups, and anti-Soviet operations. The first and third often proved complementary. In 1977 *Newsweek* estimated that Saudi Arabia provided more than $6 billion in foreign and military aid to a number of countries, including Egypt ($2.5 billion), Jordan ($500 million), Syria ($1 billion), Pakistan ($500 million), North Yemen ($150 million), Somalia ($220 million), Sudan ($250 million), and more than $1.5 billion to others.[23] These were, for the most part, American causes as well, at a time when America was recoiling from the international scene.

Saudi Arabia's newly acquired economic power corresponded with an acute crisis in American foreign policy. The one-two punch of Vietnam and Watergate severely handicapped the White House's ability to pursue its foreign policy interests. On August 8, 1974, two months after signing the military and economic joint agreements, Richard Nixon resigned. Most of Nixon's relevant foreign policy team stayed on board, but they faced a new challenge in an emboldened Congress. After Watergate, and in response to perceived executive-branch excesses in covert operations, Congress began actively circumscribing the president's authority. Most notably, it passed the Clark amendment, named for Senator Richard C. Clark, the chairman of the Senate's Subcommittee on African Affairs. The amendment restricted Ford's ability to provide covert aid to Angola, a country that had been steadily spiraling toward civil war.[24] Ford had called for increased U.S. spending after the Soviet Union contributed $300 million to the Popular Movement for the Liberation of Angola (MPLA) and sent the largest deployment of Soviet matériel to a non-Warsaw Pact country until that time. Ford reluctantly signed the Clark amendment in January 1976, characterizing its passage as a "deep tragedy." Correctly fearing that American restraint would encourage Soviet adventurism in Africa, the president warned that "responsibilities abandoned today will return as more acute crises tomorrow."[25] The amendment tied the president's hands while at the same time acknowledging that Soviet and Cuban action in Angola was "completely inconsistent with any reasonably defined policy of detente."[26] The Clark amendment remained in effect until 1985.

On December 21, 1975, referring to "recent congressional action," Kissinger sent a top-secret back-channel message to Jeddah asking for $30 million for Angola to further "the parallel interests which the U.S. and Saudi Arabia share in this matter."[27] He suggested that Saudi Arabia's king pass the money through Zaire's president, Joseph Mobutu, for disbursement to Angola. Kamal Adham, Saudi Arabia's intelligence chief who oversaw such matters, scoffed that such a route would leave the kingdom owing money to Angola's rebel leader, as Mobutu was sure to pocket a considerable portion of the funds flowing through. Mobutu, Adham noted, "has a poor record for dependability in the delivery of assistance to the Angolans." Instead, Saudi Arabia would consult with Iran and Egypt and provide assistance in a manner of its own choosing. As we will see in chapter 9, Saudi Arabia did step up aid to Angola's Jonas Savimbi, albeit through a very different route —Egypt and Morocco.

Throughout Africa, the Soviet Union advanced, testing the limits of American restraint. Saudi Arabia considered ways to raise the cost of Soviet advancement in Africa. Turki al-Faisal, Saudi Arabia's director of intelligence from 1977 to 2001, recalled that in the 1970s "Saudi Arabia's activities in Africa expanded dramatically—at a time when American activities in the rest of the world were shrinking because of Watergate and the restrictions placed on the government, particularly CIA activity."[28] Independent of American efforts, Saudi Arabia set out to thwart Soviet ambitions.

At a time when U.S. decision makers were hemmed in by the sway of domestic politics, Saudi Arabia's newfound oil wealth found its way into anti-Soviet, anti-Libyan activities. Angola, Chad, Sudan, Eritrea, and Somalia all benefited from Saudi largesse. At times American leaders actively sought donations, as they did in Angola. At other points Saudi Arabia acted independently, often with the tacit support of those in Washington who were otherwise constrained by domestic restrictions.

According to the Saudi Arabian finance minister, Saudi Arabia doled out $5.7 billion in foreign aid in 1975.[29] The U.S. figure for its own foreign assistance that year amounted to $4.9 billion.[30] Between 1972 and 1975, Saudi Arabia's Ministry of Finance and National Economy estimated that foreign aid jumped from 2.7 to 13.8 percent of GDP.

The Safari Club

e most creative foreign policy initiatives that the Saudi lead-
ndertook to beat back Soviet advancement was to join the Safari
e brainchild of France's Alexandre de Marenches, head of the
Service de Documentation Extérieure et de Contre-Espionnage
E), the French equivalent of the CIA. The Safari Club provides
d example of Saudi Arabia's self-defined anti-Communist inter-
Independent of American urging, although often with American
port, Saudi Arabia sought out opportunities to thwart growing
viet influences in its wider region.

Marenches, an ardent Cold Warrior, believed that "we are at war
nd our enemy is the Soviet Empire." In this war, Libya's Colonel
Qadhafi played a particularly troublesome role, something with which
Saudi Arabia fully agreed. "Of all the Soviet Empire's foreign agents,
none is more precious to Moscow [in Africa] than Colonel Qadhaffi,"
he concluded in his 1982 memoirs.[35] Marenches was acutely conscious
of the threat Communism posed and was troubled by what he perceived
as America's sudden withdrawal from containment. "Since Watergate,
the CIA has had enormous problems in organizing operations which
require total secrecy," he despaired.[36] If the United States would not step
up to combat Moscow and its allies, Marenches himself would build
an alternative power bloc to do so. In response, Marenches enticed Saudi
Arabia, Morocco, Egypt, and Iran to join the Safari Club, a name
chosen because it sounded African and conveyed a whiff of adventure.
Kamal Adham, who now directed Saudi Arabia's Egypt and Iran port-
folios, among his other responsibilities, signed the club's initial charter
for Saudi Arabia, as other heads of intelligence did for their own country. The club held its first meeting in Saudi Arabia in 1976. The club's
charter stated that "recent events in Angola and other parts of Africa
have demonstrated the continent's role as a theatre for revolutionary
wars prompted and conducted by the Soviet Union,"[37] The group
intended to reverse the trend.

Each Safari Club member brought unique capabilities. France supplied technical equipment for communications and security. Egypt
and Morocco provided weapons and manpower. Saudi Arabia financed
the group's efforts. The club worked because it reinforced preexisting
arrangements. The Saudis were already buying French Mirages for
Egypt's arsenal and providing Morocco with financial aid, which by 1980
amounted to around $1 billion a year.[38] Since it appeared to many in
the region that America was not going to lead the anti-Communist fight

Foreign Aid Committed by ~

Year	Bilateral		Inter. Regiona.
	Grants	Loans	
1972	143.1	77.8	—
1973	650.2	343.6	—
1974	1,130.6	747.6	2,203.3
1975	1,363.5	2,037.6	2,262.9
Total	**3,287.4**	**3,206.6**	**4,466.2**

Source: Ministry of Finance and National Economy

Jim Hoagland deftly summed up the situation in a \
Post article, writing that "the Saudis are spending billio.
an arc of influence that extends from Morocco eastward
and the Middle East and deep into Asia. It is an arc that, b.
by accident, could easily have been traced by an American ad.
tion eager to help [overcome] new difficulties in persuading C.
to appropriate money for such causes."[32] Such activity is most likely
Henry Kissinger was referring to in his memoirs when he recalled \
"often I found through other channels a helpful Saudi footprint place.
so unobtrusively that one gust of wind could erase its traces."[33]

Washington did not welcome all of Saudi Arabia's international
giving—some went to causes that greatly troubled Washington. Saudi
Arabia provided significant support to Palestinian groups including the
PLO, which at the time the United States viewed as a terrorist organization. Many of the states Saudi Arabia supported, particularly in
Africa, also cut official relations with Israel. Oil wealth helped fuel a
"Zionism equals racism" campaign at the United Nations that not only
singled out Israel as an international pariah but also caused U.S. organizations such as the Ford Foundation, which had been operating for
decades in the kingdom helping to create a more efficient bureaucracy,
to pull up stakes and relocate.[34] But such policy difficulties were often
overshadowed by Saudi support for anti-Soviet activity. Differences over
Israel, while deep and profound, were but one set of problems in an
otherwise fruitful relationship.

in what it considered the "periphery," the Saudis sought out others to engage in the anti-Soviet/anti-Libyan effort.

The Safari Club executed its first operation in Zaire. In March 1977 a political opposition group supported by Angola's MPLA and hostile to Mobutu launched an attack from Angola on Zaire's economically vital Shaba province. The Safari Club, financed by Saudi Arabia, jumped into action. Morocco provided troops to Zaire to stave off the invasion.[39] Thereafter, Mobutu owed his existence to Arab support.

Although the club was largely France's brainchild, Washington was supportive, from a distance. Alfred L. "Roy" Atherton Jr., the assistant secretary of state for Near Eastern and South Asian affairs, recalled that the Americans approached the Saudis, saying, "It sure would be helpful if [Morocco's] King Hassan had a way to get his troops to Zaire."[40]

Fresh from its victory in Zaire, the Safari Club turned its attention later that year to the Horn of Africa and the strategic countries of Ethiopia, Somalia, and Djibouti, located along the western banks of the Red Sea.

Until 1974 the United States had had strong relations with Ethiopia's emperor, Haile Selassie, while the Soviets had been on better terms with Ethiopia's archrival, Somalia. In that year Selassie was overthrown, and within two years the new Ethiopian leadership, under Mengistu Haile Mariam, began exploring relations with the Soviet Union. Tensions escalated between the United States and Ethiopia and exploded in the late winter of 1977 when President Jimmy Carter lambasted the Mengistu regime for grave human rights abuses. Largely in response, Mengistu ordered the closure of Kagnew station (an important regional U.S. intelligence communications center in Asmara), the United States Information Service offices and libraries in the country, the U.S. consulate in Asmara, and the Naval Medical Research Unit in Addis Ababa.[41] The Soviet Union soon replaced the American presence.

The U.S. Defense Department began searching for an alternative basing location, eventually leasing space at Diego Garcia, a British-controlled island in the Indian Ocean. When ousted from Ethiopia, Washington and its allies lost, and the Soviets gained, access to seven hundred miles of strategic Red Sea coastline. For a brief moment it appeared that the Soviets had scored a huge victory in sewing up good political relations with Ethiopia, Somalia, and the People's Democratic Republic of Yemen, just across the strategic Straits of Bab el Mandeb at the mouth of the Red Sea.

The turn of events in Ethiopia and the Ethiopian leadership's courting of Soviet aid "petrified" the Saudi leadership.[42] It also worried Washington. Fidel Castro's trips to Yemen, Ethiopia, and Somalia and his efforts to mediate a federation between the latter two did little to alleviate Saudi and American concerns. Zbigniew Brzezinski, Carter's national security advisor, pointed out that "if Ethiopia and South Yemen become Soviet associates, not only will access to Suez be threatened, and this involves the oil pipeline from Saudi Arabia and Iran, but there will be a serious and direct political threat to Saudi Arabia. This is something we simply cannot ignore."[43] The Soviets were encircling Saudi Arabia. Defense secretary Harold Brown and secretary of state Cyrus R. Vance saw events in the Horn of Africa more in regional and somewhat less urgent terms, although Brown's views changed as the decade progressed.

As Ethiopian-Soviet relations improved, the United States and Saudi Arabia both began exploring closer relations with Somalia. Marina S. Ottaway, once a close observer of the Ethiopian-Somali struggle, observed that Saudi Arabia

> had not been particularly interested in a close relation with Somalia. It was only the presence of the Soviet Union after the coup [in 1969] that heightened Saudi interest in Somalia. Islam facilitated relations between Somalia and the Arab countries but was not sufficient by itself to lead to a close relation unless other factors intervened.[44]

Encouraged by Saudi Arabia, Safari Club members approached Somali president Siad Barre and offered to provide the arms he needed if he stopped taking Russian aid. Barre agreed. Egypt then sold Somalia $75 million worth of its unwanted Soviet arms, with Saudi Arabia footing the bill.[45] It was the same strategy that Saudi Arabia had used to pry Egypt out of Soviet clutches.

Saudi Arabia's influence was not limited to Zaire and the Horn of Africa, but extended throughout Africa. Its goals were to beat back Libyan and Soviet influence while promoting a Saudi ascetic interpretation of Islam, two goals that proved markedly compatible. In the mid-1970s the kingdom acted to repel Libyan incursions in Chad's northern border area. The Saudis watched nervously as Qadhafi pursued his goal to become a great African and Muslim leader by subverting neighboring countries. Saudi Arabia viewed Libya's Chad adventure as a means to extend Libyan influence into sub-Saharan Africa and put pressure on Sudan, a neighbor of Saudi Arabia, separated by the Red Sea. Never enamored of Qadhafi, Saudi leaders became more leery of him when his right-hand man, Major Abdul Salam Jallud, traveled to Moscow in 1974 and concluded the first in a decade-long series of arms deals that earned the Soviet Union $20 billion in hard currency.[46] The Saudis were also perturbed by Qadhafi's easy relationship with Cubans, Russians, and radical Palestinians, whom he invited in as advisors to train dissidents from Chad and Sudan. French spymaster Marenches shared the Saudi assessment. By the mid-1970s, Saudi Arabia began paying the bills for the Chadian army to beat back Libyan, and Soviet, influence.[47]

Saudi Arabia also aided Sudan and its leader Jaafar al-Nimeiry. Sudan spanned strategic territory, separating Libya and Ethiopia and keeping Libyan agents far from the strategic Red Sea coast. Riyadh, Cairo, Paris, and Washington warily eyed expanding Libyan influence in Sudan's Darfur region. Within a decade, Libyan agents were able to traverse northern Sudan unmolested and mine the Red Sea, a secret operation that required Britain and America to deploy minesweepers as a countermeasure. Saudi Arabia also worried about Sudan's Communist Party, once the largest in any Arab country. In 1975 the CIA observed that Saudi aid helped the government of Sudan "survive leftist efforts to bring it down."[48]

Between 1975 and 1976 Saudi aid to Sudan increased from $25 to $164 million.[49] In 1977 Qadhafi denied, but could not disguise, his role in supporting a coup attempt against Nimeiry.[50] That same year Saudi Arabia dispersed an estimated $250 million to Sudan in economic and military aid.[51] Roy Atherton, the assistant secretary of state for Near Eastern and South Asian affairs, remembers that "we encouraged the Saudis to help Nimeiry . . . he didn't even have enough money to import food, and we felt Congress would not be sympathetic to any large foreign aid bill."[52] In Sudan, as elsewhere, Saudi proselytizing accompanied its Cold War funding. In 1977 the Faisal Islamic Bank opened a branch in Sudan, and the bank became a financial provider for local Islamists.[53] Equally as important, Saudi Arabia welcomed Sudanese workers into the kingdom to fill jobs in its quickly expanding economy. From 1973 on, more than a million Sudanese came and worked inside the kingdom.[54] In 1977 Saudi Arabia also poured significant resources into Sudan's African Islamic Center, a center focused on training young Africans in fundamentalist interpretations of Islam.[55]

Throughout the 1970s and 1980s the Saudis dispersed cash to a range of groups and countries, with Syria, Jordan, the PLO, North Yemen, Angola, Sudan, Somalia, Djibouti, Uganda, Mali, Nigeria, Zaire, and Guinea receiving the largest share. In Asia, sacks of cash were given to Pakistan, Bangladesh, South Korea, Malaysia, Taiwan, and the Philippines. After one trip to Pakistan in 1976 the Saudi king reportedly left behind a donation totaling $30 million in cash.[56] Before its collapse, some reports suggest that even South Vietnam was a Saudi aid recipient. Saudi Arabia maintained close ties with Europe and funded efforts against "Eurocommunism."[57] Saudi aid went to anti-Communist, pro-Islamic, and pro-Palestinian causes. Aid was at its most forthcoming when all three justifications overlapped. Entrepreneurial states would often adjust their policies to fit more easily into Saudi Arabia's preferred criteria.

Saudi covert operations during the 1970s, particularly Safari Club operations, demonstrate that Saudi Arabia was not only doing America's bidding, or its dirty work, as many Saudi's today describe it. In a 2002 speech at Georgetown University in Washington, DC, Turki al-Faisal made clear that

> the Kingdom stood fast by the United States as a supporter of the United States' policies against communism. That steadfastness was not simply because the United States was asking the Kingdom to do that, but because the Kingdom always looked upon the principles and the ideas of communism as being anathema to human thought and well being. There was a total rejection of Marxist ideas by the Kingdom, and for that reason we supported US policies against communism. We never asked for any credit for that, because we thought we were serving ourselves as well.[58]

As the United States pursued a more introspective foreign policy during the mid- to late 1970s, Saudi leaders looked toward others such as France's Marenches to help beat back Soviet influence. The fact that such activities were perfectly compatible with American global interests made them much less complicated to carry out. As we will see in chapter 9, when such Saudi-funded covert activities were made public, especially in areas where U.S. decision-makers seemed to solicit Saudi support, it would draw the ire of Congress. Outside funding diluted Congress' power of the purse, the legislature's most powerful instrument for influencing U.S. foreign policy.

The King Is Dead

On March 25, 1975, the Prophet Muhammad's birthday, King Faisal's nephew Faisal bin Musaid entered a royal meeting to which he had not been invited. Slipping in behind the Kuwaiti minister of petroleum, the Saudi youth drew a pistol over the shoulder of the Kuwaiti, who was bowing to convey his greetings, and shot the king multiple times at point-blank range. The king was pronounced dead on arrival at the hospital.

Rumors quickly spread about the assassin's motives. They ranged from vengeance on behalf of his maternal ancestry, which traced back to Muhammad ibn Rashid (King Abdul Aziz's early rival), to Zionist or CIA conspiracy theories. The most likely explanation is that Musaid killed King Faisal to avenge his brother Khaled's murder. Ten years prior,

King Faisal's decision to introduce television into the kingdom was resisted by some who believed that such modern technology, especially one that broadcast images, was contrary to the example set by the Prophet Muhammad. Khaled bin Musaid led a group of saboteurs dressed like King Abdel Aziz's Ikhwan warriors to destroy Riyadh's transmitter. After consultation with King Faisal, the police were given orders to shoot to kill, an order that resulted in Khaled bin Musaid's death.

Henry Kissinger eulogized the king, saying that the Muslim world had lost a moral compass. Other State Department officials bemoaned that Faisal's death "removed a major force for moderation in the Middle East."[59] The international dignitaries who arrived at the kingdom to mourn the king's passing represented the major emphases of the king's foreign policy. Those paying their respects included Egypt's Anwar el-Sadat, Jordan's King Hussein, Sudan's Jaafar al-Nimeiry, PLO chairman Yasser Arafat, U.S. vice president Nelson Rockefeller, and U.S. assistant secretary of state for Near Eastern and South Asian affairs Roy Atherton. Libya's Qadhafi did not attend.[60]

Crown Prince Khaled, King Faisal's half brother, who would have preferred pursuing falconry in the desert to ruling the kingdom, replaced the deceased monarch within three days. His accession established that age alone did not dictate who the kingdom's monarch would be. After Faisal, the next oldest of Abdul Aziz's sons was Muhammad, a powerful figure within the Saudi royal family. But Muhammad drank and was a renowned womanizer. For key elements within the Saudi ruling elite, Muhammad's lifestyle choices were too reminiscent of the former king Saud's. Few believed the kingdom could weather a repeat of Saud. Although he was ill at the time, Khaled, Abdel Aziz's next oldest son and Muhammad's full brother, emerged as the alternative.

The real power behind King Khaled, however, by either design or necessity brought on by Khaled's failing health, was Prince Fahd, Khaled's half brother, who along with Prince Muhammad had been instrumental in the leadership transition from Saud to Faisal. Such an arrangement suited Khaled, who had never coveted the kingship and assumed his post largely to signal stability and a legitimate transition process after Faisal's assassination. Shortly after his accession Khaled issued a royal decree telling Fahd that "we would like you to take measures, hand down directives, both foreign and domestic, and issue administrative decisions in accordance with policies which are in effect, and after consulting with us."[61] King Khaled crafted a job description more similar to that of England's Queen Elizabeth II than King Faisal's. This was a notable difference from his older brother Saud, who had refused to share power with then Crown Prince Faisal, claiming, "I am not the Queen of England."[62]

Fahd was viewed at the time as more determined than Faisal to modernize the country full steam and less concerned with Faisal's delicate balancing act between the conservative and progressive forces within society. He was willing to expand local infrastructure and development programs far beyond what Saudis themselves could create. Fahd's unabashed modernization required tens and later hundreds of thousands of non-Saudi laborers, imported to build the state. Internationally, he threw himself behind the United States wholeheartedly.

Fahd was neither as worldly nor as strategic as Faisal, although Faisal had long trusted him for his intelligence and prowess in navigating intrafamily politics. Unlike Faisal, who had traveled to Europe in 1919 as a fourteen-year-old and represented the Arab world at the UN in 1947, Fahd had not left Saudi Arabia until the age of forty, though when he finally did, scandalous stories of gambling and womanizing accompanied him. Faisal had greatly admired Fahd's intelligence and bureaucratic abilities—indeed, had made him minister of the interior at a time when the regime was nervously watching growing domestic protests. Unlike Faisal, who always insisted on something in return for Saudi Arabia's contribution, Fahd was less skilled as a negotiator. Faisal expected to get something in return for a Saudi Arabian contribution. For instance, although he lifted the 1973 oil embargo, it was "not because of our baby blue eyes," remembers the CIA station chief in Saudi Arabia at the time. He insisted that Kissinger commit to reviving the peace process. Fahd, on the other hand, was willing to give generously with few strings attached and thus became in many ways a darling of the West, the United States in particular. He was much more accommodating to American requests and let Saudi money flow more freely to gold-plated industrial and defense programs. One senior U.S. intelligence officer once referred to Fahd as a "marshmallow," because he was so easily squeezed.[63] The officer was banished from the kingdom shortly thereafter.

The Carter administration would do little to encourage Fahd's looser purse strings, although Riyadh increased its foreign aid spending for its own reasons, as we have seen. But when President Reagan took office in the 1980s, he encouraged Fahd to support his ambitious and costly global agenda, and the king responded with alacrity by increasing Saudi support for American weaponry and foreign operations by billions of dollars.

Another area of obvious difference between Faisal and Fahd was their view of Israel. Faisal was consumed by the threat of Israel, ranking Zionism alongside Communism and, as we have seen, entwining the two. Fahd would pursue a more pragmatic approach. He sent multiple back-channel messages to Washington that Israel was not his overarching priority and that Saudi Arabia and the United States should work to reduce or at least avoid tension generated by the Arab-Israeli conflict. He made clear to the CIA's station chief in Saudi Arabia that Israel was of lesser concern than southern Arabia (with Yemen and a rebellion in Oman) and the growing power of the Baath party in Iraq. Fahd was frustrated that "every time my national guard gets a new boot" it becomes a debate of regional balances.[64]

Fahd was checked in part by Prince Abdullah, today's king but by 1982 crown prince. Abdullah represented the more conservative wing of the family, more concerned about the breakneck pace of development and its consequences on local society. Abdullah's power rested on the fact that he commanded Saudi Arabia's National Guard. Throughout the late 1970s Fahd's full brothers would try to strip Abdullah of this role, something the conservative elements in society sought to prevent.[65]

The leadership change from Faisal to Fahd further deepened the U.S.-Saudi relationship. Although some, like Abdullah, remained skeptical about the close embrace, Fahd and his full brothers oversaw the institutionalization of relations with the United States, which seemed to benefit both sides. Domestic dissent, it was hoped, would slowly dissipate as modernization brought economic benefits to most Saudi citizens. Fahd surely did not expect—although perhaps he should have, given Abdullah's warnings—that the first real protests, ones with an extreme religious twist, would come later within the same decade as Saudi Arabia accrued its vast oil wealth. They led him to actively court the most radical elements within Saudi Arabia's domestic society. The year 1979 would prove a turning point in Middle East history. It would also lead to the further deepening of U.S.-Saudi relations as Saudi religious zeal brought with it obvious geopolitical benefits for both sides.

7

Mobilizing Religion

The Carter White House intended to downplay the U.S.-Soviet rivalry and cultivate relations with the "new influentials"—national security advisor Zbigniew Brzezinski's term for newly modernizing states.[1] The administration, which took power in January 1977, adopted a philosophical approach to Communism that was more similar to that of the Kennedy administration than to what it had been under Nixon and Ford. As in Kennedy's time, major regional countries such as India received increased attention. Unlike during Kennedy's time, however, Saudi Arabia was categorized by Carter as part of the modernizing camp. The gushing revenue stream allowed Saudi Arabia to invest heavily on infrastructural development, a component of modernization that attracted Washington policy makers. Political liberalization inside the kingdom, however, did not follow in the wake of such investments. Such funds also contributed to a widening array of foreign operations.

The outgoing Ford and incoming Carter administrations agreed that the Middle East was in need of constant monitoring. Kissinger's electrifying shuttle diplomacy had pried the region out of its strategic morass, but it seemed that by the end of 1976 bilateral step-by-step negotiations between Israel and the Arabs had gone as far as they were going to go. Progress toward peace, many believed, now required a regional framework. Briefing papers left by the outgoing administration recommended that Saudi Arabia, Egypt, and Jordan continue to be approached as helpful moderate states. Saudi Arabia's influence over the oil market and Arab states such as Syria, Jordan, and Egypt made it vitally important to the incoming administration.

In his first meeting with President Carter, in May 1977, Prince Fahd assured the president that he believed Israel had the right to exist and that he would try to push along Arab-Israeli negotiations to the best of his ability. Joseph L. "Jody" Powell, the president's spokesman, reported that the "process by which you would reach a secure home-land for Palestinians and a secure state of Israel with recognized boundaries in each case was a major topic."[2] This was not the first time that Saudi officials voiced quiet, if qualified, statements supporting Israel's right to exist, but for the first time the message was conveyed at the highest political level. In their first meeting, Fahd also agreed to help contain the escalating price of oil by increasing production.

In addition to conceding a sovereign Israel, Fahd advocated an inde-pendent Palestinian state. Carter stressed the importance of the PLO's acceptance of UN Resolution 242, the land-for-peace resolution in which the Arabs were to recognize Israel's sovereignty and territorial in-tegrity in response to an Israeli withdrawal from territories conquered during the 1967 war. Carter believed that such acceptance would help sway American public opinion toward a favorable Palestinian settle-ment. Fahd agreed to try to convince the PLO to accept it. The Saudis carried through on their pledge and pushed the issues in bilateral meetings with the PLO several months later.

The first Carter-Fahd meeting ended on a positive note. At the meet-ing's conclusion Carter announced:

> I've said several times since I've been President of our country that I don't believe there is any other nation with whom we've had better friendship and a deeper sense of cooperation than we've found in Saudi Arabia.
>
> There have been many times unpublished when we saw a particular problem, either in our country or around the world, and as soon as this need became known by the leaders of that great country, the need has been met in a quiet but very effective and friendly way.[3]

The statement is remarkably similar to Kissinger's "helpful Saudi foot-print" comment. It is one of the few cases in which Kissinger and Carter saw eye to eye.

The two and a half years following the meeting were enormously complicated for U.S.-Saudi relations. It would mark one of the high points in the countries' relationship when the two worked in tandem on the peace process. In appreciation, Carter agreed to help push through a major arms deal for the kingdom. But it also encompassed profound lows, in particular Saudi Arabia's withholding of support for Egypt and a rapid oil price escalation.

Egyptian president Anwar Sadat's unprecedented trip to Jerusalem in 1977 took both the United States and Saudi Arabia by surprise. Sadat had sent hints to the United States that a major initiative was in the offing, but no one in Washington suspected such boldness. "We knew that Sadat was getting restless and was thinking of a big move," recalled Carter's NSC senior Middle East advisor, Bill Quandt, "but we did not know specifically that he was planning the dramatic trip to Jerusalem. I doubt if the Saudis knew much more than we did at this point."[4] Saudi Arabia's Prince Fahd was livid when he heard about it, mostly because he was caught by surprise, but also because he believed that the Middle East crisis would continue in perpetuity unless the Palestinian problem was effectively solved, and for that a united Arab front was needed. He immediately summoned the CIA's station chief in Jeddah. Fuming and pacing, the prince demanded to know what role the United States had played and why he had not been better informed. The agent, however, had been as much in the dark as Fahd. Fahd did not at that moment sever Saudi Arabia's relationship with Egypt. Within two years, however, Saudi Arabia would slice its aid to Egypt and lead the Arab world in an anti-Egypt boycott.

Carter met with King Khaled on January 3, 1978, in an attempt to broaden and deepen the circle of support for Sadat and outline what the Americans would be willing to push for on the Palestinian side. Khaled called for a two-state solution, and he emphasized the importance of establishing a fully independent state for Palestinians.

Carter's meeting with Khaled also produced one of the most controversial and time-consuming problems faced by his administration. Impressed with Khaled's flexibility over Palestine, Carter agreed to support a long-standing Saudi request for F-15 planes. At a considerable cost, Carter was true to his word. Pro-Israel groups, who were also agitating for a robust arms package to Israel, mobilized against the sale, worried as they were about the huge weapons flows pouring into the Persian Gulf region. They were joined by domestic groups disappointed by Carter's backtracking from campaign pledges to reduce arms exports.

Saudi Arabia dispatched its best and brightest to lobby for the sale. Saud and Turki, two sons of the late King Faisal, descended on Washington. There they met up with their first cousin, the future Saudi ambassador to Washington, Prince Bandar bin Sultan, a favorite of King Fahd and the Gatsby-like son of Prince Sultan, the Saudi minister of defense and aviation. The princes were the epitome of a new breed of Saudi diplomat—outgoing, sociable, and articulate.

At one point during the lobbying campaign, Oil Minister Yamani, threatened to link a rejection of the arms deal to higher oil prices and Saudi investment policy, a threat the Saudi information minister recanted two days later.[5] King Khaled advocated for the packages because of "recently stepped-up communist expansion in the area," a likely reference to Saudi Arabia's involvement in Yemen and activities in the horn of Africa that were discussed in chapter 6.[6] To circumvent domestic pressure, the White House announced its intention to submit to Congress the arms request in combination with one for sophisticated equipment for Israel and Egypt. The package was to be approved or rejected in toto.[7] In May 1978 Congress approved an arms sale including seventy-five F-16s and fifteen F-15s to Israel, sixty F-15s to Saudi Arabia, and fifty F-5Es to Egypt. Secretary of State Cyrus Vance justified the $2.5 billion sale as one "of immense importance in promoting a course of moderation."[8] Saudi Arabia was the only one of the three countries granted the entirety of its original request. Saudi Arabia was expected to pay for Egypt's portion, something that became a contentious issue inside the kingdom after Sadat signed the Camp David accords.

The arms sale did not buy quiescence. Relations deteriorated first between Israel and Egypt and later between Egypt, Saudi Arabia, and the rest of the Arab world. In negotiations leading up to the meeting at Camp David, Egyptian and Israeli positions seemed irreconcilable. Israel sought a bilateral peace deal. Sadat wanted some linkage between an Egyptian-Israeli peace deal and a final Palestinian settlement. At the Camp David talks in September 1978 it became clear to Sadat that he would not achieve his desired preference. He settled for a deal that brought peace between his country and Israel, and pushed the Palestinian issue off to future negotiations. In spite of a certain negative reaction, Sadat pursued the agreement to achieve peace for his country. Days before the accords' official signing in March 1979, Brzezinski obtained a Saudi pledge to continue providing arms to Egypt.[9] Unfortunately, Riyadh did not keep its promise.

Saudi Arabia at that time provided Egypt substantial yearly assistance and other perks such as underwriting Egyptian weapon stocks. Its support was essential to Egypt. Bill Quandt urged Brzezinski to be mindful of Saudi Arabia and noted that "the Saudi role will be crucial, unreliable, and unpredictable."[10]

But Egyptian-Saudi relations did not easily survive the signing of the Camp David accords. Saudi leaders argued that Sadat's failure to explain his actions to the Arab world after Camp David left them exposed and proved that the United States had produced only a bilateral peace treaty.[11] The royal family was split on how to proceed, with Fahd arguing for a temperate response against the wishes of his family, in particular his brother Abdullah and nephew Saud. Prince Saud traveled to Baghdad on March 31, 1979, and joined other Arabs in pledging to sever relations with Egypt and impose sanctions on it. The Saudi decision came despite Prince Fahd's statement at the end of March that "the Saudi government's relationship with Egypt does not hinge upon a single issue."[12] Sadat responded with a series of bitter statements targeting Saudi Arabia, arguing that the Saudis were leading a covert effort to destroy Egypt financially. In May the Arab League cut its aid to Egypt, $500 million of which came from the kingdom. Prince Sultan announced the liquidation of the $1 billion Arabs arms manufacturing consortium based in Egypt.[13] Saudi Arabia stopped its yearly economic grants (ranging from $200 million to $700 million) and military grants, and in July the State Department announced a "postponement" in delivering the F-5Es to Egypt that had been agreed to in May 1978 because of financing issues. Saudi Arabia was to have underwritten the arms transfer. Although the kingdom allowed long-term deals to continue and never evicted the two hundred thousand or so Egyptians living inside Saudi Arabia who sent home nearly $2 billion per year, the situation grew ever worse.[14]

Prince Fahd left the kingdom for a six-week vacation in Spain, leading many to speculate that he was protesting the anti-American drift in Saudi Arabia's foreign policy.[15] American decision makers were shocked at the full extent of Saudi Arabia's response. Relations registered yet another low.

Watershed

Preparations for the signing of the Israel-Egypt accords in 1979 were fraught with diplomatic difficulty and monopolized Washington's attention. Then the last eight weeks of 1979 saw a dizzying series of external events and internal challenges that directly challenged the Saudi royal family and greatly concerned the United States. As scholar David W. Lesch correctly observed, "1979 constitutes a major watershed, if not the major watershed, in modern Middle East history."[16] It had profound implications for Saudi Arabia and, by extension, the U.S.-Saudi relationship.

On November 4, 1979, Iranian students seized the U.S. embassy in Tehran and took American hostages. Two weeks later religiously inspired Saudi rebels seized the Grand Mosque of Mecca and took hostages, sparking a very public two-week domestic crisis, one of the worst in the kingdom's history. The Saudi leadership emerged shaken and insecure. Iranian-inspired protests later erupted in eastern Saudi Arabia. Three weeks after Saudi Arabia's domestic siege ended, and as Washington was seeking a solution to the hostage crisis in Iran, the Soviet Union invaded Afghanistan, placing Moscow within three hundred miles of the Persian Gulf. Ten months later Iraq would invade Iran, leaving all Arab Gulf states vulnerable to Iranian retaliatory attacks. These events proved a calamity for Saudi and American policy makers and resulted in unprecedented cooperative efforts between the two. It also set the stage for a "strategic revolution" in America's global posture and a religious upheaval inside the kingdom.

The situation in Iran had begun deteriorating in late 1978, when massive anti-shah rallies brought out thousands of protesters.[17] King Khaled and Prince Fahd eyed events there warily, but the United States was preoccupied elsewhere. As late as September 1978, American attention was almost entirely focused on Camp David negotiations, Afghanistan's political devolution, SALT II negotiations with the Soviets, and the normalization of relations with China.[18] When it could focus on Iran, the Carter administration was divided about how to interpret and approach events unfolding there. Brzezinski argued to strongly back the shah. In the view of Brzezinski, and eventually that of secretary of defense Harold Brown, America's strategic reliance on the Gulf, as well as the Nixon-era commitment to the shah, required nothing less. In addition, they argued that should the United States fail to act, and should the shah fall, it would send a powerful message to America's friends around the world that Washington was an unreliable partner either unwilling or unable to assist friends in need. Others such as secretary of state Cyrus Vance and many of his advisors at the State Department worried that an aggressive U.S. posture would both ignite a serious crisis with the Soviet Union, undermining all the hard work that U.S. and Soviet negotiators had undertaken to negotiate SALT II, and run counter to Carter's commitment to human rights. Between 1978 and 1980 Iranian oil exports fell 4 million barrels per day as a result of domestic instability. Between 1979 and 1981 oil prices tripled, due in part to this collapse in its production.

On New Year's Day 1979 the shah went into exile, foreshadowing a disastrous year for the Carter administration. With "frantic concern," Saudi leaders beseeched Washington for a highly visible demonstration of support. They wanted to send a message to their own people, and neighbors, that monarchies were not easily toppled, and that the United States would support long-standing friends in the region. Unwilling to send an aircraft carrier, Washington dispatched a dozen F-15 fighters and about three hundred members of the U.S. Air Force. In order not to provoke Iran and stir up U.S. domestic protest, the fighters were sent to Saudi Arabia without their missiles.[19] Saudi Arabia's future ambassador to the United States, Prince Bandar, would remember this halfhearted show of support and question American credibility eleven years later, when the two countries began preparing to expel Iraq from Kuwait.[20]

One month after the shah's departure, Ayatollah Khomeini swept into the country from his exile in Paris determined to use the mantle of Islam to validate his position and define a new Iranian foreign and domestic policy. Representing a new kind of Islamic legitimacy (Shi'a as opposed to Sunni), the ayatollah's return to Iran posed a direct threat to the House of Saud. It challenged Saudi Arabia's position as the international mouthpiece for the Prophet Muhammad. At its core, the Sunni-Shi'a divide is about the process of succession and who should succeed the Prophet Muhammad: those chosen by knowledge-able members of the prophet's inner circle, or his son-in-law and sub-sequent descendants. The ayatollah reminded the world that the Shi'a, now represented by Iran, could claim Islamic legitimacy. The ayatol-lah's rise to power also made clear that a religiously inspired leader could overturn a long-standing monarchy. Neither boded well for the Saudi leadership.

The situation deteriorated throughout 1979 and culminated in November when Iranian students took the American embassy staff hostage. As Vance recalled, somewhat surprisingly given his attempts to pursue a moderate policy toward Iran, "the removal of Iran from the ranks of American allies and its control by an unfriendly regime was a blow to our political and security interests in Southwest Asia."[21] This echoed Prince Fahd's assessment that "power vacuums, especially in the world's most strategic area, are always dangerous."[22] Both American and Saudi leaders' eyes were now fully trained on Iran.

Iranian leaders actively tried to spread their revolution into neigh-boring states. Neighbors with large Shi'a populations were targeted, including Bahrain, Kuwait, and eastern Saudi Arabia where the king-dom's Shi'a population is disproportionately located. Throughout 1979 and 1980 Iranian radio broadcasted anti-Saudi messages into the kingdom and encouraged local dissent. The Iranian broadcasts added fuel to the growing fire in the Eastern Province. The kingdom's mas-sive oil wealth had not benefited the Shi'a community because of deeply prejudicial state policies. Throughout 1977 and 1978 there had been reports of oil infrastructure sabotage and labor unrest in the Eastern

Province, which were in part stoked and redefined by growing Shi'a religious empowerment in Iran.[23]

In January 1980 Iran urged the Shi'a of Qatif, a major city in eastern Saudi Arabia, to oppose Saudi royal authority. On February 1, the first anniversary of Ayatollah Khomeini's return from exile, the Friday sermon in Qatif's main Shi'a mosque incited a mob to attack the town's central market. A branch of the Saudi British Bank was damaged. During the incident, Radio Teheran's shortwave Arabic channel, the Voice of the Islamic Republic of Iran, beamed a daily series of escalating propaganda attacks against the Saudi state, including bitter diatribes about the immoral behavior of particular princes and a specific summons to Shi'a listeners to take up arms and rebel. In March it continued to broadcast messages that "the ruling regime in Saudi Arabia wears Muslim clothing, but inwardly represents the U.S. body, mind and terrorism."[24] Saudi Arabian intelligence officials later blamed the early incitement in the Eastern Province as one reason for their failure to anticipate the seizure of the Grand Mosque in November 1979.[25]

Two and a half weeks after the hostage taking in Iran and reports of Shi'a unrest, Saudi and non-Saudi Sunni religious zealots led by Juhayman al-Utaybi, seized the Grand Mosque of Mecca. During the dawn prayers, rebels took hold of the microphone and announced to the world that the messiah had come. Utaybi's followers occupied the mosque's courtyard, which contained the Kaaba, a cube-shaped structure considered the spiritual center of the Muslim world. A charismatic Saudi preacher, Utaybi called for the abolition of radio, television, professional soccer, and employment of women outside the home. He also urged the downfall of the royal family, decrying its corruption and close relationship with infidel powers.[26] It was the first time since the 1929 battle of Sibila that an organized political opposition openly challenged the royal family on religious terms.[27] It was an early salvo in the domestic religious war Saudi Arabia is currently fighting.

The majority of Utaybi's followers had been students at the Islamic University of Medina, where the Egyptian Muslim Brotherhood's influence had been strong, a result of King Faisal's decision to welcome them to Saudi Arabia to challenge Nasser during the 1960s.[28] These "neo-Ikhwan" argued that Muhammad ibn Abdullah al-Qahtani, who was with them inside the mosque, represented the kingdom's true spiritual leader, not Sheikh Abdel Aziz bin Baz, Saudi Arabia's grand mufti. After days of trying to resolve the situation on their own, including fighting their way into the mosque and starving out those inside, Saudi princes sought both a fatwa from the ulema and French assistance to end the siege. They received both. Turki al-Faisal called on none other than

Alexandre de Marenches and his SDECE spy service for training in gas warfare.[29] That old intelligence connection, used so effectively during Safari Club operations several years back, proved itself unexpectedly useful in this direct challenge to Saudi rule. The siege ended with Qahtani killed and Utaybi and his followers captured.

The Saudi regime squelched the Grand Mosque uprising but proceeded to adopt much of the religious radicals' agenda. So threatened was the House of Saud by Iran's religious turn and the domestic critique that it was not religious enough that the Saudi leadership sought to outbid domestic and neighboring extremists. It began pouring money into religious institutions at home and abroad. While King Abdel Aziz fought the Ikhwan in 1929 to establish the dominance of the political over the religious elements in government, in 1979 his sons attempted to co-opt a dangerous religious revival. Saudi Arabia has yet to recover from this turn to aggressive state-sponsored religious zealotry.

Three weeks after Saudi leaders emerged from the dual crises, they were confronted with yet another challenge. On December 27, 1979, Soviet forces invaded Afghanistan with nearly a hundred thousand troops and installed Babrak Karmal as Afghanistan's new leader. It was the first time that Soviet troops had massed inside a non-Warsaw Pact country, and the invasion represented a dramatic emboldening of Soviet policy. For Turki al-Faisal, Saudi Arabia's intelligence chief, the Soviet pincer movement against the kingdom was "completing something they had started in Africa."[30] To make matters worse, the "godless Communists" had invaded a Muslim country. On January 7 Saudi Arabia became the first country to withdraw from the 1980 Moscow Olympic Games in protest over the invasion.

Saudis and others had been monitoring the situation in Afghanistan for over a year, ever since a group of Marxist officers overthrew the Afghan leader and replaced him with Nur Muhammad Taraki in April 1978. In March 1979, prior to the Soviet invasion, Taraki began appealing for direct Soviet aid, unnerving Pakistan, Saudi Arabia, and the United States. A senior Pakistani government official approached a U.S. intelligence officer to explore Washington's receptivity to providing small arms and support to the Afghan resistance.[31] Saudi officials also began probing American interest in aiding the Afghan resistance.[32]

Riyadh offered financial support for any anti-Soviet effort and indicated that they could perhaps get others to tacitly support an American-led effort. In July President Carter signed a presidential finding that began a modest covert action program of propaganda and "non-military supplies" to insurgents.[33] Over the next decade, the aid program would grow into a multibillion-dollar covert operation that relied on Saudi financing and Pakistani logistical support.

Carter's director of central intelligence, Stansfield Turner, urged the United States to proceed cautiously. He was outargued by Brzezinski, who for three years had advocated a more determined stand against the unrelenting Soviet onslaught across the third world. The CIA was ordered to put $100 million into covert activity. Saudi Arabia agreed to match America's contribution.[34] Harold Brown activated Chinese support, which he and Brzezinski had been cultivating since at least the mid-1970s, when the Soviets began aiding Ethiopia. Within days of the Soviet invasion, the United States began putting small arms into Afghanistan via Pakistan.

Brzezinski and deputy secretary of state Warren Christopher arrived in Islamabad on February 1, hoping to shore up a nervous and potentially endangered Pakistan. From Pakistan, Brzezinski and Christopher flew to Saudi Arabia in what ultimately became a well-trodden American path. Brzezinski was struck by "the degree of apprehension" within the highest Saudi ranks over the Soviet invasion.[35] Fahd and the foreign minister, Saud al-Faisal, agreed to be "cooperative both inside their country and outside."[36] Just as important, if not more so, the king also agreed to provide serious economic support. In Riyadh, Saudi Arabia and the United States agreed to a matching program, in which the kingdom would match dollar for dollar American financing of anti-Soviet activity in Afghanistan.

It is unclear whether it was American or Saudi officials who first initiated what was to become a multibillion-dollar partnership to challenge the Soviets in Afghanistan. What is apparent is that both parties had their own vested interests in hurting the Soviets. For his part, Brzezinski was determined to bleed them for their activity in Africa and Southeast Asia. The Saudis, religiously motivated and viscerally anti-Soviet, were natural partners given the vast resources at their disposal and the ease with which they would fund religious groups. In the words of Robert "Bob" M. Gates, a future director of the CIA, "The stage was set for the vast future expansion of outside help, all run by CIA."[37]

For Saudi Arabia's leaders, a particularly zealous and fundamental form of Islam became the chosen instrument to respond to all three monumental events that transpired at the end of 1979. Contrary to Faisal's cautious attempt to marginalize the most extreme Nejdi religious leaders, Khaled and Fahd expanded their powers. Spending vast sums on religious institutions both at home and abroad, appearing with local clerics (often the most radical ones), and giving more airtime to local preachers, the Saudi leadership hoped to outflank its growing indigenous religious opposition, reclaim the mantle of Islam from Iran's

Ayatollah Khomeini, and eventually mobilize vast numbers of Saudi foot soldiers to head off to Afghanistan and fight to reverse atheism's expansion. For the most part, U.S. officials did not see major drawbacks to this approach. In fact, it had a lot to commend it.

"The Vital Interests of the United States of America"

The events of 1979 shifted the balance within the administration from those who preferred negotiation and deescalation to others advocating a more muscular response. One of those urging stronger action was none other than undersecretary of defense Robert Komer, who, it will be recalled, had argued for the Kennedy administration to keep its distance from the Saudi monarchy, nearly two decades earlier. On January 23, 1980, in his annual State of the Union address, Carter announced that any "attempt by any outside force to gain control of the Persian Gulf region will be regarded as an assault on the vital interests of the United States of America, and such an assault will be repelled by any means necessary, including military force."[38] It was the strongest commitment to the Persian Gulf ever uttered by a U.S. president. According to Brzezinski, Egypt, Saudi Arabia, and other Gulf states all privately conveyed relief upon hearing Carter's new policy initiative.[39]

The Carter doctrine, as the declaration came to be called, was conceived as a direct descendent of the Truman and Eisenhower doctrines. The Truman doctrine had extended American protection to Greece, Turkey, and by extension the rest of the Middle East. The Eisenhower doctrine offered assistance to those who were fighting Communism and Egyptian subversion, particularly in the heart of the Middle East. The Carter doctrine completed America's geographical march east by committing America to the defense of Southwest Asia. Nine years after British forces withdrew from "east of Suez," America explicitly and intentionally assumed responsibility for the area's defense.

As the words of the Carter doctrine rolled off the president's tongue, planners and analysts alike began actively debating whether, and how, the United States could defend such distant commitments. With no command headquarters in the region, the military required better strategic mobility and more pre-positioned assets. Under President Carter, the United States defense establishment embarked on a concerted effort to improve American strategic mobility. The U.S. Defense Department accelerated its efforts to create a rapid-reaction force to deploy forces quickly to the region. When Caspar W. Weinberger, President Reagan's secretary of defense, came to office, he built on the

Carter administration's efforts, assigning the Persian Gulf region "a very high priority."[40]

Still, for all the new military planning and political commitments, the United States and its partners were unable to prevent continued regional instability. On September 22, 1980, in the waning weeks of the presidential campaign between President Carter and his rival Ronald W. Reagan, Iraq invaded Iran, immediately drawing to its side Saudi Arabia and other Arab states, along with their money and in some cases arms.

The Aftershocks of 1979

The decade of the 1970s dramatically altered the U.S.-Saudi political dynamic. In decades prior, American decision makers had vacillated between courting and resisting Saudi support. Especially after the 1973–74 oil embargo and the accompanying oil price increases, leaders on both sides had worked to broaden and deepen the bilateral relationship. The benefits from stanching Communism versus the economic costs of allowing relations to deteriorate drove senior Saudi and American policy makers to champion closer contacts.

The Saudi proselytizing that accompanied many of its Cold War investments did not factor heavily into American political debate. It had been a persistent feature of Saudi foreign policy, but one usually understood to have a marginal, yet positive, utility. After 1979, however, Saudi preaching brought distinct advantages. Like the Eisenhower administration before it, American decision makers actively sought to encourage Saudi religious efforts. In particular, it helped to recruit fighters to Afghanistan to stem the Soviet tide.

In response to the dramatic events of 1979 and the need to shore up his own domestic base, Crown Prince Fahd turned to religion, increasing the hold that radical religious clerics had over society. He poured resources into the international and regional religious institutions created by King Faisal back in the 1960s. He also adopted many of the demands put forward by those who had stormed the Grand Mosque, dragging Saudi social and political life back toward the seventh century. Economically, Fahd continued to push forward with his modernization plans. This two-track approach unleashed a radical religious tidal wave that flooded over Saudi Arabia and the wider region. The effects of this transformed the Middle East and helped to bring down the Soviet Union. It would also directly contribute to the malignant Islamic radicalism that challenges the world today.

8

Begin or Reagan

When Reagan assumed office in 1981, oil prices were at an unprecedented high. Between 1972 and 1980 prices had skyrocketed from $1.90 to $37.96 per barrel, a nearly 2,000 percent increase in real terms. As the zealously anti-American Shi'a leader Ayatollah Khomeini incited revolutionary movements across the Arabian Peninsula, he effectively terminated Nixon's decade-long twin pillars policy, which relied on Iran and Saudi Arabia to patrol the Gulf. At the same time, the Soviet Union continued to reinforce its position in Afghanistan and elsewhere in Saudi Arabia's neighborhood. Moscow was now one step closer to the oil-rich Persian Gulf and its historic objective of securing a warm-water port. In the words of Jeanne J. Kirkpatrick, Reagan's foreign policy advisor during the 1980 presidential campaign and U.S. ambassador to the UN in the mid-1980s, the Soviet Union had "progressed from a continental power to a global power."[1]

Both Reagan's ideological fervor and his successor George H.W. Bush's realpolitik would benefit from Saudi cash and political support to manage the global tumult. Saudi Arabia, for its part, welcomed in Ronald Reagan, a president willing to pursue a muscular foreign policy. Over the next decade, at the highest levels, on the most strategically central issues, the two countries worked to hasten Communism's defeat and then reverse Iraq's invasion of Kuwait. The confidence that high-level American officials had in this highly classified relationship did not trickle down to the American people, where skepticism about Saudi intentions ran high. The result of such competing views was a series of politically costly disputes between the U.S. executive and legislature over whether or not to go forward with massive arms sales to the kingdom.

"A Potential Bulwark Against Further Soviet Moves"

Ronald Reagan wanted not only to contain the Soviet Union but also to "reverse the expansion of Soviet control and military presence throughout the world."[2] The Reagan doctrine, as Reagan's approach came to be known, aimed to increase the cost of Moscow's expansionist foreign policy by championing democracy, escalating defense spending, and supporting anti-Soviet insurgencies in the developing world. Key figures in the Reagan administration viewed Saudi Arabia as a useful partner in carrying out this doctrine, which Saudi Arabia for its part eagerly supported.

The problem for Reagan was that his doctrine was expensive and Americans, still recovering from Vietnam, had little enthusiasm for third-world adventures. But Reagan believed that his predecessors' failure to turn back Moscow's advances in Angola, Ethiopia, and elsewhere in the mid-1970s had only emboldened the Soviet Union.

To high-level administration officials it became clear that to roll back Communism "you had to be able to fund it and we simply couldn't do that alone." Saudi Arabia was seen as "a potential bulwark against further Soviet moves."[3] Director of Central Intelligence William "Bill" J. Casey set out to find third party contributors who would provide arms and money. Robert "Bud" C. McFarlane, one of President Reagan's future national security advisors, remembered that the possibility of "Saudi Arabian assistance occurred very early in the administration."[4]

Reagan recalled in his memoir *An American Life* that he "thought it was important to strengthen ties with this relatively moderate country, not only because its oil exports were essential to our economy, but because, like Israel, it wanted to resist Soviet expansion in the region."[5] Not surprisingly, he made no mention of the seizure of the Grand Mosque and rising religious fervor inside the kingdom, an oversight that would come to have profound consequences for American national security. Such issues were still a decade or so away from appearing on the White House's radar screen. Reagan also emphasized his determination to overcome what he saw as America's reputation of abandoning key allies during moments of crisis: "To put it simply, I didn't want Saudi Arabia to become another Iran."[6] And then there was Saudi Arabia's potential to contribute to peace in the Middle East. "The basis for such stability" in the Middle East, the president wrote, "must be peace between Israel and the Arab nations. The Saudis are a key to this."[7] Finally, Caspar Weinberger, Reagan's influential secretary of defense, wanted to cultivate allies in the region in addition to Israel, and Saudi Arabia was the "only country in the region that would speak to us."[8] As Weinberger told King Fahd during a visit to Riyadh in 1982, "the United States needs more than one friend in the region." Crown Prince Fahd responded that he believed U.S. policy in the Middle East was more balanced than at any time in the previous fifteen years; he was clearly hoping that closer defense ties would translate into broader political ones.[9]

Congress did not share Reagan's affinity for Saudi Arabia and objected strongly to Saudi Arabia's role in ostracizing Egypt after the Camp David accords. Many lawmakers were also doubtful of either the Saudi regime's moderation or longevity. When the administration acted to improve relations with the kingdom, as it did by continually offering enormous weapons sales, it almost always met resistance. The different lenses through which Congress and the White House viewed Saudi Arabia set the stage for a series of epic battles, particularly around arms sales to the kingdom.

In spite of public and congressional resistance, the Reagan administration pursued close relations with Saudi Arabia, in particular around the funding of highly sensitive operations in the developing world, from Central Asia to Central America. The partnership became even more effective, and controversial, when the pro-American, sixty-one-year-old Crown Prince Fahd became king in 1982, after Khaled died.

King Fahd and other high-ranking Saudis had their own reasons for working closely with the United States. The kingdom was still awash in cash and needed reliable markets in which to invest. In 1980 oil revenues brought in over $100 billion, of which the country could absorb only about $60 billion. Not only that, but oil demand was expected to increase in the near future from 11 to 20 mbd.[10] Saudi Arabia continued investing its newfound wealth in its own domestic infrastructure, security forces, and foreign (particularly U.S.) markets. It looked to U.S. expertise to help in the modernization of the country.

The United States was also instrumental in protecting Saudi Arabia's oil fields. Like his half brothers and father before him, King Fahd believed that Saudi Arabia's safety was best protected by close ties to America. He was able to act on this belief as Saudi Arabia's security environment grew increasingly dire throughout the 1980s, with Iran threatening Saudi Arabia's oil facilities, exports, and territory.[11]

Saudi Arabia was also gravely concerned about the advancing Soviet Union. Riyadh interpreted Moscow's Afghanistan adventure as part of a Soviet-directed campaign to encircle the Arabian Peninsula with radical regimes and subvert the oil-rich monarchies.[12] For decades the Soviet Union had backed an antimonarchical insurgency in Yemen, on Saudi Arabia's southern border. Eventually a thousand Soviet advisors and five hundred Cuban trainers took up residency in South Yemen. To the north and east, the kingdom worried that the

Soviets would take advantage of the destabilizing Iran-Iraq War. To its west in Ethiopia, Riyadh remained fixated on the seventeen thousand Cuban forces and Soviet aid that poured into Ethiopia after the downfall of America's ally Haile Selassie. Also of concern was Soviet penetration in Angola and Mozambique. As one CIA operative active at the time remembers, during the 1970s and 1980s "the Saudis had independent motives to fund anti-Communists anywhere they were in need."[13]

Finally, and perhaps most important, a new attitude toward Israel arrived, one that was more compatible with U.S. goals, when King Fahd took over the reigns of power in 1982. Shortly before becoming king, the crown prince offered an eight-point plan that became known as the Fahd Plan, which proposed that "all states in the region should be able to live in peace in the region." This seventh point, which even today is posted on the late king's official Web site, created a firestorm inside Saudi Arabia and the larger Arab world about whether Saudi Arabia had officially recognized Israel's right to exist.[14] Although filled with caveats and shrouded in anger at American policy toward Israel, a clarification issued by the then deputy prime minister and commander of the Saudi National Guard, Crown Prince Abdullah, announced that "our plan recognizes the right of Israel to exist only after the acceptance of a Palestinian state, the return to the 1967 borders and the end to the state of belligerency. If these conditions are met, then the recognition of Israel will be de facto. How can we deny them that right?"[15] In 1982, at an Arab summit at Fez, delegates adopted a watered-down version of the Fahd Plan, which was renamed the Fez Plan. The Fahd and Fez Plans were welcomed in Europe, and in some quarters of the White House, as a very important step along the path to peace. In a letter to Congress, President Reagan wrote,

> The Fez Communiqué significantly and irreversibly modified the Arab consensus of the three "no's" ... (i.e., no recognition, no negotiation, and no conciliation with Israel [put forward at the 1967 Khartoum conference]) ... The Fez Communiqué moved the formal Arab position from rejection of peace to consideration of how to achieve peace with Israel ... it was an implicit acceptance of the right of Israel to a secure existence ... the Plan remains the single largest step toward peace on which the Arab world has been able to agree.[16]

Fahd and others hoped such a statement would help facilitate U.S.-Saudi relations, reduce regional conflict, and more immediately allow Saudi Arabia to import higher-quality American-made weapons.

Fahd, the seventh son of King Abdel Aziz, had risen to power through his bureaucratic skill.[17] Having served as minister of education and interior, he was a consummate political insider, effectively building consensus out of the competing views of his half brothers. Back in the early 1960s, Fahd had helped Faisal, to Saud's detriment, solidify political power. He was the power behind Khaled's throne. Fahd, along with his six full brothers (including today's minister of defense, minister of interior, governor of Riyadh, deputy minister of interior, and vice minister of defense), formed a formidable bloc within the extended royal family. Fahd's weakness, one that would haunt Saudi Arabia and the United States in years to come, was his detachment from domestic political life. He advocated the rapid modernization of Saudi Arabia's infrastructure and expected the kingdom's traditional institutions to evolve along with it. As we will see, he was completely unprepared for the violent public resistance that accompanied his programs.

Although he had witnessed the 1979 protests firsthand, he neither built institutions for managing dissent nor slowed his modernization efforts. Instead, he carried out his preferred policies while granting religious radicals increased latitude within society. Washington greatly appreciated Fahd's Western orientation. In Saudi Arabia, however, powerful members of the royal family, led by Prince Abdullah, worried that Fahd's programs, devoid of Faisal and Khaled's nuanced appreciation for Saudi Arabia's domestic political limits (including tribal sensitivities and religious sensibilities), would drive the kingdom to ruin.

In 1981 Fahd sent to Washington a group of young representatives untainted by intransigent positions vis-à-vis Israel and representing the next generation of Saudi leaders, the grandsons of Abdel Aziz. Turki al-Faisal, Saud al-Faisal, and Bandar bin Sultan would become regular visitors to the United States, and there was a sense of excitement that this new breed of Saudis would bring good things to the kingdom. In particular, Prince Bandar, the son of the defense minister, Prince Sultan, emerged as one of the most important figures in U.S.-Saudi relations. Throughout the 1980s he came to personify the relationship, single-handedly representing the kingdom as the Saudi ambassador to the United States. All bilateral communications went through him. As his cousin Turki al-Faisal recalled, "He conducted secret operations out of normal channels, with King Fahd's permission and blessing."[18] Brent Scowcroft, President George H.W. Bush's national security advisor, characterized Bandar's role as "the troubleshooter for King Fahd."[19] Because Bandar had the ear of the king, he became a trusted interlocutor at the highest levels of the White House and assumed the post of Saudi Arabia's ambassador to the United States in 1983.

Born to a Sudanese concubine and a son of the founder of Saudi Arabia (Prince Sultan, the long-serving minister of defense), Prince Bandar grew up in his mother's home and then in the home of his paternal grandmother, in the shadows of his brothers with more reputable maternal lineages. King Faisal is reputed to have taken a shine to Bandar, a bright and precocious little boy. Faisal made him a coffee server, an apprenticeship that would provide his young nephew glimpses into the world of power and diplomacy at a very early age. As a young adult, he was sent off to the Royal Air Force College at Cranwell, England where he trained as a pilot. He spent 1969 training in Texas. Upon his return home in 1972 he married King Faisal's youngest daughter, Haifa, who became the subject of a terrorism financing scandal after the September 11 attacks.

The charismatic Prince Bandar made his diplomatic debut during the Carter years, when he helped to secure the sale of sixty F-15 fighter jets to Saudi Arabia. Given Bandar's military background, Turki al-Faisal asked him to help lobby for the sale, which he did successfully. In the early 1980s Bandar made at least a half dozen trips to Lebanon with Bud McFarlane, the president's special representative to the Middle East, in an attempt to broker a Lebanese cease-fire during the bloody civil war. The two worked together closely, although not much came from their effort. When 241 U.S. Marines were killed in a bombing in Lebanon in 1983, Reagan held Saudi Arabia and other Arab states partially responsible for dragging the United States into Lebanon in the first place. Two decades later, Osama bin Laden would use America's hasty withdrawal from Lebanon as proof that America was a paper tiger.

Bandar fast became a fixture in Washington, aggressively lobbying Congress on Saudi Arabia's behalf. He had strong relations with many influential members of government and would eventually become the dean of the Washington diplomatic corps. During the 1970s he had frequently played squash with Colin Powell, who would become Reagan's last in a series of national security advisors. Bandar's relations with Vice President Bush became so close that some have charged that the Bush family put Saudi Arabia's interests above America's—a charge for which there has been much speculation but little evidence. The author Craig Unger, for example, speculates that on matters of urgent national policy, Washington gives Saudi Arabia "a pass" because "$1.4 billion has made its way from the House of Saud to individuals and entities tied to the House of Bush."[20] Although Unger does not explore it, such financial ties go back further than the Bush administration, to at least the Reagan administration (although even before that the Saudi arms dealer Adnan Khashoggi reportedly contributed to Richard Nixon's presidential campaign), and cannot explain major decisions around the

peace process and more recently Iraq that cut against Saudi Arabia's preferred policies.

In many ways, the king's loose spending habits and Reagan's need
for funds were a comfortable match, at least for those operating at the
very highest levels of their governments. Over the course of the 1980s,
the Reagan administration, followed by the George H. W. Bush administration, figured out ways to integrate Saudi Arabia's global concerns
and surplus cash into American foreign policy, particularly in the developing world. The White House acknowledged and at times encouraged
Saudi Arabia's support for Iraq in its war against Iran, Afghan fighters
opposing Soviet aggression, the government of Sudan, and Angolan and
Nicaraguan rebels. In such instances, Saudi and American actions were
mutually supportive. Prince Bandar helped facilitate Saudi Arabia's
assistance.

In his 1986 State of the Union address, Reagan made the promise
that "you are not alone Freedom Fighters. America will support with
moral and material assistance your right not just to fight and die
for freedom, but to fight and win with freedom—to win freedom in
Afghanistan; in Angola; in Cambodia; and in Nicaragua."[21] What few
Americans at the time realized was that Saudi Arabia was involved in
three of these four cases, and others as well. The highly secretive partnership inspired Prince Bandar to tell a journalist about his belief that
if the American people fully understood the nature of the U.S.-Saudi
covert relationship, they would urge a more pro-Saudi policy. "If you
knew what we were really doing for America," stated Prince Bandar, "you
wouldn't just give us AWACS, you would give us nuclear weapons."[22]
When the American public did discover Saudi Arabia's financial contribution to places such as Nicaragua, its response was considerably less
charitable than Bandar anticipated.

AWACS and F-15s

One of the first challenges Reagan faced was selling sophisticated
American weaponry to Saudi Arabia. A bruising political battle, the fight
over AWACS and F-15 upgrades would occupy a significant portion of
his time. With the exception of a few votes on taxes and spending cut
legislation, Reagan recalls in his memoirs that he "spent more time in
one-on-one meetings and on the telephone attempting to win on this
[Saudi arms] measure than on any other."[23]

In 1978 Jimmy Carter had pushed through a controversial F-15 deal
by linking their export to the sale of high-end U.S. aircraft to Israel and

by assuring Congress that sophisticated offensive capabilities would be withheld from Saudi Arabia's portion of the package. Carter had denied a Saudi request to buy AWACS, an all-weather surveillance and command-and-control plane, although he did deploy American-owned and -operated AWACS to the kingdom to monitor Iranian movements at the outbreak of the Iran-Iraq War. Still, Saudi Arabia coveted the AWACS, which represented state-of-the-art American weaponry and would provide them with a new capacity to gain intelligence on neighboring forces. Riyadh also wanted bomb racks and external refueling tankers to increase the lethality and range of its recently purchased F-15 fleet.

At the time of the sale Carter made it clear to Congress that he would not authorize the sale of enhancements or AWACS to Saudi Arabia. By 1980, however, President Carter began to change his mind. After the invasion of Afghanistan and the beginning of the Iraq-Iran War, the Carter administration came to believe that Saudi Arabia's defense required further augmentation, and so the White House was "favorably disposed" toward the sale. President Carter had hinted that the weapons that Saudi Arabia sought would be forthcoming after the election, but he made no formal commitment. When Reagan came to office he was confronted immediately with Carter's promises to Congress but a dramatically different political context. The *New York Times* described the weapons issue as "the first item of controversial Middle East business for the incoming Reagan Administration."[24]

To make matters worse for the administration, the Saudis and Israelis were actively lobbying for and against the sale. Riyadh once again dispatched to Washington its young guard, those who had been so effective in securing the earlier F-15 sale. Prince Bandar pointed to the fact that Saudi Arabia had the cash to pay for the $8.5 billion ($18.4 billion in 2005 dollars) package and also shared the United States' threat perception in the Persian Gulf, Africa, and elsewhere. Israeli leaders feared that such sophisticated weaponry would be used against them in the event of another war—and that such a sale would be seen as rewarding Saudi Arabia's anti-Sadat stance vis-à-vis the Camp David accords. They also feared a weakening in the special U.S.-Israel friendship.

Like the outgoing Carter administration, the incoming Reagan administration by and large supported Saudi Arabia's AWACS and F-15 enhancements request. Secretary of Defense Weinberger took an early lead, arguing hard for the sale. Before his appointment to Reagan's cabinet, Weinberger had been a senior executive at Bechtel Corporation (an infrastructure development company with deep ties to Saudi Arabia), had traveled often to Saudi Arabia, and had strong ties with the Saudi royal family. It was no surprise, therefore, that he was among the strongest pro-Saudi voices in the Reagan administration. Two and a half weeks after Reagan took office, Weinberger declared that "we want to do everything we can to assist [the Saudis] in providing the additional security that they need."[25]

In March Reagan announced to Congress the details of the sale, which included AWACS, Sidewinder air-to-air missiles, and fuel tanks, although not the requested bomb racks.[26] Congress could override, but not amend, the sale with a majority of votes in both the House and Senate.[27] Senator Robert W. Packwood, the arms sale opponents' ringleader, began organizing to block the sale.

Six months later Reagan turned his full attention toward supporting the sale. He argued that AWACS were needed if the United States was to be seen as a reliable security partner, and also because it would help Saudi Arabia and the United States defend the Kingdom. In public and private sessions he pointed out that an attack on Saudi oil fields could halt the flow of oil for over a year, which would have a devastating effect on the U.S. economy. The president argued that the decision about foreign aid and major military sales should ultimately reside in the office of the president, not congress. When one leading senator arranged to speak with Prince Bandar to better understand Riyadh's position, Bandar arrived at the meeting accompanied by Richard V. Allen, the president's national security advisor.[28] Bandar had Reagan's full support. Reagan beseeched lawmakers to go through with the sale, telling them that if they voted against him, he would be rendered powerless on the world stage. In a meeting with forty-three Republican senators in the White House dining room, the president decried their opposition to the sale. "You're going to cut me off at the knees. I won't be effective in conducting foreign policy," he warned.[29] At a 1981 news conference he publicly criticized Israeli efforts to influence Congress' vote, stating, "It is not the business of other nations to make American foreign policy."[30] As Richard Nixon put it in an editorial in the *New York Times*, the fight came down to an ugly competition between either "Begin or Reagan."[31] This became the battle cry for those favoring the sale.

Between September and October, the president met with seventy-five of the one hundred senators to argue against blocking the sale. He met individually with forty-four of them, ten at the last minute. He offered the undecideds carrots, including not campaigning against them in upcoming elections, and judicial appointments. He also used sticks. One Minnesota Republican, Senator Rudolph E. Boschwitz, who opposed the sale, had his district punished with a base closure.[32]

Multiple pressures pushed Reagan to invest the time, including his desire to roll back congressional intervention in foreign policy. But it was the mounting security challenges in and around the Persian Gulf that focused the executive's attention in new and determined ways. While Congress tended to focus its opposition to the sale on Saudi Arabia's instability—the likelihood that new arms exports would fall into the hands of insurgents, and the balance of power with Israel on Saudi Arabia's northwest border—the White House and Pentagon supported the arms sale to increase the regime's security and alleviate mounting security challenges to its north and east. Without Iran as a pillar of U.S. support, the Reagan administration looked to bolster Saudi Arabia.

The president solicited support from former secretaries of state and defense, national security advisors, and chairmen of the Joint Chiefs of Staff. Those vocally advocating for the sale constituted a powerful bipartisan phalanx that included Henry Kissinger, Donald Rumsfeld, McGeorge Bundy, Zbigniew Brzezinski, and Maxwell Taylor. Secretary of State Alexander M. Haig Jr., testified before Congress that "our friendship with Saudi Arabia is not based solely on its role as an oil supplier. Saudi Arabia is proving itself an essential partner in our broader interests" and that it therefore should receive American military support. His sentiments were echoed three days later by Richard Allen in an opinion piece in the *Washington Post*.[33] As the issue went up to vote, one undecided senator confided to Reagan that he was seeking divine guidance for how to vote. The president mused that if he got "a busy signal it was me in there ahead of [you] with my own prayer."[34]

On October 28, 1981, the Senate failed by a razor-thin margin, 52 to 48, to pass the resolution necessary to stop the sale. The executive branch promised Congress that the upgraded F-15s would not be based at the Saudi airfield at Tabuk, close to Israel. Saudi Arabia would comply with this restriction for two decades, until March 2003, when it repositioned the aircraft during Operation Iraqi Freedom.

The Saudis were both elated and furious: elated that they had the weapons, furious that they had been dragged through a bruising public squabble to obtain something that both the current and previous administration had agreed they should have. The U.S. domestic battle caused Riyadh to doubt the United States as a reliable partner in defense and modernization.[35] The frustration was mixed with satisfaction, however. Prince Bandar and others were elated that Saudi Arabia had defeated Israel and its supporters in Congress. Bandar, as instrumental in sealing this deal as he had been in 1978, reveled in the Associated Press headline that followed the president's October 1 press conference: "Reagan Telling Israel to Butt out of American Affairs."[36]

But the sale was much more than a victory over Israel or a one-off weapons sale. It reflected a changing view of Saudi Arabia's role in the defense of America's strategic interests. The Reagan administration, following on the heels of the Carter administration, profoundly altered America's role in the Persian Gulf. As one State Department official explained when justifying the sale,

> the Soviet invasion of Afghanistan, the turmoil of the Iranian revolution, the Iran-Iraq war and the Soviet presence in South Yemen and Ethiopia underscore the instability in the region and the dangers of Soviet penetration and exploitation . . . circumstances in the region have changed dramatically.[37]

It was a nice side benefit that with the sale the White House reasserted the president's role in the making of American foreign policy. Congress, however, as we will see, did not go down without a fight. But the sale marked a larger transformation in America's security calculations along the eastern edges of the Arab world.

The AWACS and F-15 sale were also part of a larger military reorganization to put teeth into the rapid reaction force initiated by Carter, which transitioned into the unified Central Command (CENTCOM) in January 1983. Headquartered in Tampa, Florida, CENTCOM today is still charged with controlling U.S. military operations within the area spanning from Sudan in the west to Pakistan in the east, and from Iraq and Jordan in the north to Kenya and the Arabian Sea in the south. During the 1990s it also took responsibility for Central Asia. Saudi Arabia sits at the center of CENTCOM's responsibilities. Throughout the 1980s, the Defense Department worked tirelessly to increase America's ability to surge forces into the region by purchasing transport ships and planes and pre-positioning military hardware in the region. The Defense Department established bilateral security arrangements with Oman, Pakistan, Egypt, Jordan, and others. Caspar Weinberger recalled that the Persian Gulf, and Saudi Arabia in particular, was given a "very high priority. We worried about Soviet domination. We needed firm friends in the region."[38] "We weren't neglecting the Israeli alliance," he noted. The United States just wanted "to have more than one friend in the Middle East."[39] The Saudis eventually agreed to build a state-of-the-art facility outside of Riyadh that became instrumental in fighting Desert Storm in 1991.

The sale of the AWACS and the F-15 add-ons were part and parcel of the changing strategic environment in the Persian Gulf and around the globe. It signaled a tightening relationship between the United States and Saudi Arabia. For those more focused on the U.S.-Israel partner-

15. *A rare photo of Kamal Adham, King Faisal's brother-in-law and director of general intelligence until 1977. Adham would oversee many of Saudi Arabia's covert actions, particularly in Africa. He would also mentor his nephew Turki al-Faisal, his successor and current Saudi ambassador to the United States.* Photo by Robert Azzi/ Woodfin Camp Associates.

16. *In December 1974, during Christmas vacation in Vail, Colorado, President Ford gathered key advisors to discuss economic problems accompanying the high price of oil. Left to right, front row: William E. Simon, treasury secretary; President Ford; Alan Greenspan, chairman of the President's Council of Economic Advisers. Left to right, back row: Ron Nessen, press secretary; Dick Cheney, deputy chief of staff; Donald Rumsfeld, chief of staff.* Courtesy of the Gerald R. Ford Presidential Library, Ann Arbor, Michigan.

17. Prince (now King) Abdullah bin Abdel Aziz, second deputy prime minister and commander of the National Guard, sits next to a standing King Khaled in February 1979, days after Ayatollah Khomeini returned to Iran from exile. The religiously inspired overthrow of a long-standing monarchy next door greatly concerned Saudi leaders. Central Press Photos, courtesy of the Information Office, Embassy of Saudi Arabia, Washington, D.C.

18. Vice President Walter F. Mondale speaks with Crown Prince Fahd and Ahmed "Zaki" Yamani, the oil minister (center), at the White House, May 24, 1977. A close confidante of the late King Faisal, Yamani was the chief architect behind the 1973–74 oil embargo. Courtesy of the Jimmy Carter Library and Museum, Atlanta, Georgia.

19. *Demonstrators outside the White House protest the Carter administration's 1978 sale of F-15s to Saudi Arabia. Similar protests would hound President Reagan in 1981 and 1986 around controversial arms sales to the kingdom.* Photo by Wally McNamee/CORBIS.

20. *After the seizure of American hostages in Iran and the Soviet invasion of Afghanistan weeks later, President Carter defined the Persian Gulf region as a vital U.S. interest during his January 1980 State of the Union address. The Carter doctrine was deliberately designed as a follow-on to the Truman and Eisenhower doctrines. Each pushed the definition of American national interests further east.* Courtesy of the Jimmy Carter Library and Museum, Atlanta, Georgia.

21. On February 3, 1980, national security advisor Zbigniew Brzezinski looks into Afghanistan through the sights of a machine gun at a Pakistani army outpost. Brzezinski's trip would establish a decade-long joint effort between the United States, Saudi Arabia, and Pakistan that would ultimately defeat the Soviet Union in Afghanistan. Photo by Bettmann/CORBIS.

22. President Reagan carefully follows the vote on whether to allow the controversial 1981 AWACS sale to Saudi Arabia. The Senate came within two votes of blocking the sale. Left to right: Alexander M. Haig, secretary of state; James A. Baker, chief of staff; Richard V. Allen, assistant to the president for national security affairs; Richard G. Darman, assistant to the president and deputy chief of staff; Michael K. Deaver, deputy chief of staff; David R. Gergen, assistant to the president for communications. Courtesy of the Ronald Reagan Presidential Library, Simi Valley, California.

23. President Reagan and King Fahd meet in Washington, February 1985. One month later Reagan would sign an executive order that intensified America's commitments to a Soviet defeat in Afghanistan. That year also saw increasing American and Saudi commitments to Angola. Courtesy of the Ronald Reagan Presidential Library, Simi Valley, California.

24. On March 30, 1986, the Washington Post announced the sale of Stinger missiles to Angola and Afghanistan. Both sales were quietly subsidized by Saudi funds. Months earlier, Reagan dropped a Stinger request for Saudi Arabia, anticipating congressional opposition. Courtesy of the Washington Post Writers Group.

U.S. Sends New Arms To Rebels

Afghans, Angolans Get Stinger Missiles In Change of Policy

By David B. Ottaway
and Patrick E. Tyler
Washington Post Staff Writers

The Reagan administration, after hesitating for years to send sophisticated U.S. weapons to insurgent forces in the Third World, has begun supplying several hundred Stinger missiles covertly to anticommunist rebels in Angola and Afghanistan, informed sources said yesterday.

The decision, which has been closely held among the president's national security affairs advisers since it was made earlier this month, marks a major shift in U.S. policy. Shipments of top-of-the-line American arms to such insurgents had been barred in favor of furnishing largely Soviet- and Chinese-

25. On August 16, 1990, two weeks after Iraq invaded Kuwait, President Bush walks with Saudi foreign minister Saud al-Faisal at Walker's Point, Kennebunkport, Maine, discussing the region's dramatic developments. Behind the two, left to right: Brent Scowcroft, national security advisor; Richard N. Haass, senior director for Near East and South Asian affairs at the National Security Council; John E. Sununu, chief of staff. Courtesy of the George Bush Presidential Library and Museum, College Station, Texas.

26. President Bush meets with Saudi Arabia's ambassador to the United States, Prince Bandar bin Sultan, in the Oval Office of the White House, February 28, 1991. Bandar was given easy access to the Oval Office, and the president's and ambassador's families became so close that they occasionally shared small holiday dinners. Courtesy of the George Bush Presidential Library and Museum, College Station, Texas.

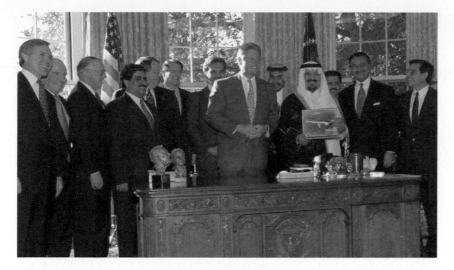

27. *President Clinton and Saudi Arabia's minister of defense and aviation, Prince Sultan bin Abdel Aziz, conclude a massive deal for Boeing planes, October 26, 1995. Prince Bandar, in the back, hoped the deal would allow Washington to view the kingdom as "a strategic asset and not a strategic liability." The commerce secretary, Ron Brown, is to the right of Prince Sultan, and General Electric's CEO, Jack Welch, stands second from the left.* Courtesy of the William J. Clinton Presidential Library and Museum, Little Rock, Arkansas.

28. *On June 25, 1996, a bomb ripped through Khobar Towers, a housing complex in eastern Saudi Arabia for U.S. service members. The blast killed 19 Americans and injured more than 260 others.* Photo by Sean Worrell, courtesy of the Defense Visual Information Center.

29. *Exactly one month after the attacks on the World Trade Center, Prince Alwaleed bin Talal bin Abdel Aziz handed New York mayor Rudolph Giuliani a check for $10 million for the Twin Towers Fund in New York. Giuliani later returned the check to him.* Photo by Stan Honda/Reuters/CORBIS.

30. *U.S. President George W. Bush walks hand in hand with Crown Prince Abdullah on his ranch in Crawford Texas, April 25, 2005. The meeting marked an easing of U.S.-Saudi relations after more than four years of significant tension.* White House photo by David Bohrer.

ship, there was concern that America's support for Israel was slipping as a result, although the president regularly asserted this was not the case.

The Iran-Iraq War and Difficulties in Obtaining Weaponry

The Iran-Iraq War gave the fight over arms particular salience in U.S.-Saudi relations. On September 22, 1980, four months before Reagan assumed the presidency, Iraq invaded Iran to reclaim the Shatt al-Arab, the border between the two states, and overran Iranian-held Khuzestan, an oil-rich area along the northern reaches of the Persian Gulf. The Iran-Iraq War threatened the flow of oil out of the Gulf, provided opportunities for Soviet adventurism, and presented a serious ideological challenge to Saudi Arabia. The two sides struggled for eight grinding years, which resulted in staggering carnage. Both Riyadh and Washington shared a strategic interest in preventing an Iranian victory.

Officially, Washington remained neutral, content to watch Iraq and Iran slug it out. In practice, however, it assumed a more biased posture. Shortly after the war began, Washington began probing Iraq to reestablish relations, which had been cut off after the 1967 war. Such efforts were pursued more vigorously after 1982, when Iran fought Iraq back to the border and then continued pressing into Iraqi territory. America's closest Arab friends in the region, Saudi Arabia and Jordan in particular, urged the United States to improve its relations with Iraq. For such states, the war not only had strategic importance but ethnic (Arab versus Persian) and religious (Sunni versus Shi'a) dimensions as well. Over time Iraq and the United States exchanged increasingly higher-level delegations. In 1983 Donald Rumsfeld, President Reagan's special envoy to the Middle East, met with Saddam Hussein; Rumsfeld was the first executive branch member to meet with the Iraqi president. Although U.S. officials were adamant that his visit did not constitute a "tilt" toward Baghdad, it clearly elevated the status of American-Iraqi relations.[40] Upon his return to Washington, Rumsfeld cautioned that failure to think seriously about Iranian aggression in the area "would make Lebanon look like a taffy pull."[41] American-Iraqi relations were reestablished in late 1984, after much prodding by Jordan and Saudi Arabia, even though Iraq was by then using chemical weapons against Iran.

The Saudis, for their part, reacted nervously to the war. According to one account, Saudi Arabia's King Khaled telephoned Iraq's leader, Saddam Hussein, three days after the war began to pledge the kingdom's support.[42] In the first two years Saudi Arabia undertook a massive Arab funding drive to underwrite Iraq's defense. Saudi Arabian officials also facilitated weapons transfer into Iraq. For example, the kingdom purchased weapons for Egypt, some of which were later reshipped to Iraq according to plan.[43] Egypt offered to assist Iraq, in large part to get back in Saudi Arabia's good graces in light of Riyadh's efforts to isolate it after Camp David. In 1982 Iraq and Saudi Arabia exchanged a dozen top-level visits.

By the end of the war Saudi Arabia had extended at least $16 billion in loans, excluding indirect support. Soviet-bloc countries, China, Germany, Japan, France, and the United States also extended billions of dollars in loans and grants to Iraq.[44] At the start of the war Iraq had been in sound fiscal condition, but by 1987 Iraq's debts ran between $65 and $85 billion, three times its GDP. At least half the amount was owed to Gulf Arab States, Saudi Arabia and Kuwait in particular.[45] These loans formed the basis for Iraq's post-Desert Storm, post-Iraqi Freedom debts, which gave Iraq the distinction of being the world's most indebted country.

The Iran-Iraq war dramatically altered the security environment on Saudi Arabia's eastern shores. In early 1983 Iran launched its third major offensive against Iraq, resulting in the largest buildups of ground forces since World War II, with nearly two hundred thousand men on each side. To help shift the military balance toward Iraq, the United States launched Operation Staunch, an effort to stem the weapons flow to both Iran and Iraq. In practice, Washington exerted significantly more effort in keeping weapons from Iran than it did Iraq. American officials never issued a démarche against those shipping weapons to Iraq, such as France or the Soviet Union.[46] Washington did, however, pressure its partners and allies to refrain from exporting arms to Iran. Operation Staunch's effect on Iran's military, built by the shah with U.S. hardware and technology, was particularly deleterious.

The fighting continued to intensify. In 1984 Iran and Iraq engaged in what became known as the "Tanker War," putting at risk Persian Gulf oil traffic. Because a significant portion of Iraq's oil was exported over land, Iranian decision makers made the choice to target tankers heading to and from Iraq's allies, Saudi Arabia and Kuwait in particular. Iran also targeted Saudi Arabia's Ras Tanura, the choke point of Saudi Arabia's petroleum industry, where oil is refined and loaded.[47] As if the Tanker War weren't destabilizing enough, in 1985 the "War of the Cities" erupted, during which each side targeted the other's capital with deadly missiles. It became clear to those in the region that their own citizens and capitals were vulnerable.

Over Memorial Day weekend 1984, as the Tanker War evolved, Reagan secretly shipped to Saudi Arabia four hundred Stinger missiles, which provided for short-range air defense, and an Air Force aerial tanker to extend the distance of Saudi fighters. The Saudis had made an urgent request for the transfer shortly after Iran had targeted Saudi and Kuwaiti ships in the Gulf. As Michael H. Armacost, undersecretary of state for political affairs, explained, the equipment was needed to build an effective layered defense against hostile forces, specifically Iran. "Both items," Armacost argued, "were urgently needed, and we were determined to act immediately."[48] It provided a firm signal to Iran of America's commitment to defend Saudi Arabia's territorial integrity.

Congress was livid. In light of the administration's seemingly underhanded tactics, lawmakers from both parties criticized the administration. Senator Robert W. Kasten Jr., the Republican chairman of the Senate's Subcommittee on Foreign Operations, told the administration it had jeopardized its goodwill in Congress. Democratic Senator Daniel K. Inouye, the panel's ranking Democrat, questioned how effective Stingers would be against Iranian attacks. Others, including the influential Republican senator Warren B. Rudman, raised concerns that the Stingers would fall into terrorists' hands, particularly the PLO.[49]

A few days later Saudi F-15 pilots engaged two Iranian fighter jets inside Saudi airspace. Saudis and their defenders in Washington used the opportunity to show that American weaponry was successfully helping to ensure the territorial integrity of Saudi Arabia, a goal that every administration since Truman had supported. Saudi Arabia used the opportunity to request more weapons: fighter jets, missiles (including Stingers), and bomb racks.[50]

Both Republicans and Democrats determined to stop the sale. The Saudi request sat pending for a year. In September 1985 the White House recognized it would not get Congress' permission to ship sophisticated weapons to Saudi Arabia. Accordingly, the White House dropped the Stinger and F-15 portion of the sale. Even though Iran and Iraq were targeting the other's capitals, Congress was reluctant to send weapons to Saudi Arabia unless more explicit ties were made to the Arab-Israeli peace process and the administration could credibly demonstrate that such weapons would not end up in terrorist hands, either by export to the PLO or as a result of a collapse of the Saudi monarchy. What was perhaps most galling for the Saudis was that Congress was fighting to withhold Stingers from them while at the same time it was urging the White House, through Republican senator Robert J. Dole among others, to deliver Stingers to Angolan and Afghan fighters, groups receiving Saudi financial assistance, and surely as unstable as Saudi Arabia, if not substantially more so.

Eventually the Saudis pulled their request and signed a $4.8 billion deal for Tornado fighters and other weaponry with Great Britain. In a letter to King Fahd, Reagan acknowledged that he understood the Saudi decision.[51] What no one in Washington foresaw was that in addition to publicly turning to the British for a massive weapons infusion, Saudi Arabia began a top-secret effort to buy missiles from China, missiles designed to carry a nuclear warhead. As we shall see, Saudi efforts, when discovered, created a firestorm.

In January 1986, in response to Iranian advancements against Iraq, Saudi Arabia submitted a pared-down $450 million arms request, which was eventually further reduced to $300 million. "I'm going to be leading the fight against this sale," announced Democratic senator Alan M. Cranston. "Saudi Arabia is still bankrolling the PLO and Syria—the protectors of terrorists who have murdered Americans and torn Lebanon asunder."[52] The administration countered that weapons to Saudi Arabia were needed precisely to combat the scourge of terrorism. In May, the assistant secretary of state for Near Eastern and South Asian affairs, Richard W. Murphy, wrote in the *New York Times* that "the current struggle against the state terrorism of Libya makes this sale particularly important . . . blocking Saudi purchases of American arms would hand Col. Muammar el-Qaddafi a victory he does not deserve."[53]

Both the House and Senate voted to stop the sale. As the *Los Angeles Times* reported, many members voted against the sale in the "belief that the Saudis had failed to help U.S. efforts to bring peace to the Middle East."[54] It was the first time that a presidential arms request had been flat-out rejected. Not much was said about events in the Persian Gulf. Reagan threatened to veto the resolution and agreed to drop the controversial request for Stinger missiles to allay congressional concern.

In an effort to override the rejection, the president once again became personally involved, making phone calls and spreading promises. Iranian attacks on Saudi oil tankers during the weeks prior proved that in the Iran-Iraq War, there was no particular sanctity for oil facilities. The president urged senators to consider that Iran was putting enormous pressure on the kingdom to cut back oil production and increase prices. Reagan tried to disarm his critics by arguing that the "Saudis have sometimes joined in Arab criticism of US action out of a sense of Arab unity. I realize all of us disagree with Saudi policies and public statements from time to time. But, we have also disagreed with many of our other allies on other specific issues, such as terrorism."[55] In the Senate, Reagan needed thirty-four votes to override the congressional veto. When the Senate voted on June 5, the vote was 34–66. The president sent the weapons to the Arabian Peninsula, albeit after a bruising fight and as a much diluted package.

The cycle of battles between the U.S. legislature and executive branches continued for the rest of Reagan's tenure. Another one occurred around a 1987 request to sell Saudi Arabia more fighter jets. The Saudi arms requests were usually submitted after an Iranian breakthrough against Iraq, domestic sabotage such as Iranian pilgrims rioting during the hajj, or a direct attack on Saudi Arabia's interests. Congress continued to resist or reduce all entreaties.

Iraq and Iran declared a cease-fire on August 20, 1988. But the bruising arms battles the war had spawned between Riyadh and Washington seemed to have strained the fabric of U.S.-Saudi relations. For the Saudi king and defense minister, the public squabbles led them to question the steadfastness of America's long-standing commitment to the territorial integrity of Saudi Arabia. At the same time, debates about the long-term stability of the House of Saud encouraged others in the region and inside Saudi Arabia to ask similar questions. Even King Fahd's trip to Washington, which he took in early 1985, did not help facilitate Saudi arms requests. All this was on the surface, however—in newspapers, talk shows, and radio programs. What was hidden from most citizens on both sides, and from those inside the government except at the highest level, was a set of top-secret operations in which the United States and Saudi Arabia worked in tandem as never before.

9

"We Support Some, They Support Some"

When Reagan took office in January 1981 he inherited from Carter a number of nascent covert operations. Along with his director of central intelligence, Bill Casey, Reagan aggressively sought to bolster them.

Casey urged the NSC and State Department to explore third-party funding when domestic restrictions threatened ongoing operations. In almost all cases, the Reagan administration turned to Saudi Arabia to help overcome financial shortfalls. Hints were dropped and suggestions made about areas of particular concern. As Ambassador Robert G. Neumann characterized it, Saudi Arabia financed "all sorts of operations all over the world. . . . We support some, they support some . . . we talk about it . . . but it's an individual decision."[1]

After a decade of détente, a policy Saudi Arabia never supported, King Fahd welcomed Reagan's determination to confront Soviet pressure more directly. Riyadh appreciated Reagan's refocus on the "periphery," an area that included Saudi Arabia's backyard. Unlike during earlier periods of American third-world activity, this time Saudi Arabia had something to offer—money. Riyadh began pouring it in, often anticipating Reagan's preferred projects. Saudi resources were particularly attractive in places such as Nicaragua, where Congress was systematically reducing financing for policies near and dear to the president's heart. In Afghanistan, Angola, the horn of Africa, and elsewhere, Saudi Arabia's contributions helped the Reagan administration aid and abet anti-Communist activities on a worldwide scale.

Giving the Soviets Their Vietnam

The Reagan administration viewed Russia's entanglement in Afghanistan with nervous enthusiasm. With nearly a hundred thousand Soviet soldiers occupying the country, Afghanistan offered Washington the opportunity to directly confront Soviet troops. Elsewhere, in places such as in Ethiopia and Angola, the Soviets and Americans confronted each other through proxies. Casey told his deputy director of operations, John N. McMahon, that a policy of harassing the Russians in Afghanistan was not only something Reagan would likely continue, but something he would probably intensify.[2]

King Fahd was receptive to America's determination to increase the pressure on the Soviets in Afghanistan, as was Turki al-Faisal. Bearing a striking resemblance to his father, the late King Faisal, Turki would become the point man for U.S.-Saudi relations in Afghanistan, and the CIA's key liaison in the kingdom. Two decades later, he would become Saudi Arabia's new ambassador to the United States. Turki easily operated in the secretive world of intelligence. Mentored in his youth by Kamal Adham, Turki replaced his uncle as the director of the General Intelligence Department in 1977. The CIA and other American officials identified Turki as perhaps the most reliable individual in the Saudi government. He also developed close ties with Osama bin Laden and other fighters in Afghanistan. His hatred for Communism, in addition to his facility with colloquial English, made him a natural interlocutor with the United States. On Afghanistan, he was "the man to see."[3] Today, in Turki's modest home in Jeddah, below a portrait of his father, stands a plaque memorializing the late King Faisal. It is inscribed in Arabic and recalls the final words of Afghanistan's King Abdul Rahman Khan on his deathbed in 1901:

> My heart remains in Afghanistan, although my soul is moving towards God. My last words to you my son and my successor: Do not trust the Russians, and never have any confidence in them.

Anti-Communist endeavors occupied a considerable portion of Prince Turki's activity, and he received King Fahd's backing to fund efforts to roll back Soviet aggression.

In addition to fighting Communism, the Saudi leadership sought to combat expanding Iranian influence in Afghanistan. Ten to 15 percent of the Afghan population is Shi'a, although local claims put the number somewhat higher. Most are Hazara, a Persian-speaking ethnic group, and many of those have ties with Iran. During the 1970s tens of thousands of Hazara went to Iran as day laborers. Located mostly in the central part of Afghanistan, many Afghan Shi'a were inspired by the Iranian revolution and ultimately received assistance from Tehran. Already aiding Iraq to stop Iran's western expansion, Saudi Arabia supported Afghanistan's most radical Sunni groups to halt Iran's eastern drift. According to Olivier Roy, a French expert on political Islam and Afghanistan, the Saudis linked up in Afghanistan with the Muslim Brotherhood and Pakistan's Jama'at-i-Islami to: promote the more radical Islamist parties among the Afghan fighters (also known as mujahideen), check Iranian influence, and prevent Western cultural influences from spreading among refugees and the mujahideen. Writes Roy, "the first two objectives had the full support of the Pakistani ISI [Inter-Services Intelligence] and the CIA."[4]

The Afghan war would dramatically alter Saudi society by bringing to the surface and encouraging the most ascetic and fundamentalist religious interpretation. Whereas King Faisal had laid the foundations of Saudi Arabia's global religious influence but tried to temper the excesses of Wahhabi purists within society, King Fahd unleashed them for political ends. Occurring against the backdrop of the Iranian revolution, the seizure of the Grand Mosque of Mecca, and Shi'a rioting in Saudi Arabia's Eastern Province, Afghanistan provided Fahd an opportunity to mobilize domestic support along religious grounds—no small task for a king with a well-known appetite for drinking and womanizing. During the 1980s, flyers, pamphlets, and propaganda proliferated, all urging young Saudis to fight the jihad in Afghanistan. Clerics in the mosques and teachers in the schools did the same. By 1986 more than sixteen thousand of the kingdom's one hundred thousand students were pursuing Islamic studies. By the early 1990s one-fourth of all university students were enrolled in religious institutions.[5] The most violent and radical messages were not only tolerated but often encouraged at the highest levels. Saudi Arabia's grand mufti, Sheikh Abdel Aziz bin Baz, and the governor of Riyadh, Prince Salman, a son of King Abdel Aziz, organized the official and charitable funds flowing toward Afghanistan. In the words of one now reformed Saudi ideologue, during the 1980s "society was given an overdose of religion."[6]

Over the course of the decade, Saudi Arabia developed a robust system for recruiting Saudi fighters, one that was left in place after the war ended and contributed to the Saudi militant presence in places such as Bosnia during the 1990s. "I felt as if I had missed Afghanistan because I was too young," remembered one prospective fighter in Riyadh who came of age during the early 1990s. "It made me want to sign up to go to Bosnia. In the end I didn't, but my friend did, and he was killed there."[7]

Three months into his new job, Casey flew to Pakistan and then Saudi Arabia. This trip was repeated annually, according to the CIA division chief at the time, "to ensure that both were still interested [in] and supportive of the Afghan program."[8] Pakistan's president, Zia ul-Haq, who had been aiding the Afghan resistance from the beginning, was eager to continue the fight in Afghanistan. Accordingly, Zia gave Casey his "red triangle briefing"—so named because of a red triangle he laid atop a map of the region. Zia positioned the point of the triangle in Afghanistan and the base across the Persian Gulf. It effectively illustrated Zia's concern that the Soviets intended to drive a wedge between Iran and Pakistan and then push south to secure their historic ambition of a warm-water port. If this was achieved, the Soviets would significantly influence oil transit from the Persian Gulf. After Pakistan, Casey then traveled to Saudi Arabia to solicit funding, a trip he would repeat many times over the next several years.

Congress supported Casey's efforts in Afghanistan. From 1982 to 1983 combined military and economic aid to Pakistan, the main conduit to Afghanistan, increased fourfold, from $101 million to $461 million.[9] Unlike in Nicaragua, where Congress relentlessly restricted aid and reduced the CIA's ability to act, in Afghanistan Congress pushed to expand operations. Determined legislators such as Representatives Charles N. Wilson (D-Tex.) and I. William McCollum Jr. (R-Fla.) and Senators Gordon J. Humphrey (R-N.H.) and Orrin G. Hatch (R-Utah) fought to increase both the program's size and budget. Congressman Wilson urged his Democratic counterparts to support the Afghan cause in order to demonstrate to their constituents back home their real anti-Communist credentials while still opposing the administration's Latin American policies.[10] Early in the 1980s the goal in Afghanistan was to stop rather than roll back Soviet advancement. As Zia ul-Haq said in December 1979, "The water in Afghanistan must boil at the right temperature."[11] Such moderation would change dramatically in 1985 when the United States decided to make an all out attempt to eject Soviet forces from, and thus win in, Afghanistan. In 1985 the Afghan program received over 50 percent of the CIA's entire operations budget.[12]

Early on, however, America wanted to maintain the shill of "plausible deniability." The CIA scoured the globe for Soviet weaponry to supply the mujahideen, those fighting against the Soviet aggression. Soviet weaponry would help hide America's hand. It would also allow the mujahideen to integrate more easily captured Soviet weapons and ammunition.

With its inventories full of aging Soviet equipment, Egypt eagerly joined the U.S.-Saudi-Pakistani joint venture. Very early on, the Saudis and Americans offered Egypt "very generous" terms for supplying Afghan fighters.[13] Providing weaponry and ordinance to Afghanistan provided Cairo hard currency it desperately needed after Saudi Arabia and the other Arabs cut off support in response to the Egyptian-Israeli peace agreement. Afghanistan also offered Egypt the opportunity to work its way back into Saudi Arabia's good graces after being ostracized. In this Cairo was largely successful.

Some forty anti-Soviet guerrilla groups existed inside and around Afghanistan and appeared too fractured to pose any significant threat to Soviet influence. Accordingly, Prince Turki took many trips to Pakistan, the country that maintained the closest relations with the mujahideen, to urge better Afghan organization. According to a U.S. intelligence summary report, Saudi Arabia was particularly skeptical about the prospects of the resistance, having been disappointed in supporting rebels against leftists in Yemen and elsewhere. Saudi officials repeatedly insisted on unity among Islamic parties as a condition for giving or expanding aid.[14]

In 1982 Pakistan, with Saudi urging, successfully organized the Afghan resistance into six parties: three Islamic fundamentalist parties, led by Yunis Khalis, Gulbuddin Hekmatyar, and Burhanuddin Rabbani, and three more-moderate parties, led by Maulvi Mohammed Nabi Mohammadi, Syed Ahmed Gailani, and Sibghatullah Mojadedi. A seventh party, headed by Abdul Rasul Sayyaf, was later formed under pressure from Saudi Arabia. Sayyaf, swashbuckling and unrelentingly doctrinaire, was born in Pahman, Afghanistan, around 1944. He earned a master's degree from al-Azhar University in Cairo and returned to Kabul University, where he became active in the burgeoning Islamic movement. He was one of the two most educated Afghan warlords. After Afghanistan's 1973 coup he was imprisoned, and fled to Pakistan in 1979 upon his release. Around that time he was recruited by Saudi Arabia and founded the Ittehad-i-Islami party, a fundamentalist party devoted to spreading a militant interpretation of Islam. Osama bin Laden joined Sayyaf when bin Laden came to Afghanistan for jihad. Today, Sayyaf's followers fill key posts in the Afghan government, including the influential position of chief justice.

Sayyaf had virtually no indigenous Afghan support, but he, along with the virulently anti-American Gulbuddin Hekmatyar, who in his youth had thrown acid on the faces of unveiled women, received the largest amount of outside Arab funding, in large part because of their radical and religiously puritanical beliefs. During the Afghan war, Hekmatyar received 50 percent of the arms flowing through Pakistan's intelligence services, paid for largely by American and Saudi funds. For both Pakistan and Saudi Arabia, Sayyaf and Hekmatyar were appealing figures, as both were Pashtun, rather than Tajik, a Persian-speaking ethnic group. They were thus believed to be less susceptible to Iranian influence.[15] Sayyaf's organization absorbed most of the non-Afghan Arab fighters.

All seven of the warlords were anti-American to a greater or lesser degree, with Hekmatyar the most strident. After the 2001 war in Afghanistan, the United States tried twice to kill him after it became apparent he was organizing against the United States.

In February 1984 Zia urged Casey to increase U.S. financial assistance. Casey then traveled to Saudi Arabia, where his hosts agreed to raise their contribution from $75 million to $100 million in fiscal year 1985. Upon returning home, Casey and his supporters in Congress were able to increase U.S. support by a similar amount.

The U.S.-Saudi matching program, put in place by Brzezinski in 1979, was still active. For every dollar raised for Afghanistan in the United States, Saudi Arabia agreed to contribute a similar amount.

By late 1984 the United States would increase its support to $250 million. Saudi Arabia matched it.[16] In mid-1986 U.S. assistance again jumped to $600 million. Between 1981 and 1986 U.S. and Saudi bilateral aid grew tenfold, from a combined $120 million to $1.2 billion per year. The money went to weapons and to the ISI for distribution to the foreign fighters in the manner of Pakistan's choosing.

The CIA was happy to receive Saudi funds that required "literally, no oversight." Saudi officials never asked for an accounting of the money once it was deposited. The head of the CIA's Afghan Task Force remembers that we "never got a call from the Saudis asking about where things were going, or what we were doing. There was no attempt to manage the account—unlike Congress, and the Pakistanis."[17] The pernicious effects of such whimsical Saudi accounting practices would explode two decades later in debates around Saudi Arabia's role in terrorist financing.

The CIA used the cash to purchase weapons for Afghan fighters. Each month the CIA also transferred funds to ISI-controlled bank accounts to facilitate logistics and support. In addition to Saudi Arabia's official matching of America's dollar-for-dollar contributions, a second, more amorphous funding stream operated through religious institutions and privately funded charities inside the kingdom. Such funds entered Afghanistan in addition to official funding. As the Pakistani general running the operation later recalled:

> It was largely Arab money that saved the system. By this I mean cash from rich individuals or private organizations in the Arab world, not Saudi government funds . . . it all went to the four Fundamentalist parties. . . . Sayyaf, in particular, had many personal religious or academic contacts in Saudi Arabia, so his coffers were usually kept well filled. This meant the moderates became proportionately less efficient, lack of Arab money being one of the causes of their inability to match the Fundamentalists in operational effectiveness.[18]

The fact that the ISI also preferred these fundamentalist parties further enhanced their status.

Saudi Arabia's grand mufti, Abdel Aziz bin Baz, a blind cleric with considerable domestic support and legitimacy who ran the World Muslim League (the organization created under King Faisal in his quest for "Islamic solidarity"), used that organization to raise money for Afghanistan. In 1981 bin Baz reportedly transferred $25 million to Sayyaf to start a new party in Afghanistan.[19] Prince Salman helped to recruit fighters destined for Sayyaf's group through such institutions, blurring the line between government and nongovernment sponsorship.

According to one of Sayyaf's Afghan associates, "Sayyaf raises millions of dollars from businessmen and charities in Saudi Arabia, Kuwait and the United Arab Emirates."[20] By the end of the war, such aid amounted to between $20 million and $25 million per month. The money helped ensure that Sayyaf's fighters had generators to keep them warm and that they were outfitted in "lavish equipment and camouflage fatigues."[21] It also built the foundation for al-Qaeda.

Over time it became ever harder to distinguish between money earmarked for Sayyaf and money intended for the larger mujahideen effort. For example, in 1984 the BBC reported that "the Saudi ambassador to Pakistan, Tawfiq al-Alamadar . . . delivered a check for $10,000,000 to Prof. Abdorrasul Sayyaf."[22] It was never clear whether this was delivered to Sayyaf in his capacity as a liaison to the wider mujahideen movement or as leader of the Ittehad-i-Islami party. Privately, Afghan intellectuals expressed their worries that Arabs, and especially Saudis, were using their aid to gain religious influence in Afghanistan.[23] Their fears were realized less than a decade later.

The Muslim Brotherhood also raised money for the Afghan fighters. The Brotherhood's efforts were led by a Palestinian Jordanian, Abdullah Azzam, who had close links with both Sayyaf and Hekmatyar. Azzam headed the Maktab al-Khidmat (Services Center), a center established in Peshawar in 1984 to support the Arab recruits heading to Afghanistan. Donations from Saudi intelligence, the Saudi Red Crescent, the World Muslim League, and Saudi princes and mosques were channeled through the Maktab. When Azzam was blown up in 1989, he was replaced in his leadership role by Osama bin Laden.[24]

The nature of Afghan operations changed dramatically in 1985 when on March 11 of that year Mikhail Gorbachev replaced Konstantin Chernenko as general secretary of the Soviet Communist party. The White House was reliably informed that Moscow had decided to try to win the war within the next two years. To underscore his determination, Gorbachev accused Pakistan's President Zia of directly waging war against the Soviet Union and threatened retaliatory action unless Pakistan altered its course almost immediately. Gorbachev also turned command of the Afghan operations over to General Mikhail Zaitzev, the brutal military leader who had ended the "Prague Spring" in Czechoslovakia in 1968.

Soviet Hind helicopter gunships began mowing down Afghan fighters. As one brave Canadian reporter remembers from her time on the ground, the gunships would come so close "you could see the whites of the pilot's eyes."[25] The Soviets also deployed the Spetsnaz, their elite fighting force. Thousands of Soviet elite soldiers poured into Afghanistan. The vehement new commitment of the Soviet Union in 1985 focused Washington's attention. "This was the escalation that scared us," remembered a key CIA operative.[26]

In March 1985 the White House decided on one more push. On March 27 Reagan issued the highly secretive U.S. National Security Decision Directive 166, officially reorienting U.S. policies, programs, and strategies in Afghanistan.[27] The goal was no longer to "harass" the Russians but rather to "make the Russians get out."[28] The CIA was reorganized to give well-regarded operatives such as Milton Bearden and John "Jack" Devine a more prominent role.[29]

The new directive and subsequent efforts profoundly altered the balance of power on the battlefield. No longer concerned with hiding its involvement, Washington began providing weaponry made in the United States. This included the powerful Stinger missile, at the time regarded as America's most sophisticated shoulder-fired missile and one that had never before been used in combat. The Stinger was an awesomely effective weapon, able to neutralize the highly destructive Soviet Hind gunships by forcing them to fly higher and out of range. Still, many warned presciently that once distributed, the Stingers could one day be used against the United States and its allies. Those arguing for its introduction responded, also correctly, that Stingers would alter the course of the war. From 1986 to 1987 the United States provided the mujahideen with around nine hundred Stinger missiles.[30] This was no doubt viewed by the Saudi defense establishment with some irony given that they were providing funds for a ragtag group of fighters to buy sophisticated U.S. weaponry that the U.S. Congress would not allow Saudi Arabia to buy.

Arab support for the mujahideen increased alongside the 1985 U.S.-Soviet escalation. Around that time the CIA became aware of a significant increase in the number of Arab nationals traveling to Afghanistan to fight the holy war against the Soviets. Robert Gates, the deputy director of the CIA at the time, recalls that "they came from Syria, Iraq, Algeria and elsewhere and most fought with the Islamic fundamentalist Muj[ahideen] groups, particularly that headed by Abdul Rasul Sayyaf. We examined ways to increase their participation, perhaps in the form of some sort of 'international brigade,' but nothing came of it."[31]

The escalation against Soviet forces, particularly the introduction of Stinger missiles, convinced the Soviets they could not win in Afghanistan. After taking more casualties, undergoing considerable diplomatic wrangling, and pouring ever more arms and money into Afghanistan, the Soviets signed the Geneva accords on April 14, 1988, to end the war. On February 15, 1989, Lieutenant General Boris Gromov strode north across the bridge spanning the Amu Dar'ya River, the frontier between Afghanistan and the Soviet Union. This terminated Moscow's ill-fated nine-year Afghan military adventure. Between ten thousand and fifteen thousand Soviet soldiers had died —nearly one-quarter the number of Americans who perished in Vietnam. The devastation to Afghanistan was incalculable.

Saudi Arabia had played an important role in raising the costs for Moscow. It bought a considerable portion of the weapons that were eventually poured into Afghanistan and generously supplied Sunni Arab and Pashtun Afghan fighters. For every dollar the United States committed, Saudi Arabia provided another one through official channels. Through unofficial channels such as highly opaque and largely unaccountable charities, Saudi Arabia contributed even more. Afghanistan became the most visible example of close U.S.-Saudi cooperation in the developing world. As we will see, however, it was by no means the only one.

Although the Soviets withdrew their forces at the end of the decade, Saudi Arabia continued to confront security threats in Afghanistan as Iran attempted to influence politics there. Throughout the 1990s, Saudi Arabia and Iran competed for influence in Afghanistan and within the wider field of Central Asia, where the political vacuum created by the collapse of the Soviet Union posed new challenges for each.

The chaos in Afghanistan had profoundly altered Saudi Arabia's international environment and domestic fabric. To recruit fighters for Afghanistan and beat back Iran's growing influence, the ruling family allowed local clerics to saturate society with Wahhabi religious doctrine. The local environment was further radicalized by the return home of Afghan fighters, many of whom wished to continue their fight to impose a literalist and selective interpretation of Islamic law. Such changes at home made it increasingly difficult for the House of Saud to work closely with the United States. According to Professor F. Gregory Gause, III, a keen observer of Saudi Arabia, "the crucible of the development of bin Ladenism was the jihad against the Soviet Union in Afghanistan in the 1980s. Among the Arab volunteers there, the retrograde social views and theological intolerance of Saudi Wahhabism came to blend with the revolutionary political doctrines developed in the 1960s by Muslim Brotherhood thinkers, particularly in Egypt."[32] The means by which both the United States and Saudi Arabia promoted their shared interests in the 1980s would destabilize their relationship in the years ahead. It also set the stage for a violent jihadi movement that today targets both countries and their global partners.

An "Ideological Super Bowl": Aiding Jonas Savimbi in Angola

Saudi Arabia was not only helpful to the administration in Afghanistan, but also active in Africa, drawing on nearly a decade of its own anti-Libyan anti-Communist activities there. Reagan inherited Carter's Angolan policy, which withheld recognition from Angola but attempted low-level reconciliation with the Popular Movement for the Liberation of Angola (MPLA)-led Angolan government. The Reagan administration looked on Communist support for the MPLA with concern, particularly the twenty-one thousand Cuban troops active there. However, because the Clark amendment prohibited U.S. aid and involvement in Angola, the Reagan administration would require third-party funds to counter Soviet and Cuban influence. Saudi Arabia became one of the many countries that proved helpful in this regard.

On March 19, 1981, two months after taking office, the Reagan administration announced that it would seek the repeal of the Clark amendment, which Ford had originally considered a "great tragedy." As far as the Reagan team was concerned, Ford's and Carter's inability to block Soviet advances in Angola had only emboldened Moscow to push into other African countries, such as Ethiopia. When Jonas Savimbi, the leader of UNITA, one of the Angolan rebel groups fighting the MPLA, came to Washington in 1981, he received a much better reception than when he had visited during Carter's time.[33]

But on Angola, the Reagan administration continued to face many critics. UNITA's South African backing deterred many in Congress who believed that associating with the South African apartheid regime, besides being of questionable morality, risked wider American interests in Africa. Even within the Republican party Angola became a controversial issue. According to one leading conservative at the time, Angola and Nicaragua "work[ed] well inside the church of the Republican Party in dealing with heretics . . . they became tests of orthodoxy and validity."[34] One State Department official described the policy fight over Angola as an "ideological Super Bowl" within the Republican party.[35]

In the spring of 1981 Jonas Savimbi met quietly with American officials in Morocco to provide them with information about what was happening in his country.[36] However, because of U.S. funding limitations imposed by the Clark amendment, Savimbi began seeking support from other countries. In particular, he looked to Safari Club members such as Saudi Arabia, Morocco, and Egypt.

In 1981 Savimbi told *Business Week* that UNITA's "biggest aid donors were Morocco and Saudi Arabia" and that Morocco housed "a key training base" for UNITA.[37] To *Le Figaro*, a French daily, Savimbi stated that "some 80% of our officers were trained in Morocco."[38] Savimbi also told the *Washington Post* in August 1984 that he received "as much as $60 million to $70 million a year, from many Arab friends, including Saudi Arabia, Egypt and Morocco." Savimbi was clear that "the Americans are giving us absolutely nothing. But, it is just that American sympathy is a little more active, and they say to friendly countries that support us, carry on, you are doing the right thing."[39] Savimbi's comments suggest that behind the scenes, Washington was at a minimum supporting third-party assistance to Angola.

Given Kissinger's back-channel message to the Saudis in 1976, which asked explicitly for the Saudis to provide $30 million for Angola, there was every reason for the Saudis to believe that through their assistance to Angola, they were furthering not only their own interests, but American ones as well. In December 1984 Casey penned a memo to senior CIA officers noting that, "as in Afghanistan, we need the involvement of other countries which have a stake in checking Communist expansionism in the less developed world." He noted that the Saudis, Moroccans, French, Zaireans, and South Africans were all already involved in Angola.[40]

Savimbi's accounts and Casey's memo correlate with the congressional testimony of an American businessman of Palestinian descent, Sam Joseph Bamieh. In July 1987 the House of Representatives' Subcommittee on Africa convened a hearing on the CIA's "possible violation or circumvention of the Clark Amendment." Bamieh testified that

Ali bin Musallam, a close confidant of King Fahd, had discussed with him a $50 million grant that was to be used for training UNITA troops in Morocco.[41] In his testimony, Bamieh also claimed that Musallam met with CIA director William Casey in New York in the fall of 1983 about the Angolan operation. Although the subcommittee was never able to marshal enough proof to implicate the CIA, Bamieh's testimony seemed to confirm what many had been seeing for some time: UNITA was receiving training and significant financial support that had Moroccan and Saudi Arabian fingerprints all over it. One American intelligence agent confirmed to the *New York Times* that Casey and Musallam had "dealings on a number of covert projects in Africa," although he did not explicitly mention Angola.[42]

As in Afghanistan, 1985 proved a turning point in Soviet activity in Angola. By the mid-1980s, the Soviets had cranked up their operations in Angola, with thirty thousand Cuban soldiers and at least twelve hundred Soviet advisors stationed there in support of the MPLA. Republicans in Congress began building pressure to repeal the Clark amendment. Representative Bill McCollum and Senator Orrin Hatch, the same congressmen urging increased support to the Afghan fighters, sent a letter to the president urging him to dispense "substantial amounts" of excess Defense Department supplies to Savimbi's forces. Congress rolled back the Clark amendment in August 1985. While it never went to a vote, its legal predecessor, which ensured the repeal, passed the Senate in a vote of 63 to 34.[43] Between 1986 and 1991 the United States provided Angola with $250 million in covert aid, making it the second-largest U.S. covert program, exceeded only by aid to the Afghan mujahideen.[44]

In January 1986, five months after the Clark amendment's repeal, Savimbi flew to Washington to solicit U.S. support. He was given the royal treatment, meeting with senior members of Reagan's cabinet, including Weinberger and Secretary of State George P. Shultz, and briefly with the president. The day after Savimbi's meetings, Reagan formally notified Congress of his intentions to provide $10 million to $15 million in covert aid to Angolan rebels.

Two months later, Congress began pushing the White House to approve Stinger missiles to Angola. Senator Bob Dole met with Shultz, and key U.S. senators to push the sale. At four different points in the conversation a reluctant Shultz asked, "Are you sure you want me to go back to Bill Casey and tell him you want Stingers?" All this happened in the same month that Congress rejected the provision of Stingers to Saudi Arabia.

Fighting between MPLA and UNITA continued until Savimbi was assassinated in 2002, but the international community, including the

United States and Saudi Arabia, largely lost interest in the country when the Cold War ended.

The Horn of Africa

As noted above, many in the Reagan administration saw the Communist advance in Ethiopia and its neighbors in the late 1970s and early 1980s as a direct result of the 1976 Clark amendment. In an effort to stem the tide, the Reagan team funneled small amounts of nonlethal aid toward the opposition to Ethiopia's leader, Mengistu Haile Mariam. However, the most meaningful covert assistance, albeit in limited amounts, came from Saudi Arabia.[45] Ethiopia provided another example of converging U.S.-Saudi Cold War interests.

Although other Arab states such as Morocco, Iraq, and the United Arab Emirates were also supporting anti-Mengistu insurgents, the Ethiopian government was primarily concerned with Saudi activity. Ethiopian officials characterized Saudi involvement in their domestic affairs as "more dangerous and complex than the attack directed against Nicaragua."[46]

In 1982 the White House rolled out its Horn of Africa policy in National Security Decision Directive 57. The area was designated "important" to the United States "because of its strategic location with respect to the Persian Gulf/Southwest Asia region." The report identified Sudan as "key" to holding back Libya and challenging the Marxist government in Ethiopia. Saudi and American leaders were concerned about Qadhafi's interests in the Mengistu regime in Ethiopia in particular, and his grand designs on the African continent more generally. A secret State Department document prepared by a U.S. ambassador to Saudi Arabia concluded that "Khartoum's chronic inability to maintain internal order or to resist Libyan blandishments (or even, as on several occasions during the Libyan war with Chad, to prevent the free passage of Libyan forces across Sudanese territory) has disturbed the Saudis."[47] Thus, as far as Sudan and Ethiopia were concerned, the 1982 security directive advised working in consultation with key friendly states, specifically Egypt and Saudi Arabia.[48]

Here too, Saudi Arabia provided meaningful foreign assistance.[49] The Saudi government contributed up to $500 million a year in aid to Sudan throughout the 1970s and 1980s.[50] Sudanese expatriate workers continued their employment in Saudi Arabia, sending home almost $400 million annually.

In 1982 U.S. economic and military assistance to Sudan nearly doubled, from $141 to $253 million. From 1982 to 1985 American aid and arms flowed into Sudan. By 1985 U.S. assistance to Sudan had reached $350 million. Throughout the 1980s that country was the largest African recipient of overt U.S. assistance.[51]

But Saudi Arabia, not the United States, was central to Sudan's economic survival. Saudi Arabia sent cash and oil to prop up Sudan's wobbling economy. During the 1980s Saudi investors channeled billions of dollars into Sudan's agricultural sector in an effort to create a regional "breadbasket." Nonetheless, by 1985 Sudan's international debt hovered around $9 billion. That year the International Monetary Fund declared Sudan bankrupt. President Nimeiry was replaced by a caretaker government that maintained a less pro-Western, more Islamist caste. Both the United States and Saudi Arabia remained engaged, although support weakened. By 1988 U.S. aid had dropped to $65 million per year, similar to Ethiopia's allocation.[52]

Yemen

Washington and Riyadh also shared concerns about growing Soviet activity in South Yemen. During a 1986 interagency meeting Reagan officials concluded that in Yemen

> our best bet, in a long term PD [public diplomacy] strategy, is to make Communism the issue . . . we should stress the diametrical opposition of Communist and Islamic values, making this the leitmotif of our propaganda throughout the region. Such an approach should strike a resonant chord in the strongly anti-Communist Arabian peninsula as well as appeal to pious Moslems generally who should be reminded of the USSR's militant atheism.[53]

About that same time, King Fahd sent Reagan a letter, inquiring how the two countries could work together in Yemen.

As early as the beginning of the 1960s the Soviets had shown an interest in the area, most specifically during the proxy war between Egypt and Saudi Arabia in North Yemen. Although Cairo ultimately withdrew its forces as a result of the 1967 Khartoum summit, a new opportunity presented itself on the Arabian Peninsula in November 1967 when the United Kingdom withdrew its forces from South Yemen. Quickly the Soviet Union sought to replace British influence, much as Saudi Arabia had feared would happen. Three years later South Yemen renamed itself the People's Democratic Republic of Yemen (PDRY), indicating a pro-Soviet tilt.

Throughout the 1970s, the Soviet Union supported PDRY. The Soviet outpost became particularly important after 1978, when Moscow lost a valued base in Somalia, something Saudi Arabia helped facilitate in the hopes of reducing Soviet influence in the area. Shortly thereafter, Soviet ships began refueling and undergoing repairs in the PDRY capital, Aden, and Socotra Island (in the Gulf of Aden) became a major Soviet anchorage point for its operations in the Indian Ocean, the Red Sea, and the Horn of Africa.

In October 1979, much to the chagrin of the Saudi leadership, the PDRY signed a twenty-year treaty of friendship and cooperation with the USSR. The PDRY subsequently signed similar protocols with East Germany, Ethiopia, and Bulgaria. In 1981 it concluded a tripartite agreement with Saudi Arabia's nemeses Libya and Ethiopia. Reagan's National Security Council concluded that "these arrangements bind the PDRY as closely to the Communist bloc as it is possible to be bound without actually being a member of the Warsaw pact."[54] According to Caspar Weinberger, who traveled to the kingdom in early 1982 and met with King Fahd, "Saudi Arabia saw [a] Soviet backed effort to encircle [the] Kingdom and disrupt entire region" because of relentless Soviet activity in PDRY, Ethiopia, and Afghanistan.[55]

Soviet-PDRY ties grew ever stronger. By 1986, around the time of the interagency meeting discussed above, PDRY debts to the Soviet Union were nearly 80 percent of GNP. In the words of one Soviet foreign ministry official, USSR-PDRY relations were "not merely multifaceted . . . they are characterized by their completeness, by their totality. Do you understand what I mean? They are all-embracing."[56]

The Saudis looked toward Washington for support, much as they had done during the Yemen crisis during the Kennedy administration. As did its Democratic predecessor, the Reagan administration sought to assist Riyadh. In October George Shultz dispatched a message to Walter L. Cutler, then the U.S. ambassador to Saudi Arabia, outlining Washington's policy. He wrote:

> The USG believes that Saudi Arabia and North Yemen [YAR] are best positioned to play a direct and immediate role. Should action be taken, the US will support Saudi Arabia politically and will support the territorial integrity of the Kingdom including the provision of assistance; we would help with arms re-supply if necessary and would also be prepared to allow Saudi transfer of US origin equipment to the YAR if the SAG believes such a step useful . . . we are providing as detailed as possible an intelligence briefing to the YARG (at their request) but are not coordinating any action with the YARG . . . You may inform the Saudis that we want to stay in close touch and examine in detail any opportunities which may be presented.[57]

Yemen was yet one more place where the United States and Saudi Arabia worked to beat back the Soviet tide.

Aiding the Nicaraguan Contras "Body and Soul"

As we have seen, Saudi Arabia's financial clout extended far beyond its immediate neighborhood, to areas as distant as Afghanistan and Zaire. By the mid-1980s, its influence was further extended to include Central America. The White House sought out Saudi assistance to deny Soviet penetration in a region considered within America's sphere of influence since the Monroe doctrine of 1823.

In 1979 Marxist Sandinista guerrillas came to power in Nicaragua during a short-lived civil war. Throughout much of the 1980s the United States sponsored anti-Sandinista guerrillas, known as "contras." Nicaragua became a clear test for the president's commitment to side with those "struggling to prevent their incorporation into the Soviet empire or to regain their freedom." Jeanne Kirkpatrick characterized the Reagan administration's support for the contras as "the most dramatic single example of the implementation of this key aspect of [the] Reagan doctrine."[58]

Many in Congress were skeptical about American tactics and the contras' abilities. In 1982 the chairman of the House Intelligence Committee, Representative Edward P. Boland, submitted an amendment forbidding the Department of Defense or CIA to provide military equipment, training, or advice "for the purpose of overthrowing the Nicaraguan regime." It passed the House on December 8 by a vote of 411 to 0.[59] In May 1983 the House Intelligence Committee went even further and voted to cut off all U.S. aid to the contras. The Senate did not support such drastic action but eventually capped aid to the contras at $24 million, considerably less than what the administration had hoped for.

To compensate for the quickly depleting financial support and the Boland amendment's restrictions, Reagan asked the NSC as early as January 1984 to raise between $10 million and $15 million in private donations and foreign funding.[60] President Reagan gave his national security advisor, Bud McFarlane, responsibility for keeping the contras alive "body and soul." In March 1984, CIA director Casey hand-carried a memo to McFarlane urging him to contact Israel and other countries to help raise weapons, equipment, and financial aid for the contras in Nicaragua. High-level Reagan officials quickly explored the kingdom's receptivity.[61] In May McFarlane visited Prince Bandar in his home and explained Reagan's determination to ensure a constant stream of funding to the contras. According to McFarlane, "It became pretty obvious to the Ambassador that his country, to gain a considerable amount of favor and, frankly, they thought it was the right thing to do, they would provide the support when the Congress cut it off."[62] Israel had refused a similar request the month prior, although in time it too would play a covert role. A few days later Bandar got back to McFarlane, announcing that his country would provide $1 million a month to the contras. Oliver L. North, McFarlane's deputy director of political-military affairs, then established a bank account number where a donation could be made, and McFarlane gave the number to Prince Bandar.

During the summer of 1984 Saudi Arabia began depositing money into the bank account of contra leader Adolfo Calero in order that he could purchase necessary arms.[63] "As in Afghanistan," wrote Casey, "we need the involvement of other countries which have a stake in checking Communist expansionism in the less developed world."[64] Although Casey and McFarlane strongly believed in pursuing third-party funding, others were concerned that it violated American law. Chief of staff James A. Baker III suspected that such activity could constitute an "impeachable offense." The White House brought the matter to the attorney general, who determined that such third-party funding was legal under very specific criteria.

In October 1984 Congress passed a third, much stricter Boland amendment in response to the CIA's mining of the Nicaraguan harbor in the spring of 1983. The mining incensed even long-term CIA backers. Senator Barry M. Goldwater, an influential but now "pissed off" CIA supporter, did not go to bat for the agency inside the Senate's Intelligence Committee, which he chaired. With the loss of Goldwater's support, Reagan's Nicaragua team was in further financial trouble. As Bob Gates, a senior CIA official, recalls, "The slender thread that sustained the Contra program in Congress had snapped."[65] The 1984 Boland amendment cut off all funding for military and paramilitary operations in Nicaragua and prohibited solicitation from other countries.[66]

According to the Walsh report, the independent counsel investigation that evaluated the criminality of America's Nicaragua policy, "Third-country funding, particularly from the Saudis, was by far the biggest source [to the contras], amounting to $32 million."[67] The other controversial source of money came from an unsuccessful arms-for-hostage swap between the United States and Iran, which became known as the Iran-contra scandal. The scandal, which prompted the Walsh report, came to represent the worst excesses of Reagan's anti-Communist policies.

Saudi Arabia's contribution was small change for Riyadh but meaningful to the contras and about half of what the United States was already contributing.[68] Although further afield than usual, Saudi Arabia's decision to fund the contras made strategic sense. It served the twin purposes of pleasing Washington and furthering Riyadh's own interests in combating worldwide Communism. Saudi money secretly helped to salvage the NSC's floundering Nicaraguan policy. When its role was uncovered, it provided even more fodder for those skeptical about the U.S.-Saudi relationship.

The Costs

Such foreign operations came with a price tag. Throughout the early 1980s the Saudi government could rely on its vast oil fortune to meet international obligations, fuel its massive modernization program, and co-opt domestic critics. But such comforts came to a crashing halt in the mid-1980s. Between 1980 and 1985 the price of oil fell from $37.96 to $27.99 a barrel as a result of greater energy conservation, increasing production by non-OPEC exporters, and quota cheating by OPEC members. In 1986 West Texas Intermediate, the benchmark for what U.S. consumers paid for oil, collapsed to $15.04 per barrel.

Inside the kingdom, oil minister Yamani drastically reduced production to shore up prices. Attempting to stabilize prices, Saudi Arabia decreased oil output from 10–11 mbd to 2 mbd, and still prices fell as other OPEC members continued to produce above their assigned quotas. This decrease in production combined with lower prices drastically reduced Saudi Arabia's oil export revenue. Yamani and others sent signals to other OPEC members that the kingdom would not continue to prop up even the very low price by continuing to restrict Saudi production unless more restraint was demonstrated. Until that point, Saudi Arabia had been playing the role of swing producer, decreasing production when prices fell too low and increasing it if they went too high. But by the mid-1980s that role was causing the kingdom to lose market share to its competitors, whose quota-busting production further dampened prices.

Seemingly overnight, the dazzlingly rich Saudi Arabia confronted budgetary problems and outstanding debts. Saudi planners had to devise ways to service the colossal modernization program they had created. The sheer maintenance of the kingdom's infrastructure had become much more expensive to run than most had anticipated. Training and paying for personnel capable of managing the runaway monster was an equally serious problem.

Huge defense deals with the United States, products of the 1974 Joint Security Commission and massive oil profits, required constant injections of suddenly scarce cash. For nearly a decade Saudi Arabia's

Ministry of Defense had undertaken long-term deals and delayed payments while also skimming a considerable amount of cash. By the mid-1980s, with low oil prices, such arrangements were putting excessive pressure on Saudi Arabia's finances.

In an effort to defend market share, if not price, Saudi Arabia followed through on its threat to increase its production and engaged in a complicated scheme of "netback" arrangements, involving Saudi Arabia's flooding the oil market with its own product and increasing its volume sold, thereby slightly raising its revenue while hurting the bottom line of other oil producers. Saudi Arabia was teaching OPEC nations a lesson: comply with OPEC regulations or else everybody loses. Prices, as expected, collapsed.

One American who was working on contract for the Saudi Arabian Monetary Agency recalls that as early as 1981 it was clear that the price of oil would start to go down, which in turn would put pressure on existing contracts.[69] The U.S. ambassador to Saudi Arabia, Walter Cutler, later recalled feeling like a "bill collector." Every time he met with the king or another high-ranking Saudi official, he raised problems of broken financial agreements and unfulfilled financial obligations.

Amid the uncertainty around prices, King Fahd shocked the oil world by suddenly firing Sheikh Yamani, the man who had directed Saudi oil policy for the past twenty-four years, was credited with engineering the 1973 oil embargo, and had graced the covers of international magazines for almost a decade. According to Wanda Jablonski, the well-respected reporter for *Petroleum Intelligence Weekly* who maintained close ties to Yamani, the minister was dismissed because he refused to carry out a two-pronged proposal to raise both production and prices (something that Yamani considered "economically suicidal") and a request to authorize a set of oil-based barter deals.[70] Two decades later Yamani confirmed that the *Petroleum Intelligence Weekly* account of his showdown with King Fahd was complete and accurate.[71] Other close observers at the time speculated that Fahd used the oil price collapse as an excuse to remove Yamani. The king had never quite trusted the long-serving oil minister, viewing him as more loyal to his ex-boss, the late King Faisal, than to the current monarchy.

The oil price collapse took the luster off day-to-day U.S.-Saudi relations. The Saudis were struggling to meet their financial obligations, and U.S. representatives now assumed the uncomfortable role of calling in debts. Still, at the highest political levels, geopolitical realities kept the two countries in each other's good standing. Overlapping interests allowed the relationship to weather low oil prices as well as one of the last major crises of the Reagan administration: the discovery of

West Texas Intermediate
(USD/bbl)

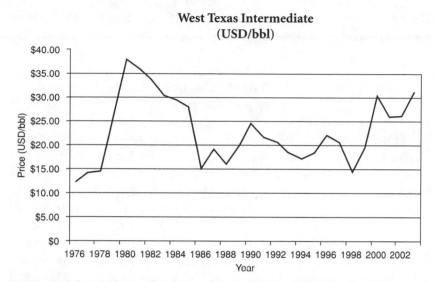

Source: British Petroleum, *BP Statistical Review of World Energy, June 2005.* Data available at http://www.bp.com/liveassets/bp_internet/globalbp/globalbp_uk_english/publications/energy_reviews_2005/STAGING/local_assets/downloads/pdf/statistical_review_of_world_energy_full_report_2005.pdf. 1976–1983 Posted WTI Prices; 1984–2003 Spot WTI (Cushing) Prices.

OPEC Net Oil Export Revenues, 1972–2006

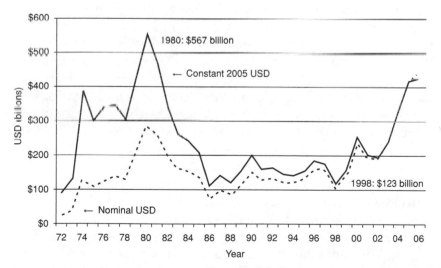

Source: Energy Information Administration, "OPEC Revenues Fact Sheet," Country Analysis Briefs. Available at http://www.eia.doe.gov/emeu/cabs/opecrev.html

Chinese missiles designed to carry nuclear warheads in the deserts of Saudi Arabia.

"You Have Put Saudi Arabia Squarely in the Targeting Package of the Israelis"

In March 1988 the *Washington Post* broke the story that Saudi Arabia had secretly purchased CSS-2 (East Wind) intermediate-range surface-to-surface ballistic missiles from China.[72] The news stunned Washington's defense and policy community. Capable of carrying nuclear warheads, the CSS-2s maintained a range of between 1,550 and 1,950 nautical miles, making them capable of striking all of Saudi Arabia's neighbors, including Israel. Saudi officials claimed that the kingdom intended to equip them with conventional (non-nuclear) warheads. King Fahd eventually sent a letter to Reagan assuring him of this. But knowledgeable observers were skeptical. The CSS-2s had never carried anything other than a nuclear warhead. The missile's inherent inaccuracy meant that it was only useful if extensive damage, not precision, was the goal of an attack.

As the story unfolded, it became clear that Saudi Arabia had been in negotiations with China since 1985, during the same time that the Saudis turned to Britain for Tornado fighter jets after Congress denied an American sale. In July 1985 Prince Bandar traveled to China, ostensibly to end that country's weapons exports to Iran, something the United States supported. Bandar suggested to the Chinese suppliers that their weapons should instead be delivered to Iraq instead of Iran. Saudi Arabia would compensate China. Because the Persian Gulf had become treacherous waters in light of Iranian targeting of transiting oil tankers, Riyadh also offered a land route across Saudi territory to facilitate trade between China and Iraq. China agreed to the $1 billion arrangement.

What Washington did not know was that buried in the Saudi-purchased weapons en route to Iraq were somewhere between thirty-five and sixty CSS-2 intermediate-range ballistic missiles and nine launchers. When they were unloaded, the CSS-2s were diverted southward into Saudi Arabia's Rub al-Khali ("the empty quarter"). American intelligence only discovered Saudi Arabia's covert operation two and a half years later when U.S. satellites picked up questionable vehicle activity heading south, rather than north into Iraq as expected.[73]

Senior Saudi officials explained the decision as a response to the escalating Iran-Iraq War and Saudi vulnerability to the missiles exchanged between the two. In addition, Saudi representatives pointed to the fact that Congress had scuttled a 1985 Saudi purchase of jet fighters and short-range missiles. Adel al-Jubeir, a representative to then Crown Prince Abdullah based in Washington, explained that "Saudi Arabia wanted a short range missile, but the United States would not sell it." The CSS-2s were the next best thing.[74]

Washington responded with an unexpected ferocity. Middle East matters were usually left to the handful of bureaucrats closely following local trends. Saudi officials may have thus expected a stern but low-level response.[75] But the consequences of nuclear proliferation went far beyond the Middle East. Suddenly the entire Washington community tracking nuclear proliferation focused its attention on Saudi Arabia. The State Department lodged complaints through traditional challenges. Men such as Richard L. Armitage, then assistant secretary of defense for international security affairs, chastised Bandar: "I want to congratulate you," Armitage said sarcastically. "This is the law of unintended consequences. You have put Saudi Arabia squarely in the targeting package of the Israelis. You are now number one on the Israeli hit parade. If the balloon goes up anywhere in the Middle East, you're going to get hit first.[76]

Washington demanded transparency. Until this day, Saudi Arabia has refused to allow American inspections and implied that the request was unseemly—Riyadh would never allow China to inspect Saudi's AWACS facilities.

The revelation reverberated throughout the Middle East and Asia. The United States was stunned that Saudi Arabia would import weapons designed to carry nuclear weapons. Indian planners argued that the acquisition showed the need for it to continue pushing its indigenous capability. Taiwan, a country with close ties to Saudi Arabia, was shocked that Riyadh would work so closely with Taipei's enemy. Israel interpreted it as a direct threat and, like Taiwan, was frustrated that China, a country with which Israel had good technical relations, would arm its enemy. Israel began undertaking low bombing runs simulating a strike on Saudi Arabia's missile facility. Saudi Arabia urged the White House to intervene and prevent Israel from undertaking a preemptive attack.

The CSS-2 acquisition violated at least three unwritten rules in the U.S.-Saudi relationship. First, Saudi Arabia had not informed the United States of its purchase. Until that point, Washington had always been apprised of Saudi Arabia's non-U.S. weapons imports prior to purchase. Reagan, for example, had given his blessing for the massive Saudi purchase of British Tornados. Second, Saudi Arabia seemed to now be dabbling in nuclear proliferation. Third, for the first time in its history, Saudi Arabia appeared willing to seriously engage a

Communist state. The United States had for over a decade pursued a nuanced policy toward Communist China, but Saudi Arabia had been even more circumspect. Riyadh now seemed prepared to rely on a Communist country for its ultimate defense.

The crisis illuminated Saudi Arabia's limited options. Confronted by a U.S. Congress unwilling to sell requested arms during the on-going Iraq-Iran War while the Soviets exerted pressure through its neighbors, Saudi leaders had turned first to Britain, with American approval, and then to China, without it. It did not turn to the Soviet Union, a more obvious source for weapons. The crisis also highlighted the costs of the constant struggle between the executive and legislative branches of the American government. Different threat perspectives and views on the stability of the Saudi leadership drove the kingdom to explore other options for promoting its defense. In this, however, they were unsuccessful. The CSS-2s antagonized Saudi Arabia's neighbors and undermined the confidence that the United States had in the kingdom. Both probably cost Saudi Arabia's reputation more than any tangential security benefits brought by the CSS-2s themselves. Almost immediately, in an effort to convince Washington of its continued trustworthiness, Saudi Arabia joined the Nuclear Nonproliferation Treaty signatories. Still, the message was clear. The Saudi leadership was beginning to question America's willingness and ability to come to its defense in times of need.

Within months the Reagan administration was out of power, and the CSS-2s became something for the incoming Bush administration to manage. The matter receded in importance as Washington grappled with the collapse of the Soviet Union and Iraq's invasion of Kuwait in 1990. Still, even today, when considering the likelihood of Saudi Arabia one day purchasing nuclear weapons, experts recall the Reagan-era precedent and Saudi Arabia's ability to proceed in a secretive manner at odds with American interests.

Ultimately the CSS-2 crisis had little lasting impact on U.S.-Saudi relations. With Afghanistan dominating the news and the Soviets clearly struggling, the 1980s ended on a high note in U.S.-Saudi relations, at least at the most senior official levels. In the words of United Press International's chief political correspondent, Martin Sieff, Reagan's eight-year tenure "was the golden age of the special relationship."[77] But with the CSS-2 purchase, cracks were beginning to show.

10

The Cold War Ends with a Bang

On August 3, 1990, Prince Bandar bin Sultan, Saudi Arabia's ambassador to the United States, arrived at the White House. There he met with the U.S. secretary of defense, Richard B. Cheney, and the chairman of the Joint Chiefs of Staff, Colin L. Powell, who were preparing to show him America's top-secret war plans to defend Saudi Arabia against a possible Iraqi invasion. The importance of this meeting was lost on no one. Saudi Arabia was in serious trouble, and America was lining up squarely behind it. The attack put at risk Saudi Arabia's vast oil resources and the stability of the entire region. "How many [men] are you talking about?" Bandar wanted to know. Powell calculated that it would be between one hundred thousand and two hundred thousand. Within six months, more than half a million American men and women would arrive in the kingdom and its Persian Gulf neighbors. Upon hearing Powell's estimation, Bandar let his breath out audibly.[1]

American war planners had been preparing for the massive defense of Saudi Arabia ever since President Carter defined the Persian Gulf as a vital American interest during his 1980 presidential address. The Reagan administration had adopted Carter's designation and ardently committed to building a credible defense. Initially, American war plans had focused on reversing Soviet aggression. But by 1989 U.S. military planners, led by General H. Norman Schwarzkopf Jr., began considering the possibility that local actors, particularly Saddam Hussein's Iraq, could threaten Saudi Arabia and destabilize the region.[2] In the summer of 1990, U.S. plans and preparations were put to the test.

A year and a half earlier, the incoming George H. W. Bush administration had ranked Middle East a third-order priority. The collapse of the Soviet empire, the dissolution of the Warsaw Pact, and the re-unification of Germany grabbed headlines and Washington's attention. The Middle East hardly registered. Developments in Central America and a massacre at Tiananmen Square in China crowded out remaining issues. To the extent that the administration did get involved in Middle East politics, it did so by withholding loan guarantees from Israel to protest settlement construction in the West Bank and Gaza Strip. "From day one" of assuming office, Bush's secretary of state, James Baker, recalls, "the last thing I wanted to do was touch the Middle East peace process. . . . I frankly saw the Arab-Israeli dispute as a pitfall to be avoided rather than an opportunity to be exploited."[3] But as prior administration officials could have predicted, the Middle East soon absorbed high-level attention.

Middle Easterners barely had time to absorb the new post-Cold War reality when the region was rocked by Iraq's invasion of Kuwait. On August 2, 1990, seven hundred tanks and a hundred thousand troops rolled across the Iraq-Kuwait border. Rather than hewing closely to its OPEC quota, Kuwait had been actively producing oil well beyond its allotment, not withstanding the disastrous price collapse in 1986. Iraq's economy was particularly vulnerable, staggering as it was from the costly Iran-Iraq War. The Iraqi leadership, which maintained historical irredentist claims against Kuwait, viewed such deliberate overpumping as an act of war. Having just concluded a devastating eight-year war with Iran, cash-strapped Baghdad required higher oil prices. With the invasion of Kuwait, Iraq sat in control of 19 percent of the world's oil. Treasury secretary Nicholas F. Brady estimated that Iraq would benefit from an extra $20 million per day as a result of the Kuwaiti conquest.[4]

Few anticipated the violence. Until early 1990, "none of us considered policy toward Iraq to be an urgent priority," remembered Baker. "It was simply not prominent on my radar screen, or the President's."[5] Saudi Arabia's King Fahd, Egypt's President Mubarak, and Jordan's King Hussein all considered Iraq's threats against Kuwait to be mere muscle flexing. Iraq's military activity on the Kuwaiti border appeared to them a clumsy attempt to compel Kuwait's leadership to rein in its oil production. Most in the region believed that Saddam Hussein could be bought off and the crisis averted until Iraq faced its next cash crunch.[6] The Arab assessment of Iraq's intentions coincided with Russian and Israeli ones. All were wrong.

In the days immediately after the invasion, Saudis and Americans nervously sized each other up. President Bush recalled that the period between the third and fifth of August were "the most hectic 48 hours since I have been President."[7] Washington weighed heavily the possibility that Saudi Arabia would capitulate and pursue its traditional foreign policy of buying off adversaries. President Bush worried that Saudi Arabia would "bug out."[8] Both Prince Bandar and King Fahd were themselves concerned that America would prove unreliable. Memories of Reagan's 1984 withdrawal under fire from Lebanon and Carter's 1979 deployment to Saudi Arabia of an unarmed F-15 squadron provided little confidence in America's steadiness.[9] For Riyadh, the prospect of the United States stirring up local opposition and then cutting and running was a disturbing possibility.

In the first interagency meeting after the invasion, national security advisor Brent Scowcroft confronted many who seemed convinced that America could do little to reverse the attack. Richard N. Haass, the president's special assistant and senior director for Near East and South Asian affairs at the National Security Council, remembered that it was a "discouraging meeting. We were unfocused in our response. People were all over the place."[10] Notions of embargoing Iraqi oil were floated, although ultimately dismissed as ineffective. Very quickly, however, a consensus emerged that at minimum Iraq had to be deterred from moving into Saudi Arabia. Iraq's seasoned military boasted more men under arms than Saudi Arabia had men of fighting age. Whether Iraq would be compelled to withdraw from Kuwait, however, remained an open question for the next three days. The United States had a strategic interest in defending Persian Gulf oil, although some within the administration believed it would make no difference whether Iraq or Kuwait pumped Kuwait's oil. Layered on top of this, however, was a very real concern about the future of the post-Cold War order. Deputy secretary of state Lawrence S. Eagleburger argued that "this is the first test of the postwar system . . . as the bipolar world is relaxed, it permits this [kind of assault] . . . [if Saddam] succeeds, others may try the same thing."[11]

Ultimately, American satellite imagery that showed Iraqi troops fortifying their lines, sending reconnaissance teams across the Saudi border, and aggressively arraying its troops, in addition to savage Iraqi behavior during the initial stages of the occupation, compelled Saudi Arabian and American decision makers to stand firmly together.[12] An attack on the kingdom appeared very real, if not imminent.[13] Khaled bin Sultan, the soon-to-be-commissioned joint forces commander and son of Saudi Arabia's defense and aviation minister, Prince Sultan, remembered:

> If Saddam were allowed to get away with the seizure of Kuwait, the independence of Saudi Arabia, and indeed the whole Arab Gulf, would be threatened. The combination of Iraq and Kuwait together would be so powerful as to dominate the Gulf and indeed the whole Middle East system. Once he had digested Kuwait, Saddam would

become the undisputed master of the area—and Saudi Arabia would face pressure to bend to his will.

From this perspective, whether or not Saddam attacked the Kingdom was in a sense irrelevant. On all important matters—particularly oil policy and foreign affairs—he would be in a position to dictate terms.[14]

President Bush shared this assessment. In an August 5 news conference in Washington he publicly ended the debate about whether to compel Iraq to leave Kuwait or simply deter Iraqi forces from attacking Saudi Arabia: "This will not stand. This will not stand, this aggression against Kuwait."[15] Colin Powell, the chairman of the Joint Chiefs of Staff, anticipated that ejecting Saddam from Kuwait would be exceedingly hard and warned, "This would be the NFL, not a scrimmage."[16]

On August 3, two days before the president's public announcement, Scowcroft instructed the secretary of defense, Dick Cheney, to show Prince Bandar America's top-secret intelligence on Iraqi movements and allow him a look at potential U.S. war plans. Two days later Cheney, deputy national security advisor Robert Gates, General Norman Schwarzkopf, undersecretary of defense for policy Paul Wolfowitz, and American ambassador to Saudi Arabia Charles "Chas." W. Freeman were dispatched to Riyadh to brief the king.

Several hours after they landed in Riyadh, the Americans joined the king and a small battery of senior Saudi princes. Cheney began the session by reminding the king that the United States had on several occasions defended the territorial integrity of Saudi Arabia, harking back to the 1962 deployment of aircraft during the Saudi Egyptian proxy war in Yemen. The defense secretary made clear that the situation for Saudi Arabia was grave and that a serious and determined response was appropriate. He proposed a two-pronged strategy—defense of Saudi Arabia and strangulation of Iraq.[17] He then turned the session over to Schwarzkopf. Bent on one knee in front of the king, Schwarzkopf methodically presented the war plans to King Fahd and Crown Prince Abdullah, the foreign minister, Prince Saud, the deputy defense minister, Prince Abdel Rahman, and the chief of staff, General Hamad. The plan included approximately 250,000 members of the American armed services to be located on Saudi territory, although the exact figure was neither asked for nor provided. According to Robert Gates, the king was "appropriately impressed."[18] However, just as the king was about to permit the deployment of American servicemen and women to Saudi territory, an animated conversation broke out in Arabic. Prince Bandar, interpreting for both sides, fell silent and did not translate the internal Saudi discussion. However, Ambassador Freeman understood what was being said.

The more risk-averse Crown Prince Abdullah wanted more time to consider Saudi Arabia's appropriate response. He urged the king to consult with other influential Saudi players before making such a monumental decision. Abdullah was concerned that king Fahd had not built the internal consensus among key tribal leaders and religious leaders that would be necessary to sustain such a controversial decision. All previous leaders had required ulema support for such monumental undertakings, and there was no reason to believe the current situation presented any fundamental difference. Abdullah's concerns were subsequently borne out in later years when the presence of American troops in the kingdom became a lightning rod for Osama bin Laden, al-Qaeda, and other disgruntled Muslims to lash out against the royal family.

King Fahd's decision to welcome American troops ignited an internal battle with religious extremists that continues today. But with Iraqi troops at his doorstep, the king did not have the luxury of time to build the consensus Abdullah was calling for. As far as the king was concerned, Kuwait, whose leadership had fled its homeland, existed now solely in "hotel rooms in London, Cairo, and elsewhere."[19] He then polled those in the room for their support on inviting in Americans to help defend the homeland. All present, including Abdullah, supported the decision to seek American assistance. Then and there they declared their fealty: "At your orders, your majesty."

The king reengaged with the Americans in English and announced that Saudi Arabia would accept American support. He later described it as one of the swiftest decisions he had ever made.[20] Saudi Arabia eventually hosted nearly half a million members of the American armed services at massive state-of-the-art military installations erected over the previous decade. Upon leaving the meeting, Freeman confided to Gates that he was scared to death about the first time an American soldier "inadvertently pissed on a mosque."[21] The situation was that fragile.

Belatedly, the royal family turned to the ulema to help legitimatize the decision to allow foreign forces to defend the kingdom. The king sought and received a fatwa from Grand Mufti, bin Baz, that sanctioned the U.S. deployment. In the coming years, this fatwa would be used by younger clerics to discredit not only the royal family but the political-religious condominium that forms the basis of the regime's legitimacy. The fatwa, coming as it did after an intense and pervasive decade-long religious campaign, did not quell domestic opposition. Opposing fatwas were issued arguing that the deployment ran counter to Islam and violated the ruling family's obligation to protect the Muslim community. According to one close observer, these "drew wider public support than did the official" ones.[22] As we will see, the Gulf War in general, and the fatwa in particular, served as a catalyst for a potent Islamic opposition that vexed the royal family throughout the 1990s and continues today.

One vocal critic of King Fahd's open invitation to the Americans was Osama bin Laden. By 1989, when he returned from Afghanistan, bin Laden had developed a committed following among "Afghan Arabs," Arabs who had fought the Soviets to victory. After the Iraqi invasion of Kuwait, bin Laden approached several key Saudi decision makers with an offer to deploy his Afghan fighters to reverse the aggression. Turki al-Faisal reportedly laughed when he heard bin Laden's proposal. Prince Turki knew better than anyone else that Afghanistan's mujahideen had proved victorious over the Soviets largely as a result of international support, not their religious conviction. They would not be able to reverse Iraqi aggression single-handedly.

Undeterred, bin Laden met with others from the royal family. With maps and diagrams, bin Laden approached Prince Sultan and offered him up to a hundred thousand fighters. "There are no caves in Kuwait," Sultan reportedly told bin Laden. "You cannot fight them from the mountains and caves. What will you do when he lobs the missiles at you with chemical and biological weapons?" Bin Laden's solution, that "we [will] fight them with faith," did not impress the defense minister.[23] The royal family's rejection proved costly. Bin Laden has been violently challenging the Saudi royal family, and the United States, ever since.

"Can You Help Get Some Money from the Saudis for Us?"

With American and Saudi commitment to oppose Saddam in place, the next challenge was to convince other states to join the effort. James Baker hopscotched the globe, forging an international coalition that he hoped would set a post–Cold War precedent. The president gave Baker—his campaign manager, first cabinet appointment, and tennis partner for over thirty years—considerable latitude. In less than six months the secretary of state logged over a hundred thousand miles and convened more than two hundred high-level meetings with presidents, prime ministers, and foreign ministers to lock in international assistance. He also spread around considerable amounts of Saudi cash.

As had been true for nearly two decades, Saudi foreign assistance once again proved a central factor in promoting its, and American, national interests. This time it helped secure one of Baker's finest achievements in his remarkable diplomatic tour de force: lining up Russia alongside the United States.[24]

Immediately after Iraq's attack, Baker flew to Russia from Mongolia, where he was rumored to be engaged in a secret hunting trip. In Russia he quickly secured a Russian UN vote to condemn Iraq's assault on Kuwait and demand its complete withdrawal. The vote, and all subsequent joint decisions, were no small feat. After Sadat expelled Soviet forces from Egypt in 1972, Iraq became Russia's most important Middle East client state. The reorientation in Russian foreign policy from Iraq toward the United States intensified an already ongoing domestic battle over the future direction of Russian foreign policy. Foreign Minister Eduard Shevardnadze, a Western-leaning member of Gorbachev's cabinet, encouraged cooperative relations with the United States. Opposing him was, among others, Yevgeny Primakov, a fluent Arabic-speaker with close ties to Saddam Hussein and a member of the Politboro and Central Committee of the Communist Party. Primakov argued vociferously against distancing Moscow from Baghdad.[25]

In mid-September President Mikhail Gorbachev revealed that such political infighting, alongside ongoing economic problems, was undermining his authority. "Can you help get some money from the Saudis for us?" he asked Baker.[26] This request came even though no Soviet ambassador had been resident in Saudi Arabia since 1938. Still, Gorbachev needed money so that those associated with the Shevardnadze camp could show the tangible benefits of aligning with Moscow's former rival against a former friend. With the Cold War over and Communism discredited, new partnerships were now possible.

Two weeks later at a meeting at the United Nations in New York, Baker pulled aside Princes Saud and Bandar and prodded, "I can't tell you what to do, but Gorbachev's situation is difficult. He's under a lot of pressure from the old guard, and it's important to help sustain him in the face of that pressure." Shortly thereafter Saudi Arabia responded with a $4 billion Russian credit line. The money would help the financially strained Russian government retain consensus at home and at the same time muddle through a bitterly cold Russian winter. For Baker, Saudi Arabia's financial assistance was "instrumental in solidifying Soviet support for the use-of-force resolution and keeping them firmly in the coalition throughout the [Iraq] crisis."[27]

Other countries also received substantial financial assistance for helping to defend the kingdom. Riyadh dug deep into its coffers and provided billions of dollars in cash and in-kind support for Operations Desert Shield, the phase of operations aimed at deterring Iraq from heading further south, as well as Desert Storm, the effort to expel Iraq from Kuwait. Along with Kuwait, Saudi Arabia agreed to underwrite $800 million in economic aid to Turkey and $1 billion over five years for a

Turkish special defense fund. Riyadh directed $800 million to Eastern Europe to help offset the dramatic rise in energy costs that resulted from the international embargo on Iraqi oil.[28] Such spending drove the kingdom into debt, from which it is still recovering.

Saudi Arabia also covered billions of dollars' worth of in-country expenses for American and European forces during Desert Storm, including American fuel and water costs, construction, and transportation. The kingdom underwrote the transportation of American troops traveling from the United States around the world to Saudi Arabia. The Saudi treasury also paid for moving a Syrian and Egyptian brigade closer to the front. As the American ambassador observed, Saudis "paid for the transportation and, indeed, the equipment of many of the Third World forces who arrived, essentially in jock straps and flip flops, requiring everything from uniforms to guns to Jeeps to artillery, all of which the Saudis provided, along with salaries and housing and water and food."[29] By the war's end, Saudi Arabia's contribution and outstanding commitments would surpass $60 billion. "There's a cancer in the region," warned Fahd. "For everyone's sake, we must eliminate it."[30]

Saudi Arabia's finances came to be seen as a bottomless pit from which to draw. Baker was adamant: "American blood will be spilled. If you think we're not going to ask the Saudis to pay for this, you've got another think coming." The king viewed the situation similarly, stating, "Money is worth much less than lives. What is money for, if not to serve us as we do our duty? How can you put a dollar value on people's lives who are fighting? Your requests will be met."[31] Any suggestion that the kingdom might not be able to pay the mounting bill was met with disdain. In his memoirs Baker recalled that when Ambassador Freeman raised with him the possibility that the war would place financial hardships on Saudi Arabia, he balked, viewing it as "a classic case of clientitis from one of our very best diplomats."[32] In other words, Baker believed that Freeman was beginning to represent the interests of Saudi Arabia, rather than the United States, a devastating charge to launch against an ambassador.

Baker's skepticism about Saudi Arabia's limitations was underscored by the analysis emerging from within various planning cells at the State Department that believed the Saudis had "all kinds of money squirreled away."[33] Many suspected that corruption had wiped out a good portion of Saudi Arabia's financial holdings, and so were even less receptive to warnings about financial limitations. It was believed that if the Saudis felt pressed, Saudi money would "magically" appear, drawn from personal accounts.

Still, Ambassador Freeman worried that the exorbitant requests would break the kingdom, preventing it from supporting future American foreign policy goals, limiting the House of Saud's ability to outspend the kingdom's ever-powerful religious establishment, and causing future resentment against the United States. Freeman's analysis proved prescient. Saudi Arabia's financial problems throughout the 1990s, which had their roots in the 1986 oil price collapse and were further strained by Desert Storm expenses, ran deep, making it difficult for the royal family to buy off growing domestic opposition and meet growing commitments, including major outstanding debts to the United States. At this juncture, in 1990, Baker did not foresee the long-term consequences of relying on Saudi Arabia to foot most of the bill from Desert Shield and Storm.

In addition to money, Saudi Arabia provided political and religious cover in the Arab and Muslim world. Baker worked to ensure that when the fighting started, Arabs would stay committed to America's course of action. During his prewar diplomatic dance, he posed three questions to each Arab leader he met, asking if they would guarantee their support if all military operations remained firmly under American control, if America attacked Iraqi territory, and if Iraq attacked Israel and Israel retaliated. In Saudi Arabia, King Fahd readily answered yes to all three questions, assuring Baker that "the United States and the kingdom are in the same bunker."[34]

Saudi Arabia's response was exactly what the Bush administration wanted to hear, unlike the Kuwaiti response. Reversing the story of almost a century prior, when Saudi Arabia's future king, Abdel Aziz, fled to Kuwait and was offered sanctuary, Kuwait's royal family was now living in exile in Saudi Arabia. Outrageously, Kuwait's crown prince had great difficulty answering affirmatively to Baker's third question, notwithstanding the fact that his country was now occupied by foreign forces. Baker pressed the matter: "We need to know if Saddam Hussein attacks Israel, where will you be?" As Baker recalls:

> "You are right to raise this question," the Crown Prince acknowledged. "Our position is clear." But, it wasn't. All that was clear was the difficulty he was having in formulating a response. The Crown Prince kept turning to his advisers and conversing in Arabic.
> "We know this is a very hard subject," I gently prodded. . . . "I must know the answer."
> Finally, I got the only acceptable response. "With regard to the position of the Kuwaiti people, if Saddam Hussein attacks Israel, since you are trying to liberate our country, I do not believe that any Kuwaiti will say anything. If he starts it—okay."[35]

From the outset the Saudis, not the Kuwaitis, were "the most aggressive member of the coalition."[36]

In the Arab and Muslim world, sides were being taken. Jordan, Yemen, and the Palestinian Liberation Organization aligned decisively with

Iraq. Jordan's leadership later argued that with so many Palestinians living inside Jordan and its economy umbilically tied to Iraq, King Hussein had little choice but to side with the PLO against the kingdom. The Saudi leadership viewed Jordanian motivations quite differently. They saw it as revenge against the House of Saud for the time when King Abdel Aziz had chased King Hussein's grandfather out of the Hejaz three-quarters of a century earlier. Many senior Saudis viewed Jordan's decision to align with Saddam as an attempt to win back the Hashemites' historical homeland. Indeed, stories were passed to the king that Jordan's Crown Prince Hassan was actively soliciting support inside the Hejaz for a return of Jordan's ruling family.[37]

Saudi Arabia took solace in the fact that its traditional allies Morocco and Egypt lined up strongly behind it. But this did not fully compensate for the fact that many religious leaders whom Saudi Arabia had for years supported were now allying with Saddam Hussein. Saudi-funded warlords such as Gulbuddin Hekmatyar and Abdul Rasul Sayyaf in Afghanistan, as well as others in Indonesia, the Philippines, and North Africa, did not come to Saudi Arabia's aid in its time of need.[38]

Those who knew King Fahd well during this time remember a dramatically different king before and after Iraqi tanks rolled across the border. Iraq's assault challenged everything King Fahd believed about the world: the calculations of his Arab neighbors, the loyalty of former allies, and the logic of world politics. The king could barely accept that one Arab state would so brazenly invade another, even though Egypt had attacked his own country three decades earlier. Saudi Arabia had only recently provided Iraq billions of dollars during its war with Iran, and still Baghdad menaced his border. Compounding his shock was King Hussein's betrayal. Several months earlier, King Fahd and King Hussein had reenacted the loyalty ceremony that Abdel Aziz had performed with the Hashemite ruler after the latter had fled the Hejaz. Layered on top was the treachery by Muslim clients scattered across the globe. For King Fahd, such perfidy was a wrenching experience that made him reexamine everything he had held to be true. "It was as if he went into a long depression," recalled one of the king's nephews.[39] It underscored the importance of the close relations with the United States that he had been sowing for more than a decade.

Desert Storm commenced on January 17, 1991. Six weeks later, on February 28, the president announced a cease-fire. Saudi and other Arab fighters had all participated in the victory. The U.S. role was made immeasurably easier by existing Saudi military infrastructure, access to its airspace, and the long-standing history between the two states. The decision to declare a cease-fire rather than allow allied forces to occupy

Baghdad was a very controversial one. Since then, some have argued that the Saudis, anxious to stop the killing of Iraqi soldiers by allied troops, had pressed Bush to end the war rather than to continue fighting. In fact, Riyadh urged Washington not to end the war prematurely, even if that meant allying with Shi'a and Kurdish forces inside Iraq, groups with which Saudis had been reluctant to engage traditionally. The Saudis were deeply agitated when war ended with Saddam still in power.[40] Until then, the Saudis "thought we [the Americans] knew what we were doing."[41]

Still, Desert Storm marked the high point in U.S.-Saudi relations. Publicly, the two sides were solidly aligned, with much of the world standing in support. Seventy-seven percent of Americans supported the movement of U.S. troops into Saudi Arabia.[42] The defense capabilities that the United States had been building in the region since the 1980 Carter doctrine served the needs of the United States, Saudi Arabia, and the smaller Gulf countries along the western coast of the Persian Gulf.

But Desert Storm also catalyzed extreme Saudi popular opposition to the House of Saud. Coming as it did a decade after the 1979 triple threats of the storming of the Grand Mosque, the Iranian revolution, and the Soviet invasion of Afghanistan, events that propelled King Fahd and his supporters to stoke the worst excesses of religious radicalism, Desert Storm galvanized the regime's religious opponents. With debts mounting to pay for the war, traditional resources were not available to co-opt local opposition, a common Saudi tactic for managing serious problems. Many Saudis also began questioning where the billions of dollars in defense expenditures had gone, if not toward building a robust and effective fighting force to defend the homeland. For these reasons the decade of the 1990s proved an exceedingly difficult one for the Saudi leadership. At the war's end in 1991, however, there seemed reasons for optimism. The U.S.-Saudi relationship was strong and a victory had been achieved. In addition, Washington appeared poised to begin a new round of Middle East peace process consultations, ones that resulted in the Madrid process, which saw Arabs and Israelis sit down together publicly to hammer out differences.

Tin-Cupping

With the Cold War and Desert Storm behind them, Saudi Arabia and the United States had an opportunity to forge a new relationship. Fifty-two percent of Americans reported that they had "gained respect for Saudi Arabia."[43] Nonetheless, the seeds of future problems were being sown almost as soon as Desert Storm ended. In terms of Iraq policy, the survival of Saddam Hussein and his relentless efforts to disrupt regional stability would strain relations between the two partners in the decade to come. The Saudi leadership had hoped that overwhelming American military force would have swept the Iraqi leader from power.

During and after the Iraq war, Saudi Arabia poured billions into defense contracts. King Fahd gave Prince Bandar and Prince Sultan authority to purchase anything deemed necessary for the war effort, which brought the kingdom's representatives to South Africa and elsewhere. In the autumn of 1990 President Bush waived a number of congressional bans and provided Saudi Arabia with F-15s (the same planes that Congress had denied Saudi Arabia in 1985, compelling Riyadh to turn toward the United Kingdom), Stinger missiles and launchers, depleted-uranium shells, M-60A-3 tanks, Patriot missiles, and other equipment. Between August and December 1991 the administration submitted more than $10 billion worth of requests. In September 1992 President Bush formally submitted a proposal to sell seventy-two F-15s to the kingdom. A $9 billion arms package was signed under the auspices of the Clinton administration in May 1993.[44] In the glow of Desert Storm, Saudi defense officials recognized a momentary window of opportunity in which Congress would not aggressively contest each defense sale they sought. They bought and bought feverishly.[45] The American chief of the USMTM, the military training program initiated under Truman, walked around "shaking my head, wondering how the hell are they going to pay for this stuff?"[46] Little did Major General Thomas G. Rhame know at the time that within a couple of years he would be promoted to director of the Defense Security Assistance Agency and would have the honor of collecting those bills.

Given such loose spending, Washington looked to Riyadh to also fund many of its pet projects, much as it had before the war. At one point in the early 1990s the United States ambassador to Saudi Arabia, Chas. Freeman, was tasked to persuade the Saudis to buy surplus Polish ham to help the starving—now defined as friendly—Russians through that year's harsh winter and at the same time provide foreign exchange to the hard-pressed Poles. Exasperated by the constant unfocused requests from Washington and outraged that Washington was asking the de facto leader of the Muslim world to purchase pork products, Freeman replied that this would be "a bit like asking the Pope to buy condoms from the Lutherans for distribution to Muslims in Bangladesh," and that he was not about to attempt it.[47]

The requests became known inside Washington's Beltway as "tin-cupping."[48] After 1991 there seemed no rhyme or reason to American requests, other than that the Saudis had a lot of money and appeared indebted to the United States. Unlike during the Cold War, when Saudi Arabia directed its aid toward a mutually agreed-upon goal of fighting Communism, the postwar requests became increasingly ad hoc. Washington solicited money for places ranging from Argentina to Zambia. Anger mounted inside the kingdom, especially as Saudi Arabia's spending during Desert Storm put an enormous strain on the state's coffers.

In the Twilight of the Cold War

The Reagan/Bush period was a high-water mark in U.S.-Saudi relations. Desert Storm was the crowning achievement of more than a decade's worth of close bilateral engagement. The U.S.-Saudi partnership helped contribute to the Soviet Union defeat in Afghanistan, Soviet losses in Africa, and the reversal of Iraq's conquest of Kuwait. The peace process was also once again moving in the right direction. The twilight of the Cold War promised new opportunities.

But as was true with many of the political relationships the United States constructed during the five decades of the Cold War, the end of the Cold War also wiped away much of the justification for the U.S.-Saudi partnership. At the time, neither side recognized this fact. The relationship simmered along for another decade or so without a fundamental reassessment of either the ends or the means of the two countries' ties. The United States would pay a high price for this neglect when the planes hit the Pentagon and Word Trade Center towers on September 11, 2001.

11

Parting Ways

In 1994 President Clinton's national security advisor, W. Anthony "Tony" Lake, outlined the administration's thinking on Persian Gulf security. In the prestigious journal *Foreign Affairs* he argued that "the end of the Cold War simply eliminated a major strategic consideration from our calculus. We no longer have to fear Soviet efforts to gain a foothold in the Persian Gulf."[1] Unrestrained by the Soviet Union, but also unable to count on Moscow's control over its regional partners, the administration designed a new policy, dual containment, aimed at deterring both Iranian and Iraqi aggression. The policy assumed a prominent American military role in the Persian Gulf, one aided by "regional allies." Saudi Arabia would be key to this new effort. It would become characteristic of the Clinton administration to expect Saudi Arabia to dutifully follow American plans. The kingdom was also expected to pay for them.

The end of the Cold War would bring a slow but steady deterioration in U.S.-Saudi relations. Oil remained a pressing concern, but the shared anti-Communism that had traditionally bound the partnership became a relic of the past. Furthermore, relations worsened at the personal level, as Clinton's team regarded Saudi Arabia's ambassador, Prince Bandar, a Bush loyalist. It had not gone unnoticed by Clinton's friends that the Saudi ambassador had been a fixture at the 1992 Republican National Convention parties.[2] While Prince Bandar expected the easy access to the president that he had received during the past two Republican administrations—he was rumored to have held a White House pass during Bush's tenure—Clinton's new gatekeepers, including Lake and his deputy, Samuel "Sandy" R. Berger, wanted him treated like any other ambassador. His access would be limited to more traditional ambassadorial functions, such as conveying messages to and from the king and escorting other Saudis in to see the president. The Saudi ambassador repeatedly tried to circumvent such restrictions and establish direct contact with the president. At one point he even took a trip to Africa that conveniently overlapped with a presidential visit, and he managed to obtain a private meeting with Clinton. Sandy Berger was incensed when he discovered the lengths to which Bandar would go to see the president.

Exacerbating existing problems between the two countries were a host of new challenges that arose during the 1990s with no mutually understood strategic context in which to place them. After Desert Storm, Iraq's president, Saddam Hussein, unexpectedly held on to power. This caused the United States to regularly amass forces in the region, something that irritated growing Saudi domestic problems and unnerved the Saudi leadership. A political vacuum developed in Afghanistan, which drew in Saudi Arabia while America focused its attention elsewhere. As America turned inward to reap the benefits of the Cold War's end, Saudi Arabia's finances weakened and its domestic environment unraveled. Then in 1995 Saudi Arabia underwent a leadership transition: King Fahd had a stroke, which gave more power to Crown Prince Abdullah, who had always been more skeptical than King Fahd of the kingdom's close relations with the United States. Each event further strained the U.S.-Saudi relationship.

Democracy, Growth, and Peace

The Clinton administration came to power focused primarily on its domestic agenda. To the extent that they did look internationally, incoming Clinton officials focused on two areas: the global economy and the promotion of democratization. A strong and growing American economy, they believed, provided the best chance for elevating the economic output of other states, improving economic conditions worldwide, and relieving some of the more intractable development challenges devastating a good portion of the globe. Accordingly, Clinton pushed through Bush's North American Free Trade Agreement, backed the "Washington Consensus" (a neoliberal set of economic policies), and established the National Economic Council, designed to serve as the sister to the National Security Council.

Promoting democracy dovetailed nicely with Clinton's economic agenda. Healthy democracies, after all, require a free marketplace of ideas, political transparency, and accountability, conditions also supportive of economic growth. Well-respected foreign policy scholars generated new theories linking the spread of democracy with peace. Drawing on the work of philosopher Immanuel Kant, Princeton professor Michael W. Doyle generated an entire research agenda when he suggested that "liberal republics will progressively establish peace among themselves."[3] In his 1994 State of the Union address, Clinton highlighted America's commitment to democracy, acknowledging that "democracies don't attack each other. They make better trading partners and partners in diplomacy."[4]

The Middle East—an area of stagnant economies and sclerotic political systems—hardly factored into this optimistic agenda and received only passing reference in Clinton's speech. Some, such as Morton H. Halperin, special assistant to the president and senior director for democracy at the National Security Council, argued that the Middle East should not be excluded from Clinton's ambitious democratizing program. But to the extent that anyone was paying attention to the region early in the administration's first term, a countervailing argument prevailed. As Martin S. Indyk, Clinton's senior Middle East director at the National Security Council, recalled, the Arab-Israeli settlement, not economic and political reform, took priority. If achieved, an Arab-Israeli settlement would free up local resources for political reform and undermine the long-standing arguments that fighting in Palestine prevented political evolution.[5] The engine for change in the region was not democratization but peace.[6] This emphasis on the Arab-Israeli problem was something that Saudi leaders had long advocated. Still, it did not result in easier U.S.-Saudi relations.

The Saudi Scene

Inside Saudi Arabia times were significantly more troublesome. The 1990s proved a devastating decade for the kingdom, both economically and politically. The kingdom's vast financial resources had been seriously compromised by the costs of Desert Storm, which totaled around $60 billion, and by the need to pay for huge arms contracts arranged before and immediately after the fighting. Politically, the royal family witnessed rising opposition from within the religious establishment, and a new younger group of clerics operating on the fringe of the official establishment. Saudi citizens were angered by their leadership's reliance on foreign (particularly American) forces for its own defense, especially in light of the government's costly arms investments of the previous decades. This anger provided a ripe environment for the government's more outspoken critics. Not without reason did governmental opponents such as Safer al-Hawali, dean of the Islamic college at Umm al-Qura University in Mecca, and Salman al-Auda, an Islamic scholar at Imam Muhammad ibn Saud University in Riyadh, question whether the regime was effectively defending the homeland. When directly tested by a threatening Iraq, Saudi Arabia's defense program had come up short, notwithstanding huge annual defense budgets. In August 1996 Osama bin Laden would embody this concern in his first major internationally publicized fatwa. Bin Laden condemned the "expensive deals [that] were imposed on the country to purchase arms." He wanted the Saudi regime to fully understand that "people [are] asking what is the justification for the very existence of the regime then?"[7]

Financial Troubles

The cost of Desert Storm and the outstanding defense contracts, on top of the Iran-Iraq War (which cost Saudi Arabia anywhere between $15 billion and $30 billion), strained the kingdom financially, emboldened the regime's domestic opposition, and ultimately irritated the kingdom's relations with American companies doing business in Saudi Arabia. During and immediately after Desert Storm, Saudi Arabia's Ministry of Defense and Aviation (MODA) went on a massive spending spree, ordering $50 billion worth of arms between 1990 and 1994. Total military spending increased even further.

Saudi Arabia's Military Expenditures

Current dollars, in billions

1985	21.3	1991	35.5
1986	17.3	1992	35.0
1987	16.2	1993	20.5
1988	13.6	1994	17.2
1989	14.7	1995	17.2
1990	23.1		

Source: U.S. Arms Control and Disarmament Agency, *World Military Expenditures and Arms Transfers* (Washington, DC: GPO, 1996), 89.

Fulfilling outstanding defense contracts with the United States, Great Britain, France, China, and others caused chronic Saudi budget deficits. According to Anthony H. Cordesman and Nawaf E. Obaid, two close observers of the kingdom, "The Gulf War pushed Saudi military and security expenditures to the crisis level. Saudi security expenditures rose from 36 percent of the total national budget in 1988, and 39 percent in 1989, to nearly 60 percent in 1990 . . . [and] around 70 percent in 1991–1992—including the cost of aid to allied governments during Desert Storm."[8] In late 1993 and early 1994 the U.S. Department of Defense found itself a day or two away from issuing a stop-work order to American defense contractors serving Saudi Arabia. Given the financial magnitude of the existing contracts, such a decision would have shut down the entire U.S. Defense Department.

Ever since the kingdom's massive oil windfall and the subsequent 1974 U.S.-Saudi Joint Security Cooperation Commission, Saudi Arabia had played an important role in sustaining the U.S. arms industry. Saudi Arabia's huge F-15 purchase made just after Desert Storm, for example, had kept open McDonnell Douglas' main plant in St. Louis, which had been slated for closure due to sustained losses and cost overruns.[9] Saudi purchases also helped to keep down the price for the Abrams tank. A 2003 congressional report noted that the "Saudi arms market has helped maintain the U.S. industrial base and create jobs."[10]

During the 1980s and early 1990s Riyadh kept up to $4 billion at the Federal Reserve Bank in non-interest-bearing accounts to cover its defense needs. When Saudi Arabia placed an arms order, the Defense Department withdrew money from the Federal Reserve fund and paid Lockheed, Raytheon, Boeing, or whichever contracting company was owed. This made the U.S. Defense Department the ultimate guarantor of Saudi Arabia's huge contracts. It gave the U.S. companies confidence in expanding production lines and increasing staff size while giving Saudi Arabia direct access to the American spare parts pipeline.

But in early 1994 Saudi Arabia's account was on the "bare edge of staying solvent."[11] The task of managing the account fell to the recently promoted Lieutenant General Thomas Rhame, who had moved from his position as chief of the U.S. Military Training Mission in Saudi Arabia, the overseer of all U.S. Department of Defense agencies in the kingdom, to become the director of the Defense Security Assistance Agency, the agency charged with overseeing all American arms contracts. In 1994 Rhame was responsible for America's worldwide foreign military sales. Almost every Monday he called his boss, Chas. Freeman, recently elevated from ambassador to Saudi Arabia to assistant secretary of defense for international security affairs, and updated him on Saudi Arabia's troubled account. Together they measured solvency in days, sometimes as few as just one.

To better assess Saudi Arabia's financial problems, General Rhame began making regular trips to Saudi Arabia. He had an inkling of the situation's severity, since he had been serving in the kingdom when the vast contracts were signed. However, all that Saudi MODA officials would tell him was that they did not want to cancel the contracts and would find a way to fulfill their contractual obligations. Given the historical precedent of a restrictive U.S. Congress, Saudi defense officials feared that once canceled, certain requests would never be renewed. Raymond E. Mabus, Jr., America's ambassador to Saudi Arabia from 1994 to 1996, recalled that "it was always a question of whether they could pay or not."[12]

Saudi Arabia's finance minister, Muhammad Abu Khail, thus had a problem. "A voice of reason inside the kingdom," Abu Khail was a "guy who knew how to say no 23 different ways without offending anyone" yet was as "hard as woodpecker lips."[13] On his desk sat a growing pile of bills without the resources to meet them. Oil prices, which had rebounded to $25 per barrel in 1991, had again fallen over the following years. In 1994 oil traded at a little over $17 per barrel. Abdullah Suleiman, King Abdel Aziz's treasurer who hauled the kingdom's wealth around in a tin box in the 1930s, would have been empathetic. The money leaving state coffers far exceeded that coming in. Abu Khail began pressuring the Ministry of Defense to forgo future contracts and reduce current spending, leaving even less available cash to fulfill existing contracts.

Tensions between Saudis and Americans mounted over outstanding accounts. Eventually Prince Bandar, the man regularly called upon to ease existing friction between United States and Saudi Arabia, stepped in to help resolve the growing crisis. Bandar had been looking for ways to engage the White House, given that his access to the president had been highly restricted. In 1994 he invited Rhame and representatives from Saudi Arabia's Ministries of Finance and Defense to his secluded estate in Aspen, Colorado. Abu Khail's people and the U.S. Department of Defense devised a plan by which MODA and the Americans would undertake a serious inventory of outstanding contracts (until then there had been no good accounting of the entire Saudi commitment to the United States), stretch out payment plans, and put new requests on hold. The Saudi account remained solvent, the Defense Department did not issue a stop-work order, and the arms industry hummed along contentedly. But Saudi Arabia's close call would continue to fuel the ire of the young clerics who had been sermonizing and disseminating cassettes accusing the leadership of blasphemy and incompetence because of their need to rely on non-Muslim forces to defend the homeland. This did not stop Washington from asking the king to subsidize heating oil for North Korea, contribute to the Mexican peso bailout, or give money to other pet projects.[14]

"Catastrophes Are Coming at Us One After the Other"

During and immediately after Desert Storm in 1991, Western-leaning Saudi reformers hoped that the international spotlight focused on the kingdom would catalyze Saudi Arabia toward a more modern political structure, one in which women were more visible and laws applied equally across the population, including the royal family. Their optimism was furthered in September 1990 when King Fahd urged government agencies to train women to work in the civil defense and medical services sectors. Hundreds of women from across the country volunteered for such training.[15] Believing that the king's endorsement represented a true shift toward equality, forty-five well-to-do women, some of whom were professors at prestigious universities, held a public protest on November 6, 1990, calling for their right to drive.[16] There was no precedent in Saudi history for women politically organizing to protest their position in society.

The women, many of whom had their husbands' support, met at a mall parking lot, ordered their drivers out of the cars, and drove around in circles until they attracted the attention they sought. As one Saudi political scientist told the *New York Times*, "In this country, you've got to think of us, the liberals, as the silent minority coming out of its shell."[17] As anticipated, the mutawa—the religious police whose power had grown under King Fahd and who operated somewhat elusively under the control of the interior minister, Prince Naif, a son of King Abdel Aziz and one of King Fahd's full brothers—arrived to shut down the protest. Shortly afterward the national Saudi police appeared and dispersed the crowds, claiming that the situation was a routine traffic violation and therefore under their jurisdiction. The women considered it a small victory that they were able to answer to the national rather than religious police.

For a few days it appeared that the king would use the opportunity to check the power of the more radical among the religious establishment. The governor of Riyadh, Prince Salman, another son of King Abdel Aziz and a full brother to Fahd, assembled a commission that rapidly decided that the women had not actually committed a crime. The moment for leniency, however, quickly passed.

Labeling the drivers "Communist whores," Islamic activists agitated for greater punishment.[18] Clerics distributed leaflets throughout Riyadh's mosques that included the drivers' names, ages, and phone numbers.

The Council of Senior Ulema (officially the highest religious authority in the kingdom) issued a fatwa banning women drivers, and Prince Naif declared that "driving by women contradicts the Islamic traditions followed by Saudi citizens." The protest participants lost their jobs, had their passports confiscated, and were restricted to virtual house arrest until King Fahd quietly exonerated them a few years later. Women in Jeddah who had hoped to bring the liberal reform movement to their city canceled a driving protest scheduled for a few weeks later. "After what has happened, none of them is willing to risk her career," said one woman who had considered joining the canceled Jeddah protest. "When they heard those women in Riyadh were being suspended from their jobs they said, 'Forget it.' "[19]

The protests succeeded in capturing international attention, but also galvanized the Islamic opposition. The driving protest, and with it any hope for increased liberalization in Saudi society, was easily and effectively snuffed out. The same cannot be said for the increasingly radicalized Islamic opposition.

Like their liberal counterparts, members of the religious establishment exploited international attention to further their goals. Religious clerics, many in only their mid-thirties, began issuing fiery statements against the foreign military presence and the exploitation of Islamic lands by Western invaders, and they warned of a coming clash of civilizations between Islam and the West. This new generation of Islamic leaders, referred to as the Sahwa, or "awakening sheikhs," had come of age as Saudi Arabia was first benefiting from dizzying oil wealth and when calls for jihad permeated Saudi society, encouraged by the Saudi political leadership.[20]

Two of the most prominent of the Sahwa were al-Auda and Hawali. Young, intense, and politically astute, these men represented a generational shift in Saudi Arabia's traditional religious hierarchy. Relentlessly they attacked the kingdom's precarious economic situation, drew attention to corruption within the royal family, and called for a more ascetic religious state. They portrayed the arrival of American troops on Saudi soil as symptomatic of the kingdom's moral, economic, and physical decrepitude. "If Iraq has occupied Kuwait, then America has occupied Saudi Arabia," argued Hawali in one of his many taped sermons that circulated throughout the kingdom via cassette during the late 1990s. "The real enemy is not Iraq. It is the West."[21] Al-Auda similarly warned that Americans had come to assume responsibility for the failing Saudi state.[22]

Ideologically, the Sahwa clerics viewed their role as significantly less compliant than their older mentors in the ulema. Unlike their elders, the new generation of clerics did not limit their sermons to religious topics, but rather publicly criticized the leadership's domestic and foreign policies. As one dissident explained, "The old clergy believe that the ruler is the vice-regent of God on earth. Advice can only be given in private and in confidence. The new clergy reject the idea of vice-regency. Rather it is the duty of the clergy to criticize the rule and work for change."[23] In comparison to the ulema, the Sahwa clerics were far less deferential to the political establishment, and their efforts often resulted in violence. The fact that the grand mufti had issued a fatwa approving the Gulf War American military deployment fueled the conviction among many that the older members of the established ulema simply rubber-stamped government policy. Along with the United States and Western culture more generally, the ulema itself became the subject of severe attacks.

In May 1991 a group of about four hundred Islamists, including Hawali and al-Auda, signed a "letter of demands" addressed to the king. The signatories, predominantly from the Nejd, were well-educated men of religion—prayer leaders, preachers, professors of religion.[24] In the letter they called for, among other things, cleansing the state apparatus of corrupt individuals, a foreign policy that avoided any alliances that might violate Islamic law, and improving the country's institutions of religion and religious dissemination. In short, they argued for the religious establishment to assume a supervisory role to the government, rather than a subordinate one.

Anti-Western religious sermons resonated with many inside the kingdom, especially those nervous about Saudi Arabia's rapid modernization and those who had recently returned from Afghanistan battle-hardened and determined to establish a true Islamic state. One of those returnees was Osama bin Laden, the son of a Yemeni-born construction tycoon, who was inspired by the Sahwa's preaching. Bin Laden had been speaking out against moral laxity since the 1980s, when he went to Afghanistan to fight the jihad.

Bin Laden had not always opposed the Saudi regime. During his time in Afghanistan he had close ties with Saudi Arabia's director of general intelligence, Turki al-Faisal, and was the beneficiary of Saudi largesse. He had used his family-derived access to the royal family in 1990 repeatedly to offer the regime the services of his Arab Afghan fighters to eject Iraqi soldiers from Kuwait. His offers were dismissed outright. Although rebuffed, bin Laden did not give up. Shortly thereafter he returned with yet another proposition, offering the services of his fighters to smash the Communist government in South Yemen—a cause that might well have generated support among the Saudi leadership during an earlier period. This too was deflected. Bin Laden's anti-Communist message was now antiquated. He was not able to convince the royal family to adopt his increasingly ascetic view of the Islamic religion or to accept his offer to provide fighters to their cause. He stewed in Saudi Arabia for another year until he left for Sudan in the spring of 1991 under pressure from the Saudi government.

Bin Laden's exile did little to quell opposition within the kingdom. In 1992 107 religious figures built upon their 1991 demands and signed a "memorandum of advice" that called for outlawing the teaching of Western law, creating a half-million-man army aimed at fighting Jews and helping Muslims, and ending foreign aid to "atheistic" regimes such as Iraq (to which Saudi Arabia had contributed during the Iran-Iraq War), Jordan, and Egypt. As F. Gregory Gause III, a Saudi expert at the University of Vermont, recalled, the letter was unprecedented in recent Saudi history in "the bluntness of its tone, its detailed critique of a wide-range of the government's policies, and the public nature of its dissemination."[25] It received only one-quarter of the original letter's signatures and represented a smaller, more radical fringe within the religious establishment. In retaliation, the Council of Senior Ulema released a statement defending Grand Mufti bin Baz, and condemning the "so-called 'Memorandum of Advice.'" Hawali and al-Auda, two of the memorandum's prominent supporters, were arrested.

Even these arrests did not quiet the opposition. In May 1993 Abdullah al-Masari, Saad al-Faqih, and four others established the Committee for the Defense of Legitimate Rights (CDLR). Five of the six had signed the memorandum of advice. The CDLR cloaked itself in the language of human rights. International human rights groups rushed to support the new Saudi organization. When pressed, however, the CDLR leadership made clear that their commitment was based not in universal human rights standards (women's equality, religious tolerance, etc.) but rather within the "legitimate" confines of sharia and a strict Islamist interpretation. Masari was arrested shortly after the group's formation. Eventually Masari and Faqih escaped to London, a destination for many dissidents from the Arab world, in order to avoid the continued wrath of the Saudi regime. They blasted faxes home to the kingdom broadcasting their continued opposition and attempted to mobilize the Saudi population against the regime. The Saudi government now confronted at least one source of opposition operating outside its borders, protected by the government of Great Britain, and using cutting-edge technology to further challenge the ruling family. Today the Saudi government is still seeking their extradition.

By the mid-1990s Saudi Arabia's political landscape, like its financial one, was in turmoil. In one notable case, five hundred men demonstrated in front of the governor's quarters in Buraida, northwest of Riyadh, demanding the release of jailed Islamic leaders. Then in 1994 the Islamic opposition protested Saudi Arabia's participation in a UN population conference. Believing that they were trespassing on its mandate to conduct foreign policy, territory traditionally ceded by the religious establishment to the ruling family, the government again responded. In 1994 Hawali, al-Auda, and hundreds of their sympathizers were (again) arrested. Hawali and al-Auda were not released until 1999, when Crown Prince Abdullah, by then the de facto ruler, sought to co-opt the two firebrands by freeing them as a goodwill gesture.

In addition to pressuring dissidents to leave and issuing prison sentences, the government tried to blunt the opposition's appeal by increasing salaries for civil servants, further rewarding citizens for their loyalty to the regime. They doled out subsidies for electricity, telephone service, free housing, and free loans to buy land, all undertaken in an effort to rebuild the popular support they feared they were losing. Such lavish spending was used by American officials back in Washington as evidence that the Saudi government had money stashed away to meet its financial obligations.

Still, the protests persisted and took a deadly anti-American turn. In November 1995 terrorists struck a joint U.S.-Saudi facility that housed a U.S. military mission helping to train Saudi Arabia's National Guard. Different groups claimed credit for the attack, which killed five Americans. One Saudi group, the Islamic Movement for Change, had issued a statement earlier in the year warning of attacks if non-Muslim Western forces did not withdraw from the Gulf region.[26] Six months later Saudi officials executed four suspects who accepted responsibility and who claimed inspiration from Osama bin Laden and his quest to rid the kingdom of American forces. The Americans only learned of the suspects' incarceration three months after their capture, when the news was made public. The four were executed before U.S. officials could interview them, which rankled Americans working on the case and undermined their confidence that Saudi Arabia was committed to jointly fighting terrorism. Subsequent to the attacks, American officials learned that bin Laden's followers had been planning an attack on Americans inside the kingdom for at least a year and had even shipped explosives into the kingdom from abroad for this purpose.[27] Saudi officials had kept that information close to their chests.

News of the attack stunned King Fahd. "Catastrophes are coming at us one after the other," he confided in a close associate.[28] Two weeks later Fahd suffered his debilitating stroke. Responsibility for day-to-day operations transferred from King Fahd to Crown Prince Abdullah.

King Fahd's stroke set in motion one of the worst, though largely underreported, crises in Saudi Arabia's political history. Although Crown Prince Abdullah quickly took charge of day-to-day operations inside the kingdom, he was not made king—an honor that remained vested in Fahd. Strong currents within the Saudi ruling elite, most notably the king's full brothers, his wife, and his youngest son, seemed determined to prevent the crown from passing fully to Abdullah, fearing a diminution in their political stature.

Prince Sultan, today's crown prince, is a full brother of King Fahd, as are Princes Naif (the interior minister), Salman (the governor of Riyadh), and Ahmed (the deputy interior minister). They, along with two others—Abdul Rahman and Turki, the latter an uncle of Turki al-Faisal—are often referred to as the "Sudairi seven," because they are seven full and powerful brothers, sons of Hassa bint Ahmad al-Sudairi, one of King Abdel Aziz's favorite wives. For decades, stretching back to the battles between King Saud and Crown Prince Faisal in the 1950s and 1960s, the Sudairi seven worked together intimately. King Abdullah is only a half brother to the Sudairis, as his mother hails from the Shammar tribe, a result of a long-ago effort by King Abdel Aziz to subdue the powerful house of Rashid, who were Shammar. Abdullah's base of support comes from some of Saudi Arabia's most powerful tribes, particularly in the north, who also tend to populate the National Guard, which he commands even as king. As long as King Fahd was alive, Crown Prince Abdullah could rule but not reign. His authority among leading members of government would remain circumscribed. Between 1995 and 2005 Saudi Arabia was a monarchy without a functioning monarch. This slowed progress toward political change.

Nonetheless, the leadership change did have an impact on U.S.-Saudi relations. Fahd had been reflexively pro-American, seeing American and Saudi interests as overlapping. Even as the Clinton administration came to power, and with joint U.S.-Saudi Cold War operations over, Fahd looked for ways to engage the United States. Prince Bandar, his right-hand man in the United States, continued to probe for areas in which Saudi Arabia could be effective. King Fahd, for example, made it very clear that the kingdom would continue to sell oil at a discounted rate to the United States in order to maintain a strategic relationship, a perk that was stopped under Abdullah. When the U.S. foreign policy establishment recoiled at the prospect of a massive Boeing plane sale to Iran but domestic advisors pointed out that twenty thousand American jobs were at stake, Clinton made a flurry of calls to King Fahd, urging him to buy the planes. Stating that Saudi Arabia wanted to be seen as "a strategic asset and not a strategic liability," Prince Bandar and President Clinton announced the $6 billion sale in February 1994. Bandar did not mention publicly that the Saudis were considering buying planes from Airbus if the U.S. deal fell through. Still, Saudi Arabia's existing economic problems were given only passing reference, although the Export-Import Bank of the United States was brought in to provide financing.

Crown Prince Abdullah was more circumspect than his half brother. From his vantage point as commander of the National Guard, the close U.S.-Saudi embrace seemed only to undermine Saudi domestic stability. Abdullah sought to put some daylight between the United States and Saudi Arabia. Soon after Abdullah assumed day-to-day control, an almost imperceptible but significant shift began taking place. Those most closely associated with King Fahd and the United States began to lose their influence. Bandar did not have Abdullah's ear as he had had Fahd's. According to one senior U.S. administration official, Bandar appeared "on the outs." Others with close ties to the United States, such as Turki al-Faisal, also did not wield the same kind of influence with Abdullah. In August 2001 Prince Turki al-Faisal stepped down as director of general intelligence, eventually becoming Saudi Arabia's ambassador to Great Britain, and most recently ambassador to the United States. (Turki's recent posting and Bandar's October 2005 appointment as secretary-general of the National Security Council suggests that both men have risen in their uncle Abdullah's estimation.)

A month after the four terror suspects were executed for the Riyadh bombing, a truck bomb exploded outside Khobar Towers, an apartment complex housing two thousand members of the U.S. armed forces. The explosion killed 19 U.S. servicemen and wounded another 372. Although technically the case remains unsolved, strong evidence suggests that an arm of Hezbollah operating inside Saudi Arabia perpetrated the attack with significant assistance from Iran.[29] The prestigious 9/11 Commission has also since speculated that bin Laden and his followers "played some role, as yet unknown."[30]

Within the U.S. administration, fissures emerged between the Federal Bureau of Investigation and the National Security Council on how to handle Saudi Arabia. The Saudis had information linking Iran to the Khobar bombing but were not fully forthcoming, and the FBI and NSC differed on how to approach the problem. Prince Bandar, sensing the internal turmoil, appeared reluctant to present the United States with Saudi information without a clear U.S. commitment for how the administration would respond. Bandar and his father, the defense minister,

Prince Sultan, worried that a halfhearted U.S. military response would only antagonize Iran, which would then likely retaliate against the kingdom. Washington, however, was not prepared to predetermine its response and viewed the Saudi motivation for withholding information somewhat differently. Sandy Berger recalled that "Bandar would always say, 'Tell me what you are going to do with the information if we share it with you.' I wouldn't play that game. I knew if we said we were going to whack the shit out of Iran we would never get anything from the Saudis—plus we had not made a decision about what we were going to do."[31] In Saudi Arabia the leadership feared that Clinton's definition of "whack the shit" was much weaker than they would prefer.

The kingdom was in turmoil, but until the late 1990s its problems did not register clearly on Washington's radar screen. Even after the 1996 attack on Khobar, the second anti-American attack on the kingdom's soil in so many years, administration officials responsible for counter-terrorism looked toward Iran as their principal source for concern. Although NSC officials recount their enormous frustration that Saudi leaders had not been more forthcoming about the 1995 attacks—executing the perpetrators before the United States was able to undertake its own interrogations—the kingdom's domestic crisis was not yet a central concern.

Still, Saudi stonewalling was disturbing to the Americans involved. U.S. law-enforcement officials expressed frustration about Saudi evasiveness. Richard Clarke, who in 1998 became the president's national coordinator for security, infrastructure protection, and counterterrorism at the NSC, believed that Saudi officials never intended to cooperate with the FBI. This was due in no small part to the fact that the 1995 and 1996 attacks exposed Saudi Arabia's domestic weaknesses, something Saudi officials there were desperately trying to hide and rectify.[32]

Riyadh's lack of cooperation exacerbated a growing list of international problems in which the United States and Saudi Arabia no longer saw eye to eye. Even on pressing international matters that had once conjoined the United States and Saudi Arabia, including events in Iraq and Afghanistan, problems emerged. Tensions mounted between the two Cold War partners.

The International Scene

Nineteen ninety-four, the same year that America's Saudi account almost ran dry and key Islamic opposition figures in Saudi Arabia were imprisoned or driven out, was the last year of smooth relations between Saudi Arabia and the United States. After that year, Americans and Saudis struggled to develop a consensus on how to deal with the Iraqi regional threat, and Saudi leaders lost confidence in American military planning.

Four years prior, in August 1990, the secretary of defense, Dick Cheney, assured King Fahd that American troops would depart the kingdom immediately after the victory over Iraq. Contrary to accusations hurled by men such as Hawali, al-Auda, bin Laden, and others, Cheney was by and large true to his word. After Iraq's withdrawal from Saudi Arabia, the United States did in fact significantly reduce its forces throughout the region. By 1993 America had fewer than one thousand military personnel deployed on Saudi soil, down from nearly half a million two years earlier.

But in 1994, in a now almost forgotten episode, Saddam Hussein again threatened Kuwait's northern border. In early October, a division of Republican Guard troops began marching south and joined up with two other Republican Guard divisions shifting toward the border with Kuwait. Suddenly seventy thousand Iraqi military personnel, an increase of twenty thousand over the regularly situated forces, were moving toward the Kuwaiti border. The United States and its coalition partners rushed troops to the region. The Pentagon dispatched thirty-six thousand ground troops to the Gulf. France and Britain also sent forces to join in what would come to be known as Operation Vigilant Warrior. Kuwait, Saudi Arabia, and Qatar pledged over $370 million in monetary and in-kind support. Unlike the experience after 1991, however, this time troop levels did not come down. After 1994 American force levels inside and around Saudi Arabia rose steadily, out of concern that Saddam would otherwise continue to menace the region.[33]

Simultaneous with rising troop levels and Saudi internal problems in justifying the American presence, the political consensus on how to deal with Saddam Hussein's Iraq began deteriorating. One year prior to Operation Vigilant Warrior, President Clinton's special advisor to the Middle East, Martin Indyk, articulated the new administration's approach in the Persian Gulf in a speech he gave to the Washington Institute for Near East Policy, a think tank focused on America's Middle East policy.[34] Tony Lake endorsed these ideas in his 1994 *Foreign Affairs* article. The dual containment policy outlined a determined effort to contain both Iran and Iraq. It never had robust Saudi Arabian support, as it went directly against the Saudis' long-standing preference of playing Iran and Iraq off each other. (In fact, by the late 1990s, Riyadh began improving its relations with Iran, another policy

US Troops in Saudi Arabia, 1992–2000

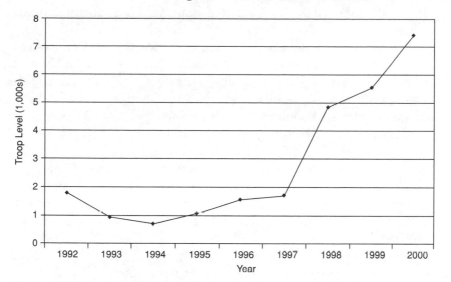

Source: Work Force Publications, Statistical Information Analysis Division, Directorate for Information Operations and Reports, Department of Defense, http://www.dior.whs.mil/mmid/pubs.htm.

decision that irked Washington.) Worse, dual containment offered no solution to the serious regional problem of how to reduce two of the region's gravest threats. It froze the status quo rather than ridding the region of either regime or providing incentives for them to work toward improving relations with the United States.

Focusing his rhetoric on international sanctions, Saddam Hussein manipulated America's Iraq policy to benefit his regime at the expense of the United States, its partners, and the larger Iraqi population. Stories of Iraqi malnutrition, desolation, and need were particularly heartbreaking for those in the region who remembered Iraq as the engine of economic growth and modernization only a few decades prior. The plight of the Iraqi people became daily fodder for local news reports in the kingdom. America's highest diplomats tried to convince those in the region that Iraq's problems were the responsibility of the Iraqi government and ought to be dealt with internally. There was, in fact, enough money to provide for the Iraqi population if resources were more equitably distributed. Nonetheless, Arab public opinion laid the blame for Iraqi suffering on America's doorstep. After all, how could the United States justify a sanctions policy that relied on a megalomaniac such as Saddam Hussein acting in the best interest of his own people?

The introduction of Arab satellite television in the early to mid-1990s also magnified the Iraqi suffering and riveted Arab attention much as coverage of the Vietnam War did for Americans more than twenty years prior. The need to manage media stories skeptical of government policy was virgin territory for both the Saudi leadership and the American military operating inside the kingdom. The best-known station, al-Jazeera, began broadcasting in 1996 and became a 24-hour station in 1999. Its popularity surged during Operation Desert Fox in 1998 when it aired live footage of American attacks on Iraq. Two competitors, Abu Dhabi Satellite Channel and Arab News Network, began reporting in the late 1990s.[35] Now Arabs could receive uncensored news reported by other Arabs. Iraq and Palestine featured prominently on the stations, with the two stories often fusing into one. It further stoked the Saudi population's anger at the United States and at its own government for partnering with it.

As the 1990s wore on, the strain between the United States and Saudi Arabia around Iraq policy became increasingly obvious. After Iraqi forces violated the northern no-fly zone and decimated Kurdish opposition and CIA outposts in 1996, the U.S. secretary of defense, William J. Perry, approached regional leaders to support a limited military response. For the first time, America's stalwart partners Saudi Arabia and Turkey both refused. Riyadh declined to allow the U.S. Air Force to fly strike missions from Saudi bases. Prince Sultan told reporters that the use of Saudi bases "was not requested from us. If it was requested we would have rejected it."[36] America attacked without Saudi overt support. In 1998 as America geared up to hit Iraq again, Saudi Arabia's defense minister made clear that his country did not favor such strikes. The new U.S. secretary of defense, William S. Cohen, did not even bother to ask for the use of the more than one hundred American aircraft based inside Saudi Arabia, to avoid the possibility of a politically embarrassing Saudi refusal.[37]

By most accounts, Saudi defense officials viewed the no-fly zone in southern Iraq and its required forces inside Saudi Arabia as a regrettable fact of life. But America's "pinprick" strikes, as the regular shelling of Iraqi targets from very high altitudes came to be called, seemed only to win the Iraqi president increasing regional support without resolving the Iraq problem. Saudi decision makers also began questioning American resolve.[38]

In December 1998, after UN weapons inspectors left Iraq in frustration, President Clinton launched Operation Desert Fox, a four-day military campaign against Iraq. Saudi leaders opposed the operation, which they thought would only antagonize their wounded but still dangerous neighbor. Saudi Arabia's preferred plan, a coup led by Iraqi Sunni Baathists, did not inspire confidence within the American establishment given that a number of coup attempts already had been tried but had failed.

By the end of the 1990s there was little agreement between the two countries about how to manage the Iraqi threat. Defense Secretary Cohen made regular trips to the kingdom, but the secretary of state, Madeleine K. Albright, and most of the rest of the administration focused their attention elsewhere: on the Balkans, on trying to resolve the Arab-Israeli conflict, and on American economic growth. Riyadh continued paying for food, fuel, water, and most everything else that American operations in Saudi Arabia required. But restrictions mounted around U.S. military activity. As Kenneth M. Pollack, Clinton's director for Gulf affairs at the National Security Council, remembered, "By any measure, the Saudis ha[d] become less supportive of limited U.S. military operations against Iraq."[39]

Afghanistan Is Not a One-Way Street

The failed state of Afghanistan and the terrorism it spawned provided another area of tension between the two countries. During the 1980s Afghanistan had represented the height of American-Saudi cooperation and shared interests. But with victory and the end of the Cold War, there was no agreement on how to manage post-conflict Afghanistan.

When, in September 1991, the U.S. secretary of state, James Baker, and the Soviet foreign minister, Boris Pankin, agreed to suspend the aid and arms that continued to trickle into Afghanistan (belying the formal end of the war two years prior), Washington's political agenda was already crammed full with other issues such as the reunification of Germany, domestic calls for a "peace dividend," and Somalia's devastation due to internecine political warfare. American officials expected that if left to its own devices, Afghanistan would return to its pre-Soviet-era political configuration, a strong tribal society with a weak political center.[40] Throughout the mid-1990s, the United States had "no policy" toward Afghanistan.[41]

Not so for Saudi Arabia, Pakistan, and Iran, whose leaders all tried to affect Afghanistan's abysmal political landscape. Although the Soviets had withdrawn their forces, a durable political solution among Afghan's warlords proved impossible. Renewed fighting among the warlords pushed yet more refugees into Pakistan's refugee camps. Warlords seemed bent on raping and pillaging the very populations they claimed to represent. To make matters worse for Saudi Arabia and Pakistan, it appeared that Iran sought to take advantage of the chaos and further extend its influence over Afghanistan. Paying little heed to the changed global context, Pakistan and Saudi Arabia continued working through the more fundamentalist anti-American fighters such as Hekmatyar and Sayyaf, as they had done alongside the United States during the 1980s. Islamic organizations continued raising considerable funds inside Saudi Arabia and the rest of the Gulf to assist.

Private Saudi donors, along with well-established Saudi charities, continued pouring money into Afghanistan and the wider region. In the early 1990s, the kingdom's Ministry of Pilgrimage and Religious Trusts announced that the government had spent about $850 million on mosque construction worldwide in recent years, employed fifty-three thousand religious leaders in mosques around the globe, and planned to hire another seventy-three hundred prayer leaders. King Fahd announced his intention to ship millions of free Qurans to the newly independent, predominantly Muslim countries of Central Asia.[42] Religion continued to serve as Saudi Arabia's weapon of choice.

In the early 1990s, long before most Americans or Saudis recognized the extent of the problem, the U.S. ambassador to Pakistan, Robert B. Oakley, asked Prince Turki if he was worried about the radicalization of Afghan Arabs. They hated both the Saudis and the Americans, Oakley warned: "Afghanistan won't be a one way street, these guys will come home." In fact, men such as Gulbuddin Hekmatyar and Abdul Rasul Sayyaf who the U.S. and Saudi Arabia had funded during the 1980s, actively campaigned against the U.S.-Saudi alliance during Desert Storm. Prince Turki answered that yes, he was indeed worried; the problem was that he could not get anyone back home to see things in quite the same way.[43]

The situation in Afghanistan became particularly severe when Osama bin Laden, fleeing Sudan, once again took up residency there in 1996. During his time in Sudan, bin Laden's rhetoric had become increasingly anti-American and anti-Saudi. He had used his time in Africa to build a base of anti-American anti-Saudi operations. During the 1990s, Arab states, particularly Egypt, Algeria, and Saudi Arabia, were actively pursuing Islamic militants within their borders.[44] The return home of Afghan war fighters fomented domestic unrest throughout the region and governments began actively pursuing such fighters. Osama bin Laden welcomed Islamic refugees to Sudan, at times paying for their transport there. Bin Laden had the active support of the Sudanese religious leader Hassan al-Turabi, a man who had benefited from Saudi funding during the 1980s. Those fleeing to Sudan were added to al-Qaeda's growing roster of recruits.

Bin Laden had set up al-Qaeda somewhere "around [the] area [of] 1989" in the waning days of the Afghan war, according to testimony provided by Jamal al-Fadl, a turncoat al-Qaeda operative.[45] The reason was in part logistical, an effort to keep track and support Arabs fighting in Afghanistan.[46] By 1989, with the Afghan war over, al-Qaeda came to serve a grander purpose. Its goal was to keep Afghan fighters together to "make Jihad" and "change the Arab government[s] because there's no Muslim government."[47] Al-Qaeda's organization eventually included an intelligence component, military, financial, political, and media committees, and an advisory council.[48] Over the next decade bin Laden's database would grow and al-Qaeda's support and logistical abilities would become increasingly sophisticated. Over time it became apparent that al-Qaeda was drawing significant financial support from wealthy citizens on the Arabian Peninsula. By 1998 al-Qaeda sympathizers were able to mount near-simultaneous bombings in Kenya and Tanzania, hundreds of miles apart. No previous terrorist operation had shown the kind of skill that was evident in the destruction.[49]

The Saudi government grew increasingly worried and urged bin Laden's family members to convince him to come home so that authorities there could better monitor and control him. At different points his mother, his brothers, and even his eighty-year-old uncle traveled to Sudan to encourage his return. He rebuffed all requests. In 1994 the Saudi government reversed course, freezing bin Laden's assets and stripping him of his citizenship.

In 1996 Saudi officials engaged in secret discussions with their Sudanese counterparts, urging Sudanese president Omar Hassan Ahmed al-Bashir to expel bin Laden.[50] America and Egypt followed suit. In spring 1996 a Sudanese official in the Defense Ministry, Elfatih Erwa, indicated to American officials that Sudan was prepared to give bin Laden to Saudi Arabia. But Saudi officials turned down the offer, as bin Laden had become a far more recognized and popular figure and they feared that his return would only further embolden his followers to focus attacks on the regime. As two former members of Clinton's NSC staff recall, "The Saudi option was a calculated nonstarter." Saudi officials feared that bin Laden would reassume his star status if allowed back home. The United States did not want him either, "for the simple reason that since he had not yet been indicted the Justice Department had no grounds to hold him."[51]

In May 1996 bin Laden departed Sudan, refueled in the United Arab Emirates, and landed in Afghanistan. Few believed then that he could cause more problems in Afghanistan, a landlocked, remote, and devastated country, than he had in Sudan or Saudi Arabia. But his return to Afghanistan was something like a homecoming. Bin Laden knew the country well and still had contacts there. He was able to plan, scheme, train, and operate outside the reach of most of the world's intelligence services.

Three months later bin Laden issued a lengthy, meandering fatwa that was published by *Al-Quds al-Arabi*, a respected London-based Arab newspaper. It was the first formal enunciation of his views. In it he repeatedly decried the dangers of the "Zionist-Crusader alliance" and targeted the House of Saud. Bin Laden protested the incarceration of al-Auda and Hawali, the plundering of Saudi Arabia's financial reserves, and the presence of American troops in the kingdom. He singled out Saudi Arabia's interior and defense ministers, Princes Naif and Sultan, for particular opprobrium.

It was also during 1996 that some high-level Clinton officials began seeing the orchestrated Arab Sunni, rather than Persian Shi'a, terrorism threat. One CIA official described Tony Lake as "foaming at the mouth about bin Laden" as early as 1996, especially after bin Laden returned to Afghanistan.[52] Between 1996 and 1999 Washington's attention slowly shifted from Iran to Saudi Arabia. With that shift, bin Laden's cash nexus on the Persian Gulf's western shores came more into focus. Vice President Albert A. Gore, Jr., raised the problem with Crown Prince Abdullah for the first time in 1999.

Bin Laden's arrival in Afghanistan in 1996 could not have been better timed. Two years before he arrived, the Taliban, a fundamentalist Islamic student movement, had successfully seized one of Afghanistan's few cities, Kandahar, with relatively little loss of life. The population, exhausted by a decade and a half of fighting and the violence that continued to plague the country after the Soviets' withdrawal, welcomed their entry. Various political arrangements between the different warlords throughout the early 1990s, brokered by Saudi Arabia and Pakistan, had not held, and the country had descended further into violence and chaos.

The extent of Afghanistan's political weakness is best displayed by the fact that a simple student movement, albeit one backed by Pakistan and Saudi Arabia, could garner popular support and sweep out battle-hardened warlords. The Taliban's foot soldiers were drawn from the Afghan refugee camps just over the Pakistani border. In the camps, young boys, often orphaned, were schooled in Saudi-funded Pakistani madrassas in little other than religion and violence. They knew hardly anything about their old country's tribal structure, customs, or culture. In the words of the Pakistani journalist Ahmed Rashid, "These boys were what the war had thrown up like the sea's surrender on the beach of history."[53] What these students did know was jihad, and they were easily mobilized to fight for their country, which was as foreign to them as any other. Four months after bin Laden arrived, in November 1996, the Taliban executed Afghanistan's reviled former president, Muhammad Najibullah, solidifying their power over all of Afghanistan. In Saudi Arabia, nostalgia further justified supporting the Taliban.[54] For some, the Taliban were echoes of the early Nejdi fighters, reminiscent of the zealous warriors that Abdel Aziz had deployed to subdue unruly Arabia.

Early in bin Laden's stay, the new-to-power Taliban were unsure how to handle their internationally renowned Arab guest. Taliban representatives contacted Saudi intelligence asking what they should do with the itinerant bin Laden. "If you have already offered him refuge," Prince Turki told Taliban representatives, you should keep him there, but "make sure that he does not operate against the kingdom or say anything against the kingdom."[55] Bin Laden's anti-American statements did not seem to faze anyone.

Bin Laden proved useful to the Taliban. Through his wealth and construction expertise, he was able to fund and build roads, training camps, and other necessary infrastructure. For the next six years the Taliban sheltered bin Laden. They resisted international efforts to dislodge him, arguing that he was their guest, and custom prevented them from compelling any guest to leave.

As is now known, bin Laden and the Taliban turned Afghanistan into a lethal international terrorist recruitment and training camp. Between 1996 and 2001 U.S. intelligence estimates suggest that between ten thousand and twenty thousand recruits passed through al-Qaeda's Afghan training camps.[56] Bin Laden's followers hailed from all over the Middle East, Europe, and beyond. Although the actual number of Saudis passing through the camps is hard to gauge, one expert on al-Qaeda estimates that about 66 percent of al-Qaeda's foot soldiers were Saudi, although the leadership was dominated by Egyptians.[57] Al-Qaeda required about $30 million per year to operate. The funds were generated largely through charitable donations. According to the 9/11 Commission's report, "Al Qaeda found fertile fund-raising ground in Saudi Arabia, where extreme religious views [hardened by Saudi domestic instability] are common and charitable giving was both essential to the culture and subject to very limited oversight." The charitable institutions that had been mobilized to serve Afghanistan in the 1980s were still well established and, drawing heavily on Saudi donors, continued to pump money into that country throughout the 1990s.[58]

Back in the late 1990s, however, these facts were just emerging. Neither the CIA nor the FBI was able to produce a clear picture of al-Qaeda's funding sources. Although the United States made some high-level representations to Saudi officials as early as 1997, and Vice President Gore spoke with Crown Prince Abdullah about the problem of Gulf money funding al-Qaeda during a meeting in Washington in 1999, there was little certainty and much confusion. The 9/11 Commission acknowledged that "before the September 11 attacks, the Saudi government resisted cooperating with the United States on the al-Qaeda financing problem, although the U.S. government did not make this issue a priority or provide the Saudis with actionable intelligence about al-Qaeda fund-raising in the kingdom."[59]

Twin Bombings in Africa

On August 7, 1998, an event occurred that would further strain U.S.-Saudi relations and push terrorism to the front of the Clinton administration's foreign policy concerns. Two powerful bombs, later traced back to al-Qaeda, exploded simultaneously at the U.S. embassies in Kenya and Tanzania. The carnage was extensive and mostly affected locals in Nairobi and Dar es Salaam. The attacks took place on the eighth anniversary of American troops entering the kingdom and six months after bin Laden issued his "jihad against Jews and Crusaders," which urged followers "to kill the Americans and their allies—civilians and military."[60] Immediately after the attacks President Clinton announced that "we will use all the means at our disposal to bring those responsible to justice, no matter what or how long it takes."[61] In November of that year the Justice Department handed down a 238-count indictment charging bin Laden with conspiracy to kill Americans.[62] He became America's most wanted fugitive.

In response to the attacks, the United States launched missiles into Afghanistan. Several of the missiles misfired, and only one of the six facilities struck was a bin Laden training camp that was nearly empty.[63] Washington did not warn either Riyadh or Islamabad (whose territory the missiles overflew), in part because American officials did not fully trust their counterparts. Saudi officials were livid that the Americans had not consulted them beforehand. Upon hearing of the attack, Prince Bandar immediately boarded a plane and returned home from the United States in order to manage the political fallout that he rightly anticipated. Not only were the Saudis kept in the dark, but rather than deal bin Laden a decisive blow, America's actions seemed only to provoke bin Laden and, as far as the Saudi leadership could tell, stir regional sympathies. For Saudi Arabia, limited action was worse than no action. Washington did not share this assessment. The U.S. ambassador to Saudi Arabia, W. Wyche Fowler Jr., remembered this episode as a "major flashpoint" in U.S.-Saudi relations.[64]

In June before the Africa bombings, Turki al-Faisal met in Afghanistan with Mullah Muhammad Omar, the Taliban's leader, to discuss Osama bin Laden. Bin Laden had become more, rather than less, powerful after his two years in Afghanistan—an outcome few had expected. Omar reportedly agreed to turn bin Laden over to Saudi officials. After the attack Turki returned to pick up bin Laden, but the Taliban leader expressed a change of heart. "Why are you doing this?" Mullah Omar asked Prince Turki. "Why are you persecuting and harassing this courageous, valiant Muslim? Instead of doing that, why don't you put your hands in ours and—let us go together and liberate the Arabian Peninsula from the infidel soldiers?"[65] A furious Prince Turki left empty-handed, and bin Laden remained sheltered in Afghanistan. The Taliban had shown that they could operate independent of Saudi Arabia, an important financial backer. In response, the Saudis expelled Taliban representatives in the kingdom and pulled their ambassador from Afghanistan. There is some evidence to suggest that in October 1998 the Saudi government dispatched a hit team to kill bin Laden.[66]

It was not until a 1999 visit to the White House by Crown Prince Abdullah that Americans formally raised the issue of bin Laden and his Saudi financial support at the highest level. Vice President Gore and the crown prince agreed to set up a meeting on the issue between U.S. counterterrorism experts and high-ranking Saudi officials, which resulted in two NSC-initiated trips to Saudi Arabia in 1999 and 2000. During these trips NSC, treasury, and intelligence representatives spoke with Saudi officials, and later interviewed members of the bin Laden family.[67] Still, U.S. officials focusing on counterterrorism were frustrated by the lack of information provided by Saudi counterparts on bin Laden and al-Qaeda. In 1999, the same year that Gore met Abdullah, the State Department formally designated al-Qaeda a foreign terrorist organization. Afghanistan was another area in which the United States and Saudi Arabia seemed no longer to work off the same page.

Oil

Oil policy offered no balm to the irritated U.S.-Saudi relationship. In 1997–98, as a result of spiking Venezuelan production, decreasing global demand attributed to the Asian financial crisis, and increased OPEC quotas, oil prices collapsed to $12 per barrel, at points falling even lower.

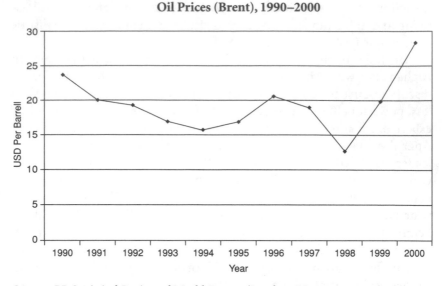

Oil Prices (Brent), 1990–2000

Source: BP Statistical Review of World Energy (London: BP Amoco, 2005), 14.

Given Saudi Arabia's precarious domestic situation, the price slide was a disaster. For Crown Prince Abdullah, America's response was just as troubling. Washington reveled in low energy prices, which spurred consumption and economic growth. Little heed was given to how declining prices exacerbated domestic turmoil halfway across the globe.

Crown Prince Abdullah responded by authorizing discussions between Saudi and Iranian OPEC representatives (something Washington viewed as a troubling development in its own right), which resulted in remarkable cooperation between the two energy producers. Improved Iranian-Saudi relations allowed OPEC members to tighten OPEC quotas and reverse declining prices. At the same time, Saudi Arabia made the strategic decision not to increase its production capacity despite forecasts of growing global demand. Many oil analysts interpreted this reluctance as a Saudi desire for higher prices. According to Edward L. Morse and Amy M. Jaffe, two well-regarded oil experts, "OPEC governments [led by Saudi Arabia], reacting to the financial suffering caused when oil prices dropped precipitously in 1998, became cautious about expanding capacity, realizing instead that greater revenue would be best achieved not by bringing new oil production capacity on line but rather by curtailing output."[68]

As prices rose throughout 1999 and 2000, the U.S. secretary of energy, William B. Richardson, made several highly publicized trips and phone calls to the kingdom urging a more flexible oil policy. Senator Charles

E. Schumer (D-N.Y.) and others called for Washington to release its strategic petroleum reserve, an act that would have immediately eased prices. Still, Riyadh hardly budged, and by 2000 oil prices rose to nearly $30 per barrel, a threefold increase in two years. Abdullah appeared intent on fueling his country's economic recovery rather than underwriting the U.S.-Saudi partnership. As Morse and Jaffe conclude, Abdullah "exhibited more reluctance to cater to U.S. wishes than Fahd demonstrated in the 1980s and early 1990s." Oil prices became another divisive issue in U.S.-Saudi relations.

The Peace Process

The role of Saudi Arabia in the Arab-Israeli peace process would follow the general trend of deteriorating U.S.-Saudi relations. Ellen Laipson, who covered the Middle East at the NSC from 1993 to 1995, remembered that in the early Clinton years "we did think Saudi Arabia was a real powerhouse in the Arab world . . . to me there was no question Saudi Arabia was a heavyweight."[69] But Saudi Arabia's role in the peace process was viewed only instrumentally by the Clinton team. Unlike Ronald Reagan, who saw Saudi Arabia as the key to peace between Israel and Arab states, Clinton's team viewed the kingdom as merely an important supporting actor.[70] Under Clinton, the Arab-Israeli peace process was ultimately reduced to a series of bilateral negotiations between Israel and Syria, on one hand, and Israel and the Palestinians, on the other, with America as the crucial mediator. To underscore this point, Clinton's special representative to the Arab-Israeli crisis, Dennis B. Ross, stated in no uncertain terms, "I am a firm believer in focusing first on developing relationships between the two key protagonists."[71] Dialogue between other regional actors was a secondary concern.

The administration did call upon Saudi Arabia, but only when specific problems arose. Prince Bandar, for example, provided Washington a useful back channel to Syrian president Hafez al-Asad when the Syrian-Israeli negotiation track appeared promising in the mid-1990s. Ross recalled Prince Bandar unfurling a list of Syrian demands in order to communicate them to the Americans and Israelis.[72] Still, Ross spent most of his time shuttling between Israel, Palestinian territories, Syria and Jordan, the real focus of his attention. When he engaged the Saudis, it tended to be at one of Bandar's estates in London, Aspen, or Virginia.

This instrumentality failed the administration. When, for example, peace talks between Israelis and Palestinians bogged down over prisoner exchanges in 1998, at the Wye River Plantation on Maryland's

Eastern Shore, President Clinton picked up the phone and called Egyptian president Hosni Mubarak, urging him to release a high-profile Israeli prisoner. Having not been part of the original conversations, Mubarak balked. A similar situation arose with Crown Prince Abdullah during the high-stakes Camp David talks in 2000, when the Israelis and Palestinians drew painfully close to reaching a final-status agreement. One key sticking point emerged around parsing the holy city of Jerusalem's sovereignty. At the eleventh hour Clinton called the Saudi crown prince, hoping he would undertake some gesture to make it easier for Arafat to complete a deal on Jerusalem. While Saudis and Palestinians disagree over whether the Saudis followed through, there is little doubt that the Saudis were reluctant to seriously engage, having been frozen out of earlier conversations. As Robert A. Malley, the special assistant to the president for Arab-Israeli affairs at the NSC, recalled, "We undervalued how important it was to get Saudi Arabia on Arafat's side."[73] This view was echoed by Martin Indyk, who in 2000 was appointed U.S. ambassador to Israel. He too recalled that "we did not have a policy of bringing the Arabs to the table."[74]

Keeping Saudi Arabia, Egypt, and others at arm's length from peace negotiations was partly a function of design and the belief that peace would be achieved through bilateral, rather than multilateral, discussions. But the design was reinforced by a structural reality. By 2000, Washington had few effective communications channels open with Saudi Arabia. Bandar had neither the ear of the crown prince nor easy access to the president. Dennis Ross was already overloaded in his efforts to cultivate strong bilateral relations between the United States and Israeli, Palestinian, and Syrian leaders. The assistant secretary of state for the Near East, Edward S. Walker Jr., had been effectively cut out of the peace process policy loop.

"Going Our Own Ways"

Saudi Arabia under Clinton was part of a larger Middle East policy. It was brought in when Americans needed a channel opened with Syria, or when Palestinians needed last-minute cover on Jerusalem. One senior administration official recounts that after negotiations failed, "Bandar was dismayed. He thought we were a bunch of idiots."[75] To be fair, the administration did not think that, given the option, either the Saudis or Egyptians would be terribly helpful. The peace process proved yet one more area in which the United States and Saudi Arabia were moving in different directions.

The Cold War glue that had held the two countries together for so long was dissolving. "Common interests were over time being reduced," remembered Martin Indyk, and the two nations were "gradually going our own ways."[76] Although for most Americans the nineties were a buoyant, heady time, they also turned into a lost decade of American foreign policy. Many of America's Cold War relationships lost their rationale. They were not reconstituted to handle the threats emerging from the new and complicated security environment, including terrorism, terrorist financing, and Saudi Arabia's religious proselytizing. Clinton never built a comprehensive strategy to deal with such problems. It is unlikely that a rejectionist Congress would have supported him even if he had.

Only a decade after the United States had built a global coalition to defend Saudi Arabia's oil and territorial integrity, the relationship was in tatters. Without a shared vision of the threats and the means to protect against them, oil interests alone could not sustain the strong high-level working relations of the prior decades. Over the course of the 1990s Saudi leaders lost confidence in America's regional policies, and close U.S.-Saudi relations became increasingly unpopular inside the kingdom. U.S. officials chafed under increasingly restrictive rules of engagement in its operations against Iraq, and limited Saudi Arabia cooperation in matters of counterterrorism. There was little agreement about how to proceed in Afghanistan. Volatile oil prices undermined each side's faith in the other. Fighting in the Palestinian territories emerged as a major point of tension. The attacks of September 11 would raise even more questions about the rationale for continued U.S.-Saudi relations.

12

September 11 and Beyond

On August 27, 2001, at a White House meeting with Condoleezza Rice, President George W. Bush's national security advisor, Prince Bandar relayed what he recalls as "the hardest message I've had to deliver between our two countries since I started working in this country, in 1983."[1] It was a grave communiqué from Saudi Arabia's Crown Prince Abdullah. "We were your friend when it was not fashionable to be your friend," Bandar began. "We stood in the fifties and sixties with you in the region when nobody was. The biggest challenge, of course, to the two of us was Saddam Hussein's invasion of Kuwait." But now, Bandar continued, the crown prince was deeply disturbed by the escalating violence between Israeli and Palestinians, and America's apparent decision not to intervene. "In light of all that, the Crown Prince feels that he cannot continue dealing with the United States. We feel that since you have taken such a decision, then we also are obliged to take our own decision."[2]

Bandar did not specify exactly what the crown prince meant. The message left open possibilities ranging from a renewed oil embargo to reduced funding for different U.S. pet projects. The message's solemnity and open-endedness focused the administration's attention, as it constituted one of the most serious threats issued by a Saudi leader against the United States. Belying the conspiracy theories linking the House of Bush and the House of Saud, George W. Bush presided over one of the worst moments in the history of U.S.-Saudi bilateral relations.[3]

President Bush responded to the crown prince's threat with a letter promising to reexamine U.S. policy toward the Israeli-Palestinian crisis. The fighting was beginning to wear on America's relations with Arab states, and European ones as well. The two sides arranged for a high-level meeting to take place on September 13, 2001, to salvage what remained of the U.S.-Saudi relationship. When Prince Bandar met with President Bush on September 13, two days after the worst terrorist attack on American soil, the context was far more horrific than either could have imagined when the meeting was first scheduled.

For years the royal family had manipulated Saudi domestic politics to manage Cold War challenges. To build domestic legitimacy and rebuff external aggression, Saudi leaders had catered to the most radical elements of the kingdom's religious establishment. It was not that Washington had ignored Saudi Arabia's proselytizing, but rather that Washington accepted and at times actively encouraged it to secure shared geostrategic ends. There was a long-term price to pay for such policies. On September 11 those costs came due.

It took the Saudi leadership eighteen months to acknowledge the kingdom's role in the attacks and to begin aggressively pursuing homegrown extremists. American officials met Riyadh's original denials of responsibility with a steely public silence. The administration stood by while the kingdom's popularity in the United States plummeted and left local Saudi officials on their own to answer accusations of complicity. Once Riyadh recognized and began actively combating domestic terrorism, Washington publicly acknowledged the kingdom's positive contributions. Still, it will take years for Saudi Arabia to establish the kinds of institutions and norms of accountability necessary to address this new threat. It also became clear that combating Islamic extremism will not have the same kind of domestic resonance inside the kingdom that fighting "godless Communism" once did.

But in early 2001, when the George W. Bush presidency was still in its infancy, such challenges lay in the future. In those earliest days, the problems confronting the two countries were severe, but they occupied much more familiar territory.

The al-Aqsa Intifada

President Bush assumed office six months after the beginning of a new round of vicious fighting between Israelis and Palestinians. The proximate cause for the al-Aqsa Intifada, as it came to be called, was the failure of Israel-Palestinian negotiations at Camp David in July 2000. Hostilities escalated over the course of successive months, roiling the Middle East.

For the incoming Bush administration, events in the Holy Land, while violent, were a bit of a sideshow. There was a general belief that if President Clinton, who had amassed considerable knowledge about the conflict and spent significant political capital trying to resolve it, could not reconcile the two parties, it was unlikely that the new team would do any better.[4] In addition, the incoming Bush team defined the fighting as a regional problem, one that should be solved locally. The United States' primary focus at the time was on major powers such as China and Russia.[5] President Bush did not assign a special envoy to the Middle East, General Anthony C. Zinni, for a full ten months after assuming office, and once the president did name Zinni, Israel's policy of assassination and uncontrolled Palestinian violence quickly undercut his envoy's standing in the region.

For Saudis and other Arabs, the al-Aqsa Intifada emerged as a high-priority issue that necessitated urgent American attention. As had happened during the first Intifada, which began in December 1987, pictures of young Palestinian boys throwing stones at Israeli tanks sur-faced. The David-versus-Goliath images that appeared in nearly all media outlets energized Arabs in the region, particularly as violence on both sides escalated unceasingly. Arab satellite television stoked domestic outrage. Unlike the Intifada a decade earlier, this time the Saudi leadership was unable to effectively filter the pictures and messages flooding into the kingdom.

On television, violent scenes were aired continuously, the most brutal often repeated with the greatest frequency. To make matters worse for both the Saudi and American leaderships, pictures of Palestinians cowering before Israeli soldiers often blended seamlessly into pictures of ailing Iraqis. With its access to satellite television stations, the Saudi population was introduced to more gruesome pictures and a steadier drumbeat of anti-Americanism than had been allowed in the past, when the government had had more control over the media. To its citizens, the ruling family appeared impotent at resolving problems both at home and abroad.

American disengagement from the conflict deeply irritated Crown Prince Abdullah. He had expected better working relations now that the Republicans, led by the son of George H. W. Bush, were in power. Yet he was unable to focus the administration's attention on a matter that meant a lot to him and his standing at home. Crown Prince Abdullah made his fury clear when he publicly declined an invitation to the White House in May 2001. In August he sent Prince Bandar to deliver "the hardest message." For its part, the Bush administration believed that Saudi Arabia and Egypt, along with other Arabs, had to adopt a more proactive foreign policy before American intervention could ease the situation.

The ongoing Arab-Israeli conflict, one that always aggravated American-Saudi relations, was on full display during the administration's earliest days. On the bilateral U.S.-Saudi agenda, few other issues existed to sublimate it, as the U.S.-Soviet contest had done in years past.

September 11

The terrorist attacks of September 11, 2001, coming as they did when U.S.-Saudi relations were already at a low, would of course challenge the very foundation of the U.S.-Saudi relationship. Almost immediately after the attacks American intelligence concluded that the hijackers were of Middle Eastern origin and that the plot had been masterminded by Osama bin Laden and his supporters. Around 3 p.m. on the day of the attack, the director of central intelligence, George J. Tenet, told the president and his small circle of advisors that "the agency was still assessing who was responsible, but the early signs all pointed to Al-Qaeda."[6]

The post-September 11 period fundamentally challenged U.S.-Saudi relations. That fifteen of the nineteen hijackers came from Saudi Arabia turned the international spotlight onto the kingdom. In early 2001 56 percent of all Americans had given Saudi Arabia a favorable rating. By December of that year, support had plummeted to 24 percent.[7] As late as 2004 a political campaign advertisement that linked Saudi Arabia to the administration of George W. Bush increased support among focus group participants for presidential contender John F. Kerry by eight percentage points.[8]

Within the United States, a palpable anger emerged at the lack of outward Saudi contrition. Whereas citizens in other countries, including Iran, held vigils and demonstrated their support for the American people, Saudi Arabia emitted only a deafening quiet. Although senior statesmen later voiced their solidarity with Americans, the earliest and most audible Saudi spokesman was Prince Alwaleed bin Talal, a wealthy Saudi businessman, who presented New York mayor Rudolph W. Giuliani with a $10 million check and then lambasted American policy in the region. In a letter dispatched almost immediately after presenting the check, Prince Alwaleed stated, "Our Palestinian brethren continue to be slaughtered at the hands of the Israelis while the world turns the other cheek. . . . At times like this one, we must address some of the issues that led to the criminal attack." Believing that Alwaleed's letter served to justify the attack, which "invites it happening in the future," Giuliani returned the check, with considerable popular support.[9]

Senior Saudi officials further exacerbated growing anti-Saudi sentiment in the United States by failing to acknowledge the citizenship of the September 11 perpetrators. Although both Saudi Arabia's foreign minister and recently resigned intelligence chief, Saud and Turki al-Faisal, never questioned that bin Laden was behind the attacks, the skepticism of the interior minister, Prince Naif, garnered significant attention in the United States, especially because his ministry held primary responsibility for tracking down and dealing with terrorists inside the kingdom. As late as December 2002, more than a year after the attacks, Naif baldly stated, "We still ask ourselves: who has benefited from the September 11 attacks? I think they [the Jews] were the protagonists of such attacks."[10] In May 2004, in response to a spate of terrorist attacks inside the kingdom, Crown Prince Abdullah concluded that "we can be certain that Zionism is behind everything. . . . I don't say 100 percent, but 95 percent."[11]

It was not only the American general public that saw official Saudi complicity in the September 11 attacks. In July 2003, Defense Policy Board chairman Richard N. Perle invited Laurent Murawiec, an analyst at the government-funded RAND think tank, to brief board members on U.S. policy toward Saudi Arabia.[12] The Defense Policy Board, made up of elite foreign policy thinkers such as Henry Kissinger, James Schlesinger, Walter Slocombe, and Harold Brown, convened to explore U.S. policy toward the kingdom in the wake of September 11. Murawiec's presentation identified Saudi Arabia as "central to the self-destruction of the Arab world and the chief vector of the Arab crisis and its outwardly-directed aggression," and proposed targeting the kingdom's oil resources, financial assets, and holy places.[13] Although Murawiec's recommendations were not taken up by the White House, nor did RAND endorse his views, the briefing was "taken very very seriously" by officials in Riyadh, according to Faisal bin Salman, the son of the long-serving governor of Riyadh and a grandson of King Abdel Aziz.[14] It was not the first time that well-respected American strategic thinkers had entertained plans to unilaterally control Saudi oil facilities. Such contingencies had been drafted in the early 1950s and revisited in the mid-1970s.

Intense financial scrutiny also revealed a disturbing pattern of Saudi capital underwriting schools and mosques throughout the region and beyond that inculcated hate and intolerance and provided foot soldiers to al-Qaeda. Riggs Bank, used by the Saudi Arabian embassy in Washington, became the subject of an intense terrorist financing legal suit, as did the New York branch of Arab Bank. It was soon apparent that rather than drying up, funding channels created during the Afghan war had continued expanding after Washington turned its attention elsewhere.

After the attacks, Congress called a number of hearings devoted to terrorist financing. In 2002 an independent task force report sponsored by the Council on Foreign Relations, one of the nation's longest-established think tanks, found that "for years, individuals and charities based in Saudi Arabia have been the most important source of funds for Al-Qaeda. And for years, Saudi officials have turned a blind eye to this problem."[15]

The September 11 attacks exposed Americans to the dark underside of U.S.-Saudi relations. But for Saudis, tacit U.S.-Saudi cooperation around religion was hardly news. For years moderates had watched their leaders empower the most radical extremes of the religious establishment—"the shrieking owls," as one Saudi described them.[16] Not only did Washington not condemn such coddling, but often it seemed to encourage it, in order to serve larger regional goals such as rebuffing Iranian ambitions or deterring the Soviet Union. Like Americans, Saudis ignored how geostrategic interests drove their own government to take controversial decisions to secure a complicated set of national interests. This led to a complete breakdown in relations between the two populations when the terrorist attacks occurred, as each viewed the other as pursuing its own national self-interest at the expense of the other's. "We did America's dirty work," one Saudi told me over dinner, echoing a widely held belief inside the kingdom.[17] The Saudi leadership was deemed a tool of American policy makers rather than a proactive partner, though the latter is a more accurate description.

In part because the funding of religious extremism was a more complicated story than the one portrayed in the American media, Saudi anger rose against the United States, mirroring the ire that many Americans expressed toward their Saudi counterparts. In addition, increased fighting between Palestinians and Israelis and an impending war in Iraq generated a grassroots Saudi boycott of American goods and companies. Teachers sent their students home with lists of American products and suggested non-American alternatives. Procter & Gamble, among others, suffered significant short-term losses.

To protect the country from future attack, Washington issued a set of new visa restrictions that further inflamed anti-American sentiment inside the kingdom. Before September 11 Saudis had benefited from extremely lax entry procedures into the United States. They had been able to send their maids to the U.S. embassy or consulate and obtain same-day visas for the entire family. This allowed many to identify as adjunct American citizens.[18] The U.S. Department of Homeland Security, established in November 2003, instituted a much stricter set of entry regulations and embedded its own representatives within the embassy and consulates. Requesting visas became an onerous and time-consuming process, and applicants often were denied access for no apparent reason other than originating from Saudi Arabia.[19] After the attacks Saudi student visa applications fell by 80 percent.[20] Saudi businessmen with long histories of working in the United States, including Aramco officials, opted to conduct their business in Europe rather than the United States, in order to avoid entering a country they suddenly perceived as hostile. The U.S. ambassador to Saudi Arabia, Robert W. Jordan, recalled that the new restrictive visa policies greatly "upset upper-middle-class Saudis—those who had been most pro-American."[21]

At the official level, the fighting between Israelis and Palestinians became an ever more prominent topic of conversation between 2001 and 2003. In October 2001, in front of 150 influential Saudis, the crown prince reread his grave August 27 message to the president, adding, "We are at a crossroads. It is time for the United States and Saudi Arabia to look at their separate interests. Those governments that don't feel the pulse of the people and respond to it will suffer the fate of the Shah of Iran."[22] In a November 2001 interview with the *New York Times*, Foreign Minister Saud al-Faisal complained that he was "angrily frustrated" with the president, whose lack of involvement, he said, "makes a sane man go mad."[23] Ambassador Jordan and his staff were "lectured constantly" about America's policy around the fighting.[24]

In February 2002, the crown prince did try to move the Arab-Israeli discussion in a more productive direction by offering "full withdrawal from all the occupied territories, in accord with U.N. resolutions, including in Jerusalem, for full normalization of relations" with Israel.[25] But in the charged atmosphere immediately following September 11, the offer fell flat, particularly because many inside the administration interpreted it as a blatantly self-serving effort to change the subject from the September attacks. It was, however, a missed opportunity.

Even an April 2002 meeting between Bush and Abdullah at the president's ranch in Crawford, Texas, could not overcome the fissures in relations. According to one American there, the meeting was "very rocky and tense."[26] Bush approached the visit focused on terrorism. The crown prince expected to discuss the fighting between Israel and Palestinians. Periods of silence were followed by terse exchanges. In a desperate effort to establish some basis for discussion and personal rapport, the president took the crown prince on a forty-five-minute jeep ride around the farm, bringing with him only one interpreter. When the president and crown prince returned, their body language and the conversation's tone were notably improved. Conversation turned to what positive steps could be taken on the Israeli-Palestinian front and what could be done to counter terrorism. The Americans agreed to work toward securing Palestinian president Yasser Arafat's release from his confinement in Ramallah, and the Saudis pledged to crack down on Hamas and suicide bombers. The meeting marked a slight improvement in official relations. Still, there was a long way to go to restore even cordial relations between the two sides.

In a 2002 poll Saudi Arabia distinguished itself as the only country of ten surveyed in which a majority of the population (51 percent) harbored negative feelings toward the American people.[27] In the nine other countries, the majority of respondents separated their dislike for American policy from their generally more benign view of the American people. A 2003 Pew report, *Views of a Changing World*, came to the ominous conclusion that "the bottom ha[d] fallen out of support for America in most of the Muslim world."[28]

Vice President Dick Cheney experienced firsthand the costs of the relationship's decline. In March 2003 he toured the Middle East, seeking support for the upcoming military campaign against Iraq. At virtually every stop, including Jordan, Egypt, and Saudi Arabia, he heard the same message: with the fighting between Israel and Palestine, and the echoes of 9/11 still reverberating, it was an inauspicious moment to open a new front in Iraq. Crown Prince Abdullah took the unusual step of granting a television interview on the eve of Cheney's trip, in which he clarified his February proposal, the Abdullah Plan, stating that "what I said was normal relations [with Israel], just as we have with other countries." The crown prince also made clear that he believed that a campaign against Iraq "would not serve America's interests or the interests of the world."[29] The trip did little to reduce tensions between the United States and Saudi Arabia, although Saudi Arabia eventually did support American military action in Iraq to a greater degree than it acknowledged publicly.[30]

Reform in the Middle East

In addition to drawing attention to counterterrorism operations specifically, the September 11 attacks caused the administration to begin considering the political, economic, and social roots of terrorism. In time, transformation of the Middle East became one of the administration's foremost priorities and key drivers for reducing terrorism's appeal. Saudi Arabia, however, would prove vexing to Washington's reform agenda. Unlike in Eastern Europe, where the United States had long advocated democratization at the expense of the ruling government, in Saudi Arabia Washington wanted political change without fundamentally destabilizing a long-term partner that still wielded considerable influence. It would prove difficult to push too hard on the kingdom when the administration still wanted it to ensure the free flow of oil at reasonable prices, assist in its Iraq campaign, and help ease the Israel-Palestine conflict.

In December 2002 the State Department's director of policy planning, Richard Haass, gave the first official administration address on reform, arguing that

> by failing to help foster gradual paths to democratization in many of our important relationships—by creating what might be called a "democratic exception"—we missed an opportunity to help these countries become more stable, more prosperous, more peaceful, and more adaptable to the stresses of a globalizing world. It is not in our interest—or that of the people living in the Muslim world—for the United States to continue this exception. U.S. policy will be more actively engaged in supporting democratic trends in the Muslim world than ever before.[31]

Haass' speech drew broad support and reflected a "meeting of the minds" within the administration.[32]

Subsequently, the U.S. government launched a series of initiatives, including the Middle East Partnership Initiative and the Broader Middle East and North Africa Initiative, both devoted to political, social, and economic reform. Reform, and democracy in particular, became an even more prominent topic after the Iraq war. The president defined his commitment to promoting democracy in the Middle East in a major policy address at the National Endowment for Democracy in November 2003. He reiterated it in his January 2005 second inaugural address. In March 2005 he went even further by concluding that "decades of excusing and accommodating tyranny, in the pursuit of stability, have only led to injustice and instability and tragedy. It should be clear that the advance of democracy leads to peace."[33] White House officials anticipated that the president's second term would provide opportunities to press reform efforts inside the kingdom.[34]

The Fight for Saudi Arabia's Soul

Saudis met Washington's reform agenda with cynicism, questioning both American motives and resolve. There was little support for the United States interfering in local politics even from those who for years had called for a more democratically oriented foreign policy. The Saudi leadership encouraged the doubt. In a June 2005 press briefing in Riyadh, in response to a journalist's question about three human rights activists serving long prison sentences, Secretary of State Condoleezza Rice stated, "As I said exactly to the [Saudi foreign] Minister . . . the petitioning of the government for reform should not be a crime."[35] Ten days later, Prince Naif asserted that nobody had the right to interfere in "this internal matter." Prince Saud similarly criticized American intervention.[36]

Still, the September 11 attacks energized an ongoing debate within the Saudi royal family and among the wider population about the kingdom's future direction. Princeton professor Michael S. Doran depicted the split as one between then Crown Prince (now King) Abdullah, representing the more progressive elements of the royal family and society, and Prince Naif, speaking for the more conservative.[37] The two sides are grappling with how fast the kingdom should change and in what direction. Although Doran oversimplified the depth and scope of the split, both within the ruling family and the broader society, he captured better than most the kingdom's struggle. It is not about whether the religious establishment should play a role in local politics, but rather how much of a role it should play, and who should represent it. September 11 set off a renewed struggle for Saudi Arabia's collective soul, one with far-reaching consequences for its ability and willingness to address issues ranging from terrorist financing to domestic reform.

The struggle over the religious establishment's proper role has recurred throughout Saudi Arabia's history. As we saw in chapter 1, the first Saudi state fell in 1818, only to be replaced by a second Saudi state determined to rein in the excesses of the radical extremists. In the early 1900s King Abdel Aziz organized and encouraged religious fighters in order to settle the population and provide foot soldiers for territorial aggrandizement. By 1929, however, when its purpose was served, King Abdel Aziz attacked and dramatically scaled back the power of his once useful religious fighting force.

During the Cold War religious and political ends came together as increased religiosity served both the pragmatists, who understood the need to work with the United States and rebuff Soviet expansionism, and the zealots, determined to pursue ideologically pure policies. In the 1960s and early 1970s these strands merged in the person of Crown Prince (later King) Faisal. Later, in response to the dramatic events of 1979, Crown Prince (later King) Fahd, hardly known for his piety, cemented the pragmatist-extremist alliance by overseeing the unrestrained radicalization of Saudi Arabia's society-wide religious machinery to further political ends.

Throughout the Cold War political and religious ends were mutually reinforcing. After September 11 they diverged sharply and political choices became starker. Funding religious radicalism and supporting worldwide religious inculcation no longer served American, or global, interests. The Saudi leadership had to decide whether this tactic served its own.

Almost immediately after the September 11 attacks some members of the royal family attempted to subordinate the religious establishment to the political one, just as their fathers and forefathers had done. Turki al-Faisal directly challenged Sheikh Abdullah al-Turki, secretary-general of the World Muslim League and a member of the Council of Senior Ulema, the kingdom's highest religious body. In a widely read newspaper article the prince argued that "those responsible for affairs of state are the rulers," while "[religious] scholars only act in an advisory capacity."[38] He quoted a number of Islamic jurists to support his view. Soon after, Prince Turki's uncle, Talal bin Abdel Aziz, who in the 1960s had supported a constitutional monarchy, similarly challenged the "potentially very confusing" claim that affairs of state should be decided jointly by rulers and religious scholars.[39] Neither prince gained much traction in the internal debates.

The tide turned in spring 2003. In June of that year Crown Prince Abdullah supported the "National Dialogue," a broad-based series of highly publicized discussions designed to open up space within society to examine intolerance, chauvinism, and religious extremism. The series addressed some of society's grievances and questioned the most radical interpretations of Islam. While little concrete came from it, the dialogue provided reformers with some much-needed backing. Subsequently, some incorporated the dialogue's language into their own political petitions. Limited advances in liberalizing education are also an outgrowth of the dialogues.

Then, in a well-publicized op-ed piece written in June 2004 for the Saudi newspaper *Al-Watan*, Saudi Arabia's ambassador to the United States, Prince Bandar, forged headlong into the heart of the battle when he argued:

> Personally, I think this crisis can be [either] easy or difficult. If we deal with the crisis [as] the founding and believing king Abdul Aziz did at the Battle of Al-Sabla [in 1929], against those who advocated the same ideology as these deviants, and, with Allah's help, we vanquish them, [then the crisis will be] easy. [But] if we deal [with them] hesitantly, in hope that [the terrorists] are Muslim youths who have been misled, and that the solution [to the crisis] is that we call upon them to follow the path of righteousness, in hope that they will come to their senses—then we will lose this war, and this means that we will lose everything that this state and this people have accomplished over the past 600 years, and that we will enter a dark world whose end only Allah knows.[40]

What turned the tide in favor of the royal family's more pragmatic elements was a series of terrorist attacks that took place inside the kingdom beginning in May 2003, when homegrown suicide bombers simultaneously attacked three housing complexes in Riyadh. The bombings continued in November 2003 and January 2004. At that time the Saudi leadership began taking drastic security, political, and economic action against local terrorists and their support base. This was accompanied by a more streamlined American approach toward dealing with Saudi Arabia.

From the spring of 2003 until today, a steady stream of reports describe Saudi security forces hunting down militants, disbanding al-Qaeda cells, and seizing weapon caches.[41] Saudi intelligence forces also began working closely with the FBI. By late summer 2004 security forces had successfully foiled a number of potential attacks, rounded up hundreds of suspects, and killed dozens of militants, including twenty-three on their most-wanted list of twenty-six. Radical clerics were warned to tone down their fiery sermons, and more than two thousand were either banned from preaching or underwent "reeducation" programs.

After the May attacks the Saudi government also became more serious about reducing the flow of funds to the bank accounts of known terrorists and religious extremists. In July 2004 the Financial Action Task Force, an OECD organization devoted to combating money laundering and terrorist financing, judged that the kingdom was "compliant or largely compliant" with international standards in almost every indicator of effectiveness.[42]

Over a two-year period Saudi officials shut down al-Haramain, the official charity of the royal family and the organization responsible for dispersing $40 million to $50 million per year, although some recent reports suggest that some of its offices may still be operational, or operating under a different name.[43] The Saudi government instituted a series of laws making it harder for its citizens to move money internationally. It put charities under the watchful eye of state regulators and eliminated the practice of placing collection boxes in malls and other public places, in order to increase accountability. The crown prince urged Saudi citizens to keep charitable support at home. Saudi citizens are now giving more money to local causes than to ones further afield. In 2004 Saudi giving to domestic causes increased approximately 300 percent.[44]

Saudi determination in fighting domestic terror corresponded with a shift in Washington's approach toward the kingdom. In response to frustration around U.S.-Saudi counterterrorism cooperation, key members of the Bush administration met in December 2002 to overhaul America's approach toward Saudi Arabia.[45] Recognizing the need to better coordinate U.S. messages intended for Saudi leaders, they decided to appoint a high-level official with strong ties to the president to assume overall responsibility for the U.S.-Saudi counterterrorism portfolio.[46] Fran Townsend, assistant to the president at the National Security Council, became the point person for the United States. She quickly developed close working relations with Muhammad bin Naif, a dynamic and effective Saudi counterterrorism expert working at the highest levels of government; he is a grandson of King Abdel Aziz and the son of the ultraconservative Prince Naif. The high-level American group also acknowledged that on many occasions Washington had failed to give the Saudi authorities accurate and actionable intelligence, while still demanding an immediate response. The administration not only began trusting the Saudis with highly sensitive information (in turn made easier after May 2003, when Saudi Arabia became more demonstrably proactive in its counterterrorism strategy) but also demanded of itself a higher burden of proof that the information passed on to Riyadh was accurate. Furthermore, the administration came to the conclusion that many of Saudi Arabia's problems in fighting terrorism resulted from poor training, rather than malevolent intent, and it sought to rectify the situation by providing the kingdom with advanced training programs. The combination of the May attacks and the streamlined American approach produced a more active and successful Saudi response to terrorism.

Improvements in Saudi Arabia's efforts generated a positive American response. After May 2003, in congressional testimony, Ambassador J. Cofer Black, the State Department's coordinator for combating terrorism, concluded that Saudi Arabia showed "clear evidence of the seriousness of purpose and the commitment of the leadership of the kingdom to this fight [against terror]."[47] In his acceptance speech at the Republican National Convention in August 2004, President George W. Bush mentioned Saudi Arabia explicitly, stating that "four years ago . . . Saudi Arabia was fertile ground for terrorist fundraising," but now "Saudi Arabia is making raids and arrests."[48] Given a political climate in which Saudi Arabia had been so closely associated with terror, the statement was in fact remarkable.

Improved relations were best reflected in the meeting between Crown Prince Abdullah and President Bush at Crawford, Texas, in April 2005. Unlike the one three years earlier, this visit went smoothly. After leaving Crawford, one of the prince's close aides confided that "it wasn't a good meeting, it was a great meeting." Americans at Crawford described the meeting similarly.[49]

Although Saudi Arabia has made dramatic improvements in its counterterrorism efforts, ones that Washington rightly applauds, the kingdom still has a long way to go in dealing with the full extent of the problem. While Saudi Arabia has effectively focused on what goes on inside the kingdom (e.g., better regulating domestic charities, monitoring wire transfers, destroying local al-Qaeda cells, working shoulder to shoulder with the FBI inside the kingdom), it has been slower to tackle the international dimensions of the problem. The U.S. Treasury Department continues to observe that the kingdom has not yet addressed the problem of cash couriers, who easily transit the kingdom.[50] In testimony before the Senate Committee on Banking, Housing and Urban Affairs in July 2005, Treasury undersecretary-designate Stuart Levey made clear that "even today we believe that private Saudi donors may be a significant source of terrorist funding, including for the insurgency in Iraq."[51] Most troubling is the Saudi government's decision to define major Islamic organizations as multilateral organizations rather than charities. Groups such as the World Assembly of Muslim Youth, the Muslim World League, and the International Islamic Relief Organization are well-funded organizations that operate from the kingdom and receive considerable local support. Defining these groups as multilateral organizations rather than charities removes them from Saudi Arabia's post-September 11 strict account controls and monitoring requirements.[52] When pressed by Representative Sue Kelly (R-N.Y.) about the distinction, Prince Bandar likened Saudi control over the charities to U.S. control over the United Nations—that is, limited.[53] At the July 2005 hearing Senator Richard C. Shelby (R-Ala.), the committee's chair, appropriately registered his concern about this loose Saudi definition. Although the Saudi leadership claims that these multilateral organizations are no longer free to send money abroad from Saudi Arabia, both the State and Treasury Departments "have concerns about whether [such restrictions are] fully implemented."[54]

Saudi Arabia has taken significant strides toward fighting terrorism at home, but it has a way to go toward ending its support for radicalism abroad. Working closely and quietly with Saudi pragmatists those in the kingdom who understand American concerns and who view their self-interests similarly—as the White House is now doing is key to reducing the export of religious radicalism and the violence it spawns. Saudi religious institutions are deeply entwined in the fabric of the kingdom's global influence, have broad domestic support, and will be difficult to dismantle. Given the history between the two states, it is crucial that the United States do what it can to help. This will entail patience, focus, and calm, qualities that are not usually attributed to the United States in the best of circumstances and are even less evident after September 11.

In addition to improving its counterterrorism efforts, the kingdom is slowly experimenting with social, economic, and political reforms. Whether Saudi pragmatists will prevail in such efforts also remains an open question. One Saudi reformer captured the difficulty in assessing progress when he said that after 2003 "we hoped for the World Series and got the minor leagues."[55] Important steps have been taken. For example, during the winter of 2005 Saudi Arabia held its first set of municipal elections in over four decades. Although only half the seats were contested and women were not allowed to vote, the grand mufti has publicly stated that he sees no religious reasons why women could not vote during the next set of elections. Saudi and U.S. negotiations successfully completed a set of bilateral agreements necessary for Saudi Arabia's World Trade Organization bid. Articles questioning radical religious interpretations appear frequently in the Saudi press in both English and Arabic; until very recently such articles landed writers in prison. Riyadh is taking steps in the right direction, ones that Washington should encourage. Washington should celebrate progress when it occurs, and similarly point out setbacks and delays. One-sided accounting, which has been the norm in U.S. public discourse, only undermines those in the kingdom whom America needs to prevail.

Crown Prince Abdullah's elevation to king in August 2005 is one of the few unambiguously positive developments. Although by no means a liberal Western reformer, Abdullah recognizes the need for social and political evolution to both reduce the threat of terrorism and ultimately preserve the royal family's reign. As king, he has more power to undertake much-needed domestic reform, but his power is not unfettered. He will continue confronting powerful brothers, such as Prince Naif, who are more willing to cater to society's most conservative elements. In addition, he must contend with retrograde religious institutions that flourished under King Fahd and produced entrenched interests opposed to reform. Abdullah also must consider reform within a context in which nearly 40 percent of Saudi Arabia's population is under the age of fifteen (compared to 20 percent in the United States and 21 percent in China) and high levels of unemployment ensure a cadre of idle and angry youth—perfect targets for al-Qaeda recruiters.

The new king's task is made more urgent by his age—he was born around 1923. King Abdullah has limited time to reconfigure domestic structures that currently empower extremists. Given the ongoing battle between Saudi pragmatists and zealots, the king's choice of a second deputy prime minister, traditionally viewed as second in line for the throne, is all the more important. As of this writing, the position remains vacant. If Abdullah is able to appoint a pragmatic prince—

perhaps his half brother Prince Salman, the governor of Riyadh and full brother of the late King Fahd and Crown Prince Sultan, or even the more unlikely but courageous choice of someone from the next generation, a grandson of King Abdel Aziz—it will improve long-term prospects for his country and U.S.-Saudi relations. If a more conservative prince such as Prince Naif is appointed, the future for both countries will be considerably bleaker.

It is King Abdullah's fate to steer Saudi Arabia into the post-Cold War, post-September 11 era. How far he can take his kingdom and to what extent he can and will repulse powerful countervailing forces will be of considerable interest to the Bush administration, with its focus on Middle East reform.

A Fragile and Fractured Relationship Limps Toward the Future

It is ironic that the war on terror, which profoundly divides the American and Saudi people, provides an opportunity for the two leaderships to work together more closely. Since the 2003 bombings inside Saudi Arabia, and the realignment in America's approach toward that country, the two states have been in close coordination. Both states have a manifest self-interest in rooting out Saudi domestic terrorism. As Fran Townsend stated at a January 2005 meeting in Riyadh, "The world cannot defeat terrorism without Saudi Arabia defeating terrorism on its own grounds."[56]

But counterterrorism cooperation at the highest levels will not overcome profound challenges facing the bilateral relationship. Each population is against the other, and the broader set of national interests that once existed no longer prevails. Oil-hungry countries such as China and India, as well as a more independent Europe, offer new outlets for Saudi international economic engagement. At the same time, Saudi religious proselytizing no longer serves the bilateral relationship as it once did. Saudi Arabia has one of the world's fastest-growing populations and a broken education system unable to effectively train the next generation for current market demands. In short, the old bargains around oil, God, and real estate are antiquated, no longer serving the needs of either country particularly well. It will take considerable willpower and political capital from both sides to reconfigure it. It is an effort well worth making.

13

Reconfiguring the U.S.-Saudi Strategic Partnership

King Fahd's death in August 2005 marked the end of an era. Fahd's reign had spanned the pinnacle of U.S.-Saudi official relations. During the 1980s Saudi Arabia's fifth king steadfastly pursued pro-American policies, ultimately aligning the kingdom with Ronald Reagan's full-bodied anti-Communism. His stroke in 1995 occurred at the precise moment that Saudi Arabia could have, and should have, re-oriented its Cold War policies. But operating within Saudi Arabia's strict monarchical hierarchy, Crown Prince Abdullah did not have the political clout to implement necessary changes. Between the crucial years of 1995 and 2001 the kingdom's policies cruised on autopilot, following a path charted during a prior political age.

The American delegation that traveled to Riyadh in August 2005 paid homage to past political realities but offered little insight into the relationship's future direction. Days after the king died, the president dispatched Vice President Dick Cheney to Riyadh, along with former president George H. W. Bush and former secretary of state Colin Powell. This led the *New York Times* to conclude, incorrectly, that the "high-powered delegation" was "the latest signal that relations between the two countries have thawed since the strains of 9/11."[1] While indeed high-powered, the delegation was more of a backward glance at Desert Storm and overlapping Cold War interests than a current thawing. Notably absent from the delegation was Secretary of State Condoleezza Rice, Secretary of Defense Donald Rumsfeld, and Frances Townsend, the U.S. liaison with Saudi Arabia on counterterrorism. In contrast to the *New York Times'* characterization, America's delegation had the nostalgic feel of an old-timers' game, rather than the nervous anticipation of a new season.

A nuanced appreciation for the changing U.S.-Saudi partnership is still lacking today. Interests around oil, God, and real estate continue to drive the relationship but are confronting new and real challenges. The religious pillar is under the most significant duress. This is particularly troubling because any strategy for winning the war on terror would benefit from Saudi participation. As the guardian of Islam's two holiest mosques, King Abdullah wields considerable influence over the Islamic world. How Saudi Arabia's leaders manage their internal religious debates and external proselytizing will largely determine the future direction of Islam worldwide and in turn the U.S.-Saudi relationship. This is true whether or not the kingdom grants the United States lucrative oil deals or defense contracts.

The Saudi leadership today has more options than it did in the past. Its future economic and domestic well-being is no longer as dependent on the United States. Although both countries would be better off with easy working relations, such relations are not ensured and will require significant attention to achieve.

Evolving Oil Relations

Oil will remain important to U.S.-Saudi relationship, as it will to Saudi Arabia's relations with every other country. In 2003 Saudi Arabia was America's second-largest petroleum supplier, sending it 1.4 million barrels per day. According to one senior Aramco employee, the company still views the United States as its largest market, at least through the medium term.[2] But in the post-Cold War environment, Saudi Arabia's economic calculus has shifted and its interests no longer mirror America's as clearly as they once did.

Today, for example, the kingdom has more options for where to invest its profits. Both Europe and Asia boast mature markets that are competing for Saudi investment. Between 2001 and 2004 OPEC members cut the proportion of their dollar deposits by more than 13 percentage points, mainly to the advantage of the euro.[3] Although the direct effects of this have yet to be felt, changing investment patterns reduce the stakes that both Washington and Riyadh have in the other's economic well-being.

This divergence in economic interests will be compounded by Saudi Arabia's domestic problems, which are driving the leadership toward supporting higher oil prices. Saudi Arabia has one of the world's fastest-growing populations, with nearly 40 percent below the age of fifteen.[4] Between 15 and 30 percent of Saudi men and approximately

95 percent of women are unemployed. Because the kingdom relies on oil exports to meet the bulk of its budgetary needs, higher oil prices will help address many of its domestic problems. As one former Saudi deputy minister of the interior made clear, "the demographic explosion that Saudi Arabia is and will be witnessing in the next decade gives the government little room but to explore aggressively all ways of maximizing oil revenues."[5]

King Abdullah has allowed prices to rise steadily since the crash in 1997–98. Under his watch, OPEC established a target price band of between $18 and $25 a barrel. Today, Saudi officials are on record expressing their comfort with a band starting at $35 per barrel. In 1998, Riyadh also made the decision not to increase its production capacity, the deleterious effects of which are felt today through tight supply and high prices.[6]

A Saudi need for higher oil prices does not necessarily put the United States on a collision course with Saudi Arabia, although it does increase the likelihood for friction between the two states. The fact that Saudi Arabia controls the largest oil resources in the world gives it a long-term interest in stable and reasonable prices to dissuade conservation and keep alternative fuels off the market. So do its robust international investments. The kingdom's preference for higher oil prices is therefore balanced by a long-term desire to ensure global dependence and a vibrant international economy. Accordingly, Saudi Arabia routinely pursues less hawkish energy pricing than its oil-exporting counterparts.

As the world's top oil producer and its largest oil consumer, Saudi Arabia and the United States are now bound in a less political and more transactional relationship. Both states will attempt to maximize their own profits without damaging the overarching, economically beneficial relationship. While prices will likely drift higher in the future than was true in the past, the kingdom will work to cap them before the effects become too harmful to the international economy. Given that billions of dollars of Saudi investments are tied up in international markets and that global oil dependency works to its advantage, $100-per-barrel oil would be devastating to the international economy and therefore Saudi Arabia's own economic interests as well.

While oil remains fundamental to the U.S.-Saudi relationship, new actors such as China and India are playing a more prominent role in Saudi Arabia's energy calculations that will also reduce American influence. Asia's growing energy consumption provides new opportunities for Saudi economic, political, and military engagement. Oil demand in China is expected to rise from about 5 to 12 mbd between 2005 and 2030. During that same period the developing world's share of global oil demand is expected to increase from 30 to 40 percent. The

International Energy Agency estimates that fossil fuels will account for over 90 percent of the projected increase in world primary demand in the next twenty-five years. Oil will remain the single most dominant fuel in the primary energy mix.[7]

Saudi Arabia is aggressively pursuing markets in Japan, China, and elsewhere. It offers favorable terms of trade to ensure its role as a primary supplier. Military and economic relations are likely to follow in its wake. China is already an arms supplier to Saudi Arabia. As we saw in chapter 10, the Chinese supplied Saudi Arabia with controversial ballistic missile systems since the mid-1980s. Unlike the United States, China will have few qualms selling Saudi Arabia the sophisticated weaponry it requests. The United States will need to monitor closely the quantity and quality of Chinese arms sales to the kingdom.

The changing nature of the oil market cuts in two contradictory directions. First, it increases the stakes that others have in Saudi Arabia, which reduces American influence, particularly in the commercial realm. Saudi contracts are no longer reflexively decided in America's favor. Between July 2003 and January 2004 Crown Prince Abdullah supported the diversification of Saudi Arabia's economy away from the United States. American oil companies lost lucrative Saudi gas contracts to Lukoil, Sinopec, and Total, major Russian, Chinese, and French companies, respectively.

But growing demand also reduces Saudi Arabia's ability to isolate and target larger American strategic interests if it so desires. Should Saudi Arabia suddenly take oil off the market to punish the United States, as it did in 1973, the kingdom would immediately confront a hostile international coalition that includes China. A moderate Saudi oil policy is one of the few common interests that the United States and China now share. It also means that other countries will come to adopt other American interests in the Gulf including its interest in Saudi domestic security and regional stability. In a report for Andrew Marshall, the director of net assessment at the Office of the Secretary of Defense, three keen energy analysts argued:

> Enhanced and tightening ties between China and Saudi Arabia with respect to energy trade and investment could have a negative impact on both US-China and US-Saudi relations. But these consequences are not at all likely. The most likely consequences of heightened China-Saudi ties are those that will have benefits for the US and for global stability, even if there is a US loss of influence over the Kingdom as Saudi Arabia looks to the growing oil markets of East Asia. China will almost certainly have an increased concern over the stability of the Middle East region and on the protection of long haul sea-lanes.

Changed circumstances are likely to push China toward greater co-operation with the US in all of these regards.[8]

Although Washington should not take for granted that greater U.S.-Sino cooperation around Persian Gulf security is inevitable, a basis for relatively smooth U.S.-Saudi-Sino relations exists and should be explored.

Growing global energy demands offer Saudi decision makers opportunities that were not available decades ago. The collapse of Communism and poor Saudi economic fundamentals means that Saudi Arabia will likely push for higher oil prices. Still, the long-standing Saudi interest in preventing conservation and use of alternative fuels prevails. In the end, the United States and Saudi Arabia continue to share important interests that will keep them aligned. While the future oil market will look different than today's does, and the likelihood for friction between the United States and Saudi Arabia has increased, a functioning U.S.-Saudi relationship will likely remain a key feature of the global economic landscape for years to come.

The Changing Defense Relationship

New tensions also permeate the relation's defense pillar, although Saudi Arabia's troubled neighborhood will likely keep the two states working together. The blowback from King Fahd's decision to welcome half a million American troops to the kingdom continues to reverberate through Saudi society. The Saudi leadership has learned firsthand the perils of an overt American presence. Relying too heavily on American military support creates its own set of security problems. In 2003 the United States wisely pulled five thousand soldiers out of Prince Sultan Air Base, a military complex located outside of Riyadh.

Strained U.S.-Saudi relations, particularly around Iraq, have reportedly led King Abdullah and Crown Prince Sultan to begin diversifying weapons purchases away from the United States, similar to the kingdom's diversification of its oil industry. Although it is often inefficient to buy major weapons systems from different sources, it seems Saudi leaders are willing to trade a rational defense modernization program for greater political stability.

Still, Saudi Arabia's geography continues to prove useful to American military planners and Saudi leaders continue to make it available. In October 2001, Operation Enduring Freedom in Afghanistan was largely conducted by Americans at Prince Sultan Air Base. The U.S. Air Force relied on Saudi airspace to conduct its missions, and the former U.S. ambassador to Saudi Arabia, Robert Jordan, recalls a "high degree of cooperation" between the two countries.

Although Saudi leaders publicly opposed Operation Iraqi Freedom in 2003, the kingdom supported American military activity to a far greater extent than was publicly acknowledged. In the initial phases of the fighting, Americans operated from at least three Saudi air bases, launched refueling tankers, F-16 fighter jets, and sophisticated intelligence-gathering flights from Saudi soil, and relied on cheap Saudi fuel.[9] Saudi Arabia's strategic location continues to prove valuable to American planners. The United States simply cannot easily operate in Central Asia, South Asia, Iraq, or the Persian Gulf without Saudi support. Iraq is still years away from serving as a viable alternative.

Although regional threats such as a failing Iraq and a nuclear-ambitious Iran will strain the relationship, they are likely to keep the two states in coordination. Chaos in Iraq serves neither party well. The Saudi leadership is well aware that chaos in Iraq attracts Saudi citizens who will likely return home one day angry and battle-hardened. Although the United States and Saudi Arabia have differing concerns about a Shi'a-led Iraqi government, the two states share an interest in preventing Iraq's collapse and denying Iran a pronounced influence there. Saudi foreign minister Saud al-Faisal registered his country's concerns about Iraq's deterioration and the rise of Iranian influence when he told an American audience, "We fought a war together to keep Iran from occupying Iraq after Iraq was driven out of Kuwait. Now we are handing the whole country over to Iran without reason."[10] In truth, Washington has few options but to work with Riyadh in Iraq, given the poor state of relations between the United States and Syria and Iran, two of Iraq's other neighbors.

At the same time, both Washington and Riyadh are nervously tracking Iran's seemingly relentless bid for nuclear weapons. A nuclear-armed Iran would dramatically alter security arrangements in the Persian Gulf, at the expense of both the United States and Saudi Arabia. Should Iran go nuclear, Riyadh could choose either to acquire nuclear weapons secretly (similar to its CSS-2 purchase) or to underwrite the efforts of others, such as Pakistan, a more likely scenario. Both options would prove exceedingly troubling to the United States. A third option would be for Saudi Arabia to seek reinforced American security guarantees. It is strongly in America's interest to encourage Saudi Arabia to pursue this third option, especially if Iran crosses the nuclear threshold. It is one of the only possible breaks in a proliferation chain that could cascade from Iran to Saudi Arabia and then to Jordan, Egypt, and beyond. Strengthened Saudi-American relations could thus prevent the entire region from going nuclear.

The end of the Cold War has introduced new security threats for both Saudi Arabia and the United States. Differences over Afghanistan,

Iraq, Iran, and the region will cause, and have already caused, new points of tension. Still, given Saudi Arabia's strategic real estate and shared concerns about Iraq and Iran, the two states will likely seek ways to establish a strategic accommodation.

God and the Changing Global Context

Since the end of the Cold War, differences have emerged in the oil and defense pillars of the relationship. Still, the most dramatic change in the bilateral relationship has not been to the oil or defense pillar but rather to the ideological one. Saudi Arabia's religiosity, once defined by Washington as an asset, is today a political liability. The president's question of whether others are with or against the United States in its war on terror, as it applied to Saudi Arabia, was never about the kingdom's oil policy. It was, and is, about how Saudi Arabia uses its religious power in international politics.

For half a century Saudi Arabia's religiosity benefited American foreign policy. It kept oil-rich Saudi Arabia in America's political camp, helped inoculate future generations against Communist expansion, and aided American-supported causes from Central America to Central Asia. Saudi Arabia's policies did not change when the Berlin Wall came down, but the global political context did. With the collapse of the Soviet Union, the religious zealots spawned by Saudi funding and American complicity turned their wrath away from Moscow and onto Washington, Riyadh, and other capitals. The existence of radical Islamic groups is in part a legacy of past political decisions taken for once-defensible, although always controversial, reasons.

In order for the two states to work together in the future, Saudi Arabia must reverse its decades-long institutionalization of religious radicalism, both at home and abroad. Ideally Saudi Arabia could play a leadership role in perpetuating a more positive interpretation of Islam. It would be enormously helpful to today's ideological struggle if Saudi clerics used the pulpits of Mecca and Medina to preach a more tolerant, less violent version of Islam. Some are doing so, but their voices are often drowned out by others.[11] Whether U.S. decision makers (or, for that matter, other Muslim leaders) like it or not, Saudi Arabia retains enormous global influence within the Muslim community. A positive, proactive stance would yield considerable benefits.

More realistically, at least in the short and medium terms, Saudi Arabia could pursue a moderating role—neutralizing the most extreme interpretations of Islam at home while preventing the worst excesses from spilling across its borders. This would require actively breaking up terrorist cells, sharing information, reining in opaque and unaccountable charities, effectively monitoring multilateral Islamic organizations, and removing clerics preaching violence.

Most threatening would be for Saudi Arabia to adopt an adversarial role. This would include the Saudi leadership flatly denying Saudi involvement in religiously inspired terrorism, resisting calls to shut down terrorist funding sources, stoking anti-Americanism, and otherwise allowing its domestic environment to fester. Such a course would rightly draw the full wrath of the United States.

From September 2001 until May 2003 Saudi Arabia pursued adversarial policies vis-à-vis extremist support. Since May 2003, however, it has shifted toward more moderate ones. It is in America's national interest to shore up those advocating this less hostile approach and to prevent backsliding. The administration has already gone part of the way toward doing this by streamlining its approach to the kingdom and publicly praising recent Saudi efforts as discussed in Chapter 12. In the longer term, however, Washington will require a comprehensive strategy to further secure Saudi Arabia's moderating role and if possible nudge it in an even more positive direction. Smart policy would include supporting pragmatists within the royal family, and Saudi society more generally, in order to sway the domestic debate over who offers real solutions to contemporary problems. It would also include laser-like attention on Saudi Arabia's external support for radicalism, particularly in the financial realm.

A Strategic Choice

America has a strategic choice to make. It can choose to distance itself from the kingdom, deciding that the regime is corrupt, morally bankrupt, illegitimate, and irredeemable. This may earn the United States public relations points in the region, as many will applaud America's disassociation. However, the pragmatists inside the kingdom would immediately lose any standing they currently have. Even if the royal family was able to maintain power, it would likely adopt more religiously intransigent policies and reactivate its religious channels to undermine American interests in the region and beyond. Saudi defense officials would look to China for sophisticated weaponry. China would likely sell it. The American armed forces would be denied efficient transportation routes to the Persian Gulf and the small Arab countries that abut it. Oil prices would rise, although not catastrophically unless the royal family actually fell from power.

A second option is to find a way to engage the royal family to encourage more moderate policies. This option will be hard and complicated, and it might fail. But even if it does fail, Washington would be no worse off than if it pursued the first option.

Engaging Saudi Arabia does not mean appeasing it; rather, it involves defining what matters most and building appropriate policies around it. One of the most important things Washington needs from the kingdom is for its leaders to aggressively monitor and shut down Saudi-based funding streams that underwrite mosques, schools, prison programs, and other institutions promoting intolerance, xenophobia, and anti-Americanism. In this light, congressional hearings like the ones called by Senator Shelby and demands by Representative Kelly, U.S. Treasury Department officials, and others that Saudi Arabia establish better financial controls are entirely appropriate.

What is not appropriate is the general Saudi-bashing that has manifested itself in opposition to all things Saudi. For example, a congressional petition circulated in May 2005 calling Saudi Arabia's World Trade Organization accession "premature" was shortsighted and counterproductive.[12] Not only is it distracting to the focus on financing issues, but WTO accession will benefit Saudi pragmatists in their fight against more conservative elements in the kingdom. It is not a gift but a weapon. The logic for WTO support is found in a 2000 article by Condoleezza Rice, who wrote on a related topic, "Although some argue that the way to support human rights is to refuse trade with China, this punishes precisely those who are most likely to change the system . . . trade in general can open up the Chinese economy and, ultimately, its politics too."[13] The same reasoning applies to Saudi Arabia's entering the WTO. Joining the WTO will benefit those in the kingdom advocating for increased transparency and accountability. These are also goals supported by the United States. It will also provide King Abdullah the cover he needs to take some very difficult and potentially explosive actions at home, such as reducing subsidies to and restricting corrupt practices among princes.

Other gratuitous anti-Saudi measures include a congressional amendment stipulating that no funds be "obligated or expended to finance any assistance to Saudi Arabia," which specifically targets a paltry $25,000 International Military Education and Training grant for Saudi military training.[14] The amendment seeks to keep Saudi military officers from training in the United States and interacting with their American counterparts. Although politically popular, such measures are strategically counterproductive and if enacted would impede Saudi Arabia's ability to conduct its fight against terrorism.

If the United States chooses to engage the kingdom, it will have to offer something in return. There needs to be a reason for Saudi leaders to work with the United States. A key Saudi interest lies in stabilizing Iraq. As noted, chaos in Iraq draws young Saudis to fight. It also increases Iranian influence on Saudi Arabia's border. In Riyadh as well as elsewhere in the region, Iran's growing confidence is sparking concern about a rising Shi'a crescent. A fear of encirclement has driven the kingdom's foreign policy since its inception, when it was concerned with British and then Soviet activity. Iran's presence in Iraq and Lebanon and its ability to influence politics in Saudi Arabia's small Gulf neighbors is profoundly troubling to Riyadh. Washington should enter active discussions with Riyadh about its Iraq strategy and its eventual military withdrawal. Saudi decision makers should be integrated into America's planning, and the underlying justification for ongoing decisions should be explained to them. In return, the kingdom has levers of influence that it can pull in Iraq that U.S. planners may want to consider.

Saudi Arabia's other main concern is American engagement in the peace process. The Bush administration's early avoidance of the subject greatly undermined those in the region Washington most wants to help. Engaging in the peace process does not mean that Washington must cater to every Arab demand. But active involvement, even if it does not produce final resolutions, will allow for greater Saudi cooperation. The violence associated with both Iraq and Palestine directly undermines Saudi Arabia's domestic stability. A reduction in violence is something that the Saudis will expect from the United States if they are going to undertake controversial actions that the United States desires. If the United States is unable to make headway in either realm, it will receive less cooperation from the kingdom on issues Washington cares most about.

Reform: A Second Order Priority

Focusing on Saudi funding does not mean that Bush's reform efforts are irrelevant, only that they are of secondary importance. If pursued deftly, reform addresses the concerns of many in the region who should be America's natural allies and could diffuse the virulent anti-Americanism that permeates the region. The Bush administration has inaugurated several important reform efforts that are already making a difference. A $100,000 U.S. Agency for International Development grant to Effat College, a women's college in Jeddah, earned the United States a public relations victory far in excess of the money contributed. The program is designed to promote cooperation between Effat and Duke University. The grant remains popular because American educational institutions are highly regarded inside the kingdom. The Bush administration deserves credit for supporting this initiative. Until recently, it was almost impossible to get U.S. foreign aid into the kingdom, an oil-rich country that few believed (understandably) needed the aid. But if the United States does not support its potential friends, it is now clear that few others will. Providing the option for local youths to become productive members of society will help wean some away from radical religious pursuits and, just as important, is a cause many pragmatists actively support.

President Bush and King (then Crown Prince) Abdullah also made significant headway in addressing issues around educational reform during their spring 2005 meeting in Crawford, Texas. In a joint statement, the two leaders announced a commitment to increase the number of Saudi students studying in the United States, expand military exchange programs that provide education to Saudi officers, and facilitate travel to the kingdom by U.S. citizens. The statement was motivated by the fact that it had become increasingly difficult for Saudi Arabia's best and brightest to travel to the United States. Between 1993 and 2003 the numbers of exchange programs sponsored by the U.S. Department of State in Saudi Arabia, Egypt, and Yemen fell by 21 percent.[15] A recent survey found that 29 percent of U.S. colleges and universities polled registered a dramatic drop in Saudi student visa applications after the September 11 attacks.[16] The significant decrease in the number of Saudi students studying in the United States over the last few years followed an existing general decline in Saudi students studying abroad since the 1980s. According to the *Statistical Yearbook of Saudi Arabia*, the number of Saudis studying abroad reached a peak of more than 12,500 in the mid-1980s but then dropped to 3,554 in 1990 and to only slightly more than 3,400 in 1996.[17] Over time the Saudi government has offered less funding for its students to travel abroad. Since the meeting in 2005, King Abdullah has created a well-funded scholarship program designed to send young Saudis to study in America. The Bush administration continues to attend to Saudi visa problems.

There are also things Washington could do to promote greater political openness that might be well received in Riyadh. Washington should engage the winners of Saudi Arabia's first municipal elections in more than forty years, which occurred over a two-month period between February and April 2005. Although voter turnout was thin and women were excluded, the precedent of the election was significant, especially as King Fahd had previously declared Islam and voting

incompatible. Rather than chronicling the elections' shortcomings, as many did and still do, the United States should seek to institutionalize the elections and bolster the role of those who won. Washington should work with others to support regional training programs for newly elected Saudi officials. Introducing them to their regional counterparts and providing political training would acknowledge the importance of the election, help institutionalize the results, increase the benefits to participating in the future, and encourage the Saudi royal family to take this new political group seriously. By reaching out to the winners, Washington could also avoid the charge that it is "cherry-picking" supporters and thus unintentionally discrediting them.

But we should not kid ourselves. Reform will help some of our friends in the kingdom, but it will not eliminate our enemies. Violent religious fighters have not emerged simply as a response to authoritarian rule. Their domestic strength was carefully cultivated for decades to serve a particular political agenda. Quickly opening up political space will not quell their violence. It will only allow them a space in the political process.

The pragmatists are not calling for liberal democracy, fearing that it would likely sweep their adversaries into power. Rather, they are calling for slow political and economic liberalization along with greater governmental controls over the most conservative elements in society. American support for the three imprisoned Saudi activists who called for a constitutional monarchy undoubtedly played a role in their August 2005 release, as did Abdullah's ascension to the throne, and should help reenergize local momentum toward change. A strategy of engagement rather than alienation is in order, although difficult to sell to publics on both sides.[18]

In today's fight against terrorism and extremism, Saudi Arabia is both part of the problem and part of the solution. American policy should be focused on how to move it more fully into the latter category. Despite real troubles, there are dangers to allowing the relationship to deteriorate. Today Saudi pragmatists face a violent and zealous opposition. If this opposition gains complete control of the state's resources, it will direct its efforts toward confronting the United States, ushering in a true clash of civilizations.

Will the House of Saud Survive?

The prior discussion assumes that there will be a Saudi partner for American officials to work with in the coming years. And yet, on

television and radio programs the question of the House of Saud's longevity is regularly debated. So, how vulnerable is the House of Saud? Any answer to this question must at least acknowledge that history has proven the royal family surprisingly resilient.

Since the earliest days of the Saudi monarchy, outside observers have anticipated its demise. During the early 1950s American flight attendants staffing King Abdel Aziz's plane helped monitor the contents of the airplane's lavatory in order to assess the king's health, so worried was Washington about the King's mortality. There was a palpable sense of relief when power transferred seamlessly from Abdel Aziz to Saud.

Over the years, the al-Saud has shown a remarkable ability to overcome serious succession challenges ranging from palace in-fighting (between Saud and Faisal), assassination (Faisal), non-sequential power transfer (the skipping over of Mohammad for Khaled) and incapacitation (King Fahd's stroke). There are still a number of sons waiting in a somewhat orderly line to assume the title of king. This includes the aging Crown Prince Sultan, Prince Salman and others. King Abdullah is only the 13th of King Abdel Aziz's forty-three sons. There are many others waiting in the wings. Not all sons are in line for the monarchy however. Some have died. Some have opted out of politics to pursue other interests. Some are considered unfit to rule. Some were removed from the line of succession for past deeds. Still, there are many sons waiting patiently for their shot.

The real succession challenge will come not in the next few years but in the next decade or so when power transfers from the sons of King Abdel Aziz to his grandsons. The criteria of ability and age that currently steers the succession process will provide some guidance but is hardly predictive. It is likely that the Ulema will be carefully consulted, as it always has been, along with other important tribes and groups within the kingdom. The brothers will undoubtedly try to find a way to help position their sons in the transition, but generational change may well cause a period of uncertainty.

Although not fully transparent to outside observers, the transition process inside the Kingdom has traditionally been handled with political dexterity. There is reason to believe it will be similarly managed in the future. Political transitions in other strategically important countries such as Pakistan and Egypt are far more precarious than succession in Saudi Arabia. Americans would be well served by focusing their attention on the question of what kind of policy to construct toward Saudi Arabia assuming the monarchy survives.

Living with the Legacy of Yesterday's Wars

Charting the development of the U.S.-Saudi relationship through the Cold War to today as this book has done provides insights into how religion has been used to realize particular political ends. It suggests that theological explanations that trace the roots of Islamic radicalism back to the 1200s and economic theories that examine globalization's effect on traditional societies are insufficient to explain the rise of religious radicalism across the Middle East. Saudi-American efforts to beat back the Soviet Union are a key component to the story. So is the fact that other American allies, such as Egypt, Tunisia, and Israel, supported indigenous Islamic movements in order to counter local nationalist opponents, many of whom were Soviet-backed. In turn, the same leaders who underwrote local Islamist groups in the 1970s and 1980s later used their very presence to justify a resistance toward democratization.

In contrast to the support Islamist groups received in America-friendly countries in the Middle East, religious organizations suffered a crueler fate in Soviet-supported countries. The Syrian regime, for instance, annihilated twenty thousand citizens in 1982 for being associated with the Muslim Brotherhood. Saddam Hussein's Iraqi forces massacred religious leaders, especially among the Shi'a population. Egypt provides a good example of how Cold War ideological struggles shape today's politico-religious landscape. While receiving Soviet aid, Gamal Abdel Nasser persecuted the Muslim Brotherhood. American-supported Anwar el-Sadat, on the other hand, heavily backed the Brotherhood in order to counter local Nasserite opposition.

If the radicalization of Islam is an outgrowth of the Middle East's Cold War experience, then it may be worthwhile considering how the Cold War affected the rise of religion more globally. After all, U.S. decision makers actively pursued close relations with the Vatican in order to stanch Communist expansion in Latin America. Ronald Reagan's close ties with the American religious right dovetailed nicely with his anti-Communist agenda. The rise of religious fundamentalism across the globe may be as much a political story as it is an economic or theological one.

Into the Future

The long history of U.S.-Saudi relations provides some reason to be optimistic that today's radical religious context can be defused. The royal family is no longer actively promoting it, as it once did, and the United States no longer benefits from it. But history also suggests that changing the context will not be easy. The seeds of religious radicalism were planted decades ago and carefully tended for both international and domestic purposes. Undoing yesterday's damage will take time, not a luxury readily available when the risks associated with terror are so high.

Mutual recriminations are easy yet counterproductive. Both the United States and Saudi Arabia, as well as their many allies and partners around the world, have contributed to today's problems through sins of either omission or commission. Recognizing this should help to recast problematic relations and to suggest concrete steps for moving forward.

Moving away from the Cold War context is long overdue. Shared strategic interests that previously enveloped the relationship have evaporated. Today Saudi leaders must work to address issues surrounding the financing of extremist thought. In return, Washington must find ways to help the pragmatists prevail in their domestic battle. Stabilizing Iraq and making progress toward peace between Israelis and Palestinians will help neutralize the toxic anti-American atmosphere in the region. The Saudi pragmatists can succeed if the United States helps to increase the quality and quantity of their numbers. Such adjustments will provide a needed course correction to promoting a radical and fundamentalist version of Islam.

The good news is that both the U.S. and Saudi leaderships seem to generally agree with this suggested path forward. Unfortunately, it will take longer to convince their respective publics that it is worth the effort. But without such effort, both sides should prepare for a grim and dangerous future.

Notes

Prologue

1. The first American diplomatic mission in Jeddah, on Saudi Arabia's western coast, was established on May 1, 1942. In the summer of 1944, America opened the first consulate in Saudi Arabia, in the eastern oil town of Dhahran, and elevated the status of the Jeddah legation by giving it a minister in residence.

2. Hermann K. Eilts, author's phone interview, February 28, 2005. Parker Hart similarly remembers that water came from an unreliable distillery plant that sold five gallon tin containers of brackish water transported by donkey from open pits, Association for Diplomatic Studies and Training oral history (henceforth ADST oral history) of Parker T. Hart, in *Frontline Diplomacy: The U.S. Foreign Affairs Oral History Collection* (Arlington, VA: ADST, 2000), CD-ROM.

3. Eilts, author's interview, Boston, December 8, 2003.

4. In a 1981 press conference during a battle to sell Saudi Arabia AWACS, U.S. president Ronald Reagan stated, "Saudi Arabia—we will not permit to be an Iran." "Transcript of President's News Conference on Foreign and Domestic Matters," *New York Times*, October 2, 1981. This was quickly interpreted to mean that the president would support the Saudi royal family, and its oil, against domestic unrest, and was soon dubbed the Reagan corollary to the Carter doctrine—a doctrine that defined the Persian Gulf as vital to American interests. See, for example, Richard L. Stout, "Casual Words That Change the World," *Christian Science Monitor*, October 9, 1981; James Reston, "The Forgotten Debate," *New York Times*, October 18, 1981; Philip Geyelin, "Foreign Policy Jumble," *Washington Post*, October 26, 1981.

5. Egypt's president Gamal Abdel Nasser's efforts won him hundreds of millions of dollars more in aid than picking sides would have done. Miles Copeland, *The Game of Nations* (New York: Simon and Schuster, 1969), 170–71.

6. Elaine Sciolino and Patrick E. Tyler, "Saudi Charges Bush with Failure to Broker Mideast Peace," *New York Times*, November 9, 2001.

7. See, for example, Robert Baer, *Sleeping with the Devil: How Washington Sold Our Soul for Saudi Crude* (New York: Crown, 2003); Stephen Schwartz, *The Two Faces of Islam: Saudi Fundamentalism and Its Role in Terrorism.* (New York: Knopf, 2003);

Dore Gold, *Hatred's Kingdom: How Saudi Arabia Supports the New War on Terrorism.* (Washington, DC: Regnery, 2003); Craig Unger, *House of Bush, House of Saud: The Secret Relationship Between the World's Two Most Powerful Dynasties* (New York: Scribner, 2004); Gerald Posner, *Secrets of the Kingdom: The Inside Story of the Secret Saudi-U.S. Connection* (New York, Random House, 2005). Antidotes to these works include Thomas Lippman's *Inside the Mirage* (Boulder, CO: Westview Press, 2004) and David Long's *The United States and Saudi Arabia: Ambivalent Allies* (Boulder, CO: Westview Press, 1985). For a terrific review of recent literature, see Max Rodenbeck, "Unloved in Arabia," *New York Review of Books,* October 21, 2004.

8. On oil, see Daniel Yergin's *The Prize: The Epic Quest for Oil, Money & Power,* 2nd ed. (New York: Free Press, 1992); Anthony Cave Brown, *Oil, God, and Gold: The Story of Aramco and the Saudi Kings* (New York: Houghton Mifflin, 1999); Aaron David Miller, *Search for Security: Saudi Arabian Oil and American Foreign Policy, 1939–1949* (Chapel Hill: University of North Carolina Press, 1980); David S. Painter, *Oil and the American Century: The Political Economy of the U.S. Foreign Oil Policy 1941–1954* (Baltimore: Johns Hopkins University Press, 1986). On succession, see Joseph A. Kechichian, *Succession in Saudi Arabia* (New York: Palgrave, 2001); Simon Henderson, *After King Fahd: Succession in Saudi Arabia* (Washington, DC: Washington Institute for Near East Policy, 1994).

9. Several good books also exist on Saudi Arabia's threat perception and general history. See Madawi al-Rasheed, *A History of Saudi Arabia* (New York: Cambridge University Press, 2002); Madawi al-Rasheed and Robert Vitalis, eds., *Counter-Narratives: History, Contemporary Society and Politics in Saudi Arabia and Yemen* (New York: Palgrave-Macmillan, 2004); Alexei Vassiliev, *The History of Saudi Arabia* (New York: New York University Press, 2000); Nadav Safran, *Saudi Arabia: The Ceaseless Quest for Security* (Ithaca, NY: Cornell University Press, 1988); David Holden and Richard Johns, *The House of Saud: The Rise and Rule of the Most Powerful Dynasty in the Arab World* (New York: Holt, Rinehart and Winston, 1982); Sarah Yizraeli, *The Remaking of Saudi Arabia: The Struggle Between King Sa'ud and Crown Prince Faysal, 1953–1962* (Tel Aviv: Moshe Dayan Center for Middle Eastern and African Studies, 1977); and Robert Lacey, *The Kingdom: Arabia and the House of Saud* (New York: Harcourt Brace Jovanovich, 1981).

10. This is not true for Baer, *Sleeping with the Devil,* and Unger, *House of Bush,* both of which have many important things to say on the politics that contributed to 9/11. Their more interesting findings, however, are so deeply buried under rhetorical flourishes, and a seemingly visceral anti-Saudi political agenda, that it is difficult to focus on the useful parts of these books.

11. Thomas E. Richs, "Briefing Depicted Saudis as Enemies: Ultimatum Urged to Pentagon Board," *Washington Post,* August 6, 2002. For the PowerPoint slides, see Jack Shafer, "The PowerPoint That Rocked the Pentagon," *Slate Magazine,* August 7, 2002, available at http://slate.msn.com/id/2069119/.

12. John F. Kerry, "Making America Secure Again: Setting the Right Course for Foreign Policy," speech, Council on Foreign Relations, New York, NY, December 3, 2003.

13. Hassan Yassin, "U.S.-Saudi Rift Rewards Terrorists," *Los Angeles Times,* August 21, 2002.

14. Condoleezza Rice, "Remarks at the American University in Cairo, June 20, 2005," available at http://www.state.gov/secretary/rm/2005/48328.htm, accessed June 23, 2005.

15. Author's interviews, Riyadh, February 2005.
16. Ali Khalil, "Saudi Conference Focuses on Fighting Terrorism," *Arab News*, February 7, 2005.
17. Center for Religious Freedom, *Saudi Publications on Hate Ideology Invade American Mosques* (Washington, DC: Freedom House, 2005).
18. National Commission on Terrorist Attacks upon the United States, *9/11 Commission Report: Final Report of the National Commission on Terrorist Attacks upon the United States* (Washington, DC: Government Printing Office, 2004), 374.
19. Fred Halliday, *The Middle East in International Relations: Power, Politics and Ideology* (Boston: Cambridge University Press, 2005), 123. Italics in the original.
20. In Ahmed Rashid, *Taliban* (New Haven: Yale University Press, 2000), 130.
21. Gilles Kepel, *Jihad: The Trail of Political Islam* (Cambridge, MA: Harvard University Press, 2002). On page 7 he argues that "the entire decade of the 1980s was overshadowed by a power struggle between the Saudi monarchy and Khomeini's Iran. Tehran sought to export its revolution, just as the Russians had once exported theirs. Riyadh set out to contain this ploy, just as the Americans had contained the Soviets during the Cold War." See also David W. Lesch, *1979: The Year That Shaped the Middle East* (Boulder: Westview Press, 2001).
22. J. M. Cowan, ed., *The Hans Wehr Dictionary of Modern Written Arabic* (Ithaca: Spoken Language Service, 1976), 142.
23. Vassiliev, *History of Saudi Arabia*, 397.
24. U.S. Congress, Senate Committee on Governmental Affairs, "An Assessment of Current Efforts to Combat Terrorism Financing," statement by David Aufhauser, 108th Cong., 2nd sess., June 15, 2004, available at http://www.senate.gov/~gov_affairs/index.cfm?Fuseaction=Hearings.Testimony&HearingID=181&WitnessID=655, accessed July 28, 2004.
25. Rashid, *Taliban*, 89.
26. The most comprehensive book on Saudi Arabia's foreign policy is still Safran, *Saudi Arabia*, now nearly twenty years old.
27. Pew Global Attitudes Project, "16-Nation Pew Global Attitudes Survey," June 23, 2005, available at http://pewglobal.org/reports/display.php?ReportID=247, accessed July 14, 2005.
28. Peter Rodman, "The World's Resentment," *The National Interest*, summer 2000. In this prescient article Rodman, now assistant secretary of defense for international security affairs, pointed to the growing problem.

Chapter 1

1. H. St. John Philby, *Arabian Jubilee* (New York: John Day, 1953), 176. A concession is a grant of land or property usually by a government in return for services or for a particular use. The king hoped to grant the right to explore for oil, within a mutually agreed-upon and demarcated area, in return for revenue.
2. Ibid., 2005.
3. In fact, Persian Gulf oil was cheaper than any local energy source, including coal. Daniel Yergin, *The Prize: The Epic Quest for Oil, Money & Power*, 2nd ed. (New York: Free Press, 1992), 154.
4. Ibid., 171.

5. Quoted in U.S. Senate, Select Committee on Small Business, Subcommittee on Monopoly, "Development of Joint Control over Foreign Oil," in *The International Petroleum Cartel: Staff Report to the Federal Trade Commission*, 83rd Cong., 2nd Sess., 1952, available at http://www.mtholyoke.edu/acad/intrel/Petroleum/ftc3.htm, accessed September 3, 2003.

6. The area included Turkey, Iraq, Saudi Arabia, and adjoining sheikdoms, but excluded Iran, Kuwait, Israel, and what was then called Transjordan.

7. Mohammed Almana, *Arabia Unified: A Portrait of Ibn Saud* (London: Hutchinson Benham, 1980), 226. Almana was one of the king's chief translators.

8. Philby, *Arabian Jubilee*, 178.

9. Almana, *Arabia Unified*, 226.

10. Thomas C. Barger, *Out in the Blue: Letters from Arabia—1937 to 1940* (Vista, CA: Selwa Press, 2000), 5–8; ADST oral history of Walter K. Schwinn, consul general in Dhahran (1957–61).

11. Yergin, *The Prize*, 299; Anthony Cave Brown, *Oil, God, and Gold: The Story of Aramco and the Saudi Kings* (New York: Houghton Mifflin, 1999), 71–75.

12. Yergin, *The Prize*, 401.

13. On the signing, see Robert Lacey, *The Kingdom: Arabia and the House of Saud* (New York: Harcourt Brace Jovanovich, 1981), 255. For the trip see also William E. Mulligan, "A Kingdom and a Company," *Aramco World Magazine—50th Anniversary Issue*, May/June 1984.

14. "Other Common Ownerships in the Middle East," in the *International Petroleum Cartel*, available at http://www.mtholyoke.edu/acad/intrel/Petroleum/ftc5.htm, accessed September 3, 2003.

15. Philip C. McConnell, *The Hundred Men* (Peterborough, NH: Courier Press, 1985), 42.

16. "Other Common Ownerships in the Middle East," *International Petroleum Cartel*.

17. Cordell Hull, *The Memoirs of Cordell Hull* (New York: Macmillan, 1948), 2:1498.

18. Ibid., 2:1499.

19. Wallace Stegner, "Discovery! The Story of Aramco Then: Chapter 12: Air Raid," *Aramco World Magazine*, July/August 1970.

20. Arabian American Oil Company, "Aramco Annual Reports 1950–1952," 13, Box 3, Folder 45, William E. Mulligan Papers, Georgetown Library Special Collections, Georgetown, MD. Daily figures converted by author from 7.8 and 200 million barrels per year.

21. Miller, *Search for Security*, xiii.

22. As well as 70–80 percent of state revenues, and around 40 percent of the country's gross domestic product (GDP). See EIA, "Country Analysis Briefs: Saudi Arabia." According to the Economist Intelligence Unit, since the 1990 Gulf War the oil sector has accounted for 85 percent of Saudi Arabia's export receipts. Economist.com, Country Briefings, "Saudi Arabia: Economic Structure," available at http://www.economist.comcountries/SaudiArabia/profile.cfr?folder=profile%DEconomic%20structure.

23. In the first quarter of 2005, OPEC's spare capacity was between 1.6 and 2.1 mbd. Saudi Arabia's spare capacity was estimated at between 1.5 and 2.0 mbd. Energy Information Administration, "Short-Term Energy Outlook," February 2005, available at http://www.eia.doe.gov/pub/forecasting/steo/oldsteos/jan05.pdf.

24. Thomas L. Friedman, "The Gridlock Gang," *New York Times*, February 26, 2003; see also Thomas L. Friedman, "Brave, Young and Muslim," *New York Times*, March 3, 2005.
25. Kenneth Labich, "Saudi Power," *Newsweek* (International Edition), March 6, 1978.
26. Ibid.
27. Nathan J. Citino, author of an important book on U.S.-Saudi relations, gets it right when he writes, "Neither a fable of Yankee entrepreneurship in the desert, nor the sort of bare statistical record of growing oil production and profits" explains the U.S.-Saudi relationship. However, instead of concluding that the U.S.-Saudi relationship is "instead part of a more important historical epic about how the United States inherited custodianship of the global economy from Great Britain," the importance of the relationship can be seen as even greater, one that extends beyond the oil relationship and into a fundamentally political one. Nathan J. Citino, *From Arab Nationalism to OPEC: Eisenhower, King Sa'ud and the Making of U.S.-Saudi Relations* (Bloomington: Indiana University Press, 2002), 2.
28. "Extension of Lend-Lease Assistance to Saudi Arabia; Organization of a Program for Financial and Military Aid," *Foreign Relations of the United States* (henceforth *FRUS*), (Washington, DC: GPO, 1943), IV: 854.
29. "Hearings on Petroleum Arrangements with Saudi Arabia," February 16, 1948, 14, Box 8, Folder 27, Mulligan Papers. This testimony was in response to Congress arguing that wartime decisions were made at the behest of, and for the benefit of, Aramco oil executives and that the company had overcharged the U.S. Navy for oil.
30. C. L. Sulzberger, "Saudi Arabia Base Key U.S. Airfield," *New York Times*, November 24, 1946.
31. "Memorandum of Conversation, by Mr. Frederick H. Awalt of the Office of African and Near Eastern Affairs," *FRUS*, 1949, VI:1626.
32. "Statement of Policy Proposed by the National Security Council, NSC 47/5, March 14, 1951," *FRUS*, 1951, V:95.
33. Parker T. Hart, *Saudi Arabia and the United States: Birth of a Security Partnership* (Bloomington: Indiana University Press, 1998), 66.
34. Military planners see it as essential, although not a "showstopper." Author's interview, former CENTCOM war planner.
35. Bernard Lewis, "Communism and Islam," *International Affairs* 30, 1 (1954): 12.
36. George Rentz records this statement after a meeting with Ibn Saud and a friend of President Harry S. Truman's in "Memorandum to Mr. F. W. Ohliger from George Rentz," February 8, 1948, Box 1, Folder 50, William E. Mulligan Papers, Georgetown Library Special Collections, Georgetown, MD (henceforth Mulligan Papers).
37. "A Grand Conspiracy," *Newsweek*, December 21, 1970, 43.
38. Laura Kalman, *Abe Fortas: A Biography* (New Haven: Yale University Press, 1990), 98.
39. "Draft Letters," Box 1, Dulles-Herter Series, Dwight D. Eisenhower: Papers as President of the United States, 1953–61 (Ann Whitman File) (DDE), Dwight D. Eisenhower Library and Museum (henceforth DDEL), Abilene, Kansas.
40. Jacob Goldberg, *The Foreign Policy of Saudi Arabia: The Formative Years, 1902–1918* (Cambridge, MA: Harvard University Press, 1986).
41. Abdulaziz H. Al-Fahad, "The 'Imam vs. the 'Iqal: Hadari-Bedouin Conflict and the Formation of the Saudi State," in Madawi Al-Rasheed and Robert Vitalis, eds.,

Counter-Narratives: History, Contemporary Society, and Politics in Saudi Arabia and Yemen (New York: Palgrave, 2004), 35–75; Joseph Kostiner, "On Instruments and Their Designers: The Ikhwan of Najd and the Emergence of the Saudi State," *Middle Eastern Studies* 21 (1985): 299; Tim Niblock, "Social Structure and the development of the Saudi Arabian Political System," in Tim Niblock, ed., *State, Society, and Economy in Saudi Arabia* (New York: St. Martin's Press, 1982), 75–105; F. Gregory Gause III, *Oil Monarchies: Domestic and Security Challenges in the Arab Gulf States* (New York: Council on Foreign Relations, 1994), 18–19.

42. Alexei Vassiliev, *The History of Saudi Arabia* (New York: New York University Press, 2000), 230; John S. Habib, *Ibn Saud's Warriors of Islam: The Ikhwan of the Najd and the Role in the Creation of the Saudi Kingdom, 1910–1930* (Leiden: Brill, 1978), 37.

43. Hafiz Wahba, *Arabian Days* (London: Arthur Barker, 1964), 127. Some may have even been responsible for the continued traces of extremism; see Al-Fahad, "The 'Imam vs. the 'Iqal," 51.

44. Habib, *Ibn Saud's Warriors*, 37.

45. Kostiner, "On Instruments and Their Designers," 298–323.

46. Vassiliev argues convincingly that in the early days, tribal identity played a significant role in determining the choice of hijrah one decided to settle in. However, within a few years, it became clear that the strength of the Ikhwan was based on their commitment to each other rather than a particular tribe. See Vassiliev, *History of Saudi Arabia*, 228, 237.

47. Barger, *Out in the Blue*, 41. On the norms of Bedouin raiding, see also H. R. P. Dickson, *The Arab of the Desert: A Glimpse into Badawin Life in Kuwait and Sau'di Arabia* (London: George Allen & Unwin, 1951), 341–61.

48. Lacey claims that Ikhwan fighters played no role in the early battle for Hofuf and other key Eastern Province battles. Vassiliev, however, in *History of Saudi Arabia*, shows that they made up a small but growing portion of Abdel Aziz's forces. See also Kostiner, "On Instruments and Their Designers," 299–306. For the role of the townsmen, or villagers, in fighting for Abdel Aziz, see Abdulaziz H. Al-Fahad, "From Exclusivism to Accommodation: Doctrinal and Legal Evolution of Wahhabism," *New York University Law Review* 79, 2 (2004); Habib, *Ibn Saud's Warriors*, 15.

49. Habib suggests that their decision to tacitly back Abdel Aziz may have come from an implicit threat that he would turn to the French for help if they did not. See Habib, *Ibn Saud's Warriors*, 106.

50. For a good discussion see Goldberg, *Foreign Policy of Saudi Arabia*, chap. 5. On general European-Saudi relations, see Gerd Nonneman, "Saudi-European Relations 1902–2001: A Pragmatic Quest for Relative Autonomy," *International Affairs* 77, 3 (2001): 631–61.

51. H. St. John B. Philby, *Arabian Days* (London: Robert Hale, 1948), 154.

52. He continues, "We 'Ikhwan in those days were fanatical and fierce to a degree. Nothing could stop our military enthusiasm, and we feared death not at all. . . . After every repulse Bin Sa'ud's chief 'Alim (priest), Ibn Sulaiman by name, used to visit the Mutair contingent of the 'Ikhwan, and exhort us to greater deeds the next day, telling us that lovely *huris* awaited every warrior that might be killed, also that beautiful gardens with running water and a silver house with golden furniture would be our portion in the next world. . . . I thought very hard . . . why it was that he [Ibn Sulaiman] was not himself anxious to gain this delectable land of *huris* he talked so much about . . . for my pains I was next day hauled before

the great Bin Sau'd himself and accused of creating alarm and despondency among the 'Ikhwan . . . from that day [I] knew the truth . . . I determined somehow or other to escape from all the 'Ikhwan religious humbug." Dickson, *Arab of the Desert*, 314–15.

53. Vassiliev, *History of Saudi Arabia*, 261; Joshua Teitelbaum, *The Rise and Fall of the Hashimite Kingdom of Arabia* (New York: New York University Press, 2001), 241–48; Al-Rasheed, *History of Saudi Arabia*, 45–46.

54. Wahba, *Arabian Days*, 133. Habib makes the argument that Abdel Aziz cleverly bided his time. He would not destroy the Ikhwan until they helped him conquer the Hejaz, the most coveted portion of his expanding territorial holdings; see Habib, *Ibn Saud's Warriors*, chap. 9.

55. Kostiner, "On Instruments and Their Designers," 315; Habib, *Ibn Saud's Warriors*, 118.

56. Habib, *Ibn Saud's Warriors*, 140.

57. James Buchan, "Secular and Religious Opposition in Saudi Arabia," in Tim Niblock, ed., *State, Society, and Economy in Saudi Arabia* (New York: St. Martins Press, 1982), 121.

58. Joshua Teitelbaum argues that the relationship between religion and state, or rather clerics and princes, is much more complex than usually assumed, and has become more so "as Saudi society became more modernized and exposed to the West." *Holier than Thou: Saudi Arabia's Islamic Opposition* (Washington, DC: Washington Institute for Near East Policy, 2000). Similarly, Buchan states that "much of the recent history of the kingdom is a tale of conflict between religious zeal and the al-Saud's notions of political expediency and social progress" ("Secular and Religious Opposition," 120); Kostiner shows that the fight between Abdel Aziz and the Ikhwan wasn't merely one of religion but also "bore the character of a Nejdi tribal struggle against the centralizing and relatively modern regime" of Abdel Aziz ("On Instruments and Their Designers," 317).

59. Al-Fahad, "From Exclusivism to Accommodation," 505. Dickson recounts a story in which Abdel Aziz tried to placate the Ikhwan by "exerting all his diplomatic skills," but that "there can be little doubt that Abdulla bin Jiluwi, father of Fahad and Governor of Hasa, did not see eye to eye with bin Sau'd in this matter," and preferred to destroy rather than co-opt Ikhwan influence. Dickson, *Arab of the Desert*, 273. John Habib notes that in Abdullah bin Jiluwi, "the Ikhwan met their match"; *Ibn Saud's Warriors*, 37.

60. Vassiliev, *History of Saudi Arabia*, 238.

Chapter 2

1. The king's harem put on mourning clothes and cried hysterically to Prince Faisal. See William A. Eddy, *FDR Meets Ibn Saud* (New York: American Friends of the Middle East, 1954), 16.

2. Cordell Hull, *The Memoirs of Cordell Hull* (New York: Macmillan, 1948), 2:1512.

3. Robert E. Sherwood, *Roosevelt and Hopkins: An Intimate History* (New York: Harper and Brothers, 1948), 871.

4. Telegram to Sec State from Eddy, April 13, 1945, Folder: "Condolences for FDR, Saudi Arabia," Department of State, Records Pertaining to Foreign Gift Items, Franklin D. Roosevelt Library (henceforth FDRL), Hyde Park, NY.

5. Hassan Yassin, author's interview, Riyadh, February 2005.
6. Letter from FDR to King Abdel Aziz, February 10, 1944, Folder 7960: "Ibn Saud, King Abdul," President's Personal File, Franklin D. Roosevelt: Papers as President, FDRL.
7. Letter from King Abdel Aziz to FDR, April 1, 1944, ibid.
8. William M. Rigdon, "The Log of the President's Trip to the Crimea, Argonaut Conference, and Great Bitter Lake, Egypt, January-February, 1945," The Log of President Roosevelt's Trips 1937–1945, 48, Box 4: "Presidential Travel Logs," William McKinley Rigdon Papers, Georgia Southern University Library (henceforth GSUL), Statesboro, GA. Admiral Rigdon was the president's naval aide.
9. John S. Keating. "Cruise of the USS Flying Carpet," True, December 1953, 109.
10. Noel Busch, "Life Visits Arabia," Life, May 31, 1943.
11. "John S. Keating, Commander Destroyer Squadron Seventeen, to FDR. TOP SECRET Report on 'Mission to Mecca:' Ibn Saud's visit with FDR," February 20, 1945, Chronological Number 194, Accession Number 122, William M. Rigdon Inventory—1945, Rigdon Papers, GSUL.
12. Keating, "Cruise," 110.
13. Elliot M. Senn, "Taking Roosevelt to Yalta: A Personal Memoir," Washington Star, January 30, 1966.
14. Harold L. Ickes, "Oil for Aladdin's Lamp," radio speech over the Mutual Network, March 7, 1944. Folder: "Interior Department, 1944–5," Official File 6, Franklin D. Roosevelt: Papers as President, FDRL. Emphasis in the original.
15. Daniel Yergin, The Prize: The Epic Quest for Oil, Money & Power, 2nd ed. (New York: Free Press, 1992), 382.
16. Letter from Harold Ickes to FDR, August 18, 1943, Folder: "Saudi Arabian Pipeline," Diplomatic Correspondence, President's Secretary's File, Franklin D. Roosevelt: Papers as President, FDRL.
17. Letter from Harold Ickes to FDR, January 4, 1944, ibid.
18. "Investigation of the National Defense Program: Additional Report of the Special Committee Investigating the National Defense Program, Navy Purchases of the Middle East Oil," April 28, 1948, Folder: "Israel-Oil Situation in the Middle East," Papers of Henry Morgenthau Jr., FDRL. Figure includes money provided directly, as well as indirectly through the British.
19. "The Under Secretary of State (Welles) to President Roosevelt," FRUS, 1939, IV:695.
20. Letter from King Abdel Aziz to FDR, May 29, 1943, Folder: "January–May, 1943," Correspondence File, State Department, President's Secretary's File, Franklin D. Roosevelt: Papers as President, FDRL.
21. Rigdon, "The Log of the President's Trips," Annex C, 1–2.
22. "The Under Secretary of State (Welles) to President Roosevelt," February 12, 1942, FRUS, 1942, IV:562.
23. Eddy, FDR Meets Ibn Saud, 35.
24. Rigdon, "The Log of the President's Trips," Annex C, 1–2.
25. Eddy, FDR Meets Ibn Saud, 35–36.
26. "President Roosevelt to the King of Saudi Arabia (Abdul Aziz ibn Saud)," April 5, 1945, FRUS, 1945, VIII:698.
27. Edward R. Stettinius Jr., Roosevelt and the Russians: The Yalta Conference (New York: Doubleday, 1949), 289.
28. Letter from Eleanor Roosevelt to Joseph Lash, February 28, 1945, Folder 5, Box 42, Papers of Eleanor Roosevelt, FDRL.

29. "Joint Statement by President Bush and Saudi Crown Prince Abdullah," Crawford Texas, April 25, 2005, available at http://www.whitehouse.gov/news/releases/2005/04/20050425-8.html, accessed April 25, 2005.
30. "Conference of Chiefs of Mission in the Near East with President Truman on November 10, 1945," *FRUS*, 1945, VIII:18.
31. "Paper Drafted by the Officer in Charge of Egypt and Anglo-Egyptian Sudan Affairs," October 24, 1950, *FRUS*, 1950, V:221.
32. Henry Wallace led the "sphere of influence" crowd.
33. As recalled by Dean Rusk in his memoir *As I Saw It* (New York: W. W. Norton, 1990), 154.
34. "Conference of Chiefs of Mission in the Near East with President Truman on November 10, 1945," 18.
35. "Memorandum of Conversation, by the Politico-Military Advisor, Bureau of Near Eastern, South Asian, and African Affairs (Dasopit)," April 24, 1952, *FRUS*, 1952–54, IX:219.
36. Harry S. Truman Presidential Museum and Library, "President Harry S. Truman's 1947 Diary Book," January 16, 1947, Truman Library Online Documents, available at http://trumanlibrary.org/diary/transcript.htm.
37. "Policy Statement Prepared in the Department of State," February 5, 1951, *FRUS*, 1951, V:1027.
38. Yergin, *The Prize*, 425.
39. "Policy Statement Prepared in the Department of State."
40. "Memorandum of Conversation Prepared in the Department of Defense," December 17, 1951, *FRUS*, 1951, V:1072.
41. "President Truman to King Abdul Aziz ibn Saud of Saudi Arabia," October 31, 1950, *FRUS*, 1950, V:1190.
42. ADST oral history of Dayton S. Mak. Mak served as an administrative officer in Dhahran, 1948.
43. "The Minister in Saudi Arabia (Eddy) to the Secretary of State," July 8, 1945, *FRUS*, 1945, VIII:925.
44. "The Acting Secretary of State to the Minister in Saudi Arabia (Eddy)," June 25, 1945, *FRUS*, 1945, VIII:915.
45. William E. Mulligan File on William Eddy, Folder 18, Box 1, Mulligan Papers. History has largely forgotten Eddy, although he was a legend of his time. Eddy was born in Sidon, Lebanon, to missionary parents and spoke classical Arabic fluently. During World War II, Eddy was the protégé of William "Wild Bill" Donovan, the chief of the OSS, and helped facilitate the Allied invasion of North Africa. He also helped introduce basketball into Egypt, and wrote the Arabic rules for that game. Most famously, he was the interpreter on the USS *Quincy* when Roosevelt and Abdel Aziz met in February, 1945. Abdel Aziz so respected Eddy's language abilities that he did not have with him his own interpreter but rather shared Eddy with Roosevelt, a very unusual occurrence. The problem was that the translator needed to kneel, given that the king always sat. But no serving American minister—Eddy was minister in Saudi Arabia—could kneel before a sitting potentate. The problem was solved when Roosevelt briefly suspended Eddy's role as minister, reverting him back to his World War I military position of colonel. Eddy then donned his old uniform and served as translator. At the end, he reverted back to his ministerial role.
46. "Memorandum by the Acting Secretary of State to President Truman," June 26, 1945, *FRUS*, 1945, VIII:916–17.

47. "The Vice Consul at Dhahran (Sands) to the Secretary of State," July 4, 1945, *FRUS*, 1945, VIII:920.

48. "Visit of his Royal Highness the Amir Faisal to Washington July 31–August 1, 1945," *FRUS*, 1945, VIII:1003.

49. "Telegram from the Acting Secretary of State to the Minister in Saudi Arabia (Eddy)," June 27, 1945, *FRUS*, 1945, VIII:918.

50. C. L. Sulzberger, "Saudi Arabia Base Key U.S. Airfield," *New York Times*, November 24, 1946.

51. "The Secretary of Defense (Forrestal) to the Secretary of State," November 8, 1948, *FRUS*, 1948, V:252.

52. ADST oral history of Parker T. Hart.

53. Robert J. Donovan, *Conflict and Crisis: The Presidency of Harry S. Truman 1945–1948* (New York: W. W. Norton, 1977), 268.

54. Dean Acheson, *Present at the Creation: My Years in the State Department*, 3rd ed. (New York: W. W. Norton, 1987), 219.

55. "Statement by the Secretary of State," no date, *FRUS*, 1947, V:61.

56. Acheson, *Present at the Creation*, 219.

57. The British told the Jews and Arabs about their decision a few days earlier, and presented the decision to the British Parliament several days later.

58. "Memorandum of Conversation between the president and Amir Faisal, Foreign Minister of Saudi Arabia," December 13, 1946, *FRUS*, 1946, VII:729–31. Acheson, *Present at the Creation*, 125.

59. Acheson, *Present at the Creation*, 176. After that meeting, "when the boredom of presiding over public meetings would overcome me, I used to practice immobility. It requires immense self-control. The temptation to pull an ear or rub the nose can become agonizing but less so than listening to speeches."

60. Truman Library, Oral History Interview with Loy Henderson, Interviewed by Richard D. McKinzie, June 14, 1973, Truman Library Online Documents, available at http://www.trumanlibrary.org/oralhist/hendrson.htm#oh1. Dean Acheson had similar sentiments; Acheson, *Present at the Creation*, 181.

61. In a candid discussion with his secretary of state, Cordell Hull, in 1939 about confusing British policy choices in Palestine, a baffled Roosevelt confessed, "My recollection of the [Palestine Mandate is that it] did intend to convert Palestine into a Jewish home which might very possibly become preponderantly Jewish within a comparatively short time." See Hull, *Memoirs*, 2:1530. In Truman's estimation, the Balfour Declaration, committed the British to a Jewish state. In his view, Jews had waited thirty years for Great Britain to make good on its promise.

62. Harry S. Truman, *Memoirs by Harry S. Truman*, vol. 2: *Years of Trial and Hope* (New York: Doubleday, 1956), 153.

63. Rusk, *As I Saw It*, 152.

64. "The Minister in Saudi Arabia (Childs) to the Secretary of State," December 4, 1947, *FRUS*, 1947, V:1336.

65. Walter Millis, ed., *The Forrestal Diaries* (New York: Viking Press, 1951), 372.

66. Oral History of Loy Henderson, available at http://www.trumanlibrary.org/oralhist/hendrson.htm#oh1.

67. Millis, *The Forrestal Diaries*, 81.

68. John Morton Blum, ed., *The Price of Vision: The Diary of Henry A. Wallace 1942–1946* (Boston: Houghton Mifflin, 1973), 65. Cited in Donovan, *Conflict and Crisis*, 319.

69. Rusk, *As I Saw It*, 153.

70. "Minister in Saudi Arabia (Childs) to the Secretary of State," May 15, 1948, *FRUS*, 1948, V:995.

71. Nadav Safran, *Saudi Arabia: The Ceaseless Quest for Security* (Ithaca, NY: Cornell University Press, 1988), 67.

72. Painter, *Oil and the American Century*, 125.

73. Eilts, author's interview, Boston, December 8, 2003.

74. Ibid.

75. "The Minister in Saudi Arabia (Childs) to the Secretary of State," February 9, 1948, *FRUS*, 1948, V:221.

76. Painter, *Oil and the American Century*, 166.

77. Yergin, *The Prize*, 445–49. For the important role played by the State Department in these decisions, see Painter, *Oil and the American Century*.

78. Painter, *Oil and the American Century*, 171.

79. "Memorandum of Conversation," March 19, 1950, *FRUS*, 1950, V:1134.

80. ADST oral history of Raymond Hare.

81. Oral History Research Office, Columbia University, Oral History Interview with Raymond Hare, Interviewed by John Luter, June 1972, #639 PRTS, DDEL, 56.

82. Hart, *Saudi Arabia and the United States*, 88.

83. Ibid., 85.

84. David Long, *The United States and Saudi Arabia: Ambivalent Allies* (Boulder, CO: Westview Press, 1985), 34.

85. The price tag was unrealistic in the face of Saudi financial constraints, and in 1950 the Joint Chiefs of Staff recommended a scaled-down version of the report and suggested an expenditure of about $75 billion that ultimately would be paid by the Saudis. But the Saudis argued that they couldn't pay for this kind of government projects because, although foreign to the United States, the king's money was to be used for gifts for "those who, if they had no money to feed themselves would be a threat to internal stability." "Memorandum of Conversation," March 19, 1950, *FRUS*, 1950, V:1137.

86. Long, *United States and Saudi Arabia*, 35.

87. "A Report to the National Security Council by the Executive Secretary on NSC 26/5," April 13, 1951, NSC Series, DDEL. (The document has since been reclassified.) This NSC directive was approved by the president on May 3, 1951. See Steve Everly and Charles R. T. Crumpley, "Truman OK'd Sabotage Plot," *Kansas City Star*, February 25, 1996; Steve Everly, "'50s Plan Prepared for Oilfield Seizure," *Kansas City Star*, January 31, 2004; Shibley Telhami, "The Persian Gulf: Understanding the American Oil Strategy," *Brookings Review* 20, 2 (2002): 32–35.

88. Cited in "A Report to the National Security Council on NSC 26/5," 2.

89. Everly and Crumpley, "Truman OK'd Sabotage Plot"; Michael Ameen, author's interview, Houston, TX, January 25, 2005. Ameen was then a young marine from a unit that would have set off explosives if so ordered.

90. Everly and Crumpley, "Truman OK'd Sabotage Plot"; Everly "'50s Plan Prepared for Oilfield Seizure." That Eisenhower also explored "conservation," or denial operations. National Security Council. NSC 5714, "Protection and Conservation of Middle East Oil Resources and Facilities," May 29, 1957.

91. "A Report to the National Security Council on NSC 26/5," April 13, 1951, 1.

92. Steve Everly, "U.S. Considered Using Radiological Weapons, '50 CIA Document Shows," *Kansas City Star*, February 20, 2002.

93. Steve Everly, "Cold War Deal Saved Big Oil," *The Kansas City Star*, June 27, 2001; Everly, "U.S. Considered Using Radiological Weapons."
94. Eilts, author's phone interview, February 28, 2005.

Chapter 3

1. In an unpublished portion of his memoirs Eisenhower wrote that "the strongest reason of all for the United States [to stay out of Vietnam during the battle at Dien Bien Phu] is the fact that among all the powerful nations of the world the United States is the only one with a tradition of anti-colonialism. . . . The standing of the United States as the most powerful of the anti-colonial powers is an asset of incalculable value to the Free world . . . the moral position of the United States was more to be guarded than the Tonkin Delta, indeed than all of Indochina." Stephen E. Ambrose, *Eisenhower: Soldier and President* (New York: Simon and Schuster, 1990), 360.
2. Ickes struggled against others such as Max Thornburg, a State Department advisor on energy and a former oil executive who viewed oil interest more benignly. Ickes also tussled with Secretary of State Hull, who believed that Washington should remain distant from the oil companies all together. Painter, *Oil and the American Century*, chap. 5.
3. Nathan J. Citino, *From Arab Nationalism to OPEC: Eisenhower, King Saud and the Making of US-Saudi Relations* (Bloomington: Indiana University Press, 2002), 15; Painter, *Oil and the American Century*.
4. "How Dulles Averted War," *Life*, January 16, 1956, 77.
5. "Statement of Policy by the National Security Council," July 14, 1953, *FRUS*, 1952–54, IX:400.
6. "Draft Letter from the President to Abdul Aziz Al Saud King of Saudi Arabia," May 1, 1953, Box 1, Dulles-Herter Series, Dwight D. Eisenhower: Papers as President of the United States, 1953–61 (Ann Whitman File), DDEL.
7. ADST oral history of Parker T. Hart.
8. The Buraimi slave market was also important to Saudi Arabia's still existent slave trade.
9. "Discussion at the 147th Meeting of the National Security Council, Monday, June 1, 1953," Box 4, NSC series, Dulles-Herter Series, Dwight D. Eisenhower: Papers as President of the United States, 1953–61 (Ann Whitman File), DDEL; Tore Tingvold Peterson, "Anglo-American Rivalry in the Middle East: The Struggle for the Buraimi Oasis, 1952–1957," *International History Review*, February 1992, 76.
10. Eilts, author's interview, Boston, December 8, 2003.
11. Phebe Marr, e-mail message to author, April 20, 2005.
12. Marr, e-mail message to author, March 2005.
13. Thomas Lippman, *Inside the Mirage* (Boulder, CO: Westview Press, 2004), 137–54. The Ford Foundation Archives in New York has extensive documentation of its more than two decades of work in Saudi Arabia. It was the Ford Foundation's only project in which it was the recipient, rather than the provider, of financial assistance.
14. Robert Vitalis, "Aramco World: Business and Culture on the Arabian Oil Frontier," in Madawi al-Rasheed and Robert Vitalis, eds., *Counter-Narratives:*

History, Contemporary Society and Politics in Saudi Arabia and Yemen (New York: Palgrave-Macmillan, 2004), 170–71; Helen Lackner, *A House Built on Sand: A Political Economy of Saudi Arabia* (London: Ithaca Press, 1978); Fred Halliday, *Arabia Without Sultans: A Survey of Political Instability in the Arab World* (New York: Vintage Books, 1975), 77–80.

15. Brown, *Oil, God, and Gold*, 213.

16. Mulligan quoted in Anthony Cave Brown, *Oil, God, and Gold: The Story of Aramco and the Saudi Kings* (New York: Houghton Mifflin, 1999), 213. William Mulligan was the head of Aramco's Arabian Affairs division (1963–78).

17. "Discussion at the 199th Meeting of the National Security Council," Thursday, May 27, 1954, Box 5, NSC Series, Dwight D. Eisenhower: Papers as President of the United States, 1953–61 (Ann Whitman File), DDEL. See also Citino, *From Arab Nationalism to OPEC*, 47.

18. Stephen Page, *The USSR and Arabia: The Development of Soviet Policies and Attitudes Towards the Countries of the Arabian Peninsula* (London: Central Asian Research Center, 1971), 30.

19. The United Arab Emirates stayed in possession of most of the Buraimi oasis. In return, the emir of the UAE, Sheikh Zaid, ceded a valuable land corridor to Saudi Arabia that ran west and south of Qatar to an outlet on the Persian Gulf. David Holden and Richard Johns, *The House of Saud: The Rise and Rule of the Most Powerful Dynasty in the Arab World* (New York: Holt, Rinehart and Winston, 1982), 376–77; "Chronology," *Middle East Journal* 28, 4 (1974): 432; Peterson, "Anglo-American Rivalry in the Middle East," 91, argues that the UAE got the better deal. However losing the land corridor was a considerable concession, as evidenced by the UAE's recent efforts to reopen negotiations.

20. Hassan el-Fekih and Habib Trabelsi, "Tensions Emerge Between UAE and Saudi Arabia: UAE-Saudi Tensions Emerge over Border Row Dating Back to the 1970s, Trade Links with US," *Arab News.* February 22, 2005.

21. Although the date of his death is not disputed, the date of his birth is. Abdel Aziz is generally thought to have been born in 1880, although Robert Lacey states that when the king died he was seventy-seven, suggesting he was born in 1876. Robert Lacey, *The Kingdom: Arabia and the House of Saud* (New York: Harcourt Brace Jovanovich, 1981), 297. Truman's family doctors who treated Abdel Aziz in the early 1950s reported, "We didn't know how old he was because their years don't coincide with ours. . . . I think it was about 80 or something like that." Truman Library, Oral History Interview with Wallace H. Graham, Interviewed by Niel M. Johnson, March 30, 1989, Truman Library Online Documents, available at http://www.trumanlibrary.org/oralhist/grahamw.htm.

22. Recollections of HRH Prince Talal bin Abdel Aziz, *The House of Saud*, directed by Jihan el-Tahri (Paris, France: Alegria Productions, 2004), DVD.

23. Holden and Johns recount the story that Prince Faisal, in front of his brothers, took a ring from the deceased monarch's finger and passed it to Saud, making clear his loyalty to the new king. Saud passed it back, symbolically recognizing Faisal as crown prince and heir apparent. Holden and Johns, *House of Saud*, 174.

24. Madawi al-Rasheed, *A History of Saudi Arabia* (New York: Cambridge University Press, 2002), 121.

25. Gerald De Gaury, *Faisal: King of Saudi Arabia* (New York: Frederick A. Praeger, 1967), 78.

26. Faisal's group, for instance, concentrated their attacks on Saud supporter Prince Talal, thus avoiding attacks on the king's reputation directly. Vassiliev, *History of Saudi Arabia*, 359.
27. Malcolm Kerr, *The Arab Cold War: Gamal Abd al-Nasir and His Rivals, 1958–1970* (London: Oxford University Press, 1967).
28. Dwight D. Eisenhower, *Waging Peace: The White House Years* (New York: Doubleday, 1965), 24.
29. "Discussion at the 302nd Meeting of the National Security Council," November 1, 1956, Box 8, NSC Series, Dwight D. Eisenhower: Papers as President of the United States, 1953–61 (Ann Whitman File), DDEL.
30. Ibid.
31. Ibid.
32. Maximum Western reserves would last between fifteen and thirty days.
33. Letter from Eisenhower to Anthony Eden, September 8, 1956, Box 7, Dulles Herter Series, Dwight D. Eisenhower: Papers as President of the United States, 1953–61 (Ann Whitman File), DDEL.
34. Eisenhower, *Waging Peace*, 39. He goes on to say, "The inherent right of any sovereign nation to exercise the power of eminent domain within its own territory could scarcely be doubted, provided that just compensation were paid to the owners of the territory so expropriated."
35. "Memorandum of a Conference with the President, White House, Washington, October 30, 1956, 4:25 p.m.," *FRUS*, 1955–57, XVI:873–74; Stephen L. Spiegel, *The Other Arab-Israeli Conflict: Making America's Middle East Policy, from Truman to Reagan* (Chicago: University of Chicago Press, 1985), 75.
36. Telegram from U.S. Ambassador to England Aldrich to John Foster Dulles. November 19, 1956, Box 8, Dulles-Herter Series, Dwight D. Eisenhower: Papers as President of the United States, 1953–61 (Ann Whitman File), DDEL.
37. Turki al-Faisal bin Abdel Aziz al-Saud, "Special Address," speech Georgetown University, Washington, DC, February 3, 2002. available at http://ccas.georgetown.edu/files/Archives%20old%20Website/public%20affairs/Prince%20Turki%20Al.doc.
38. Dwight D. Eisenhower, "Special Message to Congress on the Situation in the Middle East," January 5, 1957, Public Papers of the President, the American Presidency Project, available at http://www.presidency.ucsb.edu/ws/index.php?pid=11007&st=&st1. For an in-depth discussion of the Eisenhower doctrine and this period in Arab-American relations, see Salim Yaqub, *Containing Arab Nationalism: The Eisenhower Doctrine and the Middle East* (Chapel Hill: University of North Carolina Press, 2004).
39. Citino, *From Arab Nationalism to OPEC*, 122.
40. "Memorandum of a Conversation, Ambassador Dillon's Residence, Paris," December 10, 1956, *FRUS*, 1955–57, XII:399.
41. "Memorandum of a Conference with the President," December 20, 1956, *FRUS*, 1955–57, XII:415.
42. "Editorial Note," *FRUS*, 1955–57, XIII:405.
43. "Briefing Book on King Saud's Visit," Folder 1, Book 2, 5, White House Central Files, Dwight D. Eisenhower: Papers as President of the United States, 1953–61 (Ann Whitman File), DDEL.
44. Eilts, author's interview, December 8, 2003.
45. Lackner, *A House Built on Sand;* Vitalis, "Aramco World."
46. Page, *USSR and Arabia*, 30.

47. Vitalis, "Aramco World," 171; Halliday, *Arabia Without Sultans*, 77–80.
48. Lackner, *A House Built on Sand*, 61.
49. Nadav Safran, *Saudi Arabia: The Ceaseless Quest for Security* (Ithaca, NY: Cornell University Press, 1988), 86.
50. De Gaury, *Faisal*, 93; Holden and Johns, *House of Saud*, 201.
51. "Editorial Note," *FRUS*, 1958–60, XII:724; Wanda M. Jablonski, "Feisal Asks 'Friendly' Oil Settlement," *Petroleum Week*, June 6, 1958.
52. In the mid-1950s, after Aramco refused to advance the king additional cash until he demonstrated some responsibility, King Saud invited the International Monetary Fund to Saudi Arabia. Prince Faisal used the IMF's recommendations as the basis for his economic policies.
53. Vassiliev writes that "Faisal wanted to give the impression that he was in favour of reforms and a rapprochement with Nasser." Alexei Vassiliev, *The History of Saudi Arabia* (New York: New York University Press, 2000), 355.
54. *Al-Hayat* (Beirut), January 1, 1961, as cited in Holden and Johns, *House of Saud*, 212; Vassiliev, *History of Saudi Arabia*, 358.
55. Vassiliev, *History of Saudi Arabia*, 359; al-Rasheed, *A History of Saudi Arabia*, 109.
56. On the different views of how the government should be structured in order to modernize and survive, see Sarah Yizraeli, *The Remaking of Saudi Arabia: The Struggle Between King Sa'ud and Crown Prince Faysal, 1953–1962* (Tel Aviv: Moshe Dayan Center for Middle Eastern and African Studies, 1997); Tim Niblock, "Social Structure and the development of the Saudi Arabian Political System," in Tim Niblock, ed., *State, Society, and Economy in Saudi Arabia* (New York: St. Martin's Press, 1982), 75–105.

Chapter 4

1. "Memorandum from Acting Secretary of State Bowles to President Kennedy," May 6, 1961, *FRUS*, 1961–63, XVII:100.
2. Parker T. Hart, *Saudi Arabia and the United States: Birth of a Security Partnership* (Bloomington: Indiana University Press, 1998), 90.
3. "Letter from Saud bin Abdul-Aziz Al Saud, King of the Kingdom of Saudi Arabia, to his Excellency, John F. Kennedy, President of the United States of America," June 25, 1961, President's Office Files, Box 123b, Folder: "Saudi Arabia, Security 1961–1963," Presidential Papers of John F. Kennedy, John F. Kennedy Library (henceforth JFKL), Harvard University, Cambridge, MA.
4. "Memorandum from Secretary of State Rusk to President Kennedy," July 13, 1961, *FRUS*, 1961–63, XVII:191.
5. The king later conveyed that the author of the letter was the notoriously anti-American pro-Palestinian representative to the UN, Ahmad Shuqairi (as Rusk had suspected all along), himself a Palestinian. The king also claimed that he had not carefully read the letter before signing it. Pushed by his advisors, the president invited the king to Washington in early 1961. But the damage had been done and the meeting was strained. "Memorandum from Secretary of State Rusk to President Kennedy," December 23, 1961, *FRUS*, 1961–63, XVII:369.
6. "Department of State for the Press," March 16, 1961, Folder: 1/1/61–8/18/8, Box 156A, Country Files: Saudi Arabia, National Security Files, Presidential Papers of John F. Kennedy, JFKL.

7. "Soviet Offer of Aid to Saudi Arabia," September 11, 1962, Folder: 7/62–9/62, Box 157, Countries: Saudi Arabia, National Security Files, Presidential Papers of John F. Kennedy, JFKL.

8. "Special Message to the Congress on Urgent National Needs," delivered by President John F. Kennedy before a joint session of Congress, May 25, 1961, available at http://www.jfklibrary.org/j052561.htm.

9. John S. Badeau, *The American Approach to the Arab World* (New York: Harper & Row, 1968), 105. Phillips Talbot recalls that "Kennedy was not much interested in the hard status quo places that didn't show any real indication of modernizing prospects." Phillips Talbot, author's interview, New York, October 24, 2003.

10. About 70 percent of the $500 million aid came through PL 480. Mordechai Gazit, *President Kennedy's Policy Toward the Arab States and Israel* (Tel Aviv: Shiloah Center for Middle Eastern and African Studies at Tel Aviv University, 1983), 21.

11. "Memorandum for Mr. Bundy from C.V. Clifton," June 27, 1962, Box 156A, Countries: Saudi Arabia, National Security Files, Presidential Papers of John F. Kennedy, JFKL.

12. After he met with President Johnson in 1966, King Faisal remarked to a Libyan Arab ambassador that "President Kennedy had brought in professors without experience to advise him, while President Johnson—with great practicality—relied upon experience—his own—and that of his advisers to formulate effective policies covering a tremendous range of world problems." Memorandum for Mr. Marvin Watson from James W. Symington, #153, July 8, 1966, Folder: "Saudi Arabia Memos [1 of 2], volume I, 12/63–4/67," Country File, Saudi Arabia, National Security File, Papers of Lyndon Baines Johnson: Presidential Papers, Lyndon Baines Johnson Library (henceforth LBJL), Austin, TX.

13. David Long, *The United States and Saudi Arabia: Ambivalent Allies* (Boulder, CO: Westview Press, 1985), 113.

14. "To Rusk from Talbot, February 13, 1962," Folder: 2/1/62–2/19/62, #2, Box 156A, Countries: Saudi Arabia, National Security Files, Presidential Papers of John F. Kennedy, JFKL.

15. "Memorandum from the Department of State Executive Secretary (Brubeck) to the president's Special Assistant for National Security Affairs (Bundy), Review of Policy toward the Yemen Conflict," February 24, 1963, *FRUS*, 1961–63, XVIII:358.

16. Mordechai Abir, *Saudi Arabia in the Oil Era: Regime and Elites, Conflict and Collaboration* (London: Croom Helm, 1988), 85.

17. Wanda M. Jablonski, "Is Arabia Moving to a New 50-50 Oil Pattern?" *Petroleum Week*, February 22, 1957.

18. Stephen Duguid, "A Biographical Approach to the Study of Social Change in the Middle East: Abdullah Tariki as a New Man," *International Journal of Middle East Studies* 1, 3 (1970): 195–220.

19. Phebe Marr, e-mail message to author, April 20, 2005; Citino, *From Arab Nationalism to OPEC*, 152.

20. Wanda M. Jablonski, "Feisal Asks 'Friendly' Oil Settlement," *Petroleum Week*, June 6, 1958.

21. Shoshana Klabanoff, *Middle East Oil and U.S. Foreign Policy* (New York: Praeger, 1974), 199.

22. Alexei Vassiliev, *The History of Saudi Arabia* (New York: New York University Press, 2000), 359.

23. David Holden and Richard Johns, *The House of Saud: The Rise and Rule of the Most Powerful Dynasty in the Arab World* (New York: Holt, Rinehart and Winston, 1982), 198–222.

24. "Situation in Saudi Arabia," CIA telegram, October 15, 1962, Box 157, Countries: Saudi Arabia, National Security Files, Presidential Papers of John F. Kennedy, JFKL.

25. "Memorandum for: McGB from RWK," June 7, 1962, Box 156A, Countries: Saudi Arabia. National Security Files, Presidential Papers of John F. Kennedy, JFKL.

26. Madawi al-Rasheed, *A History of Saudi Arabia* (New York: Cambridge University Press, 2002), 114.

27. Iranian-American Relations Oral History Project, "The Reminiscences of Robert W. Komer," Columbia University, New York, April 27 and August 27, 1987. Ambassador Hart recalls that the president "followed things in great detail. It was commonly said that he could give an excellent briefing on the Yemen to anybody." Oral History Project, "Interview with Parker T. Hart," April 15, 1969, Presidential Papers of John F. Kennedy, JFKL. See also Warren Bass, *Support Any Friend: Kennedy's Middle East and the Making of the U.S.-Israel Alliance* (New York: Oxford University Press, 2003), 98–144.

28. Hart, *Saudi Arabia and the United States*, 135.

29. F. Gregory Gause III, *Saudi-Yemeni Relations: Domestic Structures and Foreign Influences* (New York: Columbia University Press, 1990), 59.

30. The planning for the trip began a few months before. The original purpose of the trip was spelled out in a document preceding the actual trip, "Telegram from Thatcher in Jidda to Secretary of State," July 26, 1962, Box 157, Country Reports, National Security File, Presidential Papers of John F. Kennedy, JFKL.

31. "Memorandum from Robert W. Komer of the National Security Council Staff to President Kennedy," October 4, 1962, *FRUS*, 1961–63, XVIII:158, parentheses in the original.

32. "Memorandum of Conversation, President's Talk with Crown Prince Faysal," Washington, October 5, 1962, *FRUS*, 1961–63, XVIII:162.

33. Kennedy offered a port call by the U.S. Navy. He also mentioned that he would make available for purchase American supersonic F-5As, if the Saudis had the money. The Saudis had previously requested to buy F-86s but had been turned down. The United States owned the F-86s the Saudis had been training on since 1957. Even as late as 1963, the Saudi air force was "still unable [to] fly, navigate and maintain these planes effectively." See "Outgoing Telegram from the Department of State," September 17, 1963, Folder: 9/63–11/63, Box 157A, Countries, National Security Files, Presidential Papers of John F. Kennedy, JFKL.

34. "Memorandum from the Assistant Secretary of State for Near Eastern and South Asian Affairs (Talbot) to Secretary of State Rusk, Yemen Situation and Its Implications," October 9, 1962, *FRUS*, 1961–63, XVIII:172.

35. "Memorandum from Robert W. Komer of the National Security Council Staff to President Kennedy," October 4, 1962, 159.

36. "Memorandum from the Joint Chiefs of Staff to Secretary of Defense McNamara: Possible US Military Support to the Saudi Arabian Regime," November 9, 1962, *FRUS*, 1962–63, XVIII:207.

37. In yet another bizarre turn in Gulf politics, the British began lining up alongside Saudi Arabia to counter Nasser. In a meeting on October 9, British ambassador

Sir David Ormsby Gore informed Rusk of Britain's decision to covertly support Prince Hassan bin Yahya, See footnote 1 of "Memorandum from the Assistant Secretary of State for Near Eastern and South Asian Affairs (Talbot) to Secretary of State Rusk, Yemen Situation and its Implications," October 9, 1962, *FRUS*, 1962–63, XVIII:172.

38. Author's interview, Saudi Arabia, February 2005; Joseph A. Kechichian, "The Role of the Ulama in the Politics of an Islamic State: The Case of Saudi Arabia," *International Journal of Middle East Studies* 18, 1 (1986): 60.

39. "Ten Point Programme Issued by Crown Prince Faisal on 6th November, 1962," in De Gaury, *Faisal*, Appendix I.

40. Eilts, author's phone interview, February 28, 2005.

41. Hart, *Saudi Arabia and the United States*, 157–62; Gause, *Saudi-Yemeni Relations*, 60–61.

42. "Telegram from the Department of State to the Embassy in the United Arab Republic," March 2, 1963, *FRUS*, 1961–63, XVIII:391. Phillips Talbot remembers that high-level Kennedy officials actually presented Nasser with a deal. The "deal was that anything that Nasser wanted to do to modernize Egypt we could support wholeheartedly and we could probably get some funds for it. But if Nasser interfered with Israel or the conservative Arab states, we would have much greater trouble." Talbot, author's interview, October 24, 2003.

43. Parker Hart, who was an eyewitness, claims Hard Surface comprised six F-100Ds, but State Department documents claim eight; Hart, *Saudi Arabia and the United States*, 210. "Editorial Note," *FRUS*, 1961–63, XVIII:581.

44. Hart, *Saudi Arabia and the United States*, 193.

45. Bass, *Support Any Friend*, 130.

46. "Saudi Arabia Lets Jews in US Units Serve on Her Soil," *New York Times*, June 10, 1963.

47. Bass, *Support Any Friend*, 130–33. To this day some claim that the planes were sent unarmed. A careful look at the rules of engagement (ROE) approved by the president discounts it. According to the ROE, if Egyptian planes strayed into Saudi territory and shot at American planes, USAF pilots were authorized to "destroy the intruder." See "Memorandum to the President from R. W. Komer," July 2, 1963, Folder: 7/63–8/63, Box 157A, Countries: Saudi Arabia, National Security Files, Presidential Papers of John F. Kennedy, JFKL.

48. "Memorandum of Conversation," *FRUS*, 1961–63, XVII:475.

49. Talbot, author's interview, October 24, 2003. See also "Interview with Parker T. Hart," April 15, 1969, JFKL, in which he states that there was not much of a change between Kennedy and Johnson that "the death of Kennedy coincided with the end of a period, which was the period of our strongest overt support for Faisal by aircraft in the country."

50. Shortly before he died, Kennedy came to share this assessment. In a message from Kennedy to Nasser, orally transmitted through the U.S. ambassador, Kennedy made clear that "we are confident that the UKG and the SAG are honoring their assurances to us that they are not aiding the Royalists. I therefore have no leverage with Faysal when, having carried out his end of the bargain, he continues to see Egyptian troops in Yemen and hear expression of the UARG hostility from Cairo." "Telegram from the Department of State to the Embassy in the United Arab Republic," October 19, 1963, *FRUS*, 1961–63, XVIII:752.

51. Rusk, *As I Saw It* (New York: W. W. Norton, 1990), 378.

52. "U.S. Library Set Afire Over Congo Action," *Washington Post*, November 27, 1964.
53. American ambassador to Egypt Lucius Battle has an interesting account in his oral history at the LBJ library. At first he believed that the shooting down of Macom's plane was intentional. After collecting the facts, he believed it more likely an accident. By that point, however, history had moved on and the conflict between America and Egypt was exacerbated.
54. Eilts, author's interview, December 8, 2003.
55. In 1966, Saudi arms expenditures would increase from $503 million to over $1 billion (in constant 1978 dollars) and Iranian expenditures from $612 million to over $1 billion. These states purchased most of their arms from the United States. In the Saudi case, the big jump in 1964 was based on large sales to the British, orchestrated by the United States. See "Table I: Military Expenditures of Middle Eastern States," in Joe Stork and Jim Paul, "Arms Sales and the Militarization of the Middle East," in *Arms Race in the Middle East, MERIP Reports* 112 (1983): 6. Congress has slightly different numbers, but the trend lines are similar. From 1950 to 1964 the United States and Saudi Arabia agreed to $87 million in sales. In 1965 alone, that number jumped to $341 million. See also *SIPRI Yearbook of World Armaments and Disarmament 1969/70* (New York: Humanities Press), 271.
56. Stephen L. Spiegel, *The Other Arab-Israeli Conflict: Making America's Middle East Policy, from Truman to Reagan* (Chicago: University of Chicago Press, 1985), 119.
57. Ibid., 120.
58. De Gaury, *Faisal*, 132.
59. Robert Lacey, *The Kingdom: Arabia and the House of Saud* (New York: Harcourt Brace Jovanovich, 1981), 351.
60. Ibid., 352.
61. De Gaury, *Faisal*, 134.
62. "Broadcast by Ex-King Sa'ud from Cairo," in BBC, *Summary of World Broadcasts*, May 21, 1967.
63. Nadav Safran, *Saudi Arabia: The Ceaseless Quest for Security* (Ithaca, NY: Cornell University Press, 1988), 122.
64. Background paper, "Soviet and Chinese Communist Intentions in the Near East —Red Sea Area," Document 34, LBJL.
65. Abir, *Saudi Arabia in the Oil Era*, 8.
66. "From Ambassador Hart to Secretary of State," October 31, 1963, Folder: 9/63–11/63, Box 157A, Countries: Saudi Arabia, National Security Files, Presidential Papers of John F. Kennedy, JFKL.
67. Which totaled about $100 million in equipment. See Document 42, Folder: "Faisal Visit Briefing Book [1 of 2] 6/21–23/66," Country File: Saudi Arabia. National Security File, Papers of Lyndon Baines Johnson: Presidential Papers, LBJL.
68. Douglas Little, "Choosing Sides," in Robert A. Divine, ed., *The Johnson Years, LBJ at Home and Abroad* (Lawrence: University Press of Kansas, 1994), III:168.
69. Thomas F. Brady, "Britain Speeding Emergency Defense for Saudis to Deter and Egyptian Attack," *New York Times*, October 1, 1966.
70. Long, *United States and Saudi Arabia*, 44–45.
71. "Memorandum from Robert W. Komer of the National Security Council Staff to President Johnson," June 16, 1965, *FRUS, 1964–68*, XXI:480. While the F-104s worked superbly in their main mission of intercepting high-altitude bombers, they were unstable at low speeds, takeoffs, and particularly landings.

72. They were designed to defend the relatively short British defense perimeter, not extended combat roles over the vast expanses of Saudi desert.

73. "Intelligence Memorandum: Saudi Arabian Arms Purchases," May 26, 1966, *FRUS*, 1964–68, XXI:509.

74. The money deposited in British coffers would then help purchase the F-111s from the United States. As the British would later describe, "sales of military equipment can relieve the burden of defense expenditures by enabling us to produce our own weapons more economically; they provide experts; they also help to ease the difficulties of the country's balance of payments. The agreement for the sale of an air defense system to Saudi Arabia, for example . . . means an addition of 90 million to our exports." Taken from the 1966–67 Statement of Defense Estimates, cited in Mike Klare, "US Arms Sales and Military Aid to the Middle East," *MERIP Reports* 30 (1974): 18.

75. Klare, "US Arms Sales," 18.

76. Long, *United States and Saudi Arabia*, 46; Anthony Sampson, *The Arms Bazaar: From Lebanon to Lockheed* (New York: Viking Press, 1977), 174–81; Fred Halliday, *Arabia Without Sultans: A Survey of Political Instability in the Arab World* (New York: Vintage Books, 1975), 71–74. In addition to their not being able to afford them, the F-111s began to decrease in importance as the British considered their withdrawal east of Suez. Cathy Tackney, "Dealing Arms in the Middle East. Part I: History and Strategic Considerations," *MERIP Reports* 8 (1972): 11.

77. Safran argues that "after the Six Day War, in the crucial period between 1967 and 1970, the Saudis did less to build up their military combat capabilities than at any other time in Faisal's reign." Safran, *Saudi Arabia*, 203.

78. Cable from Hart to Rusk, "Delivery of President's Letter of Faysal re Yemen," August 29, 1964, #68, Country File: Saudi Arabia, National Security File, Papers of Lyndon Baines Johnson: Presidential Papers, LBJL.

79. "Memorandum from the President's Special Assistant (Rostow) to President Johnson," *FRUS*, 1964–68, XXI:518.

80. "Memorandum of Conversation, President and King Faisal, June 21, 1966," Saudi Arabia Memos [2 of 2] vol. I, 12/63–4/67," Folder 4, Country Files: Saudi Arabia, National Security File, Papers of Lyndon Baines Johnson: Presidential Papers, LBJL.

81. Eilts, author's phone interview, February 28, 2005.

82. Mem Con 2/21/66 #191 from Faisal to President, Folder: "4. Saudi Arabia Memos [2 of 2] vol. I, 12/63–4/6," Country File: Saudi Arabia, National Security File, Papers of Lyndon Baines Johnson: Presidential Papers, LBJL.

83. "Memorandum of Conversation," June 21, 1966, *FRUS*, 1964–68, XXI:523.

84. Ibid., 528.

85. John W. Finney, "Faisal Ruffled at News Parley," *New York Times*, June 23, 1966.

86. "Memorandum for the President, from WW Rostow," July 14, 1966, No. 152, Folder: "3. Saudi Arabia Memos [1 of 2] volume I 12/63–4/67," National Security File, Papers of Lyndon Baines Johnson: Presidential Papers, LBJL.

87. Local Government Relations, "The June 1967 Riots," July 26, 1967, Folder 8: "The June 1967 Riots," Box 16, Mulligan Papers.

88. Al-Rasheed, *A History of Saudi Arabia*, 129; Vassiliev, *History of Saudi Arabia*, 384.

89. "Incoming Telegram to Rusk, #10," June 3, 1967, Middle East Crisis, May 12–June 19, 1967, Box 23, National Security Council Histories, National Security File, Papers of Lyndon Baines Johnson: Presidential Papers, LBJL.

90. My thanks to Minda Arrow for her help on this point.

91. It spread because it seemed plausible. The turnaround time of the Israeli jets was much quicker than the Arab states thought possible, opening the possibility that the Israelis were being assisted.
92. Daniel Yergin, *The Prize: The Epic Quest for Oil, Money & Power*, 2nd ed. (New York: Free Press, 1992), 555.
93. "The June 1967 Riots," Mulligan Papers.
94. Ibid.
95. "Telegram from the Department of State to the Embassy in Saudi Arabia, #290," June 8, 1967, *FRUS*, 1964–68, XXI:557.
96. "CIA Intelligence Memorandum," June 9, 1967, Appendix Q [2], Document #12, Middle East Crisis, May 12–June 19, 1967, National Security Council Histories, Box 21, National Security File, Papers of Lyndon Baines Johnson: Presidential Papers, LBJL.
97. "The June 1967 Riots," Mulligan Papers.
98. United States Department of the Interior, *United States Petroleum Through 1980* (Washington, DC: 1968), 64.
99. Long, *United States and Saudi Arabia*, 116.
100. ASDT oral history of Hermann Eilts. In the end, Eilts and Yamani did not have to deal with the barges, as the ships were bunkered at a nearby port in Djibouti.
101. "Airgram from the Embassy in the United Kingdom to the Department of State," August 3, 1967, and "Airgram from the Embassy in Germany to the Department of State," August 4, 1967, *FRUS*, 1964–68, XXXIV:467–69.
102. Middle East Web, "Khartoum Resolutions, September 1967: Introduction," Middle East Historical and Peace Process Source Documents, available at http://www.mideastweb.org/khartoum.htm.
103. Thomas F. Brady, "Saudis Question Embargo on Oil," *New York Times*, July 1, 1967.
104. "McNamara to the Special Committee Meeting on Monday June 12," cited in Harold Saunders, "The Middle East Crisis; Preface," Document 2, vol. 1, Tabs 1–10, Box 17, Middle East Crisis, May 12–June 19, 1967, National Security Council Histories, National Security File, Papers of Lyndon Baines Johnson: Presidential Papers, LBJL.
105. "CIA Intelligence Memorandum," June 18, 1967, Document 45, Vol. 10, Appendix Q [IV], Box 21, Middle East Crisis, May 12–June 19, 1967, National Security Council Histories, National Security File, Papers of Lyndon Baines Johnson: Presidential Papers, LBJL.
106. Fouad Ajami, *The Arab Predicament: Arab Political Thought and Practice Since 1967* (New York: Cambridge University Press, 1981), 71.
107. Safran, *Saudi Arabia*, 123.

Chapter 5

1. "Telecon with Sec Schlesinger/Secretary Kissinger at 8:27 am," October 10, 1973, Kissinger Telephone Transcripts, FOIA Electronic Reading Room, Department of State, available at http://foia.state.gov/documents/kissinger/0000C284.pdf.
2. Jerry Markon and John Mintz, "Plot to Kill Saudi Ruler Admitted in U.S. Court," *Washington Post*, July 31, 2004; Eric Lichtblau, "Islamic Leader to Plead Guilty in Libya Plot," *New York Times*, July 30, 2004.

3. Helena Cobban, *The Palestinian Liberation Organization: People, Power, and Politics* (New York: Cambridge University Press, 1984), chap. 3.

4. James Piscatori, "Islamic Values and National Interest: The Foreign Policy of Saudi Arabia," in Adeed Dawisha, ed., *Islam in Foreign Policy* (Cambridge: Cambridge University Press, 1983), 42. Between 1967 and 1969, Saudi Arabia channeled money through Fatah, not the PLO, which was then deemed an Egyptian puppet. On the rise of Fatah, see Cobban, *Palestinian Liberation Organization.*

5. Other reasons include that Palestinians in Jordan came to believe that the leadership preferred Bedouins and East Bank families to the West Bank Palestinian population residing in Jordan. Cobban, *Palestinian Liberation Organization*, chap. 3; Mark Tessler, *A History of the Israeli-Palestinian Conflict* (Bloomington: Indiana University Press, 1994), chap. 7.

6. Mordechai Abir, *Saudi Arabia in the Oil Era: Regime and Elites, Conflict and Collaboration* (London: Croom Helm, 1988), 113–20.

7. Dana Adams Schmidt, "Saudi Arabia Ends Wave of Arrests," *New York Times*, September 10, 1969. There were reports of other attempted coups in September and November 1969 and April–May and July 1970; Alexei Vassiliev, *The History of Saudi Arabia* (New York: New York University Press, 2000), 371. On the September coup attempt, see "The King's Gamble," *The Economist*, September 1, 1973, 16; James Buchan, "Secular and Religious Opposition in Saudi Arabia," in Tim Niblock, ed., *State, Society, and Economy in Saudi Arabia* (New York: St. Martin's Press, 1982), 115. Buchan asserts that both Saudi and American intelligence officials received early information about the coup.

8. Henry Kissinger, *Years of Upheaval* (Boston, MA: Little, Brown, 1982), 196.

9. Richard Nixon, *RN: The Memoirs of Richard Nixon*, 2nd ed. (New York: Touchstone/Simon & Schuster, 1990), 477.

10. Stephen L. Spiegel, *The Other Arab-Israeli Conflict: Making America's Middle East Policy, from Truman to Reagan* (Chicago: University of Chicago Press, 1985), 179.

11. ADST oral history of Joe Sisco.

12. Cabinet Task Force on Oil Import Control, *The Oil Import Question: A Report on the Relationship of Oil Imports to the National Security* (Washington, DC: U.S. Government Printing Office, 1970), particularly 226–30. The report baldly asserts that "although we cannot exclude the possibility, we do not predict a substantial price rise in world oil over the coming decade," 405.

13. Or 20 percent of domestic energy demand. See Cabinet Task Force on Oil Import Control, *The Oil Import Question*, 414.

14. William Simon, *A Time for Action* (New York: McGraw Hill/Readers Digest Press, 1980), 63.

15. Ibid., 64.

16. Daniel Yergin, *The Prize: The Epic Quest for Oil, Money & Power*, 2nd ed. (New York: Free Press, 1992), 591.

17. By keeping cheaper Middle East oil from competing with domestic supply, the system was designed to protect domestic markets. This artificially lowered global prices to the benefit of oil consumers, Europe and Japan in particular. The system was conceived at a time when there was ample production capacity. By 1973 such conditions no longer existed and oil exporting countries became increasingly assertive.

18. Nixon also later removed international quotas.

19. Energy Information Administration, "World Oil Price Chronology (Real and Nominal Terms)," Excel version, March 2005, available at http://www.eia.doe.gov/emeu/cabs/chron_march2005.xls.
20. "Aramco 1973: A Review of Operations by the Arabian American Oil Company," Folder 4, Box 4, Mulligan Papers.
21. Jim Hoagland, "Saudis Ponder Whether to Produce the Oil U.S. Needs," *Washington Post*, July 11, 1973.
22. Yergin, *The Prize*, 584; James E. Akins, "The Oil Crisis: This Time the Wolf Is Here," *Foreign Affairs* 51, 3 (1973): 476.
23. Yergin, *The Prize*, 583–87.
24. Akins, "The Oil Crisis," 467.
25. Mohamed Heikal, *The Road to Ramadan* (New York: Ballantine Books, 1975), 268.
26. William B. Quandt, e-mail message to author, January 18, 2005. Quandt would become a senior staff director under President Carter.
27. Kissinger, *Years of Upheaval*, 854, 856.
28. Akins, *Foreign Affairs*, 1973, 490.
29. Anwar el-Sadat, *In Search of an Identity: An Autobiography* (New York: Harper and Row, 1977), 239, 151.
30. Turki al-Faisal replaced Kamal Adham as director of intelligence in 1977, shortly after King Faisal was assassinated.
31. Heikal, *Road to Ramadan*, 119.
32. Arnaud de Borchgrave, "The New Politics of Mideast Oil," *Newsweek*, September 10, 1973. Some reports, including one by Jim Hoagland in the *Washington Post*, suggest that buying Mirages on Egypt's account may have continued after the war.
33. Advisors left, but Sadat did not ask them to leave their Mediterranean bases. For Sadat, there was an important difference between "strategic presence" and "advisors." Arnaud de Borchgrave, "A Hot Autumn," *Newsweek*, August 7, 1972.
34. Heikal, *Road to Ramadan*, 184.
35. Henry Kissinger, *Years of Renewal* (New York: Touchstone/Simon & Schuster: 1999), 354.
36. Turki al-Faisal bin Abdel Aziz al-Saud, author's interview, London, April 2004.
37. Walter Isaacson, *Kissinger: A Biography* (New York: Simon & Schuster, 1992), 511.
38. Turki al-Faisal, author's interview, April 29, 2004.
39. Heikal, *Road to Ramadan*, 268.
40. William B. Quandt, "Kissinger and the Arab-Israeli Disengagement Negotiations," *Journal of International Affairs* 9, 1 (1975): 35.
41. Kamal Adham followed up with a discussion at the U.S. embassy to convey the message that he believed that Sadat would probably renew hostilities and that in such circumstances the Saudi government would feel compelled to join other Arabs in taking actions adverse to U.S. interests. Adham indicated that the Saudi government "was thinking of oil." See "Cable from Jidda to Secretary of State," May 8, 1973, Folder: Pol 15-1 Saud 1/1/71, Box 2585, General Records of the Department of State (RG 59), Subject Numerical Files 1970–73, Political and Defense, Nixon Presidential Materials Project, National Archives II, College Park, Maryland.
42. Jim Hoagland, "Faisal Warns U.S. on Israel," *Washington Post*, July 6, 1973.
43. Jim Hoagland, "Saudis Ponder Whether to Produce the Oil U.S. Needs," *Washington Post*, July 11, 1973.
44. Ibid.

45. Michael Ameen, author's interview, Houston, TX, January 25, 2005.

46. Nicholas C Proffitt, "Faisal's Threat," *Newsweek*, September 10, 1973.

47. Hoagland, "Saudis Ponder."

48. Hoagland, "Faisal Warns."

49. Recollections of James Schlesinger, *The House of Saud*, directed by Jihan el-Tahri (Paris, France: Alegria Productions, 2004), DVD.

50. Stockholm International Peace Research Institute, *SIPRI Yearbook of World Armaments and Disarmament, 1974* (New York: Humanities Press, 1974), 151, 5. Iraq and Jordan lost 125 and 20 tanks, respectively.

51. Raymond Close, author's phone interview, January 27, 2005.

52. William B. Quandt. *Peace Process: American Diplomacy and the Arab-Israeli Conflict Since 1967* (Washington, DC: Brookings Institution, 1993), 164; Isaacson, *Kissinger*, 522.

53. Robert Jordan, author's phone interview, February 2, 2005.

54. Quandt, "Kissinger and the Arab-Israeli Disengagement Negotiations," 36; Kissinger, *Years of Upheaval*, chap. 11.

55. Isaacson, *Kissinger*, 514.

56. Yergin, *The Prize*, 604–5.

57. Ibid., 606–7.

58. Nadav Safran argues quite convincingly that Faisal's decision had less to do with the $2.2 billion aid package and more with his belief that the Arabs were losing and required something to change the situation. See Nadav Safran, *Saudi Arabia: The Ceaseless Quest for Security* (Ithaca, NY: Cornell University Press, 1988), 156–59. Although it is not clear exactly why Faisal made the decision he did, and quite possibly both reasons factored into his decision, all officials operating at the time linked the aid package to Faisal's decision.

59. Frank Jungers as cited in Anthony Cave Brown, *Oil, God, and Gold: The Story of Aramco and the Saudi Kings* (New York: Houghton Mifflin, 1999), 294.

60. Mohamed Heikal, *The Road to Ramadan* (New York: Ballantine Books, 1975), 273.

61. Brown, *Oil, God, and Gold*, 295.

62. "Memorandum for Brigadier General Richard Lawson, USAF, Military Assistant to the President, 30 November 1973," Folder: "Energy Crisis, November 1973–1974," Box 321, Subject Files, National Security Council (NSC) Files, Nixon Presidential Materials Project, National Archives II, College Park, Maryland.

63. Ameen, author's interview, January 25, 2005.

64. Brown, *Oil, God, and Gold*, 295.

65. Akins to Kissinger, January 21, 1974, Folder: "Middle East—Saudi Arabia, 2 of 3," Box 139, Country Files, Papers of Henry A. Kissinger, Nixon Presidential Materials Project, National Archives II, College Park, Maryland.

66. Brown, *Oil, God, and Gold*, 296. Everyone, in fact, was not happy. What Jungers does not recall in his notes is that he leaked the agreement within Aramco's senior American leadership. When news of the leak got back to Yamani and the king, Yamani threatened to cancel the secret energy shipments. After he calmed down, the oil minister decided to continue with his decision to provide fuel to the 6th and 7th Fleets, stating that "Jungers' stupidity should not be allowed to provoke Saudi Arabia into taking action which can [cause] severe harm to the U.S." He did warn, however, that any future leaks "or additional gaffes would destroy him and would certainly severely affect our relationship with the Kingdom." As Ambassador Akins reminded Washington, Frank Jungers "is not noted for his polit-

ical astuteness." See cables from the embassy in Jidda to the secretary of state, January 21, 1974, and February 11, 1974, Folder: "Middle East—Saudi Arabia, 2 of 3," Box 139, Country Files, Papers of Henry A. Kissinger, Nixon Presidential Materials Project, National Archives II, College Park, Maryland.

67. Ameen, author's interview, January 25, 2005.
68. Brown, *Oil, God, and Gold*, 297.
69. In 1973 the shah made a similar calculation. Although he was a hawk on oil prices, his was the only country neighboring the Soviet Union that did not allow Russian planes to transit its airspace.
70. Kissinger, *Years of Upheaval*, 661.
71. Robert Hormats, author's phone interview, August 15, 2004.
72. "King Faisal: Man of the Year," *Time*, January 6, 1975.
73. "Excerpts from the Kissinger News Conference," *New York Times*, November 22, 1973, 18. The press conference took place on November 21, 1973.
74. See, for example, Glen Frankel, "U.S. Mulled Seizing Oil Fields in 1973," *Washington Post*, January 1, 2004; Alan Hamilton, "US Ready to Seize Arab Oilfields, Spy Chiefs Said," *The Times* (London), January 1, 2004; Owen Bowcott, "UK Feared Americans Would Invade Gulf During 1973 Oil Crisis," *The Guardian*, January 1, 2004.
75. Barger, "Suppose We Seized Arab Oil Fields," *Los Angeles Times*, April 13, 1975.
76. Kissinger, *Years of Renewal*, 885.
77. "King Faisal: Man of the Year."
78. "Ex-Envoy Says Kissinger Didn't Try to Stop Oil Price Rise," Associated Press, May 4, 1980. George Ball, William Simon, and James Akins all viewed the shah as the chief culprit in the oil crisis.
79. Kepel, *Jihad*, 70.

Chapter 6

1. Raymond Close, author's interview, Princeton, NJ, October 25, 2004.
2. Allan J. Mayer et al., "All About the New Oil Money," *Newsweek*, February 10, 1975.
3. Henry Kissinger, *Years of Renewal* (New York: Touchstone/Simon & Schuster: 1999), 677.
4. Bernard Gwertzman, "'Milestone' Pact is Signed by US and Saudi Arabia," *New York Times*, June 9, 1974.
5. Kenneth Labich, "Saudi Power," *Newsweek* (International Edition), March 6, 1978,
6. John Whitehead, author's interview, New York, March 12, 2004.
7. Recollections of Hisham Nazer, *The House of Saud*, directed by Jihan el-Tahri (Paris, France: Alegria Productions, 2004), DVD.
8. Labich, "Saudi Power," 13.
9. Ibid.
10. Juan De Onis, "A Multibillion Purchase of Treasury Issue Due," *New York Times*, September 7, 1974. Originally, there was speculation that Saudi Arabia would invest $5–10 billion. See Clyde H. Farnsworth, "U.S. Investments Expected," *New York Times*, July 25, 1974.
11. Don Oberdorfer, "Carter and Fahd Confer," *Washington Post*, May 25, 1977.

12. Anthony Solomon, assistant secretary of the treasury for monetary affairs, quoted in Martin Tolchin, "Foreigners' Political Roles in U.S. Grow by Investing," *New York Times*, December 30, 1985.
13. Patricia Patterson, author's interview, Dallas, TX, March 2005.
14. Close, author's interview, October 25, 2005.
15. Although the United States of course was not giving anything, but rather selling. De Onis, "US Role Grows in Arming Saudis."
16. Juan De Onis, "U.S. Aides in Saudi Arabia Study Sales of New Arms," *New York Times*, November 2, 1974.
17. Sales agreements are not the same as deliveries, which are used in the following table.
18. On naval programs see *The Military Balance* (London: International Institute for Strategic Studies, 1975–76), 91. On weapons for Egypt see *SIPRI Yearbook* (Stockholm: Stockholm International Peace Research Institute, 1973).
19. "U.S. Company Will Train Saudi Troops to Guard Oil," *New York Times*, February 1975.
20. Taken from Joe Stork, "Saudi Arabia on the Brink," *MERIP Reports* 91 (1980): 26.
21. Odeh Aburdene, then vice president, Treasury Department of the First National Bank of Chicago, calculated that the aggregate net inflow of Saudi funds into the United States averaged $5.1 billion annually over the years 1974–78. See his article "An Analysis of the Impact of Saudi Arabia on the US Balance of Payments 1974–1978," *Middle East Economic Survey*, September 24, 1979, i–iii.
22. Bandar bin Sultan bin Abdel Aziz al-Saud, interviewed by Lowell Bergman, *Frontline*, PBS, October 9, 2001 transcript available at http://www.pbs.org/wgbh/pages/frontline/shows/terrorism/intervews/bandar.html.
23. Labich, "Saudi Power."
24. International Security Assistance and Arms Export Control Act of 1976, PL 94-329, §404, 90 Stat 729 (1976).
25. David Binder, "Senate Votes to Cut off Covert Aid for Angolans; Ford Predicts a 'Tragedy,'" *New York Times*, December 20, 1975; Gerald R. Ford, *A Time to Heal* (New York: Harper and Row Publishers, 1979), 346.
26. International Security Assistance and Arms Export Control Act of 1976, §405.
27. Memo provided to author on condition of anonymity.
28. Turki al-Faisal, author's interview, April 2004.
29. According to a recently released CIA estimate, Saudi Arabia contributed less, but a still significant amount: $2 billion in official development assistance during the 1974–76 period. Central Intelligence Agency, "Trends in OPEC Economic Assistance, 1976," CIA-RDP79B00457A000600040001-3, CIA Records Search Tool (CREST), CD-ROM, 2. Obtained at the National Archives II, College Park, MD.
30. Jim Hoagland and J. P. Smith, "Practicing Checkbook Diplomacy," *Washington Post*, December 21, 1977.
31. Helen Lackner, *A House Built on Sand: A Political Economy of Saudi Arabia* (London: Ithaca Press, 1978), 130.
32. Hoagland and Smith, "Practicing Checkbook Diplomacy."
33. Henry Kissinger, *Years of Upheaval* (Boston, MA: Little, Brown, 1982), 663. Fred Halliday chronicles similar Saudi efforts in his "A Curious and Close Liaison: Saudi Arabia's Relations with the United States," in Tim Niblock, ed., *State, Society, and Economy in Saudi Arabia* (New York: St. Martin's Press, 1982), 132–33.

34. For more on the Ford Foundation's role in the kingdom, see Thomas Lippman, *Inside the Mirage* (Boulder, CO: Westview Press, 2004), chap. 8; Riyadh Office Files, Ford Foundation Archive, New York.

35. Count Alexandre de Marenches, *The Evil Empire: The Third World War Now* (London: Sidgwick and Jackson, 1982), 1, 138.

36. Ibid., 142.

37. Mohamed Heikal, *The Road to Ramadan* (New York: Ballantine Books, 1975), 113. Heikal found evidence of the Safari Club when allowed to go through the shah's files. See also Mahmood Mamdani, *Good Muslim, Bad Muslim: America, the Cold War, and the Roots of Terror* (New York: Pantheon Books, 2004), 84–87.

38. Francis Ghiles, "Saudi Aid to Morocco Put at $1 Bn This Year," *Financial Times*, April 10, 1981.

39. Turki al-Faisal, author's interview, April 29, 2004. Useful background on Marenches was provided by Arnaud de Borchgrave, author's interview, Washington, DC, August 2004. See also Helmy Sharawi, "Israeli Policy in Africa," in Khair el-Din Haseeb, *The Arabs and Africa*, (London: Croom Helm, 1985), 305.

40. Stephen V. Roberts, "Prop for U.S. Policy: Secret Saudi Funds," *New York Times*, June 21, 1987.

41. Marina Ottaway, *Soviet and American Influence in the Horn of Africa* (New York: Praeger, 1982), 108.

42. The shah of Iran reported this reaction back to Washington. See Zbigniew Brzezinski, *Power and Principle: Memoirs of the National Security Adviser 1977–1981* (New York: Farrar, Straus and Giroux, 1983), 179.

43. Brzezinski, *Power and Principle*, 181.

44. Ottaway, *Soviet and American Influence*, 161.

45. Heikal, *Road to Ramadan*, 126. Marina Ottaway gives a much lower figure of $30 million in *Soviet and American Influence*, 125. Assistant Secretary of State for Near East Alfred L. Atherton estimates that Saudi Arabia contributed $200 million to Somalia; Roberts, "Prop for U.S. Policy."

46. Robert M. Gates, *From the Shadows: The Ultimate Insider's Story of Five Presidents and How They Won the Cold War* (New York: Touchstone/Simon & Schuster, 1997), 77.

47. Close, author's interview, October 25, 2005; François Soudan, "La Menace qui vient du sud," *Jeune Afrique*, October 26, 1983, 36–37, cited in J. Millard Burr and Robert O. Collins, *Africa's Thirty Years War Libya, Chad and the Sudan 1963–1993* (Boulder, CO: Westview Press, 1999), 180.

48. Central Intelligence Agency, "Trends in OPEC Economic Assistance," 3.

49. Ibid., 13–14.

50. Ronald Bruce St. John, "The Libyan Debacle in Sub-Saharan Africa 1969–1987," in René Lemarchand, ed. *The Green and The Black: Qadhaffi's Policies in Africa* (Bloomington: Indiana University Press, 1988), 114; Ottaway, *Soviet and American Influence*, 113. The coup was led by Sadiq al-Mahdi.

51. Labich, "Saudi Power."

52. Roberts, "Prop for U.S. Policy."

53. Gilles Kepel, *Jihad: The Trail of Political Islam* (Cambridge, MA: Harvard University Press, 2002), 176–84.

54. Ibid., 400 n. 25.

55. Ibid., 181. In interviews with the author, journalists reporting from Sudan at the time remember Saudi Arabia bailing out Sudan every time it ran into significant economic difficulties.

56. Lackner, *A House Built on Sand*, 129.
57. Labich, "Saudi Power."
58. Turki al-Faisal bin Abdel Aziz al-Saud, "Special Address," speech, Georgetown University, Washington, DC, February 3, 2002.
59. "Message by Ford," *New York Times*, March 26, 1975.
60. David Holden and Richard Johns, *The House of Saud: The Rise and Rule of the Most Powerful Dynasty in the Arab World* (New York: Holt, Rinehart and Winston, 1982), 381.
61. Ibid., 386.
62. Robert Lacey, *The Kingdom: Arabia and the House of Saud* (New York: Harcourt Brace Jovanovich, 1981), 355.
63. Author's interview, U.S. intelligence officer.
64. Close, author's phone interview, August 2004.
65. Abir, *Saudi Arabia in the Oil Era*, chap. 6.

Chapter 7

1. Stephen L. Spiegel, *The Other Arab-Israeli Conflict: Making America's Middle East Policy, from Truman to Reagan* (Chicago: University of Chicago Press, 1985), 318.
2. Don Oberdorfer, "Carter and Fahd Confer," *Washington Post*, May 25, 1977.
3. Speigel, *The Other Arab-Israeli Conflict*, 333.
4. William B. Quandt, e-mail message to the author, January 18, 2005.
5. See Peter Osnos and David B. Ottaway, "Yamani Links F15s to Oil, Dollar Help," *Washington Post*, May 2, 1978, and "Information Official Says F15 Deal Not Linked to Oil," *Washington Post*, May 4, 1978.
6. Don Oberdorfer and Bill Peterson, "Saudi Leader Appeals for F15s and Defense," *Washington Post*, May 14, 1978.
7. Congress hated the notion of a package deal. In the end the administration was forced at the last minute to disaggregate the package before the final vote, but by then the White House had a majority committed not to vote against any of the components. William B. Quandt, e-mail message to author, January 18, 2005.
8. Don Oberdorfer and George C. Wilson, "US Offers to Sell 3 Mideast Nations $5 billion in Jets," *Washington Post*, February 15, 1978.
9. In his memoirs, Brzezinski states that he obtained a much stronger "secret Saudi pledge not to adopt any sanctions against Egypt. [The Saudis promised] to confine themselves to a formally negative reaction in keeping with their position against a separate treaty." Zbigniew Brzezinski, *Power and Principle: Memoirs of the National Security Adviser 1977–1981* (New York: Farrar Straus Giroux, 1983), 286. Quandt argues that Brzezinski overstated the committement; Quandt, *Camp David: Peacemaking and Politics* (Washington, DC: Brookings Institution Press, 1986), 312 n. 15.
10. Quandt, *Camp David*, 296.
11. Cyrus Vance, *Hard Choices: Critical Years in America's Foreign Policy* (New York: Simon & Schuster, 1983), 230.
12. Arnaud de Borchgrave, "The Saudis Play Their Hand," *Newsweek*, March 26, 1979.
13. Untitled report, Associated Press, May 14, 1979. The *Washington Post* reported that Egypt stood to lose fifteen thousand jobs because of this. Thomas Lippman, "Saudis to Close Arab Arms Firm to Punish Egypt," *Washington Post*, May 14, 1979.

14. Don Oberdorfer, "Frustration Marks Saudi Ties to US," *Washington Post.* May 6, 1979.
15. Nadav Safran, *Saudi Arabia: The Ceaseless Quest for Security* (Ithaca, NY: Cornell University Press, 1988), 280–81; Anthony Lewis, "Saudi Crown Prince Urges U.S. to Start Talks with P.L.O.," *New York Times*, June 22, 1979. Other scholars such as Abir viewed Fahd's extended vacation as a "prudent" decision to distance himself from what was becoming viewed as a "discredited" pro-American policy. Mordechai Abir, *Saudi Arabia in the Oil Era: Regime and Elites, Conflict and Collaboration* (London: Croom Helm, 1988), 146.
16. David W. Lesch, *1979: The Year That Shaped the Middle East* (Boulder: Westview Press, 2001), 2. Italics in the original.
17. During one in particular, the shah's forces fired into the crowd to disperse them, killing and wounding between two thousand and four thousand. Gary Sick. *All Fall Down: America's Tragic Encounter with Iran*, 2nd ed. (New York: Random House, 1986), 59.
18. Gary Sick recounts that "strange as it may seem, by the end of October 1978, after some ten months of civil disturbances in Iran, there had still not been a single high-level policy meeting in Washington on this subject. The reason for this lapse was obvious. The intense diplomatic negotiations between Egypt and Israel that began at Camp David in September 1978 and continued through the signing of a peace treaty in March 1979—precisely the time span of the climax of the Iranian revolution—occupied the full attention of US policy makers and officials concerned with the Middle East." To emphasize the point, he repeats it a few pages later: "With the Camp David negotiations, Salt II and normalization of relations with China all coming to a climax at approximately the same moment, the national security policy apparatus of the United states government was stretched to the limit . . . this coincidence in timing helps account for the curious absence of sustained attention that Iran received at the highest levels from August through October, when the crisis was brewing," Sick, *All Fall Down*, 70, 77.
19. Bernard Gwertzman, "U.S. Jets Will Visit Saudi Arabia as Show of Support in Tense Area," *New York Times*, January 11, 1979.
20. Bob Woodward, *The Commanders* (New York: Simon & Schuster, 1991), 240.
21. Vance, *Hard Choices*, 347.
22. de Borchgrave, "The Saudis Play Their Hand."
23. Abir, *Saudi Arabia in the Oil Era*, 139–48.
24. Peter A. Iseman, "Iran's War of Words Against Saudi Arabia," *The Nation*, April 19, 1980. See also James Buchan, "Secular and Religious Opposition in Saudi Arabia," in Tim Niblock, ed., *State, Society, and Economy in Saudi Arabia* (New York: St. Martins Press, 1982), 117–20.
25. Buchan, "Saudi Arabia's Shi'ite Minority Troubles Riyadh," *Financial Times*, March 2, 1980; Lesch, *1979: The Year That Shaped the Middle East*, 60.
26. For a translation of some of Utaybi's preachings, see Buchan, "Secular and Religious Opposition," 122.
27. One could also add to the list the attempt to seize the Saudi television transmitter in 1965, although it was not as organized as 1979.
28. Madawi al-Rasheed, *A History of Saudi Arabia* (New York: Cambridge University Press, 2002), 144.
29. Recollections of Turki al-Faisal, *The House of Saud*, directed by Jihan el-Tahri (Paris, France: Alegria Productions, 2004), DVD.

30. Turki al-Faisal, author's interview, London, England, April 29, 2004.
31. Robert M. Gates, *From the Shadows: The Ultimate Insider's Story of Five Presidents and How They Won the Cold War* (New York: Touchstone/Simon & Schuster, 1997), 144.
32. Prince Bandar was sent by the royal family to probe the interests of possible contributors to the fight in Afghanistan. See Kurt Lohbeck, *Holy War, Unholy Victory: Eyewitness to the CIA's Secret War in Afghanistan*. Gates refers to a Saudi official and not Bandar specifically; *From the Shadows*, 144.
33. "Finding Pursuant to Section 662 of the Foreign Assistance Act of 1961, as Amended, Concerning Operations in Foreign Countries Other than Those Intended Solely for the Purpose of Intelligence Collection," July 3, 1979, Folder: "Central Intelligence Agency Charter 2/9/80–2/29/80," Box 60, Collection: White House Office of Counsel to the President, Jimmy Carter Library, Atlanta, GA.
34. Lohbeck, *Holy War, Unholy Victory*, 19.
35. Brzezinski, *Power and Principle*, 449.
36. Stuart Auerbach, "Saudis Termed Responsive to US Needs," *Washington Post*, February 5, 1980. See also Brzezinski, *Power and Principle*, 449.
37. Gates, *From the Shadows*, 148.
38. Jimmy Carter, "The State of the Union Address Delivered Before a Joint Session of the Congress," January 23, 1980, Public Papers of the President. American Presidency Project, available at http://www.presidency.ucsb.edu/ws/index.php?pid =33079&st=&st1=.
39. Brzezinski, *Power and Principle*, 445.
40. Caspar Weinberger, author's phone interview, June 24, 2004.

Chapter 8

1. Jeanne J. Kirkpatrick, *The Reagan Doctrine and U.S. Foreign Policy* (Washington, DC: Heritage Fund, 1985), 6.
2. Robert McFarlane, author's interview, Washington, DC, May 10, 2004.
3. Ibid.
4. Ibid.
5. Ronald W. Reagan, *An American Life: The Autobiography* (New York: Simon and Schuster, 1990), 410.
6. Ibid., 41. Later in his memoirs, Reagan writes that he viewed Carter's failure to support the shah as one of Carter's greatest mistakes. Some at the time believed that this commitment to Saudi Arabia went beyond America's traditional backing for the territorial integrity of Saudi Arabia to the regime itself, and dubbed it the "Reagan corollary to the Carter doctrine." Such a commitment, however, was qualified by the president's spokesman as reflecting Reagan's "very strong" view rather than a new doctrine or commitment. The commitment to the regime did not seem to appear in formal communications between the two states and thus does not appear to represent a change in official policy.
7. In a later diary entry he writes that Arab-Israeli peace "should come through bilateral agreements just as it did with Egypt. That's why we want to start with Saudi Arabia." See Reagan, *An American Life*, 412, 415.
8. Caspar Weinberger, author's phone interview, June 24, 2004. Bahrain, Jordan and Egypt could be relied on at different times for different things, but for Weinberger, Saudi Arabia was the most steadfast partner the United States had in the region.

9. "SecDef Trip to the ME [Middle East] Feb. 4–13, 1982," Box 91987, NSC Near East and South Asia Affairs Directorate Records, Ronald Reagan Presidential Library (henceforth RRPL), Simi Valley, CA.

10. Adel al-Jubeir, author's interview, Washington, DC, June 10, 2004. This tracks with research by the Congressional Research Service and the Central Intelligence Agency. CRS estimated that by 1985 projected demand for Saudi oil would be 16.6 million barrels per day. The CIA estimated between 19 and 23 million. See "Report to the Congress: Critical Factors Affecting Saudi Arabia's Oil Decisions," 1978, Folder 27, Box 8, Mulligan Papers.

11. Author's interview, intelligence officer, 2004; author's interview, Saudi official, Washington, DC, June 2004.

12. An October U.S. Department of State cable reported that "the Saudis interpret Moscow's takeover in Afghanistan last year as part of a Soviet-directed campaign to encircle the Persian Gulf and the Arabian Peninsula with radical regimes in preparation for the subversion of the conservative oil-rich monarchies," See Marin J. Strmecki, "Power Assessment: Measuring Soviet Power in Afghanistan," Ph.D. diss., Georgetown University, 1994, 2:559. The cables went out to embassies abroad and were based on consultations with Saudi diplomats.

13. Frank Anderson, e-mail message to author, July 2004.

14. Government of Saudi Arabia, "Palestine-Israel Issue," available at http://www.kingfahdbinabdulaziz.com/main/l500.htm, accessed October, 2005.

15. Abdullah bin Abdel Aziz al-Saud, "Americans: 'The Greatest Danger'" (interview), *Time*, November 9, 1981. For an interesting discussion of its contemporary relevance see Robert Satloff, "Assessing Crown Prince Abdullah's 'Normalization' Plan," *Policy Watch* #604, Washington Institute for Near East Policy, Washington, DC, February 2002.

16. Letter to the Speaker of the House of Representatives and the president of the Senate on the sale of AWACS aircraft to Saudi Arabia, June 18, 1986, Ronald Reagan Presidential Library website, available at http://www.reagan.utexas.edu/archives/speeches/1986/61886e.htm.

17. Fahd was actually the eleventh son, but four others died before adulthood.

18. Elsa Walsh, "The Prince: How the Saudi Ambassador Became Washington's Indispensable Operator," *The New Yorker*, March 24, 2003.

19. Ibid.

20. Craig Unger, *House of Bush, House of Saud: The Secret Relationship Between the World's Two Most Powerful Dynasties* (New York: Scribner, 2004), 273; For a rebuttal see, Craig Unger and Rachel Bronson, "How Does the Saudi Relationship with the Bush Family Affect U.S. Foreign Policy?" available at http://www.slate.com/id/2103239.

21. "Address Before a Joint Session of Congress on the State of the Union," February 4, 1986, available at http://www.reagan.utexas.edu/archives/speeches/1986/20486a.htm, accessed May 31, 2005.

22. Edward J. Epstein, "The Well-Greased 'Special Relationship,'" *Manhattan Inc.*, October 1987, cited in Jonathan Marshall, "Saudi Arabia and the Reagan Doctrine," *Middle East Report* 155 (1988): 14.

23. Reagan, *An American Life*, 416.

24. Don Oberdorfer, "Arabs to Get U.S. Missiles for F15's," *New York Times*, March 7, 1981.

25. Richard Halloran, "Weinberger Asserts U.S. will Help Saudis to Buttress Forces," *New York Times*, February 4, 1981.

26. Israel was promised $600 million over two years in military sales loans plus a generous attitude toward Israeli sale of planes that contained a U.S.-designed engine.

27. This was the way the law purported to work at the time. In the mid-1980s the Supreme Court ruled such legislation unconstitutional. To block a sale Congress now has to be able to muster two-thirds of each house to overrule a presidential veto of a resolution objecting to the sale.

28. For a good discussion on the history and the specifics of the AWACS deal discussed below, see Richard Grimmett, *Executive-Legislative Consultation on U.S. Arms Sales* (Washington, DC: U.S. Government Printing Office, 1982).

29. Walter Isaacson, "Once Again, AWACS on the Line," *Time*, October 19, 1981; author's phone interview, senior American official involved in the AWACS sale, June 2005.

30. "Transcript of President's News Conference on Foreign and Domestic Politics," *New York Times*, October 2, 1981.

31. This became the battle cry of those for the arms sale. "Statement by Former President Richard Nixon, for Release Sunday 4 October 1981," AWACS Legislative Strategy (3) OA 10520, Box 1, Series 1: Subject File 1981–83, David Gergen Files, RRPL.

32. Stephen V. Roberts, "Senate 52–48, Supports Reagan on AWACS Jet Sale to Saudis; Heavy Lobbying Tips Key Votes," *New York Times*, October 29, 1981. For other carrots and sticks see Melinda Beck, "AWACS: The Final Days," *Newsweek*, November 2, 1981.

33. Alexander M. Haig, Jr, "Testimony Before the Senate Foreign Relations Committee," 97th Cong., 1st Sess., September 17, 1981; Richard V. Allen, "Why the AWACS Sale is Good for US," *Washington Post*, September 20, 1981, Folder: "AWACS Legislative Strategy (2)," Box OA 10520. David Gergen Files. RRPL.

34. Ronald W. Reagan, *Reagan: A Life in Letters*, ed. Kiron Skinner et al. (New York: Free Press, 2003), 686.

35. Anthony H. Cordesman, *The Gulf and the Search for Strategic Stability: Saudi Arabia, the Military Balance in the Gulf, and Trends in the Arab-Israeli Military Balance* (Boulder, CO: Westview Press, 1984), 256. In general, Cordesman focuses his discussion on the weakening of U.S.-Saudi ties around 1980. Although his discussion is compelling, he doesn't address the covert areas that helped counterbalance such stresses at the highest political level. His analysis also focuses more on the last year of the Carter administration rather than the Reagan administration.

36. Richard W. Murphy, author's interview, New York, March 31, 2004.

37. Oberdorfer, "Arabs to Get U.S. Missiles for F15's."

38. Caspar Weinberger, author's phone interview, June 24, 2004.

39. Ibid. Frances "Bing" West, Reagan's assistant secretary of defense for international security policy, confirmed this view in a discussion with the author, July 2004.

40. Reginald Dale, "US Envoy Visits Iraq," *Financial Times*, December 20, 1983.

41. George P. Shultz, *Turmoil and Triumph: My Years as Secretary of State* (New York: Charles Scribner's Sons, 1993), 235.

42. Majid Khadduri, *The Gulf War: The Origins and Implications of the Iran-Iraq Conflict* (New York: Oxford University Press, 1988), 124.

43. For example, in 1984, Egypt bought training aircraft from Brazil. Of the eighty aircraft assembled, forty stayed in Egypt; the other forty were exported to Iraq. Saudi Arabia paid for this, through the Gulf Cooperation Council.

44. The Soviet bloc lent Iraq about $8 billion, mostly for arms. Phebe Marr, *The Modern History of Iraq*, 2nd ed. (Boulder, CO: Westview Press, 2004). Western governments and commercial lenders from Germany, Japan, France, and the United States extended about $27 billion in loans and aid.

45. See *The Military Balance* (London: International Institute for Strategic Studies, 1986–87), 92; *The Economist*, August 20, 1988, May 20, 1980; Helen Metz, ed., *Iraq: A Country Study* (Washington, DC: Federal Research Division, Library of Congress, 1988), 126; Anthony H. Cordesman and Ahmed S. Hashim, *Iraq: Sanctions and Beyond* (Boulder, CO: Westview Press, 1997), 133. Actual figures are very difficult to pin down. Neither Iraq nor Iran was transparent in its wartime financing. Estimates are also complicated by the fact that the debt was accumulated in different ways, including the provision of cash, Saudi Arabia and Kuwait selling oil on Iraq's behalf, loans extended by lending institutions, etc. Iraq's short-term loans held a very high interest rate, and, given the low price of oil and its recent emergence from war, it was unable to repay them. By one Iraqi account, Saudi Arabia and Kuwait were supporting Iraq at a rate of $100 million per day. See Nadia el-Sayed el-Shazly, *The Gulf Tanker War* (New York: St. Martin's Press, 1998), 196. Saudi Arabia and Kuwait also sold oil on Iraq's behalf; ibid., 324.
46. Richard W. Murphy, author's interview, March 31, 2004.
47. Stephen C. Pelletiere. *The Iran-Iraq War: Chaos in a Vacuum* (New York: Praeger, 1992), 84; Nadav Safran, *Saudi Arabia: The Ceaseless Quest for Security* (Ithaca, NY: Cornell University Press, 1988), 417.
48. Michael H. Armacost, "U.S. Response to Saudi Request for Military Assistance—Transcript," *US Department of State Bulletin*, July 1984.
49. Bernard Gwertzman, "Senators Assail Arms Sale to Saudis," *New York Times*, June 6, 1984.
50. At least one Iranian plane was destroyed. David Long, *The United States and Saudi Arabia: Ambivalent Allies* (Boulder, CO: Westview Press, 1985), 67; Dilip Hiro, *The Longest War: The Iran Iraq Military Conflict* (New York: Routledge, 1991), 130. The request included 40 F-15 interceptors, 3,000 Sidewinder air-to-air missiles, 1,000 Stinger missiles, Maverick air-to ground antitank missiles, and bomb racks for F-15s that had been denied Saudi Arabia in 1981. Terry Atlas, "White House Postpones Action on Saudi Weapons Request," *Chicago Tribune*, January 30, 1985.
51. Bernard Gwertzman, "Saudis Say Reagan Cleared Purchase of British Planes," *New York Times*, September 16, 1985.
52. Sara Fritz, "U.S. May Seek $1-Billion Arms Sale to Saudis," *Los Angeles Times*, January 8, 1986.
53. Richard W. Murphy, "Sell the Saudis Defense Equipment," *New York Times*, May 20, 1986.
54. Sara Fritz, "President Trims Saudi Arms Deal: Stinger Missiles Dropped in Effort to Preserve Sale," *Los Angeles Times*, May 21, 1986.
55. This point came up repeatedly during different briefings to different constituencies. See, for example, "Talking Points for Meeting with Jewish Leaders on Saudi Arms Sale, May 19, 1986," Folder: May 20, 1986 (419720), Box CFOA 872, Office of the President: Presidential Briefing Papers, RRPL.

Chapter 9

1. "Saudis Secretly Funding Contras, U.S. Sources Say—'Kickback' from AWACS Sale Funneled to Nicaraguan Rebels, Other Anti-Leftists," *San Francisco Examiner*, July 27, 1986.

2. Bob Woodward, *Veil: The Secret Wars of the CIA, 1981–1987* (New York: Simon & Schuster, 1987), 104.
3. Stephen Coll, *Ghost Wars: The Secret History of the CIA, Afghanistan and Bin Laden, from the Soviet Invasion to September 10, 2001* (New York: Penguin, 2004), 262, 215.
4. Olivier Roy, *Afghanistan: From Holy War to Civil War* (Princeton: Darwin Press, 1995), 79–93. See also Barnett R. Rubin, *The Fragmentation of Afghanistan: State Formation and Collapse in the International System*, 2nd ed. (New Haven, CT: Yale University Press, 2002), 184–87.
5. Gwenn Okruhlik, "Networks of Dissent: Islamism and Reform in Saudi Arabia," *Current History*, January 2002, 23.
6. Author's interview, Riyadh, February 2005.
7. Ibid.
8. Charles G. Cogan, "The CIA and Afghanistan Since 1979," *World Policy Journal*, summer 1993, 79.
9. Census Bureau, "USAID: US Loans and Grants Assistance from International Organizations (Annual) & Unpublished Data," *Statistical Abstract of the United States* (Washington, DC: GPO, various years), vols. for 1980–1994.
10. George Crile, *Charlie Wilson's War: The Extraordinary Story of the Largest Covert Operation in History* (New York: Atlantic Monthly Press, 2003), chapter 19.
11. Mohammad Yousaf and Mark Adkin, *Afghanistan: The Bear Trap: The Defeat of a Superpower* (Havertown, PA: Casemate, 2001), 20.
12. Crile, *Charlie Wilson's War*, 339.
13. In an interview with NBC news, Sadat said that the United States had been "very generous" in paying for these weapons. See Dusko Doder, "Soviets Play up Sadat Disclosure to Assail U.S. for Afghan Strife," *Washington Post*, 25 September 1981. The Saudi contribution was also recognized in Leslie H. Gelb, "U.S. Said to Increase Arms Aid for Afghan Rebels," *New York Times*, May 4, 1983. Eastern European states also contributed, as did China. By 1985 China was putting more weapons into Afghanistan than Egypt and was deemed a more reliable and efficient producer of Soviet weaponry.
14. Intsum [Intelligence Summary] 914—October 11, 1979, cable #266505, item no. 694 in National Security Archive, Making of U.S. Policy, cited in Rubin, *Fragmentation of Afghanistan*, 193 n. 26.
15. Roy, *Afghanistan*, 83. Roy ascribes to Turki al-Faisal such motives.
16. Robert M. Gates, *From the Shadows: The Ultimate Insider's Story of Five Presidents and How They Won the Cold War* (New York: Touchstone/Simon & Schuster, 1997), 320.
17. Pakistani views were by no means the last word on these decisions. Jack Devine, author's interview, New York, March 9, 2004.
18. Yousaf and Adkin, *Afghanistan*, 106–7.
19. Christina Lamb, "Holy War Within Afghanistan's Battlefields," *Financial Times*, June 7, 1989.
20. James Rupert, "Arab Fundamentalists Active in Afghan War; Use of Funds and Volunteers from Mideast Watched for Disruptive Influence," *Washington Post*, March 2, 1989.
21. See Christina Lamb, "Holy War Within Afghanistan's Battlefields"; Abdel Khel, "Arab Extremists Exploit Afghan Jihad," *Christian Science Monitor*, February 23, 1989.

22. "Large Saudi Cash Donation to Resistance Leader," *BBC Summary of World Broadcasts*, May 26, 1984.

23. James Rupert, "Dreams of Martyrdom Draw Islamic Arabs to Join Afghan Rebels," *Washington Post*, July 21, 1986.

24. Ahmed Rashid, *Taliban* (New Haven: Yale University Press, 2000), 131; Rubin, *Fragmentation of Afghanistan*, 197. Some, including members of bin Laden's family, suspect Osama of perpetrating the murder.

25. Katherine Gannon, author's interview, New York, February 2004.

26. Gust Avrakotos, quoted in Crile, *Charlie Wilson's War*, 344.

27. The document is still classified. It was first reported on by Stephen Coll in "Anatomy of a Victory: CIA's Covert Afghan War," *Washington Post*, July 19, 1992. It was later confirmed by Charles G. Cogan, who had served as the chief of the Near East and South Asia Division of the CIA's directorate from 1979 to 1984. Clearly the changes in weaponry and tactics that occurred after its issuance further suggest the content of the directive.

28. Cogan, "The CIA and Afghanistan," 76.

29. Milt Bearden took over as CIA station chief in Pakistan in 1986, and Jack Devine became head of the Afghan Task Force in 1985.

30. Rashid, *Taliban*, 44–45.

31. Gates, *From the Shadows*, 349.

32. F. Gregory Gause, III, "Saudi Arabia and the War on Terrorism," in Adam Garfinkle, ed., *A Practical Guide to Winning the War on Terrorism* (Stanford: Hoover Institution, 2004), 92.

33. The Associated Press reported meetings with Secretary of State Al Haig, among others. See Lawrence L. Knutson, "Haig Held Meeting with Angolan Rebel Leader," Associated Press, December 9, 1981; Knutson, "Angolan Rebel Says Status 'Enhanced' by Meeting with Haig," Associated Press, December 10, 1981.

34. Sidney Blumenthal, "The Reagan Doctrine's Strange History; When a Small, Passionate Group Keeps Trying, It Can Change Foreign Policy," *Washington Post*, June 29, 1986. The American Conservative Union was proud to note that the repeal of the Clark amendment was something it actively supported.

35. "Angola Rebel Makes Case for U.S. Funds, Shultz, Savimbi Hold Talks," *Chicago Tribune*, January 30, 1986. Savimbi had supporters in many important corners. For example, the head of the Cuban American National Foundation, a group stridently anti-Castro and thus stridently pro-UNITA, had previously worked for Jeanne Kirkpatrick at the United Nations.

36. See, for instance, "US Relations with South Africa and Contacts with Savimbi and Mudge," *BBC Summary of World Broadcasts*, April 4, 1981; "US Contacts with Savimbi," *BBC Summary of World Broadcasts*, April 9, 1981. The meeting was authorized for the purpose of information gathering. CIA operative, author's interview, October 13, 2004.

37. Steven Mufson, "Some Familiar Echoes in Financing of Angola Rebels," *Los Angeles Times*, July 26, 1987.

38. U.S. House of Representatives, Committee on Foreign Affairs, Subcommittee on Africa, "Hearing: Possible Violation or Circumvention of the Clark Amendment," 100th Cong., 1st Sess., July 1, 1987 (Washington, DC: Government Printing Office, 1987), 115.

39. Ibid., 23.

40. Gates, *From the Shadows*, 312.

41. "Hearing: Possible Violation or Circumvention of the Clark Amendment," 93.
42. Neil A. Lewis, "Saudis Linked to Donations to Angola Rebels," *New York Times*, July 2, 1987.
43. Raymond W. Copson and Robert B. Shepard, *Angola: Issues for the United States* (Washington, DC: Congressional Research Service, 1986).
44. Human Rights Watch, *Angola Unravels: The Rise and Fall of the Lusaka Peace Process* (New York: Human Rights Watch, 1999), chap. 3, available at http://www.hrw.org/reports/1999/angola.
45. Woodward, *Veil*, 385. Ethiopian government officials issued repeated warnings about Saudi and other Arab material support flowing into northern Ethiopia. In 1985, for example, the Ethiopian foreign minister charged that banditry in northern Ethiopia had been planned and organized by Sudan and Saudi Arabia and that Syria, Iraq, and Morocco had also supported the "terrorist bandits."
46. "Ethiopia: Mengistu Report to WPE Central Committee," *BBC Summary of World Broadcasts*, March 30, 1987; "West Africa: In Brief; Ethiopian Statement on Arab Support for 'Banditry,' " *BBC Summary of World Broadcasts*, January 31, 1985.
47. Cable, FM: AMEMBASSY, Riyadh, To: SECSTATE WASHDC, "Saudi Arabia After the Thaw, Part I," April 1990, Central Foreign Policy Records, Department of State, declassified by author under Executive Order 12958.
48. National Security Council, "United States Policy Towards the Horn of Africa," National Security Decision Directive 57, September 17, 1982, available at http://www.fas.org/irp/offdocs/nsdd/23-1913t.pdf.
49. Saudi assistance to the government of Jaafar al-Nimeiry slowed shortly after Sudan endorsed the Camp David agreement between Egypt and Israel, one of the only Muslim countries to do so. In 1981, the Sudanese president stressed that "we get every economic and military aid from Saudi Arabia. However, recently the military aid has begun, not to diminish, but to take a longer time, a much longer time to arrive" ("Sudanese 'Suicide Army' to Operate in Libya," *BBC Summary of World Broadcasts*, October 17, 1981). Shortly thereafter, however, Saudi assistance picked up again.
50. Alfred Taban, "Sudan Rekindles Old Friendship with Saudi Arabia," Reuters dispatch in the *Middle East Times*. The CIA estimated that in 1976 alone, Saudi Arabia disbursed $164.5 million; "Trends in OPEC Assistance, 1976," CREST, 14.
51. USAID, "Total Economic & Military Assistance Loans and Grants in $US millions, current." US Overseas Loans & Grants [Greenbook], available at http://qesdb.cdie.org/gbk/index.html.
52. Ibid. A year after the coup, the head of Sudan's Transitional Military Council was still praising Saudi Arabia's support of Sudan and in particular the role played by King Fahd. In an anniversary speech, for example, he thanked the government of Saudi Arabia for its continued backing to Sudan. See, for instance, "Speeches by Siewar al-Dhahab and Daf'allah on Sudan's Revolution Anniversary," *BBC Summary of World Broadcasts*, April 8, 1986.
53. "Decisions Taken at Interagency Meeting on Yemen Public Diplomacy," January 29, 1986, Folder: "Iran-Iraq [South Yemen (PDRY)] 1986 [2]," Near East and South Asia Affairs Directorate, NSC: Records 1983–89, RRPL.
54. "Fact Sheet on South Yemen and the Soviet Bloc: The All-Embracing Relationship," Folder: "Iran-Iraq [South Yemen (PDRY)] 1986 (1)," Box 91950, NSC Near East and South Asia Affairs Directorate Records, RRPL.

55. "SecDef Trip to the ME [Middle East] Feb. 4–13," 1982, Box 91987, NSC Near East and South Asia Affairs Directorate Records, RRPL. Syria was also included in this list.

56. John Kifner, "Massacre with Tea: Southern Yemen at War," *New York Times*, February 9, 1986.

57. "Shultz to Amb. in Riyadh, Jan. 1986," Folder: "Iran-Iraq [South Yemen (PDRY)] 1986 (2)," Box 91950, NSC Near East and South Asia Affairs Directorate Records, RRPL.

58. Kirkpatrick, *Reagan Doctrine and U.S. Foreign Policy*, 10.

59. Gates, *From the Shadows*, 298.

60. The decision came on January 6, 1984. See Gates, *From the Shadows*, 311.

61. Gates, *From the Shadows*; McFarlane, author's interview. One aide recalls that the president authorized McFarlane to get the contras funded "in any way you can"; Lawrence E. Walsh, *Final Report of the Independent Counsel for Iran/Contra Matters*, volume 1; part IV, chap. 1. See Seymour M. Hersch, "Target Qaddafi," *New York Times Magazine*, February 22, 1987, 22. Woodward makes the claim that Saudi Arabia was mentioned specifically in Casey's memo; *Veil*, 350.

62. Walsh, *Final Report*, part IV, chap. 1.

63. Walsh, *Final Report*, part V, chap. 8; Gates, *From the Shadows*, 311.

64. Gates, *From the Shadows*, 312.

65. Ibid., 308.

66. No money was to go to the CIA, Defense Department, "or any other agency or entity of the United States involved in intelligence activities . . . for the purpose or which would have the effect of supporting, directly or indirectly, military or paramilitary operations in Nicaragua by any nation, group, organization, movement or individual," Department of Defense Appropriations Act for Fiscal Year 1985—Section 8066 of Title VIII, General Provisions, as contained in Public Law 98-473. See *International Legal Materials* 26, 2 (1987): 444.

67. Walsh, *Final Report*, part IX, chap. 27.

68. Between June 1984 and 1986, Oliver North was able to funnel about $40 million to the contras through a hazy network of private funds, international assistance, and illegal weapons sales to Iran, discussed below. James M. Scott. *Deciding to Intervene: The Reagan Doctrine & American Foreign Policy* (Durham, NC: Duke University Press, 1996), 154.

69. Author's interview, May 2005.

70. "The 'Inside Story' of Why Yamani Was Actually Dismissed," *Petroleum Intelligence Weekly*, November 24, 1986.

71. Anna C. Rubino, "Secrets of the Oil World: Wanda Jablonski and the Influence of Journalism," Ph.D. diss., Yale University, 2002, 370.

72. John M. Goshko and Don Oberdorfer, "Chinese Sell Saudis Missiles Capable of Covering the Middle East," *Washington Post*, March 18, 1988.

73. David Ottaway, "Saudis Hid Acquisition of Missiles," *Washington Post*, March 29, 1988.

74. Al-Jubeir, author's interview.

75. Author's interview, State Department official working on the issue at the time, Washington, DC.

76. James B. Mann, *About Face: A History of America's Curious Relationship with China, from Nixon to Clinton* (New York: Alfred A. Knopf, 1999), 169–70, cited in Thomas W. Lippman, "Saudi Arabia: The Calculations of Uncertainty," in Kurt

Campbell, ed., *The Nuclear Tipping Point* (Washington, DC: Brookings Institution Press, 2004), 111–14.

77. Martin Sieff, "Sand in Our Eyes," *The National Interest*, summer 2004.

Chapter 10

1. Bob Woodward, *The Commanders* (New York: Simon & Schuster, 1991), 243.
2. Until the late 1980s, the main concern of American military planners at Central Command (CENTCOM) was to prevent the Soviet Union from reaching the Persian Gulf through Iran's Zagros Mountains. General Norman Schwarzkopf, CENTCOM's commander in chief, believed the existing plans were "bankrupt," a relic of the Cold War. The real threat to the region, he argued, now came from interstate rivalry rather than outside forces. In response, CENTCOM planners began devising an exercise entitled Internal Look, which simulated an Iraqi invasion of Kuwait. Eerily, the exercise was supposed to run between July 9 and August 4, 1990. It was canceled when imagined scenarios were overtaken by actual events.
3. James A. Baker with Thomas M. DeFrank, *The Politics of Diplomacy: Revolution, War and Peace, 1989–1992* (New York: G. P. Putnam's Sons, 1995), 115.
4. Bob Woodward, *Veil: The Secret Wars of the CIA, 1981–1987* (New York: Simon & Schuster, 1987), 226.
5. Baker, *Politics of Diplomacy*, 263.
6. Khaled bin Sultan with Patrick Seale, *Desert Warrior: A Personal View of the Gulf War by the Joint Forces Commander* (New York: HarperCollins, 1995), 175. Iraq's president Saddam Hussein claimed that Kuwait's tactics had cost his country $14 billion.
7. George H. W. Bush, *All the Best, George Bush* (New York: Scribner, 1999), 476.
8. Woodward, *Veil*, 251. See also George H. W. Bush and Brent Scowcroft, *A World Transformed* (New York: Alfred A. Knopf, 1998), 321. Secretary of Defense Cheney warned that "Saudi Arabia and others will cut and run if we are weak"; Bush and Scowcroft, *World Transformed*, 317.
9. See Woodward, *Veil*, 240; ASDT oral history of Chas. Freeman; Bush and Scowcroft, *World Transformed*, 325; Khaled bin Sultan, *Desert Warrior*, 26.
10. Richard N. Haass, author's interview, New York, April 25, 2005.
11. Bush and Scowcroft, *World Transformed*, 323.
12. See George Bush's letter to Jordan's King Hussein in which he talks about the "irrefutable evidence, which I thought we had presented to you, shows that the very day he [Saddam] announced he was moving his forces out of Kuwait, vast Iraqi armor was heading south toward the Saudi border," in Bush, *All the Best*, 484–85.
13. Kenneth M. Pollack, *The Threatening Storm: The Case for Invading Iraq* (New York: Random House, 2002), 37.
14. Khaled bin Sultan, *Desert Warrior*, 19.
15. "The Iraqi Invasion: Transcript of News Conference Remarks by Bush on Iraq Crisis," *New York Times*. August 6, 1990.
16. Bush and Scowcroft, *World Transformed*, 324.
17. Ibid., 267.
18. Robert Gates, author's interview, January 25, 2005, College Station, TX.
19. ASDT oral history of Chas. Freeman.

20. Ibid.
21. Gates, author's interview, January 25, 2005.
22. Gwenn Okruhlik, "Networks of Dissent: Islamism and Reform in Saudi Arabia," *Current History*, January 2002, 26.
23. Douglas Jehl, "Holy War Lured Saudis as Rulers Looked Away," *New York Times*, December 21, 2001.
24. During the 1956 Suez crisis, the Soviet Union and the United States lined up on the same side, against Britain, France, and Israel. But it was hardly as allies. Each was trying to benefit more from the spoils of victory. Still, it was an odd alignment to find during the height of the Cold War.
25. Baker, *Politics of Diplomacy*, 206; Bush and Scowcroft, *World Transformed*, 366, 377.
26. Baker, *Politics of Diplomacy*, 294.
27. Ibid., 295.
28. Ibid., 372.
29. ASDT oral history of Chas. Freeman.
30. Baker, *Politics of Diplomacy*, 306.
31. Ibid., 373.
32. Ibid.
33. ASDT oral history of Chas. Freeman.
34. Baker, *Politics of Diplomacy*, 306.
35. Ibid.
36. Ibid., 289.
37. Khaled bin Sultan, *Desert Warrior*, 210; ASDT oral history of Chas. Freeman.
38. Not only had the most hard-line Islamic fighters in Afghanistan not backed Saudi Arabia, but in April 1991, at an Arab and Islamic conference in Sudan, leading Islamists reiterated their support for Iraq and proclaimed themselves an alternative to the Saudi-dominated Organization of the Islamic Conference. See Gilles Kepel, *Jihad: The Trail of Political Islam* (Cambridge, MA: Harvard University Press, 2002), 184.
39. Author's interview, Marrakesh, Morocco, December 3, 2004.
40. Pollack, *The Threatening Storm*, 187.
41. Chas. W. Freeman, author's interview, Washington, DC, December 15, 2004.
42. Andrew H. Malcolm, "Confrontation in the Gulf; Opponents to U.S. Move Have Poverty in Common," *New York Times*, September 8, 1990.
43. Howard Goldberg, "AP Poll Find Americans Split on Prodding Israeli Towards Peace," Associated Press, March 13, 1991.
44. For a summary of the debates and the equipment see Richard Grimmett, "Arms Sales to Saudi Arabia: 1990–1993" (Washington, DC: Congressional Research Service, December 17, 1993). The F-15 component was $4 billion. See also Steven Pearlstein, "Saudis Place Order for 72 F-15 Fighters," *Washington Post*, November 6, 1991.
45. Anthony H. Cordesman, *Saudi Arabia: Guarding the Desert Kingdom* (Boulder, CO: Westview Press, 1997), chap. 6.
46. Thomas Rhame, author's phone interview, January 19, 2005.
47. Freeman, author's interview, September 2004, Washington, DC.
48. The term was first used to describe James Baker's trip to raise money from allies for Desert Shield, "tin-cup in hand," Baker, *Politics of Diplomacy*, 287–91; Bush and Scowcroft, *World Transformed*, 360.

Chapter 11

1. Anthony Lake, "Confronting Backlash States," *Foreign Affairs*, 73, 2 (1994): 45–55.
2. Raymond E. Mabus, author's interview, New York, June 13, 2005.
3. Michael W. Doyle, "Liberalism and World Politics," *American Political Science Review* 80, 4 (1986): 1151–69; Bruce Russett, "The Democratic Peace: 'And Yet It Moves,'" *International Security* 19, 4 (1995): 164–76. Citing Doyle and Russett, Edward D. Mansfield and Jack Snyder wrote in a widely read piece that "one of the best-known findings of contemporary social science is that no democracies have ever fought a war against each other, given reasonably restrictive definitions of democracy and of war. This insight is now part of everyday public discourse and serves as a basis for American foreign policy making." Edward D. Mansfield and Jack Snyder, "Democratization and the Danger of War," *International Security* 20, 1 (1995): 5.
4. William J. Clinton, "Address Before a Joint Session of the Congress on the State of the Union," January 25, 1994, Public Papers of the President, American Presidency Project, available at http://www.presidency.ucsb.edu/ws/index.php?pid=50409&st=&st1=.
5. Martin Indyk, "Back to the Bazaar," *Foreign Affairs*, 81, 1 (2002): 75–88.
6. Martin Indyk, author's interview, Washington, DC, May 27, 2005.
7. *MacNeil/Lehrer NewsHour*, "Bin Laden's Fatwa," available at http://www.pbs.org/newshour/terrorism/international/fatwa_1996.html.
8. Anthony H. Cordesman and Nawaf Obaid, "Saudi Military Forces and Development: Challenges and Reforms," Center for Strategic and International Studies, working draft, May 30, 2004, 10–13.
9. Steven Pearlstein, "Saudis Place Order for 72 F-15 Fighters," *Washington Post*, November 6, 1991.
10. Alfred B. Prados, "Saudi Arabia: Current Issues and U.S. Relations" (Washington, DC: Congressional Research Service, April 3, 2003), April 3, 2003, 9, available at http://www.fas.org/asmp/resources/govern/crs-ib93113.pdf.
11. Thomas Rhame, author's phone interview, January 19, 2005.
12. Raymond E. Mabus, author's interview, New York, June 13, 2005.
13. Rhame, author's phone interview, January 19, 2005; Chas. W. Freeman, author's interview, Washington, DC, December 15, 2004.
14. Mabus, author's interview, June 13, 2005.
15. Eleanor A. Doumato, "Gender, Monarchy, and National Identity in Saudi Arabia," *British Journal of Middle Eastern Studies* 19, 1 (1992): 31.
16. Until that time women in Saudi Arabia did not drive, but there was no law specifically prohibiting it.
17. Youssef Ibrahim, "An Outcry from the Saudis' Liberal Minority," *New York Times*, November 8, 1990.
18. Mamoun Fandy, *Saudi Arabia and the Politics of Dissent* (New York: Palgrave, 1999), 49–50; Doumato, "Gender, Monarchy, and National Identity."
19. David Sharrock, "Women Take Back Seat as Driving Becomes Law: Plans for New Protest Are Shelved as Fatwa Is Adopted," *The Guardian*, November 15, 1990.
20. For good discussions on these individuals and their evolution, see Joshua Teitelbaum, *Holier than Thou: Saudi Arabia's Islamic Opposition* (Washington, DC: Washington Institute, 2000); R. Hrair Dekmejian, "The Rise of Political Islamism in Saudi Arabia," *Middle East Journal*, autumn 1994; Madawi al-Rasheed, "Saudi

Arabia's Islamic Opposition," *Current History*, January 1996; Toby Craig Jones, "The Clerics, the Sahwa and the Saudi State," *Strategic Insights* 4, 3 (2005); International Crisis Group, "Saudi Arabia Backgrounder: Who Are the Islamists?" *Middle East Report* 31, Amman/Riyadh/Brussels, September 21, 2004; Stéphane Lacroix, "Between Islamists and Liberals: Saudi Arabia's New 'Islamo-Liberal' Reformists," *Middle East Journal*, summer 2004; Gwenn Okruhlik, "Networks of Dissent: Islamism and Reform in Saudi Arabia," *Current History*, January 2002; Fandy, *Saudi Arabia and the Politics of Dissent.*

21. Mamoun Fandy, "The Hawali Tapes," *New York Times*, November 24, 1990.
22. Teitelbaum, *Holier than Thou*, 28–32.
23. Cited in Okruhlik, "Networks of Dissent," 25.
24. Dekmejian gives a good breakdown of the Islamist elite's demographics; "Rise of Political Islamism," 635–38. See also al-Rasheed, "Saudi Arabia's Islamic Opposition."
25. F. Gregory Gause III, *Oil Monarchies: Domestic and Security Challenges in the Arab Gulf* (New York: Council on Foreign Relations, 1994), chap. 2. See also Dekmejian, "Rise of Political Islamism," 634.
26. "Saudi Arabia: FBI Team Probe Riyadh Bombing," *Middle East Economic Digest*, November 24, 1995.
27. National Commission on Terrorist Attacks upon the United States, *9/11 Commission Report: Final Report of the National Commission on Terrorist Attacks upon the United States.* (Washington, DC: Government Printing Office, 2004), 60.
28. Elaine Sciolino, Jeff Gerth, and Douglas Jehl, "Saudi Kingdom Shows Cracks, U.S. Aides Fear," *New York Times,* June 30, 1996.
29. Richard Clarke, *Against All Enemies* (New York: Free Press, 2004), 112–13; E. Walsh, "Louis Freeh's Last Case," *The New Yorker*, May 14, 2001; *9/11 Commission Report*, 60. Earlier that month, a Hezbollah cell in Bahrain that also boasted Iranian ties tried to overthrow the government of Bahrain but was stopped by Bahraini officials. Then Saudi border guards intercepted a car on the Bahrain border carrying explosives. Under interrogation, the driver admitted his contacts with Iranian officials and ongoing training programs in Lebanon, led by a Saudi dissident. Again, the Saudis had not shared this information with American officials, preferring to quietly press Syria to shut down the camp in Lebanon, Syria ignored the message.
30. *9/11 Commission Report*, 60.
31. E. Walsh, "Louis Freeh's Last Case." On Saudi reluctance to provide evidence without a clear estimation of America's response, see also Clarke, *Against All Enemies*, 117–18, and Daniel Benjamin and Steven Simon, *The Age of Sacred Terror* (New York: Random House, 2002), 224–25.
32. Clarke, *Against All Enemies*, 114; Benjamin and Simon, *Age of Sacred Terror*, 224.
33. Rachel Bronson, "Beyond Containment in the Persian Gulf," *Orbis*, spring 2001, 196.
34. Martin Indyk, "The Clinton Administration's Approach to the Middle East," speech, Soref Symposium, Washington Institute for Near East Policy, Washington, DC, May 18, 1993, transcript available at http://www.washingtoninstitute.org/templateC07.php?CID=61.
35. Abu Dhabi Satellite Channel was relaunched in 2000. Lebanese Broadcasting Corporation was launched in 1985, but not as a satellite station.
36. "Saudi Against Hosting U.S. Raids on Iraq," *Reuters Newswire*, September 11, 1996, as cited in Prados, "Iraq: Post-War Challenges and U.S. Responses, 1991–1998,"

21; Kenneth M. Pollack, *The Threatening Storm: The Case for Invading Iraq* (New York: Random House, 2002), 82–83.

37. Steven Myers, "Standoff with Iraq: The Overview," *New York Times*, February 9, 1998, A1.

38. Prados, "Iraq: Post-War Challenges and U.S. Responses, 1991–1998," 23; Douglas Jehl, "On the Record, Arab Leaders Oppose U.S. Attacks on Iraq," *New York Times*, January 29, 1998.

39. Pollack, *Threatening Storm*, 188.

40. Robert M. Gates, author's interview, January 25, 2005, College Station, TX; Richard N. Haass, author's interview, New York, April 25, 2005.

41. Peter Tomsen, as quoted in the *9/11 Commission Report*, 110 n. 12.

42. Coll, *Ghost Wars*, 230.

43. Robert Oakley, author's interview, Washington, DC, February 1, 2005.

44. Rohan Gunaratna, *Inside Al Qaeda: Global Network of Terror* (New York: Columbia University Press, 2002), 55.

45. Jamal Ahmed al-Fadl, Testimony in *U.S. v. Usama bin Laden* (Hon. Leonard Sand, J., S.D.N.Y.), S(7) 98 Cr. 1023 (Feb. 6, 2001), 191.

46. Peter L. Bergen, *Holy War, Inc.: Inside the Secret World of Osama bin Laden* (New York: Free Press, 2001), 59.

47. al-Fadl testimony, 190.

48. *9/11 Commission Report*, 56; Gunaratna, *Inside Al Qaeda*, chap. 2. Journalist Peter Bergen likened the structure of al-Qaeda to a multinational holding company, headquartered in Afghanistan, under the chairmanship of bin Laden; *Holy War, Inc.*, 30.

49. Benjamin and Simon, *Age of Sacred Terror*, 257.

50. *9/11 Commission Report*, 63.

51. Benjamin and Simon, *Age of Sacred Terror*, 246–47.

52. Ibid., 243.

53. Ahmed Rashid, *Taliban* (New Haven: Yale University Press, 2000), 32.

54. When I asked one Saudi with close ties to intelligence whether working with the Taliban unnerved him, he answered almost wistfully, "They were like Wahhabis . . . they were like Wahhabis." Author's interview, Jeddah, February 2005.

55. Turki al-Faisal, interview by Chris Bury, *Nightline*, ABC News, December 10, 2001.

56. *9/11 Commission Report*, 67.

57. Marc Sageman, *Understanding Terror Networks* (Philadelphia: University of Pennsylvania Press, 2004), 71. The notorious terrorist Khaled Sheikh Mohammed similarly put the number of Saudis operating in Afghan training camps at 70 percent; *9/11 Commission Report*, 232. One reporter operating in Pakistan during the 1990s puts the number of Saudis much lower. In 1995 the Pakistani government required militant Arabs to register with the government. Most did not register, but the numbers provided a breakdown of the 5,902 that did. One rough estimate from 1995 puts the distribution of Arabs operating out of Pakistan at 19 percent Egyptian, 16 percent Saudi, 16 percent Yemeni, 13 percent Algerian, 13 percent Jordanian, 5 percent Iraqi, 5 percent Syrian, 3 percent Sudanese, 3 percent Libyan, 2 percent Tunisian, and 2 percent Moroccan. Because Pakistan served as a way station for Arabs heading to Afghanistan, this breakdown is a good indication of the Arab composition inside Afghanistan. See Rahimullah Yusufzai, *The News* (Pakistan), December 8, 1995, as cited in Bergen, *Holy War, Inc.*, 90.

58. *9/11 Commission Report*, 170–71. It also made clear that this concl︎
    exclude the likelihood that charities with significant Saudi gover︎
    ship diverted funds to al-Qaeda.
59. John Roth, Douglas Greenburg, and Serena Wille, *Staff Report to n.︎*
    sion: Monograph on Terrorist Financing, prepared for the National Comm︎
    on Terrorist Attacks upon the United States, 39, available at http://www.9-11︎
    commission.gov/staff_statements/911_terrfin_monograph.pdf; Clarke, *Against All*
    Enemies, 194–96.
60. World Islamic Front, "Jihad Against Jews and Crusaders," February 23, 1998, avail-
    able on Federation of American Scientists Web site, http://www.fas.org/irp/world/
    para/docs/980223-fatwa.htm.
61. "Clinton Statement on U.S. Embassy Bombings in Africa," August 7, 1998, U.S.
    Department of State International Information Programs, available at http://
    usinfo.state.gov/is/Archive_Index/Clinton_Statement_on_US_Embassy_Bombings_in
    _Africa.html.
62. Mary Anne Weaver, "The Real Bin Laden," *The New Yorker*, January 24, 2000.
63. Ibid.
64. Wyche Fowler, author's phone interview, January 14, 2005.
65. Turki al-Faisal interview, *Nightline*. See also an interview with Mullah Omar
    where he says, "We told him that as a guest, he shouldn't involve himself in any
    activities that create problems for us," in Tim McGirk, "Guest of Honor," *Time*,
    August 24, 1998; "Opposition Says Handover of Bin Ladin Impossible," *BBC*
    Summary of World Broadcasts, October 10, 1998.
66. See for example, "Afghan Taleban Arrest Plotters Planning to Kill Bin Ladin—Saudi
    Opposition," *BBC Summary of World Broadcasts*, October 21, 1998. During the
    Taliban's interrogation, it emerged that the assassination team was sent by Prince
    Salman, a son of Abdel Aziz and the long-serving governor of Riyadh province.
    There is also some evidence to suggest that Saudis sent out a hit team years ear-
    lier when bin Laden resided in Sudan.
67. Roth, Greenburg, and Wille, *Staff Report to the Commission*.
68. Edward L. Morse and Amy Myers Jaffe, "OPEC in Confrontation with Globaliza-
    tion," in Jan H. Kalicki and David L. Goldwyn, eds, *Energy and Security: Toward a*
    New Foreign Policy Strategy (Baltimore: Johns Hopkins University Press, 2005), 81.
69. Ellen Laipson, author's interview, Washington, DC, May 2, 2005.
70. In his diary, Reagan wrote that Arab-Israeli peace "should come through bilateral
    agreements just as it did with Egypt. That's why we want to start with Saudi Arabia,"
    See Ronald W. Reagan, *An American Life: The Autobiography* (New York: Simon
    and Schuster, 1990), 412, 415.
71. Dennis Ross, *The Missing Peace: The Inside Story of the Fight for Middle East Peace*
    (New York: Farrar, Straus and Giroux, 2004), 238.
72. Ibid., 568.
73. Robert Malley, author's interview, Washington, DC, May 2, 2005. Malley went on
    to state that the administration never got a straight answer whether or not Saudi
    Arabia offered to provide Arafat cover. High-level Saudis state that they made clear
    to Arafat they would support him. High-ranking Palestinians claim the Saudis were
    never forthcoming with their support.
74. Martin Indyk, author's interview. Washington, DC. May 27, 2005.
75. Author's telephone interview, May 2005.
76. Indyk, author's interview, May 27, 2005.

Chapter 12

1. Elsa Walsh, "The Prince: How the Saudi Ambassador Became Washington's Indispensable Operator," *The New Yorker*, March 24, 2003.
2. Ibid.
3. For works charting the relationship between the Bush family and the Saudi royal family, see for instance, Craig Unger, *House of Bush, House of Saud: The Secret Relationship Between the World's Two Most Powerful Dynasties* (New York: Scribner, 2004), and Kevin Phillips, *American Dynasty: Aristocracy, Fortune and the Politics of Deceit in the House of Bush* (New York: Viking, 2004).
4. Rachel Bronson, "The Reluctant Mediator," *Washington Quarterly*, autumn 2002, 178.
5. See, for example, Condoleezza Rice, "Promoting the National Interest," *Foreign Affairs*, 79, 1 (2000): 45–62.
6. National Commission on Terrorist Attacks upon the United States, *9/11 Commission Report: Final Report of the National Commission on Terrorist Attacks upon the United States.* (Washington, DC: Government Printing Office, 2004), 4, 326.
7. May 2, 2003, "Saudi Arabia: Withdrawal of Forces," Council on Foreign Relations website, available at http://www.cfr.org/background/saudiarabia_usforces.php.
8. Jim Rutenberg, "Kerry Ads Draw on Saudis for New Attack on Bush," *New York Times*, October 5, 2004.
9. John J. Goldman and Marisa Schultz, "U.S. Strikes Back," *Los Angeles Times*, October 12, 2001.
10. Alaa Shahine, "Saudi Interior Minister: Jews Were Behind September 11 Attacks," Associated Press, December 5, 2002; Matthew A. Levitt, "Who Pays for Palestinian Terror?" *Weekly Standard*, August 25, 2003.
11. Michael Isikoff and Mark Hosenball, "A New Rift?" Newsweek, May 6, 2004, available at http://msnbc.msn.com/id/4901881/print/1/displaymode/1098/.
12. Although he was an analyst associated with RAND, his briefing was not a RAND report, and Murawiec later issued a statement that he was not speaking for RAND.
13. Jack Shafer, "The PowerPoint That Rocked the Pentagon," *Slate Magazine*, August 7, 2002, available at http://www.slate.com/id/2069119.
14. Prince Faisal bin Salman bin Abdel Aziz al-Saud, author's interview, Riyadh, February 2005.
15. *Terrorist Financing, Report of an Independent Task Force* (New York: Council on Foreign Relations Press, 2002), 1.
16. Author's interview, Jeddah, February 2005.
17. Author's interviews, Riyadh, February 2005. This refrain is relatively common.
18. Gina Abercrombie-Winstanley, author's interview, Jeddah, February 2005; Robert Jordan, author's phone interview, February 2, 2005.
19. Abercrombie-Winstanley, author's interview, February 2005.
20. Author's interview, Riyadh, February 2005. As of 2005, they had yet to recover.
21. Jordan, author's phone interview, February 2, 2005.
22. James A. Dorsey, "Saudi Leader Warns U.S. of Separate Interests," *Wall Street Journal*, October 29, 2001.
23. Elaine Sciolino and Patrick E. Tyler, "Saudi Charges Bush with Failure to Broker Mideast Peace," *New York Times*, November 9, 2001.
24. Jordan, author's phone interview, February 2, 2005

Select Bibliography

Archives

Columbia University Library, New York, NY
  Oral History Research Project

Dwight D. Eisenhower Library, Abilene, KS (DDEL)
  Ann Whitman File—DDE Papers as President
    Dulles-Herter Series
    National Security Council Series
    Oral Histories
    White House Central Files

Ford Foundation Archives, New York, NY
  Riyadh Office Files

The Georgetown University Library—Special Collections, Washington, DC
  William E. Mulligan Papers

Lyndon Baines Johnson Library, Austin, TX (LBJL)
  Papers of Lyndon Baines Johnson—Presidential Papers
    National Security File
    Oral Histories

John F. Kennedy Library, Boston, MA (JFKL)
  John F. Kennedy—Papers as President
    President's Office Files
    National Security Files
      Papers of Robert W. Komer
    Oral Histories

National Archives II, College Park, MD
  Nixon Presidential Materials Project
    National Security Council Files
    Papers of Henry A. Kissinger

Petroleum Intelligence Weekly Library, New York, NY
   Petroleum Intelligence Weekly, 1973–1974; 1985–1986

Princeton University Library, Princeton, NJ
   Papers of John Foster Dulles
      Oral Histories

Ronald Reagan Presidential Library, Simi Valley, CA (RRPL)
   David Gergen Files
   National Security Council Records
   Office of the President-Presidential Briefing Papers

Franklin D. Roosevelt Library, Hyde Park, NY (FDRL)
   Department of State Files
   Franklin Delano Roosevelt-Papers as President
      Official File
      President's Personal File
      President's Secretary File
   Papers of Henry Morgenthau Jr.
   Papers of Eleanor Roosevelt

Electronic Archives

American Presidency Project
   http://www.presidency.ucsb.edu/
   Public Papers of the President

Energy Information Administration, Department of Energy
   http://www.eia.doe.gov

Federation of American Scientists—Intelligence Resource Program
   http://www.fcs.org/irp
   Congressional Material Official Documents

Jimmy Carter Library and Museum
   http://www.jimmycarterlibrary.gov/documents
   Selected Speeches of Jimmy Carter

Resources for the Study of International Relations and Foreign Policy. Mount Holyoke
College.
   http://www.mtholyoke.edu/acad/intrel/feros-pg.htm

Truman Presidential Museum and Library
   http://www.trumanlibrary.org/library.htm
   Online Documents
   Archival Collections—Oral Histories

U.S. Agency for International Development. U.S. Overseas Loans and Grants
[Greenbook].
   http://qesdb.cdie.org/gbk/index.html

U.S. Department of State—Freedom of Information Act Electronic Reading Room
http://foia.state.gov
Kissinger Telephone Transcripts (1973–1976)

Select Periodicals

U.S. Central Intelligence Agency, *World Factbook*, http://www.cia.gov/cia/publications/factbook

U.S. Census Bureau. *Statistical Abstract of the United States* Washington, DC: GPO, various years

U.S. Department of State, *Foreign Relations of the United States: Diplomatic Papers* (Washington, DC: Government Printing Office, 1941–68)

U.S. Defense Security Assistance Agency, *Foreign Military Sales and Military Assistance Facts* (Washington, DC: Data Management Division, Comptroller, 1980–81)

International Energy Agency, *World Energy Outlook 2002* (Paris: IEA, 2002), http://www.iea.org/textbase/nppdf/free/2000/weo2002.pdf

Institute of International and Strategic Studies, *The Military Balance*, London, 1986–90

Stockholm International Peace Research Institute, *SIPRI Yearbook of World Armaments and Disarmament* (New York: Humanities Press, 1969–79)

U.S. Arms Control and Disarmament Agency, *World Military Expenditures and Arms Trade* (Washington, DC: Government Printing Office, 1963–96)

Books

Abir, Mordechai. *Saudi Arabia in the Oil Era: Regime and Elites, Conflict and Collaboration.* London: Croom Helm, 1988.

Abukhalil, As'ad. *The Battle for Saudi Arabia: Royalty, Fundamentalism, and Global Power.* New York: Seven Stories Press, 2004.

Acheson, Dean. *Present at the Creation: My Years in the State Department.* 3rd ed. New York: W. W. Norton, 1987.

Ajami, Fouad. *The Arab Predicament: Arab Political Thought and Practice Since 1967.* New York: Cambridge University Press, 1981.

Albright, Madeleine, with Bill Woodward. *Madam Secretary.* New York: Miramax Books, 2003.

Algosaibi, Ghazi. *The Gulf Crisis: An Attempt to Understand.* New York: Kegan Paul, 1993.

Alice, Princess of Great Britain. *For My Grandchildren: Some Reminiscences of Her Royal Highness Princess Alice, Countess of Athlone.* Cleveland: World Publishing Company, 1967.

——. *The Memoirs of Princess Alice Duchess of Gloucester.* London: Collins, 1983.

Almana, Mohammed. *Arabia Unified: A Portrait of Ibn Saud.* London: Hutchinson Benham, 1980.

Ambrose, Stephen E. *Eisenhower, Soldier and President: The Renowned One-Volume Life.* New York: Touchstone/Simon & Schuster, 1990.

Anderson, Irvine H. *Aramco: The United States and Saudi Arabia: A Study of the Dynamics of Foreign Oil Policy, 1933–1950.* Princeton: Princeton University Press, 1981.

Arabian American Oil Company. *Aramco Handbook: Oil and the Middle East.* Dhahran: Arabian American Oil Company, 1968.

Badeau, John S. *The American Approach to the Arab World.* New York: Harper & Row, 1968.

Baer, Robert. *Sleeping with the Devil: How Washington Sold Our Soul for Saudi Crude.* New York: Three Rivers Press, 2004.

Baker, James A., with Thomas M. DeFrank. *The Politics of Diplomacy: Revolution, War and Peace, 1989–1992.* New York: G. P. Putnam's Sons, 1995.

Barger, Thomas C. *Out in the Blue: Letters from Arabia, 1937–1940: A Young American Geologist Explores the Deserts of Early Saudi Arabia.* Vista: Selwa Press, 2000.

Bass, Warren. *Support Any Friend: Kennedy's Middle East and the Making of the U.S.-Israel Alliance.* New York: Oxford University Press, 2003.

Bearden, Milton, and James Risen. *The Main Enemy: The Inside Story of the CIA's Final Showdown with the KGB.* New York: Random House, 2003.

Beling, Willard A., ed. *King Faisal and the Modernization of Saudi Arabia.* Boulder, CO: Westview Press, 1980.

Benjamin, Daniel, and Steven Simon. *The Age of Sacred Terror.* New York: Random House, 2002.

Bergen, Peter L. *Holy War, Inc.: Inside the Secret World of Osama bin Laden.* New York: Free Press, 2001.

Bidwell, Robin. *The Two Yemens.* Boulder, CO: Longman Group and Westview Press, 1983.

Bin Sultan, HRH General Khaled, with Patrick Seale. *Desert Warrior: A Personal View of the Gulf war by the Joint Forces Commander.* New York: HarperCollins, 1995.

Blum, John Morton, ed. *The Price of Vision: The Diary of Henry A. Wallace 1942–1946.* Boston: Houghton Mifflin, 1973.

Bose, Meena, and Rosanna Perotti, eds. *From Cold War to New World Order: The Foreign Policy of George H. W. Bush.* Westport: Greenwood Press, 2002.

Bradley, John R. *Saudi Arabia Exposed: Inside a Kingdom in Crisis.* New York: Palgrave-Macmillan, 2005.

Brinkley, Douglas, ed. *Dean Acheson and the Making of U.S. Foreign Policy.* New York: St. Martin's Press, 1993.

Bromley, Simon. *American Hegemony and World Oil: The Industry, the State System and the World Economy.* University Park: Pennsylvania State University Press, 1991.

Brookings Institution. *Toward Peace in the Middle East: Report of a Study Group.* Washington, DC: Brookings Institution Press, 1975.

Brown, Anthony Cave. *Oil, God, and Gold: The Story of Aramco and the Saudi Kings.* New York: Houghton Mifflin, 1999.

Brown, Harold. *Thinking About National Security: Defense and Foreign Policy in a Dangerous World.* Boulder, CO: Westview Press, 1983.

Brzezinski, Zbigniew. *Power and Principle: Memoirs of the National Security Adviser 1977–1981.* New York: Farrar Straus Giroux, 1983.

Burns, William J. *Economic Aid and American Policy Toward Egypt, 1955–1981.* Albany: State University of New York Press, 1985.

Burr, J. Millard, and Robert O. Collins. *Africa's Thirty Years War: Libya, Chad, and the Sudan, 1963–1993.* Boulder, CO: Westview Press, 1999.

Bush, George H. W. *All the Best, George Bush: My Life in Letters and Other Writings.* New York: Lisa Drew Book/Scribner, 1999.

Bush, George H. W., and Brent Scowcroft. *A World Transformed.* New York: Alfred A. Knopf, 1998.

Califano, Joseph A. Jr. *The Triumph & Tragedy of Lyndon Johnson: The White House Years.* New York: Simon & Schuster, 1991.

Campbell, Kurt, ed. *The Nuclear Tipping Point.* Washington, DC: Brookings Institution Press, 2004.

Caro, Robert A. *The Years of Lyndon Johnson: Master of the Senate.* New York: Alfred A. Knopf, 2002.

——. *The Years of Lyndon Johnson: Means of Ascent.* New York: Alfred A. Knopf, 1990.

Carter, Jimmy. *Keeping Faith: Memoirs of a President.* New York: Bantam Books, 1995.

Champion, Daryl. *The Paradoxical Kingdom: Saudi Arabia and the Momentum of Reform.* New York: Columbia University Press, 2003.

Childs, J. Rives. *Foreign Service Farewell: My Years in the Near East.* Charlottesville: University of Virginia Press, 1969.

Citino, Nathan J. *From Arab Nationalism to OPEC: Eisenhower, King Saud and the Making of U.S.-Saudi Relations.* Bloomington: Indiana University Press, 2002.

Clarke, Richard. *Against All Enemies.* New York: The Free Press, 2004.

Clifford, Clark, with Richard Holbrooke. *Counsel to the President: A Memoir.* New York: Random House, 1991.

Clinton, Bill. *My Life.* New York: Alfred A. Knopf, 2004.

Cobban, Helena. *The Palestinian Liberation Organization: People, Power, and Politics.* New York: Cambridge University Press, 1984.

Cohen, Michael J. *Truman and Israel.* Berkeley: University of California Press, 1990.

Cohen, Warren I., and Nancy Bernkopf Tucker, eds. *Lyndon Johnson Confronts the World: American Foreign Policy, 1963–1968.* New York: Cambridge University Press, 1994.

Coll, Stephen. *Ghost Wars: The Secret History of the CIA, Afghanistan and Bin Laden, from the Soviet Invasion to September 10, 2001.* New York: Penguin, 2004.

Cooley, John K. *Unholy Wars: Afghanistan, America and International Terrorism.* 3rd ed. London: Pluto Press, 1999.

Copeland, Miles. *The Game of Nations: The Amorality of Power Politics.* New York: Simon & Schuster, 1969.

Cordesman, Anthony H. *The Gulf and the Search for Strategic Stability: Saudi Arabia, the Military Balance in the Gulf, and Trends in the Arab-Israeli Military Balance.* Boulder, CO: Westview Press, 1984.

——. *The Gulf and the West: Strategic Relations and Military Realities.* Boulder, CO: Westview Press, 1988.

——. *The Iran-Iraq War and Western Security, 1984–1987: Strategic Implications and Policy Options.* London: Jane's Publishing, 1987.

——. *Saudi Arabia Enters the Twenty-First Century: The Military and International Security Dimensions.* Westport: CSIS/Praeger, 2003.

——. *Saudi Arabia Enters the Twenty-First Century: The Political, Foreign Policy, Economic, and Energy Dimensions.* Westport: CSIS/Praeger, 2003.

——. *Saudi Arabia: Guarding the Desert Kingdom.* Boulder, CO: Westview Press, 1997.

Cordesman, Anthony H., and Ahmed S. Hashim. *Iraq: Sanctions and Beyond.* Boulder, CO: Westview Press, 1997.

Crile, George. *Charlie Wilson's War: The Extraordinary Story of the Largest Covert Operation in History.* New York: Atlantic Monthly Press, 2003.

Crocker, Chester A. *High Noon in Southern Africa: Making Peace in a Rough Neighborhood.* New York: W. W. Norton, 1992.

Cutler, Robert. *No Time for Rest.* Boston: Atlantic Monthly Press, 1965.

Dallek, Robert, *Flawed Giant: Lyndon Johnson and His Times, 1961–1973*. New York: Oxford University Press, 1998.

———. *Franklin D. Roosevelt and American Foreign Policy, 1932–1945*. New York: Oxford University Press, 1995.

———. *Lyndon B. Johnson: Portrait of a President*. New York: Oxford University Press, 2004.

Daweesha, Adeed I., ed. *Islam in Foreign Policy*. Cambridge: Cambridge University Press/Royal Institute of International Affairs, 1983.

De Gaury, Gerald. *Faisal: King of Saudi Arabia*. New York: Praeger, 1966.

de Marenches, Alexandre. *The Evil Empire: The Third World War Now*. London: Sidgwick & Jackson, 1988.

de Marenches, Alexandre, and David A. Andelman. *The Fourth World War: Diplomacy and Espionage in the Age of Terrorism*. New York: William Morrow, 1992.

De Waal, Alex, ed. *Islamism and Its Enemies in the Horn of Africa*. Bloomington: Indiana University Press, 2004.

Deaver, Michael K., with Mickey Herskowitz. *Behind the Scenes*. New York: William Morrow, 1987.

Deter, Moshe. *"To Serve, to Teach, to Leave": The Story of Israel's Development Assistance Program in Black Africa*. New York: American Jewish Congress, 1977.

Deeb, Mary Jane. *Libya's Foreign Policy in North Africa*. Boulder, CO: Westview Press, 1991.

Dickson, H. R. P. *The Arab of the Desert: A Glimpse into Badawin Life in Kuwait and Sau'di Arabia*. 2nd ed. London: George Allen & Unwin, 1951.

Divine, Robert A., ed. *The Johnson Years*, Volume III: *LBJ at Home and Abroad*. Lawrence: University Press of Kansas, 1994.

Donovan, Robert J. *Conflict and Crisis: The Presidency of Harry S. Truman, 1945–1948*. New York: W. W. Norton, 1977.

———. *The Tumultuous Years: The Presidency of Harry S. Truman, 1949–1953*. New York: W. W. Norton, 1982.

Dunnigan, James F., and Albert A. Nofi. *Dirty Little Secrets of World War II*. New York: William Morrow, 1994.

Eddy, William A. *FDR Meets Ibn Saud*. New York: American Friends of the Middle East, 1954.

Eden, Anthony. *Full Circle: The Memoirs of Anthony Eden*. Boston, Houghton Mifflin, 1960.

Eisenhower, Dwight D. *Waging Peace: The White House Years*. New York: Doubleday Press, 1965.

———. *The White House Years: Mandate for Change, 1953–1956*. New York: Doubleday, 1963.

El-Affendi, Abdelwahab. *Turabi's Revolution: Islam and Power in Sudan*. London: Grey Seal, 1991.

El-Sadat, Anwar. *In Search of an Identity: An Autobiography*. New York: Harper and Row, 1977.

El-Shazly, Nadia el-Sayed. *The Gulf Tanker War*. New York: St. Martin's Press, 1998.

Emerson, Steven. *The American House of Saud: The Secret Petrodollar Connection*. New York: Franklin Watts, 1985.

Esposito, John L. *Holy War: Terror in the Name of Islam*. New York: Oxford University Press, 2002.

Fandy, Mamoun. *Saudi Arabia and the Politics of Dissent.* New York: St. Martin's Press, 1999.

Ford, Gerald R. *A Time to Heal.* New York: Harper & Row/Reader's Digest, 1979.

Fürtig, Henner. *Iran's Rivalry with Saudi Arabia between the Gulf Wars.* Reading, England: Ithaca Press, 2002.

Garfinkle, Adam, ed. *A Practical Guide to Winning the War on Terrorism.* Stanford: Hoover Institution, 2004.

Gates, Robert M. *From the Shadows: The Ultimate Insider's Story of Five Presidents and How They Won the Cold War.* New York: Touchstone/Simon & Schuster, 1997.

Gause, F. Gregory III. *Oil Monarchies: Domestic and Security Challenges in the Arab Gulf States.* New York: Council on Foreign Relations, 1994.

———. *Saudi-Yemeni Relations: Domestic Structures and Foreign Influences.* New York: Columbia University Press, 1990.

Gazit, Mordechai. *President Kennedy's Policy Toward the Arab States and Israel: Analysis and Documents.* Tel Aviv: Shiloah Center for Middle Eastern and African Studies, 1983.

Glassman, Jon D. *Arms for the Arabs: The Soviet Union and War in the Middle East.* Baltimore: Johns Hopkins University Press, 1975.

Gold, Dore. *Hatred's Kingdom: How Saudi Arabia Supports the New Global Terrorism.* Washington, DC: Regnery, 2003.

Goldberg, Jacob. *The Foreign Policy of Saudi Arabia: The Formative Years, 1902–1918.* Cambridge, MA: Harvard University Press, 1986.

Golub, David B. *When Oil and Politics Mix: Saudi Oil Policy, 1973–1985.* Harvard Middle East Papers: Modern Series #4. Cambridge, MA: Center for Middle Eastern Studies, Harvard University, 1985.

Goodwin, Doris Kearns. *Lyndon Johnson and the American Dream.* New York: Harper & Row, 1976.

Gordon, Michael R., and Bernard E. Trainor. *The Generals' War: The Inside Story of the Conflict in the Gulf.* Boston: Little, Brown, 1995.

Greenberg, David. *Nixon's Shadow: The History of an Image.* New York: W. W. Norton, 2003.

Gruening, Earnest. *Many Battles: The Autobiography of Ernest Gruening.* New York: Liveright, 1973.

Gunaratna, Rohan. *Inside Al Qaeda: Global Network of Terror.* New York: Columbia University Press, 2002.

Habib, John S. *Ibn Sa'ud's Warriors of Islam: The Ikhwan of Najd and Their Role in the Creation of the Sa'udi Kingdom, 1910–1930.* Leiden: Brill, 1978.

Haddad, George M. *Revolutions and Military Rule in the Middle East: The Arab States.* 2 vols. New York: Robert Speller and Sons, 1971.

Haig, Alexander M. Jr., with Charles McCarry. *Inner Circles: How America Changed the World: A Memoir.* New York: Warner Books, 1992.

Halberstam, David. *War in a Time of Peace: Bush, Clinton, and the Generals.* New York: Scribner, 2001.

Halliday, Fred. *Arabia Without Sultans.* New York: Penguin Books, 1974.

———. *The Making of the Second Cold War.* London: Verso, 1983.

———. *The Middle East in International Relations: Power, Politics and Ideology.* New York: Cambridge University Press, 2005.

———. *Two Hours that Shook the World: September 11, 2001, Causes & Consequences.* London: Saqi Books, 2002.

Hart, Parker T. *Saudi Arabia and the United States: Birth of a Security Partnership.* Bloomington: Indiana University Press, 1998.

Haseeb, Khair el-Din, ed. *The Arabs and Africa.* London: Croom Helm, 1985.

Heikal, Mohamed. *Iran: The Untold Story: An Insider's Account of America's Iranian Adventure and Its Consequences for the Future.* New York: Pantheon Books, 1981.

———. *The Road to Ramadan.* New York: Ballantine Books, 1975.

Henderson, Simon. *After King Fahd: Succession in Saudi Arabia.* Policy Paper #37. Washington, DC: Washington Institute for Near East Policy, 1994.

Henze, Paul. *Rebels and Separatists in Ethiopia: Regional Resistance to a Marxist Regime.* Santa Monica: Rand, 1985.

Hiro, Dilip. *The Longest War: The Iran-Iraq Military Conflict.* New York: Routledge, 1991.

Holden, David, and Richard Johns. *The House of Saud: The Rise and Rule of the Most Powerful Dynasty in the Arab World.* New York: Holt, Rinehart and Winston, 1982.

Hull, Cordell. *The Memoirs of Cordell Hull.* 2 vols. New York: Macmillan, 1948.

Humphrey, Hubert. *The Education of a Public Man: My Life in Politics.* New York: Doubleday, 1976.

Hurewitz, J. C. *Middle East Politics: The Military Dimension.* New York: Praeger, 1969.

———, ed. *Soviet-American Rivalry in the Middle East.* New York: Praeger, 1969.

Ickes, Harold L. *Fightin' Oil.* New York: Alfred A. Knopf, 1943.

Isaacson, Walter. *Kissinger: A Biography.* New York: Simon & Schuster, 1992.

Johnson, Lyndon B. *The Vantage Point: Perspectives of the Presidency, 1963–1969.* New York: Holt, Reinhart & Winston, 1971.

Kalicki, Jan H. and David L. Goldwyn, eds. *Energy and Security: Toward A New Foreign Policy Strategy.* Washington, DC: Woodrow Wilson Center Press, 2005.

Kalman, Laura. *Abe Fortas: A Biography.* New Haven: Yale University Press, 1990.

Kampelman, Max. *Entering New Worlds: Memoirs of a Private Man in Public Life.* New York: HarperCollins, 1991.

Kaufman, Burton I. *Trade and Aid: Eisenhower's Foreign Economic Policy, 1953–1961.* Baltimore: Johns Hopkins University Press, 1982.

Kechichian, Joseph A. *Succession in Saudi Arabia.* New York: Palgrave, 2001.

Kelly, John B. *Arabia, the Gulf, and the West: A Critical View of the Arabs and Their Oil Policy.* New York: Basic Books, 1980.

Kepel, Gilles. *Jihad: The Trail of Political Islam.* Cambridge: Belknap Press, 2002.

———. *The War for Muslim Minds: Islam and the West.* Cambridge: Belknap Press, 2004.

Kerr, Malcolm. *The Arab Cold War: Gamal Abd al-Nasir and His Rivals, 1958–1970.* London: Oxford University Press, 1967.

Khadduri, Majid. *The Gulf War: The Origins and Implications of the Iraq-Iran Conflict.* New York: Oxford University Press, 1988.

Khorany, Bahgat, ed. *How Foreign Policy Decisions Are Made in the Third World.* Boulder, CO: Westview Press, 1986.

Kirkpatrick, Jeanne. *The Reagan Doctrine and U.S. Foreign Policy.* Washington, DC: Heritage Foundation, 1985.

Kissinger, Henry. *White House Years.* Boston: Little, Brown, 1979.

———. *Years of Renewal.* New York: Touchstone/Simon & Schuster, 1999.

———. *Years of Upheaval.* Boston: Little, Brown, 1982.

Klebanoff, Shoshana. *Middle East Oil and U.S. Foreign Policy.* New York: Praeger, 1974.

Kostiner, Joseph, ed. *Middle Eastern Monarchies: The Challenge of Modernity.* Boulder, CO: Lynne Rienner, 2000.

Kunz, Diane B., ed. *Diplomacy of the Crucial Decade: American Foreign Relations During the 1960s.* New York: Columbia University Press, 1994.

Kupchan, Charles. *The Persian Gulf and the West: The Dilemmas of Security.* Winchester, MA: Allen & Unwin, 1987.

Kux, Dennis. *The United States and Pakistan, 1947–2000: Disenchanted Allies.* The Adst-Dacor Diplomats and Diplomacy Series. Princeton: Woodrow Wilson Center, 2001.

Lacey, Robert. *The Kingdom: Arabia and the House of Saud.* New York: Harcourt Brace Jovanovich, 1981.

Lackner, Helen. *A House Built on Sand: A Political Economy of Saudi Arabia.* London: Ithaca Press, 1978.

Lacqueur, Walter. *The Road to War: The Origin and Aftermath of the Arab-Israeli Conflict of 1967–8,* Middlesex: Penguin Books, 1968.

——. *The Struggle for the Middle East: The Soviet Union and the Middle East 1958–1968.* London: Pelican Books, 1969.

Laham, Nicholas. *Selling AWACS to the Saudis: The Reagan Administration and the Balancing of America's Competing Interests in the Middle East.* Westport: Praeger, 2002.

LeMarchand, René, ed. *The Green and the Black: Qudhafi's Policies in Africa.* Bloomington: Indiana University Press, 1988.

Lenczowski, George. *American Presidents and the Middle East.* Durham, NC: Duke University Press, 1990.

——. *The Middle East in World Affairs.* 4th ed. Ithaca: Cornell University Press, 1980.

Leverett, Flynt, ed. *The Road Ahead: Middle East Policy in the Bush Administration's Second Term.* Washington, DC: Brookings Institution Press, 2005.

Levinson, Jeffrey L., and Randy Edwards. *Missile Inbound: The Attack on the Stark in the Persian Gulf.* Annapolis: Naval Institute Press, 1997.

Lesch, David W. *1979: The Year That Shaped the Middle East.* Boulder, CO: Westview Press, 2001.

Lippman, Thomas W. *Inside the Mirage: America's Fragile Partnership with Saudi Arabia.* Boulder, CO: Westview Press, 2004.

Lohbeck, Kurt. *Holy War, Unholy Victory: Eyewitness to the CIA's Secret War in Afghanistan.* Washington, DC: Regnery Gateway, 1993.

Long, David. *The Kingdom of Saudi Arabia.* Gainesville: University Press of Florida, 1997.

——. *The United States and Saudi Arabia: Ambivalent Allies.* Boulder, CO: Westview Press, 1985.

Longrigg, Stephen Helmsley. *Oil in the Middle East, its Discovery and Development.* London: Oxford University Press, 1954.

MacMillan, Harold. *Riding the Storm, 1956–1959.* New York: Harper & Row, 1971.

Mamdani, Mahmood. *Good Muslim, Bad Muslim: America, the Cold War, and the Roots of Terror.* New York: Pantheon Books, 2004.

Mangone, Gerard J., ed. *Energy Policies of the World.* New York: Elsevier Publishing, 1976.

Marr, Phebe. *A Modern History of Iraq.* 2nd ed. Boulder, CO: Westview Press, 2004.

McConnell, Philip C. *The Hundred Men.* Peterborough: Courier Press, 1985.

McDonald, James G. *My Mission In Israel, 1948–1951.* New York: Simon & Schuster, 1951.

McGhee, George. *Envoy to the Middle World: Adventures in Diplomacy, 1948–1982.* New York: HarperCollins, 1983.

McNamara, Robert. *The Essence of Security: Reflections in Office*. New York: Harper & Row, 1968.

McPherson, Harry. *A Political Education*. Boston: Little, Brown, 1972.

Meese, Edwin. *With Reagan: The Inside Story*. Washington, DC: Regnery Gateway, 1992.

Merrill, Karen, ed. *Modern Worlds of Business and Industry: Cultures, Technology, Labor*. Turnhout, Belgium: Brepols, 1998.

Miller, Aaron David. *Search for Security: Saudi Arabian Oil and American Foreign Policy, 1939–1949*. Chapel Hill: University of North Carolina Press, 1980.

Millis, Walter, ed. *The Forrestal Diaries*. New York: Viking Press, 1951.

Niblock, Tim, ed. *State, Society, and Economy in Saudi Arabia*. New York: St. Martin's Press, 1982.

Nixon, Richard. *RN: The Memoirs of Richard Nixon*. 2nd ed. New York: Touchstone/ Simon & Schuster, 1990.

O'Ballance, Edgar. *The War in Yemen*. Hamden: Archon Books, 1971.

Obaid, Nawaf. *The Oil Kingdom at 100: Petroleum and Policymaking in Saudi Arabia*. Washington, DC: Washington Institute for Near East Policy, 2000.

Ottaway, Marina. *Soviet and American Influence in the Horn of Africa*. New York: Praeger, 1982.

Page, Stephen. *The USSR and Arabia: The Development of Soviet Policies and Attitudes Towards the Countries of the Arabian Peninsula*. London: Central Asian Research Centre, 1971.

Painter, David S. *Oil and the American Century: The Political Economy of the U.S. Foreign Oil Policy, 1941–1954*. Baltimore: Johns Hopkins University Press, 1986.

Parker, Richard B. *The Politics of Miscalculation in the Middle East*. Bloomington: Indiana University Press, 1993.

Paterson, Thomas G., ed. *Kennedy's Quest for Victory: American Foreign Policy, 1961–1963*. New York: Oxford University Press, 1989.

Pelletiere, Stephen C., and Douglas V. Johnson III. *Lessons Learned: The Iran-Iraq War*. Carlisle Barracks: Strategic Studies Institute, US Army War College, 1991.

Peterson, J. E. *Yemen: The Search for a Modern State*. Baltimore: Johns Hopkins University Press, 1982.

Petterson, Donald. *Inside Sudan: Political Islam, Conflict, and Catastrophe*. 2nd ed. Boulder, CO: Westview Press, 2003.

Philby, H. St. John. *Arabian Days*. London: Robert Hale, Ltd, 1948.

———. *Arabian Jubilee*. New York: John Day, 1953.

Phillips, Kevin P. *American Dynasty: Aristocracy, Fortune, and the Politics of Deceit in the House of Bush*. New York: Viking, 2004.

Pillar, Paul R. *Terrorism and U.S. Foreign Policy*. Washington, DC: Brookings Institution Press, 2001.

Pollack, Kenneth M. *The Threatening Storm: The Case for Invading Iraq*. New York: Random House, 2002.

Posner, Gerald L. *Secrets of the Kingdom: The Inside Story of the Secret Saudi-US Connection*. New York: Random House, 2005.

Powell, Colin L., with Joseph E. Persico. *My American Journey*. New York: Ballantine Books, 1995.

Quandt, William B. *Camp David: Peacemaking and Politics*. Washington, DC: Brookings Institution Press, 1986.

———. *Decade of Decisions: American Foreign Policy Toward the Arab-Israeli Conflict, 1967–1976*. Berkeley: University of California Press, 1977.

——. *Peace Process: American Diplomacy and the Arab-Israeli Conflict Since 1967.* Berkeley: University of California Press, 1993.

——. *Saudi Arabia in the 1980's: Foreign Policy, Security and Oil.* Washington, DC: Brookings Institution Press, 1981.

——. *Saudi Arabia's Oil Policy.* Washington, DC: Brookings Institution Press, 1982.

Rabinovich, Itamar. *The War for Lebanon, 1970–1985.* Rev. ed. Ithaca: Cornell University Press, 1985.

Ra'anan, Uri, et al., eds. *Arms Transfers of the Third World: The Military Buildup in Less Industrialized Countries.* Boulder, CO: Westview Press, 1978.

Randal, Jonathan. *Osama: The Making of a Terrorist.* New York: Alfred A. Knopf, 2004.

Rasheed, Madawi al-. *A History of Saudi Arabia.* New York: Cambridge University Press, 2002.

Rasheed, Madawi al-, and Robert Vitalis, eds. *Counter-Narratives: History, Contemporary Society, and Politics in Saudi Arabia and Yemen.* New York: Palgrave-Macmillan, 2004.

Rashid, Ahmed. *Taliban.* New Haven: Yale University Press, 2000.

Reagan, Ronald. *An American Life: The Autobiography.* New York: Simon & Schuster, 1990.

——. *Reagan, in His Own Hand.* Ed. Kiron Skinner et al. New York: Free Press, 2001.

——. *Reagan: A Life in Letters.* Ed. Kiron Skinner et al. New York: Free Press, 2003.

Rigdon, William M., with James Derieux. *White House Sailor.* Garden City: Doubleday, 1962.

Rodman, Peter W. *More Precious than Peace: The Cold War and the Struggle for the Third World.* New York: Charles Scribner's Sons, 1994.

Ross, Dennis. *The Missing Peace: The Inside Story of the Fight for Middle East Peace.* New York: Farrar, Straus and Giroux, 2004.

Roosevelt, Archie. *For Lust of Knowing: Memoirs of an Intelligence Officer.* Boston: Little, Brown, 1988.

Rostow, Eugene V. *Peace in the Balance: The Future of American Foreign Policy.* New York: Simon & Schuster, 1972.

Rostow, W. W. *The Diffusion of Power: An Essay in Recent History.* New York: Macmillan, 1973.

Roy, Olivier. *Afghanistan: From Holy War to Civil War.* Princeton: Darwin Press, 1995.

Rubin, Barnett. *The Fragmentation of Afghanistan: State Formation and Collapse in the International System.* 2nd ed. New Haven: Yale University Press, 2002.

Rubino, Anna C. "Secrets of the Oil World: Wanda Jablonski and the Influence of Journalism." Ph.D. diss., Yale University, 2002.

Rudolph, Susanne Hoeber, and James Piscatori, eds. *Transnational Religion and Fading States.* Boulder, CO: Westview Press, 1997.

Rusk, Dean. *As I Saw It.* New York: W. W. Norton, 1990.

Safran, Nadav. *Saudi Arabia: The Ceaseless Quest for Security.* 2nd ed. Ithaca: Cornell University Press, 1988.

Sageman, Marc. *Understanding Terror Networks.* Philadelphia: University of Pennsylvania Press, 2004.

Sampson, Anthony. *The Arms Bazaar: From Lebanon to Lockheed.* New York: Viking Press, 1977.

——. *Seven Sisters: The Great Oil Companies and the World They Made.* New York: Viking Press, 1975.

Schlesinger, Arthur. *A Thousand Days: John F. Kennedy in the White House*. Boston: Houghton Mifflin, 2002.

Schulz, George P. *Turmoil and Triumph: My Years as Secretary of State*. New York: Charles Scribner's Sons, 1993.

Schulze, Reinhard. *A Modern History of the Islamic World*. New York: New York University Press, 2000.

Schwartz, Stephen. *The Two Faces of Islam: The House of Sa'ud from Tradition to Terror*. New York: Doubleday, 2002.

——. *The Two Faces of Islam: Saudi Fundamentalism and its Role in Terrorism*. New York: Alfred A. Knopf, 2003.

Scott, James M. *Deciding to Intervene: The Reagan Doctrine and American Foreign Policy*. Raleigh: Duke University Press, 1996.

Sewell, John W., Richard E. Feinberg, and Valeriana Kallab, eds. *U.S. Foreign Policy and the Third World: Agenda 1985–86*. New Brunswick: Transaction Books, 1985.

Sherwood, Robert E. *Roosevelt and Hopkins: An Intimate History*. New York: Harper & Brothers, 1948.

Shichor, Yitzhak. *East Wind Over Arabia: Origins and Implications of the Sino-Saudi Missile Deal*. Berkeley: Institute of East Asian Studies, University of California, 1989.

Sick, Gary. *All Fall Down: America's Tragic Encounter with Iran*. 2nd ed. New York: Random House, 1986.

Simon, William. *A Time for Action*. New York: McGraw Hill/Reader's Digest Press, 1980.

——. *A Time For Truth*. New York: Reader's Digest Press, 1978.

Sivan, Emmanuel. *Radical Islam: Medieval Theology and Modern Politics*. Enlarged ed. New Haven: Yale University Press, 1990.

Sorenson, Ted. *Kennedy*. New York: Harper & Row, 1965.

Spiegel, Steven L. *The Other Arab-Israeli Conflict: Making America's Middle East Policy, from Truman to Reagan*. Chicago: University of Chicago Press, 1985.

Stassen, Harold, and Marshall Houts. *Eisenhower: Turning the World Toward Peace*. St. Paul: Merill/Magnus Publishing Corporation, 1990.

Stettinius, Edward R., Jr. *Roosevelt and the Russians: The Yalta Conference*. New York: Doubleday, 1949.

Strmecki, Marin J. "Power Assessment: Measuring Soviet Power in Afghanistan." 2 vols. Ph.D. diss., Georgetown University, 1994.

Takeyh, Ray. *The Origins of the Eisenhower Doctrine: The US, Britain and Nasser's Egypt, 1953–57*. New York: St. Martin's Press, 2000.

Teicher, Howard, and Gayle Radley. *Two Pillars to Desert Storm: America's Flawed Vision in the Middle East from Nixon to Bush*. New York: William Morrow, 1993.

Teitelbaum, Joshua. *Holier than Thou: Saudi Arabia's Islamic Opposition*. Washington, DC: Washington Institute for Institute Near East Policy, 2000.

——. *The Rise and Fall of the Hashimite Kingdom of Arabia*. New York: New York University Press, 2001.

Telhami, Shibley. *The Stakes: America and the Middle East: The Consequences of Power and the Choice for Peace*. Boulder, CO: Westview Press, 2002.

Tessler, Mark. *A History of the Israeli-Palestinian Conflict*. Bloomington: Indiana University Press, 1994.

Thayer, George. *The War Business*. New York: Simon & Schuster, 1969.

Truell, Peter, and Larry Gurwin. *False Profits: The Inside Story of BCCI, the World's Most Corrupt Financial Empire*. New York: Houghton Mifflin, 1992.

Truman, Harry S. *Memoirs of Harry S. Truman: 1945, Year of Decisions.* New York: Doubleday, 1955.
——. *Memoirs of Harry S. Truman: Years of Trial and Hope.* New York: Doubleday, 1956.
Truman, Margaret. *Harry S. Truman.* New York: William Morrow, 1973.
Unger, Craig. *House of Bush, House of Saud: The Secret Relationship Between the World's Two Most Powerful Dynasties.* New York: Scribner, 2004.
Vance, Cyrus. *Hard Choices: Critical Years in America's Foreign Policy.* New York: Simon & Schuster, 1983.
Vassiliev, Alexei. *The History of Saudi Arabia.* New York: New York University Press, 2000.
Wahba, Hafiz. *Arabian Days.* London, England: Arthur Barker, 1964.
Walton, Richard. *Cold War and Counterrevolution: The Foreign Policy of John F. Kennedy.* New York: Viking Press, 1972.
Weinberger, Caspar. *Fighting for Peace: Seven Critical Years in the Pentagon.* New York: Warner Books, 1990.
Weintraub, Sidney, ed. *Economic Coercion and U.S. Foreign Policy: Implications of Case Studies from the Johnson Administration.* Boulder, CO: Westview Press, 1982.
Wicker, Tom. *Dwight D. Eisenhower.* New York: Times Books/Henry Holt, 2002.
Woodward, Bob. *The Commanders.* New York: Simon & Schuster, 1991.
——. *Plan of Attack.* Simon & Schuster: New York, 2004.
——. *Veil: The Secret Wars of the CIA, 1981–1987.* New York: Simon & Schuster, 1987.
Yaqub, Salim. *Containing Arab Nationalism: The Eisenhower Doctrine and the Middle East.* Chapel Hill: University of North Carolina Press, 2004.
Yamani, Mai. *Changed Identities: Challenge of the New Generation in Saudi Arabia.* London: Royal Institute of International Affairs, 2000.
——. *Cradle of Islam: The Hijaz and the Quest for an Arabian Identity.* London: I. B. Taurus, 2004.
Yergin, Daniel. *The Prize: The Epic Quest for Oil, Money and Power.* 2nd ed. New York: Free Press, 1992.
Yizraeli, Sarah. *The Remaking of Saudi Arabia: The Struggle Between King Sa'ud and Crown Prince Faysal, 1953–1962.* Tel Aviv: Moshe Dayan Center for Middle Eastern and African Studies, 1997.
Yodfat, Aryeh. *Arab Politics in the Soviet Mirror.* New York: Halstead Press, 1973.
Yousaf, Mohammad, and Mark Adkin. *Afghanistan: The Bear Trap: The Defeat of a Superpower.* Havertown: Casemate, 2001.
Zeiler, Thomas W. *Dean Rusk: Defending the American Mission Abroad.* Wilmington: Scholarly Resources, 2000.

Articles

Ajami, Fouad. "The End of Pan-Arabism." *Foreign Affairs* 57, 2 (1978): 355–73.
Akins, James E. "International Cooperative Efforts in Energy Supply." *Annals of the American Academy of Political and Social Science* 410 (1973): 75–85.
——. "The Oil Crisis: This Time the Wolf Is Here." *Foreign Affairs* 51, 3 (1973): 462–9(
——. "What Hope America?" *Journal of Palestine Studies* 9, 4 (1980): 182–88.
Aldrich, Winthrop W. "The Suez Crisis: A Footnote to History." *Foreign Affairs* 45 (1967): 541–52.

McMillan, Joseph, Anthony H. Cordesman, Mamoun Fandy, and Fareed Mohamedi. "The United States and Saudi Arabia: American Interests and Challenges to the Kingdom in 2002." *Middle East Policy* 9, 1 (2002): 1–28.

Mansfield, Edward D., and Jack Snyder. "Democratization and the Danger of War." *International Security* 20, 1 (1995): 5–38.

Marshall, Jonathan. "Saudi Arabia and the Reagan Doctrine." *Middle East Report* 155 (1988): 12–17.

Mejcher, Helmut. "King Faisal Ibn Abdul Aziz Al Saud in the Arena of World Politics: A Glimpse from Washington, 1950 to 1971." *British Journal of Middle East Studies* 31, 1 (2004): 5–23.

"Missile Proliferation—Saudi Arabia." FAS Intelligence Resource Program, http://www.fas.org/irp/threat/missile/saudi.htm.

Mulligan, William E. "A Kingdom and a Company." *Aramco World Magazine*, May–June 1984, http://www.saudiaramcoworld.com/issue/198403/a.kingdom.and.a.company.htm.

Nadelmann, Ethan. "Setting the Stage: American Policy Toward the Middle East 1961–1966." *International Journal of Middle East Studies* 14 (1982): 446–47.

Niblock, Tim. "Social Structure and the Development of the Saudi Arabian Political Structure." In Tim Niblock, ed., *State, Society and Economy in Saudi Arabia*, 75–105. New York: St. Martin's Press, 1982.

Nonneman, Gerd. "Saudi-European Relations 1902–2001: A Pragmatic Quest for Relative Autonomy." *International Affairs* 77, 3 (2001): 631–61.

Okruhlik, Gwenn. "Networks of Dissent: Islamism and Reform in Saudi Arabia." *Current History*, January 2002, 22–28.

Peck, Malcom C. "The Saudi-American Relationship and King Faisal." In Willard A. Beling, ed., *King Faisal and the Modernization of Saudi Arabia*, 231–43. Boulder, CO: Westview Press, 1980.

Petersen, Tore Tingvold. "Anglo-American Rivalry in the Middle East: The Struggle for the Buraimi Oasis, 1952–1957." *International History Review* 14 (1992): 71–91.

Piscatori, James P. "Islamic Values and National Interest: The Foreign Policy of Saudi Arabia." In Adeed I. Daweesha, ed., *Islam in Foreign Policy*, 33–53. Cambridge: Cambridge University Press/Royal Institute of International Affairs, 1983.

Podhoretz, Norman. "Appeasement by Any Other Name." *Commentary* 76, 1 (1983): 25–38.

Pollack, Josh. "Saudi Arabia and the United States, 1931–2002." *Middle East Review of International Affairs* 6, 3 (2002), http://meria.idc.ac.il/journal/2002/issue3/jv6n3a7.html.

Polliack, Lily. "Middle East Conflict in the Shadow of President Johnson." Draft circulated at State Department Conference, "The United States, the Middle East, and the 1967 Arab-Israeli War," Washington, DC, January 12–13, 2004.

Quandt, William B. "Kissinger and the Arab-Israeli Disengagement Negotiations." *Journal of International Affairs* 29, 1 (1975): 33–48.

———. "Lyndon Johnson and the June 1967 War: What Color Was the Light?" *Middle East Journal* 46, 2 (1992): 198–228.

———. "Middle East Conflict in U.S. Strategy, 1970–71." *Journal of Palestine Studies* 1, 1 (1971): 39–52.

———. "Soviet Policy in the October Middle East War—I." *International Affairs* 53, 3 (1977): 377–89.

Rasheed, Madawi al-. "Saudi Arabia's Islamic Opposition." *Current History* 95, 597 (1996): 16–22.

Rentz, George. "The Saudi Monarchy." In Willard A. Beling, ed., *King Faisal and the Modernization of Saudi Arabia*, 15–34. Boulder, CO: Westview Press, 1980.

Rice, Condoleezza. "Promoting the National Interest." *Foreign Affairs* 79, 1 (2000): 45–62.

Rodenbeck, Max. "Unloved in Arabia." *New York Review of Books*, October 21, 2004, 22–26.

Rodman, Peter W. "The World's Resentment: Anti-Americanism as a Global Phenomenon." *The National Interest* 60 (2000): 33–41.

Ronald, Bruce St. John. "The Libyan Debacle in Sub-Saharan Africa, 1969–1987." In René Lemarchand, ed., *The Green and the Black: Qadhafi's Policies in Africa*, 125–38. Bloomington: Indiana University Press, 1988.

Russett, Bruce. "The Democratic Peace: 'And Yet It Moves.'" *International Security* 19, 4 (1995): 164–76.

Scarcia, Amoretti B. "Libyan Loneliness in Facing the World: The Challenge of Islam?" In Adeed I. Daweesha, ed., *Islam in Foreign Policy*, 53–67. Cambridge: Cambridge University Press/Royal Institute of International Affairs, 1983.

Schulz, George P. "Shaping American Foreign Policy: New Realities and New Ways of Thinking." *Foreign Affairs* 63, 4 (1985): 705–21.

Schwab, Peter. "Israel's Weakened Position on the Horn of Africa." *New Outlook*, April 1978, 21–25 (27).

Sharawi, Helmy. "Israeli Policy in Africa." In Khair el-Din Haseeb, ed., *The Arabs and Africa*, 285–319. London: Croom Helm, 1985.

Sieff, Martin. "Sand in Our Eyes." *The National Interest* 76 (2004): 93–100.

Sindi, Abdullah M. "King Faisal and Pan-Islamism." In Willard A. Beling, ed., *King Faisal and the Modernization of Saudi Arabia*, 184–201. Boulder, CO: Westview Press, 1980.

Sisco, Joseph J. "Selective Engagement." *Foreign Policy* 42 (1981): 27–42.

———. "The United States and the Arab-Israeli Dispute." *Annals of the American Academy of Political Science* 384 (1969): 66–72.

Sobel, Richard. "Contra Aid Fundamentals: Exploring the Intricacies and the Issues." *Political Science Quarterly* 110 (1995): 287–306.

Stegner, Wallace. "*Discovery!* The Story of Aramco Then." *Aramco World Magazine*. Serialized by chapter in issues from January/February 1968 through July/August 1970, available at www.saudiaramcoworld.com.

Telhami, Shibley. "The Persian Gulf: Understanding the American Oil Strategy." *Brookings Review* 20, 2 (2002): 32–35.

Telhami, Shibley, Fiona Hill, et al. "Does Saudi Arabia Still Matter?" *Foreign Affairs* 81, 6 (2002): 167–78.

Vaughan, James. "The United States and the Middle East Crisis of 1967: A British Perspective." Draft circulated at State Department Conference, "The United States, the Middle East, and the 1967 Arab-Israeli War," Washington, DC, January 12–13, 2004.

Viorst, Milton. "The Storm and the Citadel." *Foreign Affairs* 75, 1 (1996): 93–107.

Vitalis, Robert. "Aramco World: Business and Culture on the Arabian Frontier." In Karen Merrill, ed., *Modern Worlds of Business and Industry: Cultures, Technology, Labor*, 3–25. Turnhout, Belgium: Brepols, 1998.

———. "Black Gold, White Crude: An Essay on American Exceptionalism, Hierarchy, and Hegemony in the Gulf." *Diplomatic History* 26, 2 (2002): 185–213.

———. "The Closing of the Arabian Oil Frontier and the Future of Saudi-American Relations." *Middle East Report* 204 (1997): 15–21.

Walsh, Elsa. "Louis Freeh's Last Case." *The New Yorker*, May 14, 2001, 68–79.
——. "The Prince: How the Saudi Ambassador Became Washington's Indispensable Operator." *The New Yorker*, March 24, 2003, 48–65.
Weaver, Mary Anne. "Blowback." *Atlantic Monthly*, May 1996, 24–28.
——. "The Real bin Laden." *The New Yorker*, January 24, 2000, 32–38.
Winik, Jay. "The Neoconservative Reconstruction." *Foreign Policy*, 73 (1988–89): 135–52.
Woodrow, Thomas. "The Sino-Saudi Connection." *The Jamestown Foundation, China Brief* 2, 21 (2002), http://www.jamestown.org/publications_details.php?volume_id=18&issue_id=661&article_id=4680.
Wright, Claudia. "Showdown in the Sahara." *Inquiry*, April 12, 1982, 21–25.
Yaqub, Salim. "Imperious Doctrines: U.S.-Arab Relations from Dwight D. Eisenhower to George W. Bush." *Diplomatic History* 26, 4 (2002): 571–91.
Yost, Charles W. "The Arab-Israeli War: How It Began." *Foreign Affairs* 46, 2 (1968): 304–20.

Reports

Congressional Office of Technology Assessment, *Global Arms Trade: Commerce in Advanced Military Technology and Weapons* (Washington, DC: Government Printing Office, 1991).
Cordesman, Anthony H., and Nawaf Obaid. "Saudi Internal Security: A Risk Assessment." Center for Strategic and International Studies, Washington, DC, May 30, 2004.
——. "Saudi Military Forces and Development: Challenges and Reforms." Center for Strategic and International Studies, Washington, DC, May 30, 2004.
——. "Saudi Petroleum Security: Challenges and Responses." Center for Strategic and International Studies, Washington, DC, November 29, 2004.
——. "Saudi National Security: Challenges and Developments." Center for Strategic and International Studies, Washington, DC, September 30, 2004.
Djerejian, Edward, chair "Changing Minds and Winning Peace: A New Strategic Direction for U.S. Public Diplomacy in the Arab and Muslim World." Advisory Group on Public Diplomacy for the Arab and Muslim World, Washington, DC, October 1, 2003.
Financial Action Task Force on Money Laundering/Groupe d'Action Financière sur le Blanchiment de Capitaux. *Annual Report 2003–2004.* FATF, Paris, July 2, 2004, http://www.fatf-gafi.org/dataoecd/12/44/33622501.PDF.
Finding America's Voice: A Strategy for Reinvigorating U.S. Public Diplomacy: Report of an Independent Task Force Sponsored by the Council on Foreign Relations. New York: Council on Foreign Relations Press, 2003.
Freedom House, Center for Religious Freedom. *Saudi Publications on Hate Ideology Invade American Mosques.* Freedom House, New York, January 28, 2005, http://www.freedomhouse.org/religion/pdfdocs/FINAL%20FINAL%20SAUDI.pdf.
Grimmett, Richard F. "Arms Sales to Saudi Arabia: 1990–1993." Congressional Research Service, Washington, DC, December 17, 1993.
——. "Background on Delivery of AWACS Aircraft to Saudi Arabia." Congressional Research Service, Washington, DC, June 26, 1986.
——. *Executive-Legislative Consultation on U.S. Arms Sales.* Washington, DC: U.S. Government Printing Office, 1982.

International Crisis Group. "Can Saudi Arabia Reform Itself?" Middle East Report No. 28. International Crisis Group, Cairo/Brussels, July 2004, http://www.icg.org/library/documents/middle_east_north_africa/iraq_iran_gulf/28_can_saudi_arabia_reform_itself_web.pdf.

——. "Saudi Arabia Backgrounder: Who Are the Islamists?" Middle East Report no 31. International Crisis Group, Amman/Brussels/Riyadh, September 21, 2004, http://www.crisisgroup.org/library/documents/middle_east___north_africa/iraq_iran_gulf/31_saudi_arabia_backgrounder.pdf.

National Commission on Terrorist Attacks upon the United States. *9/11 Commission Report: Final Report of the National Commission on Terrorist Attacks Upon the United States*. Washington, DC: Government Printing Office, 2004.

Obaid, Nawaf, Amy Jaffe and Edward L. Morse. *The Sino-Saudi Energy Rapprochement: Implications for US National Security*. New York: The Gracia Group, 2002.

Pew Research Center for the People and the Press. "Views of a Changing World, 2003." June 3, 2003, http://people-press.org/reports/display.php3?ReportID=185.

Prados, Alfred B. "Iraq: Post-War Challenges and U.S. Responses, 1991–1998." Congressional Research Service, Washington, DC, March 21, 1999.

——. "Saudi Arabia: Current Issues and U.S. Relations." Congressional Research Service, Washington, DC, April 3, 2003.

——. "Saudi Arabia: Terrorist Financing Issues." Congressional Research Service, Washington, DC, October 4, 2004.

Preece, Richard M. and Robert D. Shuey. "Iran Arms and Contra Funds: Selected Chronology of Events, 1979–1987." Congressional Research Service, Washington, DC, February 4, 1987.

Rigdon, William M. "The Log of President Roosevelt's Trips, 1937–1945." Box 4, William McKinley Rigdon Papers, Georgia Southern University Library, Statesboro, GA.

Roth, John, Douglas Greenburg, and Serena Wille. *Monograph on Terrorist Financing: Staff Report to the Commission*. Washington, DC: National Commission on Terrorist Attacks upon the United States, 2004, http://www.9-11commission.gov/staff_statements/911_TerrFin_Monograph.pdf.

Terrorist Financing: Report of an Independent Task Force. New York: Council on Foreign Relations Press, October 2002.

Tower, John, chairman. *The Tower Commission Report: The Full Text of the President's Special Review Board*. New York: Bantam Books/Times Books, 1987.

U.S. Cabinet Task Force on Oil Import Control. *The Oil Import Question: A Report on the Relationship of Oil Imports to the National Security*. Washington, DC: U.S. Government Printing Office, 1970.

U.S. Department of Agriculture. *Public Law 480 and Other Economic Assistance to United Arab Republic of Egypt*. Washington, DC: Government Printing Office, 1964.

U.S. Department of the Interior. *United States Petroleum Through 1980*. Washington, DC: Government Printing Office, 1968.

U.S. Department of State, Bureau of Democracy, Human Rights and Labor. *International Religious Freedom Report*. http://www.state.gov/g/drl/rls/irf/2004/.

U.S. House of Representatives, Committee on International Relations, Subcommittee on Africa. "Possible Violation or Circumvention of the Clark Amendment: Hearing Before the Subcommittee on Africa of the Committee on Foreign Affairs, House of Representatives, Wednesday, July 1, 1987." Washington, DC: Government Printing Office, 1987.

U.S. Office of International Energy Affairs. *U.S. Oil Companies and the Arab Oil Embargo: the International Allocation of Constricted Supplies*. Washington, DC: Government Printing Office, 1975.

U.S. Senate, Committee on Foreign Relations. *The BCCI Affair: A Report to the Committee on Foreign Relations by Senator John Kerry and Senator Hank Brown*. 102nd Cong., 2nd Sess., Senate Print 102–140. Washington, DC: Government Printing Office, 1992, http://www.fas.org/irp/congress/1992_rpt/bcci/index.html.

U.S. Senate, Committee on Foreign Relations. "Report by the Department of State, Defense and the Interior on Security and International Issues Arising from the Current Situation in Petroleum—January 1953." *Hearings: Multinational Corporations and United States Foreign Policy, Part VIII*, 3–9. Washington, DC: Government Printing Office, 1975, http://www.mtholyoke.edu/acad/intrel/Petroleum/state.htm.

U.S. Senate, Committee on Foreign Relations, Subcommittee on Multinational Corporations. *Multinational Oil Corporations and U.S. Foreign Policy: Report Together with Individual Views to the Committee on Foreign Relations*. Washington, DC: Government Printing Office, 1975.

U.S. Senate, Committee on Foreign Relations, Subcommittee on Multinational Corporations. *Multinational Petroleum Companies and Foreign Policy: Hearings Before the Subcommittee on Multinational Corporations of the Committee on Foreign Relations*, Part 9, 93rd Cong., 2nd Sess., June 5, June 6, July 25, and August 12, 1974. Washington, DC: Government Printing Office, 1975.

U.S. Senate, Committee on Governmental Affairs. "An Assessment of Current Efforts to Combat Terrorism Financing." Testimony by David Aufhauser. 108th Cong., 2nd sess., June 15, 2004, http://www.senate.gov/~gov_affairs/index.cfm?Fuseaction=Hearings.Testimony&HearingID=181&WitnessID=655.

U.S. Senate, Committee on Governmental Affairs. "Hearing: Terrorism Financing: Origination, Organization, and Prevention." 108th Cong., 1st Sess., July 31, 2003, http://hsgac.senate.gov/index.cfm?Fuseaction=Hearings.Detail&HearingID=106.

U.S. Senate, Committee on the Judiciary, Subcommittee on Terrorism, Technology, and Homeland Security. "Terrorism: Two Years After 9/11, Connecting the Dots: Institutionalized Islam: Saudi Arabia's Islamic Policies and the Threat They Pose." Testimony by Simon Henderson. 108th Cong., 1st sess., July 10, 2003, http://judiciary.senate.gov/testimony.cfm?id=910&wit_id=2573.

U.S. Senate, Select Committee on Small Business, Subcommittee on Monopoly. "The International Petroleum Cartel: Staff Report to the Federal Trade Commission." 83rd Congress, 2nd Sess., Washington, DC, 1952, http://www.mtholyoke.edu/acad/intrel/Petroleum/ftc.htm.

Walsh, Lawrence E. *Final Report of the Independent Counsel for Iran/Contra Matters*, volume I: *Investigations and Prosecutions*. Washington, DC: Government Printing Office, 1993.

Film and Media

The House of Saud. DVD. Directed by Jihan el-Tahri. Paris: Alegria Productions, 2004.

Association for Diplomatic Studies and Training. *Frontline Diplomacy: The U.S. Foreign Affairs Oral History Collection*. Arlington: ADST, 2000. CD-ROM.

Index